CW01208656

PLAYMAKER
POLO

Dedication

To my wife, Maria Ines, and sons David and Sebastian, who have all helped me enormously in different dimensions, both with the completion of this book and in many important parts of my life.

PLAYMAKER POLO

HUGH DAWNAY

J. A. ALLEN · LONDON

© Hugh Dawnay 2004
First published in Great Britain 2004
Reprinted 2010
Reprinted 2012

ISBN 978-0-85131-900-1

J.A. Allen
Clerkenwell House
Clerkenwell Green
London EC1R 0HT

J.A. Allen is an imprint of Robert Hale Limited

www.allenbooks.co.uk

The right of Hugh Dawnay to be identified as author
of this work has been asserted by him in accordance
with the Copyright, Designs and Patents Act 1988

British Library Cataloguing in Publication Data
A catalogue record for this book is available from the British Library

Edited by Martin Diggle
Design and typesetting by Paul Saunders

Photographs by Snoopy Productions, except for page 24 (Adam Finer), pages 32, 42 (lower), 61, 141, 144, 251 (Bunny Parsons), pages 93, 113, 118, 138, 167, 213 (MacInnes Photographs Limited), pages 17, 56, 62, 71, 112, 119, 195, 217, 235 (lower), 250, 255 (Alice Gipps) and pages 13, 14, 15 (supplied by the author)

Line illustrations on pages 45, 49, 51, 53, 59, 84, 87, 162 by Mairin Grant, on pages 36, 44, 57, 68, 99, 125, 133, 149, 177, 181, 200, 226, 227, 242, 244, 300 by Susanna Holt.
All other line illustrations by Sebastian Dawnay.

Illustration enhancement by Rodney Paull

Colour separation by Tenon & Polert Colour Scanning Limited, Hong Kong
Printed in China by New Era Printing Co. Limited

Contents

Foreword by Gonzalo Pieres	xi
Foreword by James Kennedy	xii

1 An Introduction to Playmaking — 1
- The Playmaker — 1
- The Hitter and the Receiver — 2
- Speed of the Ball — 4
- Coaching — 6
- Three Unique Dimensions — 6
- Method — 9

2 A Brief History of Polo — 11
- India — 11
- Game Spread by Playmakers — 12
- The British Army and the Olympics — 12
- Polo in the USA — 15
- Polo in Argentina — 16

3 The Author's Experience — 19
- Starting to Play — 19
- Playmaking Apprenticeship — 20
- A Golden Opportunity — 20
- Marriage, Coaching and the Polo School — 21
- The Family Team and Home-bred Ponies — 24
- Authorship — 26
- Learning for Coach and Coached — 26

4 Thought Processes — 28
- Polo Pleasure — 28
- Basics of the System — 28

5 LATET for Tactics — 31
- Look — 31
- Adjust — 33
- Team — 34
- Engage — 36
- Turn — 38

CONTENTS

6 SLOSH Guidelines for Riding — 41
- Riders New to Polo — 41
- Seat — 41
- Legs — 43
- Outside the Pony — 43
- Steering — 45
- Hands Applied Softly — 45

7 PASSF for Striking — 48
- The PASSF Concept — 48
- Preparation — 50
- Approach — 56
- Swing Slowly — 58
- Sweet Spot — 61
- Follow Through — 62

8 Tactics 'A' – Playmaking Components — 65
- Three Essential Skills — 65
- Receiving a Pass — 65
- The Ride-off — 67
- Hooking Sticks — 70
- Leading Exponents — 72

9 Riding 'A' – Individual and Group Exercises — 74
- Turning and Halting Individually — 75
- Circling Individually — 75
- Copying Playmaker in One Horizontal Line — 78
- Conforming to Both Teams in Two Parallel Lines — 78

10 Striking 'A' – Half-shot — 82
- Half-shot as Second Half of Full Shot — 82
- Constructing the Half-shot Forehand with PASSF — 82
- Constructing the Open Offside Backhand Half-shot with PASSF — 86
- Exercises — 88

11 Tactics 'B' – Four Basic Tactics — 91
- Three Elements for Playmaking — 91
- The Rope — 92
- The Barrier — 96
- The Diamond — 97
- The Soft Diamond — 101

12 Riding 'B' – Team Drills — 104
- Working in a Vertical Line — 104
- Parallel Vertical Lines — 106

	Joining in Pairs	108
	Joining Vertical Lines	109

13 Striking 'B' – Straight Full Shots (First Circle) — 111
Introducing Full Shots — 111
Constructing the Straight Offside Forehand with PASSF — 112
Constructing the Straight Nearside Forehand with PASSF — 112
Exercises — 120

14 Tactics 'C' – No. 1 as Link Playmaker to Goal — 122
Tasks Defined by PRST — 122
PRST in Outline — 124
PRST in Detail — 124
Historical Examples — 129

15 Riding 'C' – Control Within a Pair — 132
Opponents as Partners — 132
Turning in Pairs — 132
Turning Inside an Opponent — 133
Pairs Joining as Foursome — 133
Coaching Assistance — 135

16 Striking 'C' – Offside Front Circle (Second Circle) — 137
Second of the Five Circles — 137
Constructing the Offside Neck Shot with PASSF — 137
Constructing the Offside Open Backhand with PASSF — 141
Exercises — 144

17 Tactics 'D' – No. 4 Shuts the Back Door — 147
Principal Roles of No. 4 — 147
PRST Outline for Shutting the Back Door — 148
Shutting the Back Door in Detail — 148
The Reverse Rope — 153
Historical Examples — 156

18 Riding 'D' – Movements at Speed — 160
Progressing from Previous Exercises — 160
Figure of Eight — 160
Ripple Turns — 162
Cavalry Charge — 163

19 Striking 'D' – Offside Rear Circle (Third Circle) — 166
Constructing the Offside Forehand Cut Shot with PASSF — 166
Constructing the Offside Tail Backhand with PASSF — 170
Exercises — 174

20 Tactics 'E' – No. 2 as Link Playmaker from Barrier to No. 1   176
Demands of a Difficult Position   176
No. 2's Role Explained by PRST   176
Goalpost Drill   180
Historical Examples   182

21 Riding 'E' – Short Races   185
Maintaining Riding Skills Under Pressure   185
Races Between Two Individuals   187
Team Relay Races   188

22 Striking 'E' – Nearside Front Circle (Fourth Circle)   190
The Value of Nearside Shots, and When to Avoid Them   190
Constructing the Nearside Neck Shot with PASSF   191
Constructing the Nearside Open Backhand with PASSF   192
Exercises   195

23 Tactics 'F' – No. 3 the Pivot Playmaker from Behind the Barrier   198
Understanding an Important Role   198
No. 3's Role Defined by PRST   198
Historical Examples   201

24 Riding 'F' – Playing Ponies   205
Considerations Before and During Play   205
Number of Chukkas Played   206
Additional Match Considerations   207
Post-match   208
Schooling Between Matches   209

25 Striking 'F' – Nearside Rear Circle (Fifth Circle)   212
Constructing the Nearside Cut Shot with PASSF   212
Constructing the Nearside Tail Shot with PASSF   214
Exercises   217

26 Tactics 'G' – Going to the Next Play   219
The Throw-in   219
Interchanging Positions   223
Recovering Ground   228
Historical Examples   229

27 Striking 'G' – Hitting the Ball Further   233
Striking Principles   233
Adapting PASSF for Greater Length   233

28	**Tactics 'H' – Facing the Hit-in**	**239**
	Opponents' Strategy	239
	One on One	240
	The Box	241
	Meeting the Ball	243
	Historical Examples	246
29	**Tactics 'I' – Rules and Penalties**	**249**
	Learning the Rules	249
	Penalties and Tactics	252
	Historical Examples	258
30	**Tactics 'J' – Team Play**	**261**
	General Concepts	261
	Pre-match Preparation	263
	Practice Sessions	263
	Patron's Role	264
	Positions and Marking	265
	Team Discipline	265
	Historical Examples	266
31	**Tactics 'K' – How to Beat a Better Team**	**269**
	Match-winning Components	269
	Tactics against Superior Opposition	269
	Historical Examples	273
32	**Tactical Critique**	**276**
	Questions	276
	Answers	279
	Remedies	279
33	**Riding Critique**	**280**
	Establishing Areas for Improvement	280
	Questions	282
	Assessing Answers	283
	Remedies	283
34	**Striking Critique**	**287**
	Problems and Their Diagnosis	287
	Questions Related to PASSF	288
	Answers	289
	A Closer Look at Remedies	289
35	**Polo Rules Test**	**292**

CONTENTS

36 Polo Riding 'G' – Pony Procurement — 296
- Buying — 296
- Breeding — 301

37 Preparation – Playmake Before the Season Starts — 305
- The Need for Preparation — 305
- Playing Plans — 305
- Pony Management — 306
- Tack — 309
- Mallets — 309
- Clothes and Equipment — 310

38 Playmaker Conclusion — 314

- Appendix 1 – Playmaker Polo Revision Booklet — 317
- Appendix 2 – Constructive Skills Challenge — 317

Hurlingham Polo Association Rules 2004 — 318

- Teams, Players and Players' Equipment, Substitution — 318
- Ponies, Tack and Pony Welfare — 321
- Tournament Committee, Private Grounds, Umpires and Referees, Goal Judges, Timekeeper/Scorer and Medical Cover — 322
- Ground, Ball and Access During Play — 324
- Start, Duration and End of Play — 325
- Changing Ends, Wrong Line-up, Scoring Goals and Winning — 326
- Restarting Play — 327
- Play Stopped/Not Stopped — 328
- Line of the Ball, Right of Way and Precedence — 329
- Riding Off, Dangerous Riding, Intimidation, Hooking, Misuse of Whip, Spurs and Stick, Rough or Abusive Play — 331
- Penalties — 332
- Annex A – Suggested Layout of a Polo Ground — 334
- Annex B – Notes for Officials — 335
- Annex C – Guidelines for Tournaments — 344
- Annex D – Conditions for Official HPA Tournaments — 346
- Annex E – Rules for League and Group Matches — 347
- Appendix to the Rules — 350

Index — 354

Foreword by Gonzalo Pieres

When playing polo at Palm Beach, I was so impressed by the successful results of Hugh Dawnay's many polo clinics that I invited him to co-host with me a group of players at my home in Argentina. Clearly, he has used our time together to further his teaching and coaching while developing the concept of *playmaking* in all its dimensions. I am delighted to have been quoted and cited as a good example of a *playmaker* on several occasions in this excellent book. I recommend that any player who wishes to improve and be raised in handicap should read and apply the contents. Also, I hope that all coaches will now include this effective and attractive philosophy in their syllabus.

Foreword by James Kennedy

James Kennedy was the pioneer manufacturer for Bausch & Lomb outside the USA, before becoming Vice President responsible for all their European plants. He was honoured by the Irish Chamber of Commerce as their President for a term. As Chairman of Whitfield Court Polo Club, he set up exchanges of polo youth between Ireland and the UK.

This excellent new book from Major Hugh Dawnay draws on over a quarter of a century of unique experience in the world of polo and ably demonstrates his complete command of all aspects and facets of the game. Hugh is, indeed, the world authority on polo – the professor, the coach and, in many respects, an innovator who pioneered developments in polo that we now regard as obvious.

In this, his latest work, his insight and depth of knowledge of the sport assist players of all levels of experience to partake in and enjoy this unique game that combines the magical elements of horse, rider, stick and ball – the ingredients that, without doubt, make polo the opera of all sports.

It has been my distinct pleasure to have played with, and been associated with Hugh and his family for the last twenty years in Waterford. During that time, as head of a European division of an American multi-national corporation and, more recently, managing my own business, I have found Hugh's teaching and support invaluable in improving my game. In addition, the considerable wisdom of his teachings can easily be adapted as lessons for work and living.

The readers of this exciting new book will first of all have much fun in reading it, and are also guaranteed greater insights into this wonderful sport. We wish Hugh many more chukkas as *playmaker* and coach in what is undoubtedly the game of his life.

JAMES KENNEDY
Waterford, 2003

1

An Introduction to Playmaking

The Playmaker — The Hitter and the Receiver — Speed of the Ball — Coaching — Three Unique Dimensions

The Playmaker

A *playmaker* is a person who creates a situation for the benefit of a team, or for other people. Polo is now played in every continent of the world and has been raised to its present-day standard as a result of the input of many *playmakers*, who contributed in important ways both on and away from the polo field.

For the individual, *playmaking* can be broken down into four main areas, which we will examine below.

In Order to Start Playing

Physical and financial courage are required to start polo:

1. To bear the rigours of horse riding (if not already accustomed to it). Initially, it may be none too pleasant and can leave you stiff and sore.

2. As a total novice, competing against experienced players is difficult and humbling. Sometimes, it is even worse than this, if you have to take unfair abuse from a team member, who expects you to do the impossible and play like a veteran.

3. To collect the wherewithal (ponies, clothes, mallets and tack) to be equipped to participate in a team necessitates guidance and, of course, expenses that you must relate carefully to your available budget (see Chapter 37 Preparation).

4. As a corollary to point 3 above, a polo player is inevitably involved in a redistribution of wealth.

On the Polo Field

During play, either the hitter and/or a potential receiver of the ball can be the *playmaker*. The former is the player in possession of the ball, who sends it either directly to a team member or to a place where it can be received by someone moving there. The latter *playmakes* either by going to a spot that is free from interference by any of the opposition, or by subduing the nearest opponent before the ball is struck. In both cases, the action enables a *playmaker* to receive a pass, if it is accurately delivered. The second scenario gives a bonus, in that the receiver also physically prevents one opponent from moving in anticipation of where the ball will go, or in the expected direction of the next play.

Away from the Polo Field

Away from the field of play, there are many dimensions of *playmaking* that necessitate detailed thought and planning, in anticipation of all that is needed to allow a team to participate and perform satisfactorily in a tournament. These include being equipped, as mentioned above, together with planning the training of both ponies and players. Various aspects of this preparation will be discussed at the relevant points in the following chapters. At a level above these issues lie the leaders of Polo Associations, the establishment of clubs, the organization of tournaments and the provision of suitably prepared polo fields, all brought about by the initiative and dedication of many indispensable *playmakers*.

Redistribution of Wealth

Whether intentionally or not, a polo player is deeply involved in the process of redistributing wealth. To assemble a team and then compete in a series of tournaments requires a considerable daily and weekly expenditure on various items, besides the employment of grooms, vets, farriers, drivers and professional players. Prior to this, over a number of years, the breeding and training of team ponies (probably in many different places), plus the production of all the equipment used, will have contributed to much employment and involved many financial transactions. All this can surely be called commercial *playmaking*, which distributes money to many pockets. When, during tournaments, cash is raised for charities, this is a further example of *playmaking* providing funds for worthy beneficiaries.

The Hitter and the Receiver

In play, who is the ideal *playmaker* – the hitter or the receiver? I frequently ask this question when coaching a group of people. The majority immediately reply 'hitter' and then, after reflection, some of them correctly change to 'receiver'. There is a much better opportunity for a *receiver playmaker* to retain possession than for a simple receiver, who has to wait to see what action the *hitter playmaker* takes. Also, the momentum of the game is thus advanced by valuable seconds. The situation can be further improved if and when there is a choice of *playmaker receivers*.

The Hidden Playmaker

A player who can contribute in a variety of ways, without touching the ball or being noticed, is a *hidden playmaker*. This is because most players and spectators, together with the operators of video cameras, only watch the ball and the players close to it. Therefore, any player who acts as a decoy or as an alternative receiver, or who subdues an opponent away from the ball, will be hidden from the majority of people, although fulfilling an essential role. Gonzalo Pieres (10), for a decade the best player in the world, was at times the supreme expert at contributing, without being noticed, while others scored goals. Then, when necessary, from being hidden, he would suddenly appear as a *visible playmaker*, to take control of the ball and score, or set up a goal.

Gonzalo Pieres, the *playmaker* legend during the last two decades of the 20th century, seen here in the *hidden playmaker* role, controlling Miguel Novillo Astrada, the emerging talent of the new century.

Speed of the Ball

Which is more important – the speed of the ball or the pony? (See Figures 1 and 2.) Again, the first answer to this question, when given by the majority, without much thought, is the speed of the pony. This is wrong. Logically, the ball can travel much faster than a pony, whose energy should, whenever possible, be conserved. The ball-chaser abuses ponies by galloping too much in pursuit of the ball. The *playmaker* spares the ponies, through clever anticipation and tactics (which involve all of the team), thereby making the ball do most

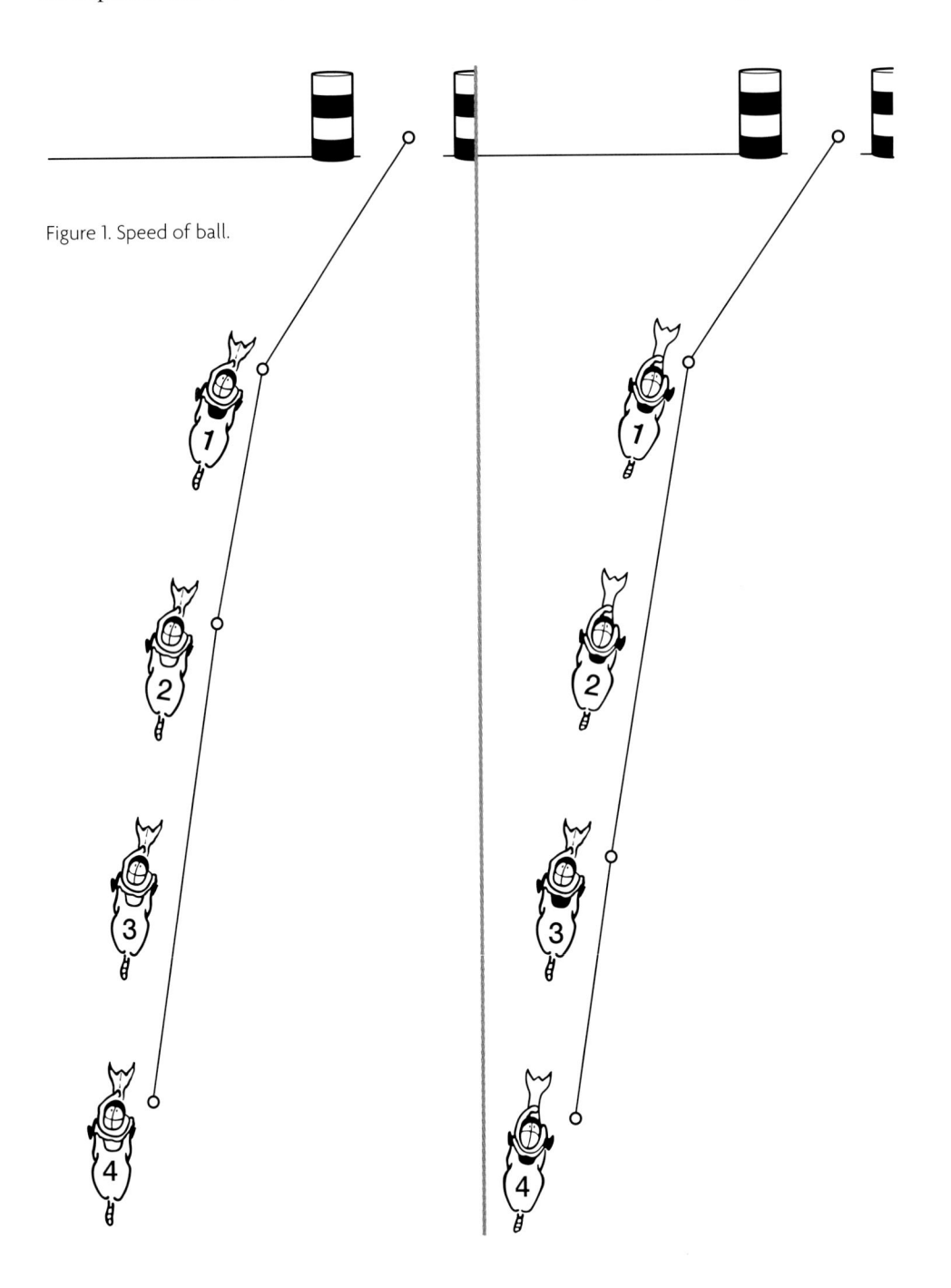

Figure 1. Speed of ball.

of the work. This underlines the importance of playing polo as a team game, with all the players combining together to apply the following three principles:

1. Fast tactical thought.

2. Excellent pony control.

3. Accurate ball striking.

For each of these there is a thought process, which will be explained in due course and frequently revisited and revised.

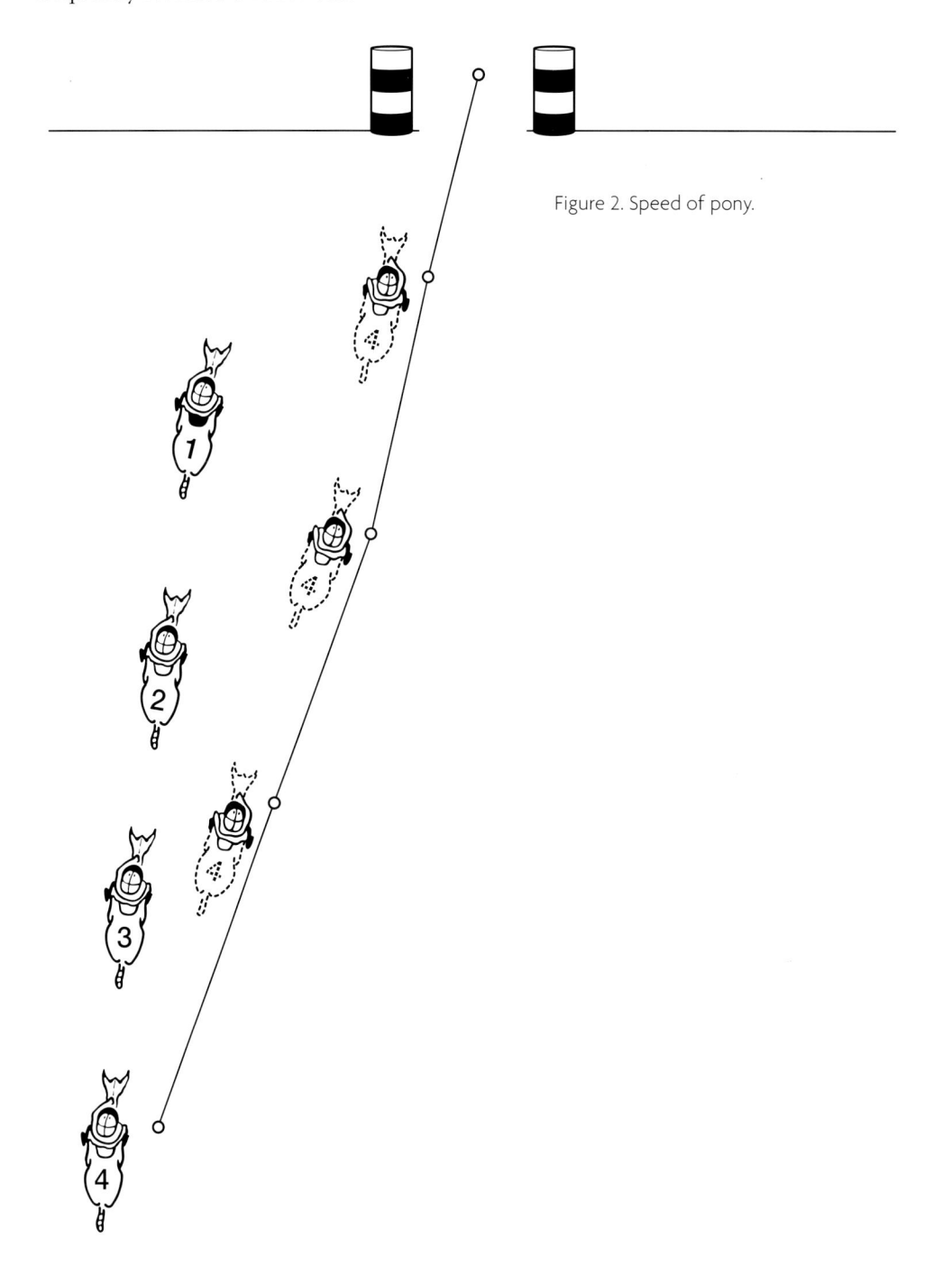

Figure 2. Speed of pony.

It should be emphasized that bursts of acceleration at selected moments of play, by good *playmakers*, can be decisive. Such players also have the ability to control their hitting at speed and to turn quickly. But, at the same time, they are skilful at preserving the energy of their ponies by cutting corners to the next play, and passing the ball to others, when possible. They know and appreciate that they are *not* riding machines.

In contrast, novice players, on fast ponies, will normally travel twice as far in the wrong direction as they would have done on a slower pony. Also, they, and other low-goal players, can only ride and strike at a slower speed than experienced, stronger players. Therefore, in order to include them in a game, the speed of the ball is the priority. This brings us to a brief consideration of the importance (to players of all standards) of coaching, with an emphasis on team play.

Coaching

Anyone who creates a sport or brings an established game to a new location, has to be a *playmaker*. The poet Firdausi described a polo match played between the Persians and Turkomans in 600 BC at Ispahan in Iran. The stone goalposts, eight yards apart, on a ground three hundred yards long, can be seen there today. The dimensions of the field have never changed and we claim that polo was the first team game ever played. We do not know whether these original participants played selfishly by ball-chasing, or as *playmakers* for the benefit of a team. But we have to suspect that individual skills were preferred to team tactics, because today, 2,700 years later, there are still too few *playmakers* and too many ball-chasers, who are playing without being coached. It seems incredible that this situation exists, since it is accepted that winning tournaments requires good team play, which in turn necessitates coaching.

It is not unnatural for people to think that unselfish play threatens to deprive them of enjoyment, or moments of glory, but, by considering such play as a form of hidden *playmaking*, you should be able to discover another way to have great fun while assisting your team. In any case, *some* sacrifices by players are required, in that they should always place their own desires second to team priorities. In the chapters on tactics, there are many references to the 25% (near the ball) and the 75% (away from ball) and when this concept is fully comprehended it becomes simpler to contribute in the 75% and to enjoy doing so.

Three Unique Dimensions

You will find it easier to become a constructive *playmaker*, if you are aware of polo's three unique dimensions. Modern-day polo skills have been developed in line with these, and their influence affected the formulation of the rules. Below, these three points are carefully examined in relationship to *playmaking*. It is important that the whole team understands their significance and connection to general polo strategy and can use them to advantage, because all three are relevant to the success of a team.

Disparity of Skills

At polo, people of very different abilities can play together, because of a handicap system which enables teams to be composed of a mixture of strong and weak players. In most other sports, all the players are segregated into various standards – International, Club, School, Junior, etc – whereby they normally compete against people who have a similar level of skills, so that they can all usefully contribute to a team.

The significance of the handicap factor in polo, is that the less skilful need courage to go onto the field with brilliant players. Hence they desperately require help from a *playmaker*, while selfish play by others will totally prevent them from participating in a constructive manner. Tactics should therefore be planned to allow all players to participate within their abilities. For example, when low handicap (novice) players are given opportunities to *playmake*, it would often be desirable to limit them to only one hit during that play. This minimizes exposure to stronger opponents and it will be sufficient – if the more skilful team members co-operate by astute positioning to receive that one strike from them. Thereby the strength of the whole team will be considerably increased and the pressure on the better players reduced, while the others should learn, from experience and mistakes, how to handle pressure in the future.

Winston Churchill, who won the 1899 inter-regimental tournament in India, with the 4th Hussars, said that loyal polo teamwork renders a true combination, so vastly superior to the individuals of which it is composed.

The Right of Way

Polo is the only ball sport that has a right of way, which at all times governs the rules of the game. Players can control the right of way by regularly moving laterally to be first on the newest line of the ball. Such domination also requires a combination of anticipation, *hidden playmaking* and accurate hitting. This should enable a team to maximize possession and minimize the number of fouls committed. Yet, because of the variety and mix of abilities, there is enormous scope for the stronger opponents to make fools out of your weaker players. This problem is exacerbated by the contradiction that the line is incredibly simple to explain, yet can appear to be highly complicated when two players both claim to be on it at the same time. The situation can be improved if, before each and every match, it is specifically planned how to keep the better opponents apart from your lower-handicapped players.

Obstruction Far from the Ball

In polo, only the *hidden playmakers* take advantage of this unique rule when they subdue opponents who are far from the ball by making physical contact with them in a ride-off (see Chapter 8). In other sports, a similar action would automatically be deemed to be a foul. In polo, not only is this permitted, but it is also an important part of the tactics frequently employed by the better players and seldom used by the weaker ones. Such action off the ball often enables their team to retain or retake possession, during the next play. It is extremely effective when strong opponents are restricted from applying their superior anticipation, when not in possession of the ball, in a fluid situation. But many players seem to be influenced by their subconscious (which wants to obey the rules of other ball games), or by the attraction of the ball itself. Hence, they only attempt to contain opponents when the ball is close, which is normally too late. Only experience and coaching will teach beginners how to *playmake* in this manner, when not involved with the ball in the 75%.

Co-ordination

Co-ordinating these three unique dimensions to your advantage requires much thought and is, itself, a form of *playmaking*. The skills which each player possesses must be proved under pressure. This can only happen if all the team members are involved in the *playmaking* plans. Then, by learning from mistakes, improvements should quickly be made and, through experience, pressure will cease to be such an obstacle.

This procedure could be developed if an infrastructure existed for coaching at every level. Players would then learn the correct guidelines from the beginning and receive an ongoing, constructive programme of revision and critique in order to develop their abilities to the optimum degree. Currently, in Great Britain, there is good instruction for the Pony Club players, and for some beginners. There is also a system, called fast

Action from the Cowdray Gold Cup Final – Sebastian Dawnay reaches wide for C.S. Brooks against Ellerston.

track, which gives the most promising youngsters valuable experience in Argentina, New Zealand, Australia and South Africa. Yet there is no follow-up to these good beginnings, and too much uncontrolled abuse from the better players destroys much of the young talent.

At the other end of the scale, for international teams – those that play in the Argentine Open and some of the high-goal American tournaments – coaches are currently employed. In England, a few high-goal teams have experimented with coaches, but there are no permanent arrangements. I believe that the rest continue to be misled by a false economy that places a higher priority on investment in ponies and professional players than on improvement through coaching. These teams clearly fail to realize that progress in individual skills and team tactics cannot be maintained without revision and good critique. Furthermore, they do not appreciate that, if all four players in a team can anticipate tactically, the perception of who can *playmake* will change.

It is indisputable that the Argentinians are so far ahead of the rest of the world that no other country can match them in open polo. But the Polo Associations of the other countries must at least wish to close the gap and so it amazes me that I have never seen them openly encourage the employment of coaches. Pete Sampras in tennis, and Greg Norman in golf – two of the most outstanding performers of all time in their respective sports – were helped by coaches throughout their careers. In all sports other than polo, it is universally accepted that, in order for a team to win, it is necessary for a coach to polish the skills of the individuals before moulding them to work together.

The managers and coaches of the best soccer clubs in the world were not normally the greatest players themselves, yet they are heeded and respected by the outstanding players of today, who are valued in tens of millions of pounds. Surely, in the polo world, there are similar people whose potential coaching skills are being wasted while, in the meantime, many high-goal players fail to achieve their potential rating, many with medium handicaps never achieve high-goal status and hundreds in low-goal polo continue to chase the ball into obscurity.

Method

In this book I am employing a system similar to that used in my polo clinics and described in my previous book, *Polo Vision*, while often emphasizing the many dimensions of *playmaking*. Thereby, the three main subjects, tactics, riding and striking, are first introduced by discussing five principles for each one. Then, to avoid too much repetition, the key subjects are alternated in successive chapters. Thus, a multitude of details are presented in a logical sequence with practical exercises included, although there is a continuing change of subject. As in most learning processes, this leads to explanations and understanding being developed steadily, over a period. In using this technique – and in order to avoid overwhelming readers with excessive explanations at an early stage – I have assumed in novice readers some knowledge of the rudiments of polo, or other sports (equestrian or otherwise), to which polo bears some relationship. However, I would encourage those who have neither to seek clarification from a polo coach, or from knowledgeable players. As you will discover, a large part of *playmaking* involves the sensible use of a coach.

REVISION

Playmaking

- **P** — creates benefit for team by hitting constructively and/or receiving to keep **P**ossession.
- **R** — *Receiver playmaker* can retain ball better, especially if helped by *hidden playmaker*.
- **B** — maximizing use of **B**all speed by often passing, gives ponies short- and long-term benefit.
- **T** — invent and often revise **T**hought processes for tactics, pony control and accurate striking.

Unique Dimensions

- **U** — relevance of three **U**nique dimensions and ways to use them for team advantage.
- **S** — disparity of **S**kills wider than other sports, limiting participation within abilities.
- **R** — **R**ight of way derived from line of ball affects possession and invites extra fouls.
- **O** — legal means of **O**bstruction when not playing, or even near, the ball.

2

A Brief History of Polo

India — Game Spread by Playmakers — Regimental Tournaments — The British Army and the Olympics — Polo in the USA — Polo in Argentina

India

Modern polo had its origins in India. Records show that, in 1859, at Cachar, members of the British Cavalry and tea-planters were the *playmakers* who founded the Sichar Polo Club. They learnt about the sport from the Manipuris, who had played it in the remote valleys of the North Indian mountains for two hundred years, untouched by the many wars of those two centuries. Once the British Cavalry discovered polo, their officers spread the game rapidly to many places across India including Calcutta, where a club opened in 1862.

First Public Polo Match

The Field, a magazine still published monthly in Britain today, was the first publication to write about polo in India. The article was read by the officers of the regiment which I joined ninety years later, the 10th Royal Hussars. By trying to hit a ball with walking sticks from their chargers, the large horses they rode on duty, they became the first polo *playmakers* in Britain. These officers were so enthused that they sent a representative to Ireland to buy a group of strong ponies, which they duly trained to play. In 1869 the 10th Hussars challenged the 9th Lancers to the first-ever public polo match, in which eight players were in each team. (The 10th Hussars won the match!) A hundred years later I played in the centenary match at Windsor, when the 9th Lancers had their revenge. The confusion caused by sixteen players competing on ponies together was unbelievable, but we were honoured that this memorable event is recorded in the renowned book *Chukka*, published by in 1971 by Herbert Spencer, who also took the photographs and wrote the editorial.

Game Spread by Playmakers

In 1873 The Hurlingham Club, in London, where tennis, squash and bowls were played, introduced polo as an extra sport. In the following year, they wrote the first rules of polo, for teams of five players. Shortly after this it was agreed that the game was too fast and dangerous for five, so teams were reduced to four a side. The game of polo rapidly spread across Britain and Ireland, before it was introduced to many other countries in Europe, Africa and the Americas. British *playmakers* taught the game as they travelled through the Colonies and their efforts extended as far as South America, including Argentina. Initially, the pony height limit was 14.2 hands and, in the rules, offside was included as a foul. When the standard improved and play became much faster, both these measures were abolished.

In 1876 James Gordon Bennett, the American media magnate of the day, returned to the United States from England carrying some polo mallets and balls. Ponies were brought from Texas to New York and American polo was born. The first Club was called Westchester and this name was later given to the famous cup which was fiercely competed for in many series of matches between England and USA.

Regimental Tournaments

Although the first public match, mentioned earlier, was between two cavalry regiments, it was in 1877 that the first recognized inter-regimental tournaments were introduced by the British Army in India. The enthusiasm and fervour shown by the soldiers in these matches not only ignited civilians and Indian nobility across the country, but established for the future a great, healthy rivalry among the regiments of the British Cavalry. I felt the effects of this when I played polo in the 1950s and '60s for the 10th Hussars in the inter-regimental tournaments, which took place every year in England and Germany. The pressure was enormous, as if we were playing for our country, and we were nervous for many days before each match.

The British Army and the Olympics

Between the two World Wars, the standard of regimental polo in India reached incredible heights, with many teams in the British and Indian Cavalry attaining handicaps of more than 20 goals. This happened because equitation and horse mastery was part of their job, giving them the opportunity to train their ponies correctly and to practise extensively. Officers who were invited to play high-goal polo with the Maharajas, not only benefited considerably themselves but many of them, especially the *playmakers*, passed on the skills they had learnt to their own teams.

The 10th Hussars, with a 25-goal team, achieved the unique feat of winning back-to-back inter-regimental tournaments in India and England in 1936 and 1937. The regiment owed this success to the generosity of the four best Indian players of that day. On two occasions, to escape from the worst heat of the summer, they all went to the

The 10th Hussars team that won the 1936 inter-regimental tournament in India. D. Dawnay, R Harvey, M. McMullen, C. Gairdner.

equivalent of a polo camp in the remote hills of India. Each time, every day for two weeks, they played twelve or more chukkas together. The result of mixing with these four 9-goal Indian players (see photograph below) for these intense spells of playing, was that the joint team handicap was raised by 8 goals. Whoever arranged this great opportunity for the 10th Hussars was a great *playmaker*.

The 10th Hussars team, with their four 9-goal Indian benefactors, *left to right*, P. Singh, Jaipur, A. Singh and Hanut Singh.

PLAYMAKER POLO

I am proud that my father, handicap 7, played for the 10th Hussars in both India and Britain and, in between, using the same ponies, captained the British Olympic team in Berlin. This team was composed of four soldiers, presumably because the likes of that exceptional player Gerald Balding (10) were deemed to be professional. After losing the final to Argentina, whose team had a string of forty ponies, my father was presented with the silver medal by Hitler, who presided over the awards ceremonies in Berlin.

The 10th Hussars team that won the last inter-regimental tournament (1939) before World War II. D. Dawnay, M. McMullen, J. Archer-Shee, W. Mallet.

below In play in the Berlin Olympics, 1936; David Dawnay in front of Humphrey Guinness.

Presentation of the Berlin Olympic medals, with silver to Britain. D. Dawnay in front of L. Hinde and F. Fowler.

Polo in the USA

In the 1930s, the standard of polo played by the Americans was the highest ever achieved by their own players in the USA. They had several 10-goal players, headed by Tommy Hitchcock, who was probably the greatest *playmaker* of all time. The reason for this may well be that Tommy's mother was a polo coach. She instilled the correct principles into Tommy and many other young Americans from an early age. Hitchcock had been a hero in the First World War after volunteering, at the age of seventeen, to be a fighter pilot in France. During combat missions against the Germans he shot down two aircraft, but then, on another day, he was forced to crash-land in Germany after being wounded. Despite being handicapped by his injury, he made a brave, dramatic escape from the prisoner of war camp and reached safety in Switzerland.

The climax of this boom in American polo was a series of matches heralded as the 'East versus the West'. The two famous Guest brothers played for the East, which was captained by Tommy Hitchcock. Charles Smith, who was rated 10 goals longer than any other American, captained the West. The polo was awesome and was watched by enormous crowds. The East won the first game and the West the second, but the third was spoilt when Tommy was badly hurt. There was a suspicion that the West had been over-aggressive in trying to mark him. He probably should not have continued but he did, after a long delay, and the West then took control to win the Series.

Polo development was considerably influenced by the Westchester Cup Series, previously mentioned. Between 1886 and 1939, England and USA battled for this prestigious prize thirteen times. England won the first three matches but, after that, the USA were victors in nine of the other ten. Throughout this period, the large crowds witnessed a very high standard of play and sportsmanship and various rule changes were as a direct result of the experience gained in these games.

The Americans have also had some epic battles against the Argentinians. In the Cup of Americas in 1922 and 1928 America won, after being inspired by Hitchcock. But he was injured at the Olympics in 1924, when Argentina secured the gold medal. In 1936 there is no explanation to be found as to why USA, whose team that year were in England for the Westchester Cup, did not compete in the Berlin Olympics. In the final, as mentioned earlier, Argentina duly won, easily defeating the British team, captained by my father. After the Second World War, the Americans were twice defeated easily in Argentina. Then, in Texas in 1980, the contest was very close, when the 40-goal team from Coronal Suarez, two Harriots and two Heguys, had pony problems caused by a flu virus and only won narrowly.

Polo in Argentina

Since 1980, the Argentinians' superiority has been undisputed and they are recognized as the kings of polo. The Spanish Conquistadors brought the first horses to Argentina and centuries later the British introduced the game to the people. Thereafter, it was discovered that Argentine farmland was perfect for breeding and raising horses because of the incredibly strong grass, which grows without adding any other nutrition. There are thousands of large, flat estancias on which, initially, the horse was essential for the control of enormous herds of cattle. During the early polo years, the same ponies were used to round up stock and play chukkas. Polo fields were easy to lay out on that flat land and it was simple for both young and old to start playing, resulting in a rapid and dramatic improvement of standard. Children in particular benefited from riding bareback and beginning stick and ball exercises before reaching ten years of age. Then the Thoroughbred was introduced to the breeding of equine stock and both cattle ponies and polo ponies began to look rather different.

Polo clubs were founded all over the country and, because of the climatic variations in such a large land, many players were able to travel and compete throughout the year. The biggest tournaments were founded during the Argentinian spring, from September to November, in the capital Buenos Aires. These are for teams of up to 40 goals and the clubs at Hurlingham (founded and named by the British), and Indios and Tortugas (jointly) have become famous for staging the first two of them. The teams then move on to the Palermo stadium, in that city, to play the Argentine Open – the climax of the world polo year.

Whichever team wins at Palermo has the right to claim to be the world team champions. Over the past three decades, four of the winning teams have been rated at 40 goals. For Coronel Suarez, Juan Carlos Harriott, regarded as the greatest player of all time, and his brother Alfredo combined so well with the Heguy brothers, Horacio and Albert, that they won throughout the 1970s except for one year. Then Santa Ana with the Dorignac brothers, Frankie and Gaston, plus Daniel Gonzales and Hector Merlos, beat them to become another 40-goal quartet. In the 1980s, Gonzalo and Alfonso Pieres, with Ernesto

A BRIEF HISTORY OF POLO

Totz and Carlos Gracida (a Mexican), held 40 goals to represent La Espadana and win several times. Next, the first-ever team of brothers to win the Open and be 40 goals, the four sons of Horacio Heguy – Gonzalo, Horacio, Marcos and Bautista – swept all before them in the early 1990s. Yet, believe it or not, all these 40-goal teams were sometimes made to battle in an extra chukka before beating other teams of up-and-coming young Argentinian players with lower handicaps, which emphasizes the amazing standard that has been achieved there. Furthermore, in recent years, the Argentine could at one time boast of having twelve players rated somewhere in the world at 10 goals. These included the seven Heguys, sons of Horacio and Alberto, who had played for the famous Coronel Suarez mentioned above.

Currently Adolfo Cambiaso is the modern polo phenomenon; at seventeen years of age he became the youngest-ever 10-goal player in the world and he has already been on the winning team in all the biggest international tournaments. However, at the time of writing, the battle for supreme team honour has been won by the four Novillo Astrada brothers who, in their first year together, delighted the polo world by winning the 2003 Argentine Open, thereby becoming the victors of the most prestigious polo triple

Modern polo phenomenon Adolfo Cambiaso who, at seventeen years of age, became the youngest-ever 10-goal player in the world.

17

crown. In achieving this victory, they gave a classical and wonderful example of team play, which makes the ball do the work.

REVISION

Polo History

- **O** — modern **O**rigins in India 1859; UK match 1869; polo introduced to Hurlingham Club in 1873.
- **H** — 1876 polo introduced in USA; 1877 Indian inter-regimental matches at **H**igh-goal level.
- **I** — **I**nter World Wars, USA standard best with Hitchcock; international matches played.
- **A** — UK, USA and **A**rgentina played influential series; **A**rgentinians became supreme champions.

3

The Author's Experience

Starting to Play — Playmaking Apprenticeship — A Golden Opportunity — Marriage, Coaching and the Polo School — The Family Team and Home-bred Ponies — Authorship — Learning for Coach and Coached

Starting to Play

At the age of twenty-three I started to play polo, having previously competed in almost all the other equestrian sports. I had also enjoyed fox hunting in Ireland, since childhood and during school holidays, throughout the Second World War. Falling into ditches, bog holes and rivers, after a frost, was a fantastic grounding for all types of sport. My father, a supreme *playmaker* in many dimensions, including the battlefield in war, had generously supplied me with good horses and had given me the benefit of his own equestrian experiences, which included multi-dimensional successes in addition to his polo triumphs mentioned earlier. His best purchase for me was Rendez-Vous II, a magnificent red bay gelding, who taught me so much, while winning point-to-points, hunter trials and showjumping, despite my woeful inexperience at that time. As I write, on the wall above my head, a beautiful painting of Rendez-Vous II reminds me how he suffered my many mistakes, while giving me sufficient prominence to be offered a number of other race rides. Hence in steeplechases and point-to-points I had the good fortune of enjoying close to two hundred rides and having twenty winners, before increased weight ended that career.

Then luck again came my way, when polo was re-introduced to my regiment to provide me with the opportunity to start this wonderful sport. Playing on Arab stallions, purchased in 1956 from Baghdad, the 10th Hussars restarted post-war polo on the beach at Aqaba, Jordan. Our Colonel at that time was Alistair Tuck, who was a vital *playmaker* in the way that he found, transported and trained the Arab ponies and then organized our polo. Furthermore, he had the patience to endure our exuberant, dangerous behaviour, as he tried to explain the intricacies of the right of way.

Playmaking Apprenticeship

When we returned to Europe, Colonel Tuck retired and I found that I had to organize and captain the regimental team. This experience, together with my father's advice, gave me a valuable apprenticeship in how to *playmake*, both on and away from the polo field, which helped me to achieve a 3-goal handicap in five years. I then had the privilege of playing for the British Army in Rome, Delhi, Nairobi, Sotogrande and Buenos Aires. These highly enjoyable polo travels, and my experiences in some English and German tournaments, opened my eyes to the unbelievable situation that there were no coaches in polo.

However, it was in this era that I met, and was influenced by, an important *playmaker* and an incredibly flamboyant character, Brigadier Hesky Baig (6) from Pakistan. In Rome, our military team was severely beaten in the first match. Hesky told us 'Don't panic – remember you are British' and offered to give us a coaching session. We gratefully accepted and, from him – besides an insight into how Allah could change his whiskey into water as it touched his tongue – I learnt the basis of all my tactical instruction. Armed with this knowledge, I also began to develop some coaching ideas for improving pony control and striking, with which I attempted to help my fellow army players in Germany.

A Golden Opportunity

Suddenly, in 1966, out of the blue, I was handed a golden opportunity to experiment further, when asked to coach the Germans in Dusseldorf and Hamburg during weekends. 'Very interesting, tell us more', they said, when I first expounded the theory of playing in a vertical, upfield line, instead of one spread laterally across the field. The British Army had taught me to instruct in five subjects, including riding, so I relished the task of designing my own structured system to cover tactics, polo riding and striking separately, before combining them in controlled instructional chukkas. This experience was incredibly valuable, because I was forced to work hard, in the knowledge that you have to be efficient to satisfy the Germans. Hence the skeleton of my earlier book *Polo Vision* was constructed, while I tasted some wonderful German hospitality from their polo players and especially from the Coffee King of Hamburg, Atti Darboven.

My confidence was boosted when I coached and captained the 10th Hussars team to win the 1966 inter-regimental tournament in Germany, for the first time. We were exhilarated by the knowledge that the polo name of this great regiment had been redeemed.

Later, after some amusing diplomacy to counter German and British objections, the two nationalities agreed to play together in teams, at polo tournaments. My last year in Germany was 1969, by which time a few German players had risen to 1-goal handicap, and I staged a match between Dusseldorf and Hamburg. Believe it or not, through the coffee contacts of Darboven, I also organized, coached the participants and played in a polo exhibition behind the Iron Curtain in Hungary. Despite a serious language problem, enormous horses and a pitch with obstacles on it, we performed to thirty thousand people, to a great reception. Finally, in August of 1969, I took three Germans with me to play in the main Dublin tournament in Ireland. Hence my last four years in Germany gave me a wonderful background for what was to become my second career.

Marriage, Coaching and the Polo School

1970 was a glorious year that had a lasting effect on my life. I was introduced to, and thrilled by, medium-goal polo in England and, for the first time, we won the English inter-regimental tournament. In November, I went with the army team to Argentina to play against a military team. We lost all the matches but I won in a wider sense because it was here that I first met Maria Ines, the amazing woman who was to become my wife, when she attended a lunch before a polo match. The following year I gained my freedom by leaving the army in October then, six weeks later, gladly surrendered it when marrying Maria Ines in Buenos Aires. Thirty years later we are still together, with two grown-up sons. The younger, Sebastian, has a polo career and to our delight has reached 5 goals, having played regularly in high-goal and being in a winning Gold Cup and British Open team. David, who made us proud by earning a good degree at Bristol, achieved 2 goals in polo, while working as a banker, before marrying another Argentinian lady and moving to Barcelona for a new career in computers.

In 1972, I intended to use my German experience to offer polo coaching in Ireland and England, but found that, with the exception of one team, with which I was playing in Dublin, it was not in demand. However, I was twice invited to play in tournaments in England. This proved to be valuable experience, because I learnt much from playing with two outstanding international *playmakers*. In medium-goal, with Tayo Astrada (who later reached 9 goals) from Argentina, we reached the semi-final of the Harrison tournament at Cowdray. Tayo's famous sons have since played much high-goal with my son Sebastian and, in 2003, emulated the Heguys by winning the Argentine Open as a team of four brothers. In the 8-goal, with patron Doug Brown (now the Club Chairman) and the experienced Indian, Kishen Singh, we won the Ruins Cup defeating two Royal Princcs in the final, much to the dismay of several smart ladies who had brought out their best hats for the prizegiving. The latter was largely won by *playmaking*, away from the field of play, when I suggested that the game should be umpired by the American Billy Linfoot (a former 9-goal international), who was renowned as a *playmaker* and for his fairness.

During the next two years, the polo seasons brought me only a few opportunities to develop my coaching system and I realized that the only way I could succeed was to become a serious *playmaker*, by establishing facilities and offering the service from my Irish home, Whitfield Court. Hence I began the preparations for opening a Polo School in 1976, which included laying out a polo field. To assist me in gathering enough ponies together for such an operation, between two winter purchasing trips to Argentina, I agreed to pool ponies with Renata and Cecil Coleman, in order to coach and play in their team during the summer of 1975. We won tournaments in both Ireland and England, where we played in two finals on one day, and had a rewarding season. After some more

Tayo Astrada and the author watching their sons in action.

learning experiences and several unexpected adventures, I returned to Whitfield happy to find the grass on my newly made polo field looking good for the following year.

In 1976, aided by the summer of drought, my Polo School and Whitfield Polo Club duly opened. From then until the end of the 2002 season, when we closed the school and the club moved to another location, I revelled in the wonderful privilege of being able to play and coach polo only a few yards away from my home. Today, it very hard to believe that more than twenty-seven years have passed by, during which I have enjoyed an incredibly exhilarating and fascinating period of my life. Players of thirty nationalities have visited Whitfield to have polo coaching and I have travelled to thirty countries, ten in Europe, ten in the Americas and ten in the rest of the world, to give polo clinics. Additionally, I have had the honour of conducting two months of clinics at Palm Beach, Florida, for twelve years in succession. There, I learnt much by watching and meeting most of the world's best players while enjoying the company of many interesting and eminent people. Some of them were in the clinics and I benefited enormously from their opinions and comments, although on occasions 'being divided by the same language' created a few amusing situations. Also, I went to Cyprus to coach enormous groups, for one week every September, over fourteen consecutive years. At Episcopy, the aptly named Happy Valley contained a sand polo field, on which many visiting international players have been entertained.

Cyprus offered me a very privileged additional experience, when I became involved, for one week, with the Superstars Circus. The group consisted of several Olympic gold

Palm Beach group.

medallists, a World Triathlon champion and two national Superstar champions. I had to devise a polo test for them and then train them to ride, and to hit the ball. Their ability to learn and apply every detail that I taught them was truly amazing and made me feel very humble. Furthermore, they reproduced the same level of concentration for seven other sports with which they were not familiar and, as a spectator, I much enjoyed their performances, which included some hair-raising adventures. This experience emphasized to me that top athletes succeed because of a combination of talent and incredible *application*. This must be linked to much dedicated revision, which I now believe constitutes a vital dimension of *playmaking*.

I have returned to Argentina many times, to watch the incredible Open polo, buy ponies and do some coaching. The latter involved bringing, from my client list, the first polo visitors to La Martina, the home of the incomparable Adolfo Cambiaso and the present-day vendors of smart polo equipment. Also, one year, I was privileged to be invited to work with Gonzalo Pieres, then the leading 10-goal player, during the Open, to give a group of Americans a luxury week of polo. The slow pace of our game clearly did not mix with the speed of the Open and, as a direct result of this, Gonzalo nearly lost the title that year. So, although we had a brilliant week, sadly it was decided that it could not be repeated.

One trip leads to another, and as a result of my Palm Beach and English contacts, I accepted invitations to sixteen clubs in the USA and sixteen locations in Great Britain, to visit and give clinics. The latter included one week of intensive work, every year for seven years, with Pony Club groups, organized with great enthusiasm by John Wright, a great *playmaker*, who is now the manager of Tidworth Polo Club. During these weeks I enjoyed an international flavour, when young foreign players from South Africa, Chile, Argentina and USA were added to the groups.

Best of all, for the past nine years, every March, I have coached in a paradise called Costa Careyes, on the Pacific coast of Mexico. There, I much enjoy the scenic polo fields, glorious beaches and wonderful swimming in the best climate that I have ever encountered – I am already looking forward to future years.

The author with clients at Costa Careyes, Mexico, March 2004.

The Family Team and Home-Bred Ponies

Throughout this period I continued to play in tournaments and enjoyed some success in Dublin during the 1980s when sharing a team with Oliver Caffrey. One year, Oliver invited Dickie Cernadas (7) to play with us and his unselfish, brilliant play gave me a significant lesson about *playmaking*, explained later in Chapter 23. Over the same period, from one stallion, sixty ponies were bred at Whitfield, all of which were broken and trained by my head man, John O'Keeffe. Some were sold abroad, others were bought by club members and the rest were useful replacements for the school and the family team which, since the late 1980s, included my sons. Our greatest joy came in 1992, when the three of us played together on twelve of the breed, to win the two principal Dublin tournaments. On each occasion, we needed a little help. First from a good professional as the fourth player and second, by a little witchcraft from behind one goal where our No. 5, Maria Ines, stood to prevent our opponents from scoring.

THE AUTHOR'S EXPERIENCE

Family team, including No. 5, Maria Ines.

below The family team in action against Craig McKinney (seen between author's two sons).

25

Authorship

Another big delight for me was the publication of my earlier book, *Polo Vision*. This has been printed twice in the original version and twice more in a revised form with five additional chapters. In total, I believe that over ten thousand copies have been sold around the polo world. Many compliments that I have received about the book have given me much pleasure. Comments, telephone calls and letters have indicated how different brains react to constructive information. Some people claim to have taught themselves, and others, directly from the text without ever meeting me. Others say that the book is extra helpful after they have been coached by me. A couple of good friends, who have never contemplated being coached, have said that they could not understand a word – one of them was joking.

One continues to learn and, in this new book, the subjects that I wrote about in *Polo Vision* have been expanded upon further, incorporating new ideas and extra knowledge, which I have acquired in recent years.

Learning for Coach and Coached

Every time I meet new clients, I sense an excitement that I can exchange knowledge, by imparting to them my new ideas, while learning from their responses and questions. This helps me in my quest to keep simplifying all the explanations in respect of the techniques, thought processes and principles which I teach. This rewarding process has been further assisted every time I try to put any of the above into writing. Better still, I find that actual coaching and working on a book are mutually beneficial. Hence I have enjoyed the advantage of an on-going learning curve. Progress was accelerated when I became involved with instigating a system of qualified coaches for the Hurlingham Polo Association (HPA) in England. The ensuing seminars, which included lectures from coaches in different sports and the exchanging of ideas with other polo instructors, widened my knowledge and scope for coaching enormously. To date, more than sixty people have qualified as coaches and instructors and are listed in the *Hurlingham Polo Association Year Book*. The main beneficiary has been the Pony Club which, at every level, has taken organized courses given by our group over the past decade. This uptake is satisfyingly reflected by the increased number of good young players who are now seen in tournaments. Many other beginners have also taken advantage of the situation by employing one or more of us, in order to learn the correct techniques and principles from the beginning.

The ages of my clients, over nearly three decades, have varied from ten to seventy, but the majority were in their thirties and had already played some polo. However, a small percentage were total novices and they proved to me that starting with no bad habits is a considerable advantage. The number of lady players has been steadily increasing, but it appears that few of them have the opportunity to play enough to achieve a significant rise in handicap.

I always find that it is most rewarding when I help anyone to improve in any dimension of the game. It is especially pleasing if they tell me that, by using my system, they have been able to take a positive part in a polo match. However, it is frustrating when I watch a promising ex-student, who has never returned for revision and has clearly forgotten 80% of what had been, at one time, learnt and applied. The following chapters give you all my latest ideas with a strong emphasis on how to *playmake* in many different dimensions. I hope that they will be helpful and put you on the road to becoming a successful *playmaker* both on, and away from, the polo field, besides assisting the process of redistributing wealth.

REVISION

- **C** — equestrian background; started polo at twenty-three; benefited from three *playmaking* **C**oaches.
- **A** — played for **A**rmy in five countries and in British and German tournaments; learnt from coaches.
- **S** — opened polo **S**chool in 1976, visited by players from thirty nations and gave clinics in thirty countries.
- **Q** — gave Palm Beach clinics for twelve winters and instigated coaching **Q**ualification in Britain.

4

Thought Processes

Polo Pleasure — Basics of the System

Polo Pleasure

Polo is a sport in which everyone, given the opportunity, can be a *playmaker* and thereby further enjoy a game that is second to none, win or lose. No other equestrian sport gives a competitor so much action time in the saddle. The shortest polo match will last an hour, during which a player should derive the pleasure of combining the thrill of speed on horseback with the sensation of hitting a ball and the benefit of tactical co-ordination with others. To maximize this enjoyment you should know how to *playmake* within a team.

Playmaking necessitates applying thought processes to three subjects:

Tactics — for good positioning through anticipation.

Riding — to enable you to react quickly.

Striking — so that you can play your part fully, with consistent accuracy.

A good coach should be able to help people individually to acquire these desired thought processes, by finding the wording that suits each of them. For a sport which incorporates such a disparity of skills, coaching must be varied for the different abilities and talents, yet applied collectively in order to instil and maintain all the basics, especially those essential for team play.

Basics of the System

At the Whitfield Court International Polo School in Ireland, I designed a method to improve players and teach beginners. In order not to bore them, I frequently changed the subject and the venue on any one day. Now I am repeating that system, while adding

above Two of the Novillo Astradas in action against Martin Aguerre and Santiago Gaztambide.

left Memo Gracida watches team mate Pite Merlos.

many new ideas that I have learnt from working with experienced players and beginners, in twenty-five years at my Polo School and while travelling to coach around the world.

My wish is to see many more people becoming *playmakers*. By working in groups – or even as a pair, with a friend or a coach – I invite you to learn the new exercises which will be explained as you read on. These will build riding and ball-striking skills, which should be combined with the tactics that I have imparted in other chapters.

By being a valuable *playmaker*, within your capacity, you can have the greatest possible fun. This necessitates taking advantage of the disparity of standards in polo instead of letting this subdue you.

Three Questions

Let me pose three questions and first reply negatively with three don'ts, before reversing them into positive answers.

Questions
1. *Tactics* — Where to go?
2. *Riding* — How to get there?
3. *Striking* — What to do when you get there?

Answers

Negatives
1. Don't *chase* the ball.
2. Don't *look* at your *pony*.
3. Don't *kill* the ball.

Positives
1. Go where the ball will chase *you*, the *playmaker*.
2. Let the pony look at and follow *you*, the *playmaker*.
3. Hit *slowly* to be an accurate *playmaker*.

To obey the three positive answers, you must learn or revise fifteen key points, five for each subject, to give you improved thought processes. To help you remember them, there are three *MNEMONICS*, which will each be discussed in detail in their respective chapters. These are:

LATET	**SLOSH**	**PASSF**
Look	**S**eat	**P**repare
Adjust	**L**egs	**A**pproach
Team	**O**utside the pony	**S**wing slow
Engage	**S**teering	**S**pot on ball contact
Turn	**H**ands used softly	**F**ollow through
Chapter 5	Chapter 6	Chapter 7

5

LATET for Tactics

Look — Adjust — Team — Engage — Turn

The mnemonic LATET describes the five headings above. By understanding and applying all of these headings you can make the ball *chase you*, and thereby learn to be an effective *playmaker*.

Look

It is the basis of your polo tactics to look around continually. If correctly applied, this gives continual 'all round vision', which enables you to see everything that happens, the current line of the ball and all that is about to be done by your three team mates and the four opponents. This is similar to driving a car in heavy traffic, where it is essential to see in front and behind to avoid being surprised by others. But, in a car, the mirror provides the rear view and the driver does not have to turn the body in the same way as required by a polo player.

How to Look

How does a player turn in the saddle to look behind? 'By moving the head or neck' is the normal (incorrect) answer I am given. Instead, try the other end of the body and turn the feet, which rotate the lower leg and knees, which in turn twist the thighs and hips, allowing effortless movement of the shoulders, neck and head. So you could say 'look with your feet' — but beware that this does not interfere with your application of the correct riding grip. Further to this, a young, supple person can start the rotation with the hips and keep the feet perfectly still.

Turning in this way will also help your striking technique, when a similar rotation of the parts of the body is applied to motivate the shoulders in order to avoid using simple arm strength.

Five looking, one turning.

When to Look

Teams in every sport have this requirement of looking, but in polo, where the ponies add extra speed, it is vitally important. When pursuing the ball you should know what is taking place behind, in front and on both sides of you, even if you are also battling in a ride-off. When far from the ball, good anticipation is aided by continual looking, and this allows you to see any opportunity to *playmake*, instead of losing the necessary all-round vision through chasing or watching the ball too much.

How to Improve

How can you make yourself improve at looking? By being regularly monitored by a coach, or anyone who is willing to watch you constructively. Also, before mounting a pony, stretch your neck muscles by looking left and right and behind you several times. Then you should extend this self-discipline to make yourself look around between each shot, both during practice and in actual matches. Even better, when doing stick and ball exercises and while playing, keep saying aloud 'look around' until you become confident that your subconscious has taken over so that you do it automatically between shots.

Adjust

This is a continual process, which can only be done correctly by first *looking*. Four players on a full-size polo field are operating on the equivalent length of three football pitches and often an enormous amount of adjustment is required. You should never be satisfied with your position, even when the rest of your team are between you and the ball. An adjustment, whether slight or large, has to be made to everything that takes place, or is about to happen, on this large field.

Direction

Often a major change of direction is necessary, but sometimes, from a minor alteration, you become the *playmaker* to score a goal, or even win a match. My riding exercises in forthcoming chapters will assist you and your ponies to respond quickly to the need to turn sharply through small and big angles. But tactical anticipation that takes you to the next play before it happens is even more helpful.

Distances

At the same time, distances between you and others must be kept as constant as possible to allow you to stay in reach, but not too close. Probably the worst mistake in polo lies in this dimension, because players are too often either huddled together or too far apart. Hence control of the field is not retained and possession is frequently lost.

Speed

The speed of the ponies has to be varied incessantly to achieve the above and maintain a correct position. High-goal players are very skilful at making minor accelerations and decelerations. *Control* of speed is much more important than pure speed and, again, good riding is a vital factor.

Mistakes

Car drivers in heavy traffic have to make endless adjustments which are similar to those of polo players, in that much of the adjustment is rooted in anticipation of what is expected, while part of it is a quick reaction to mistakes. As in life, it is mistakes that trigger the need for many adjustments in polo. These mistakes are made by you, your pony, your team, the opponents or even (in a manner of speaking) the ball, when it bounces falsely. Some mistakes can be covered, but slow or poor adjustment to them can cause disaster. However, mistakes may also become fortuitous, if you and your team react more quickly to them than the opponents do. In some situations, it is difficult to prevent the ball from hitting your pony and, when it happens, it demands an instant adjustment. However, anticipation will help to minimize the number of times it occurs.

Surprises

Brilliant plays by friend or foe produce surprises, which must be adjusted to. Bad umpiring, when an obvious foul is not blown, can unexpectedly alter situations drastically, but protesting will only delay adjusting, especially if a dramatic change of direction is needed. Often, the best way of retrieving an ugly situation is to move directly from the present play to the next one, and this will also save the pony's energy – which is the equivalent of petrol in a vehicle.

Economy

A car driver who brakes and accelerates too much will quickly run out of petrol. How big is the tank of a polo pony? Seven and a half minutes, if the pony is fit and is not over-exerted early in a chukka. Unnecessary use of speed can be avoided, and braking minimized, by cutting corners to the next play. In this way, the pony's stamina can be preserved on the day and for the future. Riding exercises to help you understand and apply these adjustments, while developing strong legs, are given later.

Critique

How do you know if you are adjusting correctly and quickly enough when playing? 'By results' you may reply. But it is possible to win playing badly or to lose playing well, and it is important to know that you can only play as well *as you are allowed to*. An effective coach, who observes constructively, can supply the answer. If you want to give consistently good performances, you will need frequent assessments to confirm your correct actions and help you to adjust more effectively in the future and thereby become a regular *playmaker*.

Team

Your position in relation to your own team should be the principal factor for adjustment. Thereby you should be able to maintain two players either side of the barrier, which moves with the game between Nos. 2 and 3, a concept that will be explained fully in Chapter 11.

Own-team Awareness

The team which most consistently fills the four positions, without leaving gaps or allowing two members to compete for the ball simultaneously, should win. Therefore, you must always know where the other three are, especially your best player. If you move out of position there are then only three operational players and territorial control is weakened. It is wrong to be too close, alongside or too far away from other team members. This happens when a No. 1 goes too far up the field or a No. 4 stays too far back and then, until they adjust, it is impossible for them to be *playmakers*.

Thought Process

The ball-chaser looks first for the ball, second at the nearest opponent, while hoping that the rest of the team are watching and admiring. This process should be reversed to *make the ball chase you*. On average, you should only expect the ball to be your responsibility to compete for during 25% of the game and hence for 75% of the game you will be adjusting as a *playmaker* off the ball. This all needs self-discipline but, if achieved, will actually increase your involvement and help you to relax more. A good way to control your subconscious is by asking yourself the following questions:

1. 'Where are my No. 3 and other team members?'
2. 'Therefore which of the opponents should I now be controlling?'
3. 'Is the ball about to be my responsibility in the 25%?'

This extra emphasis on watching your own No. 3 is enormously valuable, because it enables you to work closely with probably your best player, while absorbing much of his superior anticipation. Also, any position left empty, at any time, should be quickly noticed and filled before the opposition can take advantage.

Distances Between Players

Many people have asked me 'What is the correct distance between players?' The answer depends on the standard of polo. A perfect team, when anticipating a pass from their No. 4, should adjust positions so that:

A short strike will reach No. 3.

An average shot will find No. 2.

The best hit will travel to No. 1.

By practising team exercises, without any opposition, correct and effective distances can be established. In many teams, No. 2 is often too far from the barrier (see Chapter 11) and too close to No. 1, becoming in effect a No. 1½ to receive all passes and produce poor marking when there is a sudden turn to defence. Surely it is better when No. 3 can reach No. 1 with an average shot and No. 2 with a short, accurate delivery. This formula will increase depth in attack and defence, while encouraging the better midfield players to include Nos. 1 and 4 in the proceedings. Incorrect distances on a large field allow selfish play to flourish, with a loss of team cohesion. This bad scenario can be exacerbated by the dreaded words 'Leave it' being overused. The call 'Leave it' is wrong when it brings no definite advantage, because then at least four negatives occur:

1. Depth of attack is reduced.
2. Defence, if and when suddenly needed, is weakened.
3. The speed of the ball is replaced by the efforts of the pony.
4. Lower handicap players never learn to take pressure.

A competent coach can instil correct calls and distances between players, thereby helping to involve all the team members as *playmakers*. This will bring fast individual improvement and vastly increase team cohesion.

Engage

This is the hardest part of polo for a beginner to understand and apply correctly. However, when it is fully comprehended and practised, a polo player can develop, with experience, the ability to gain possession of the ball in many situations.

Two Alternative Ways

There are two distinct methods of engagement.

Engaging the 'line of the ball', by joining it positively without fouling (see Figure 3). This is best achieved by the principle of always moving laterally to the line in order to be clearly in the right of way well before reaching the ball. Remember that the line of the ball

Figure 3. Joining the line correctly and not fouling opponent.

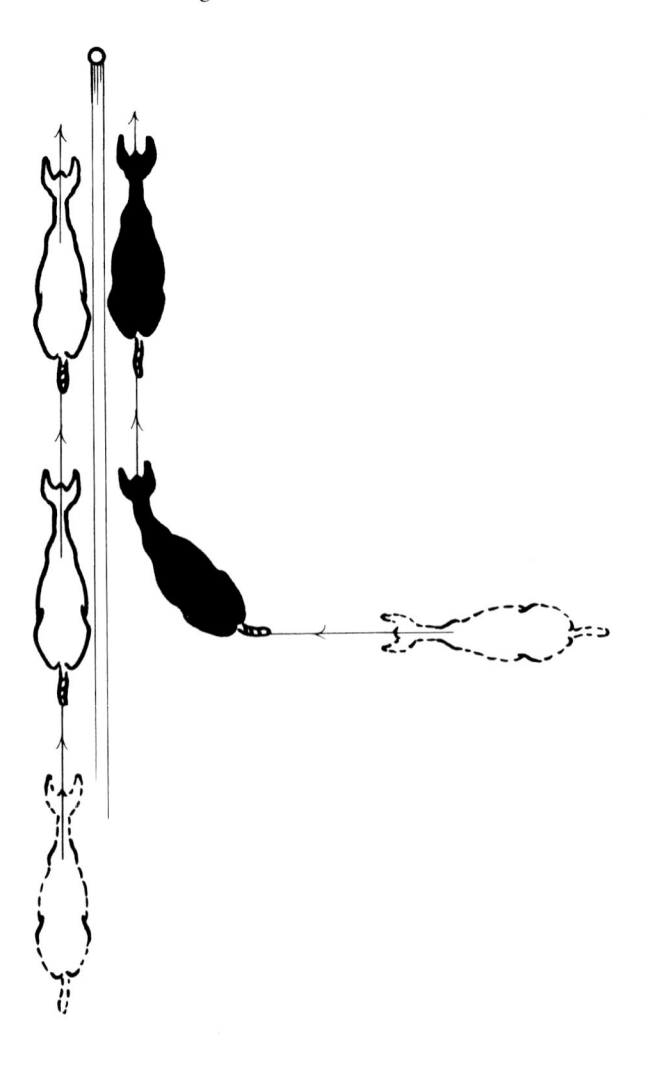

is the *line made by the ball as it travels or the line it ran before stopping*. Any player following the line with the ball on the *offside* has the primary right of way and is entitled over all others to proceed. If the ball is on the *nearside* it is the secondary right of way, with no entitlement to meet an opponent approaching with the ball on his offside. The player with the secondary right of way must give way, or he will commit a foul.

Engaging an opponent in a legal ride-off to gain control, before striking the ball. The opponent may be on or far away from the line which gives the 'right of way' The technique of a ride-off is covered in full in Chapter 8. Engaging opponents mainly applies to the 25%, when you compete directly for the ball, but is still relevant to the 75% of play, as explained below.

Uniqueness of Polo

The importance of engaging correctly and early is related to the three ways in which polo is unique among sports, already mentioned in my introduction:

1. The disparity of skills of the participating players.

2. That there is a right of way related to the path of the ball.

3. That, without relation to the ball, you can obstruct another player in the 75%.

The combination of these three factors provides great scope for one player to make a fool of another, when competing for the ball. This is because the weaker player cannot adjust to changes of the line of the ball and the actions of others as quickly as a superior opponent, who therefore wins more possession and almost all the ride-offs between them, or draws a foul. However, engaging actively during the 75% of play can effectively *limit* any superiority of opponents and (ladies please note) it will reduce the roughness which can occur when contact is made close to the ball. Basically you are wrong if you are not marking an opponent, except when you are escaping from one to try to be a *playmaker*. Therefore, you should always look to engage an opponent visually and, for much of the time, physically.

Line Complications

The line of the ball is very simple, in that it is the exact path of the ball, but deflections cause complications because then the right of way changes rapidly. The better players also muddle opponents (and sometimes umpires) by appearing from nowhere to claim the line. When in the 25%, there are four possible situations that could exist. These are covered in detail in Chapter 8 by the section Receiving a Pass. The secret lies in knowing which one of the four situations you are encountering, before engaging the line or the opponent. The Field Rules in Appendix 1 of the *Hurlingham Association Year Book* should also be read thoroughly, so that you become fully acquainted with the way all the fouls relate to right of way and the line of the ball.

Turn

Turning early is the way to win possession of the ball, to be the *playmaker* in the 25% and to be in control of your area in the 75% of play. Ideally, you should turn before the play changes direction. The player who turns earliest should win possession, but it is essential that you have first adjusted to be the correct distance to receive a pass. Thereby, you should be able either to join the line of the ball first or engage early any opponent who would otherwise threaten you. Ideally, your turn will be seen by the hitter, who then directs the ball to you, the *playmaker*.

Completing LATET

In a relay race, the anchor member of a team is in a similar situation to a polo player, who accomplishes the first four parts of LATET and then turns. If the other team members have given a poor performance, the last one cannot win. Equally, if the others are in good form, their efforts will be wasted if the last one is slow. Hence, when a polo player turns early, the whole LATET *playmaking* formula will be completed, but a late turn will waste the other four component parts.

Times to Turn

Far too many polo players consistently turn late because they are chasing or watching the ball to the exclusion of applying LATET. Also, their subconscious rules and misleads them into thinking that the ball will not reach them, until they see it actually arrive. There are four different times to turn *but only the first is correct*:

1. *Before the ball is struck, so that you can become the playmaker.*

2. One move late, *after you see the ball has been struck.*

3. Two moves late, *after you see the ball has travelled some distance* and it may even have reached or gone past you.

4. Three moves late, *after the last striker of the ball has overtaken you.*

I believe that the majority of polo players belong to the third category, normally turning so late as to be two moves behind the action of the game and thereby going into both attack and defence in a non-*playmaking* capacity. This is an enormous error, which exaggerates any disparity of skills and will not be corrected until sideline coaching becomes a regular feature in polo. Once, in a tournament in Argentina, I watched two 5- and two 4-goal players in an 18-goal team. At half-time they only led by 1 goal so I took courage to suggest that they were all turning late. They looked surprised but corrected the fault and went on to win by 6 goals.

An early turn is especially relevant when defence switches into attack, because the best way to defeat your opponent's defence is to be a move ahead of it as a *playmaker*. To turn before attack changes to defence can also be very important, but this principle is not so dogmatic because there are some variations in its application. For example, in front of the barrier (see Chapter 11) it is normally preferable for a forward to try to depreciate an opponent's backhand by harassing, impeding and blocking the shot before turning. Also, behind the barrier, one of the backs, anticipating the direction of the backhand, can sometimes meet the shot instead of turning.

Thought Process

It is negative and wrong to argue that a late turn is justified because the backhand just might be missed. With distances correctly applied, as suggested above, one player should have the possibility of adjusting quickly to a missed shot to regain possession. It is vital to prevent the following thought process:

'Will the ball be missed?'
'The ball has been hit, but will it reach me?'
'Oh yes, the ball has reached me and now I turn' (two moves late).

This should be replaced by:
'Adjust to be correct distance from the backhander.'
'Move to be free in open ground, or to where an opponent can be controlled.'
'Turn *before* backhand is struck.'

Therefore, your subconscious must be disciplined and I suggest you carry out exercises which train you to turn before backhands are struck — it is even better if you verbalize the word *playmaking* as you do it. This should create muscle memory, having a similar effect to saving some text in a computer, which can be recalled when required, and it could even be repeated in actual matches until you are confident that you have developed an automatic early turn. The watchful eye of a coach constantly assessing this dimension will help to accelerate improvement, make you into a *playmaker* and prevent you from returning to the bad habit of turning late.

Polo standards would be raised dramatically if all clubs had coaching which concentrated on the skills of *turning to be a playmaker*. In due course, this would not only make the players apply the five parts of LATET consistently, but would also convert the receiver into being the *playmaker* on many more occasions.

SUMMARY

I believe that, by understanding LATET, you can master the first stage of tactics that gives you the base upon which to build the knowledge of how to play in all four positions in a team. These will be covered in detail in individual chapters about the job and duties of each player. When those chapters, and all of what has been said here, are assimilated, you will be able to *playmake* by combining in an effective strategy with the other players. The assistance of a coach, who is unbiased, must provide a very helpful input and minimize arguments between the players The team tactics can then be adjusted as necessary for each match, to take account of the expected strengths and weaknesses of the opposition, besides correcting the faults observed in your own players. Hopefully, by then, you will often find *the ball following you*.

REVISION

Look

A	—	**A**ll-round vision.
B	—	use **B**ody to look.
B	—	look **B**ehind continually.
I	—	look **I**n front on both sides.

Adjust

S	—	**S**peed travelled.
D	—	**D**istances from others.
D	—	**D**irection travelling.
M	—	to **M**istakes.

Team

B	—	watch your **B**est player.
O	—	**O**ff-the-ball positioning is 75% of the game.
E	—	fill any **E**mpty position.
WAS	—	**W**eak, **A**verage and **S**trong passes all covered.

Engage

L	—	the **L**ine of the ball.
O	—	the relevant **O**pponent.
V	—	always engage **V**isually.
P	—	be ready to engage **P**hysically.

Turn

R	—	before the ball **R**eaches you.
H	—	before the ball is **H**it.
P	—	*P*laymaking to be sent a pass.
C	—	LATET is **C**ompleted by an early turn.

6

SLOSH Guidelines for Riding

Riders New to Polo — Seat — Legs — Outside the Pony — Steering — Hands Applied Softly

Riders New to Polo

Some people are born to be on a horse, so riding comes naturally to them. Even so, they can and do benefit from good constructive coaching and criticism. If they decide to try polo, such people will have an advantage over contemporaries who are inexperienced riders, so long as they can change their riding technique as required.

The less fortunate, who try polo as novice riders, can offset their obvious disadvantage by accepting that the average polo pony is excellently trained to *follow* them. Then, by seeking lessons and coaching that will enable them to develop legs strong enough to impart orders to a pony, they can quickly become sufficiently competent to play in a polo match.

Both of the above categories of riders should benefit enormously if they consciously apply the five headings that make up the mnemonic SLOSH, as described and explained below. The aim is to make the pony follow you, while you concentrate on tactics and hitting. Exercises described in the chapters on riding will show you how this can be done in relation to other riders and ponies.

Seat

Always sit on the front of the saddle and check regularly that you have not slipped backwards to be on the cantle. This is very important because:

1. It enables you to hit the ball *early*.
2. You will be secure in the saddle, permanently well balanced, and your body's centre of gravity will be perfectly placed to apply all the skills of polo.
3. You can move into the half-seat with minimum effort.
4. The pony is comfortable for all exertions.

Many of the best polo players are in the half-seat for most of the time, and always when striking the ball. Ideally, your fork stays permanently flush with the pommel of the saddle. You can move into the half-seat by letting your head go forward while increasing thigh pressure and pushing the pelvis forward. It is important to be able to change effortlessly from sitting on the front of the saddle to being in the half-seat.

Sebastian Dawnay in the half-seat.

Jose Suto in the half-seat playing the ball early.

Legs

The correct application of strong legs is a fundamental requirement for all types of riding. When playing polo, the squeeze from the legs is necessary before carrying out adjustments or actions such as:

Accelerating — Approaching the Ball — Changing Direction — Hooking a Stick — Riding-off Opponents — Looking behind — Slowing Down — Stopping

The weight of your head should be transmitted down the body, to the seat, through the thighs and knees, into the feet set parallel to the pony's flanks and finishing in the heels. Then the feet must tilt the pressure into the insteps. Thus, with the toes firmly up, the heels down and the feet slightly angled like a snow-plough, the squeeze will be strong and smooth. Normally the knees and toes form a vertical line, but at times in the half-seat the feet may have to move back behind this line to assist balance. Thus there is a shock-absorbing action provided first by thighs and knees and second by ankles and feet.

Outside the Pony

A good car driver looks outside the vehicle while using hands and feet to manipulate the controls without seeing them. A polo player should do exactly the same, applying legs, hands and whip, if necessary, without seeing the pony. By deliberately not observing the pony you are riding, you can effectively increase your control of that pony and, if you do this consistently, the pony will become totally dominated while you concentrate fully on the game. By emphasizing this I have helped enormously many weak riders and added extra skill to some strong ones. Possibly without realizing it, all high-goal players are completely 'outside the pony', while the majority of low-goal players and beginners, when I first meet them, are clearly 'inside the pony' – see Figure 4(a) and (b).

Once this concept has been accepted and applied, besides improving the ability to see all other players and everything that happens, pony manoeuvrability and control will increase. Ponies are non-predators with eyes on the sides of the head. Therefore they can watch and react to all your actions in order to conform to you. This is highly preferable to the reverse, which initially forces you to 'follow the pony', thereby losing valuable time, until you overrule to take control. Another way to describe this vital skill is that the heads of the rider and pony are permanently separated. The presence and absence of eye contact between rider and pony, and the relative effects upon training and riding, have been explained in more detail in *Polo Vision*.

Turning the lower limbs, especially the feet, can help you to stay 'outside the pony' and see the actions of others – but beware not to upset the correct use of the legs by overdoing this. A very supple person can turn at the waist effortlessly, without any assistance from lower down. The required result is to simulate having a rear view mirror.

Figure 4. (a) Correctly positioned, 'outside the pony'.

(b) 'Inside the pony'.

A 2-goal player once wrote to me, to say that he had won an important tournament because, in the last chukka of the final, he had extracted the best-ever performance from his favourite pony. By exaggerating the way he kept 'outside the pony', he made it react to him perfectly.

Steering

The indirect rein is the reining method used for steering a polo pony. The left hand applies the indirect rein across the pony's neck (neck-reining), which should be carried out without any contact on the pony's mouth. Yet the contact of the rein on the pony's neck should only be *confirming* any instruction to change direction. The action begins with a look behind, or sideways, before asking the pony to turn. In this way you will avoid accidentally colliding with others and making unnecessary turns, but when required, you can make the fastest possible change of direction. This is an extension of being 'outside the pony'. If you keep your eyes totally focused on the new direction, throughout the turn, the pony can follow you without difficulty. Remember, the pony likes to stay beneath your weight and to look, together with you when possible, wherever your focus is. Therefore, there should not be any confusion if the pony first feels your legs give a warning and then sees you look and lean in the new direction, before receiving the clear directive from the neck-rein to turn and follow you.

Hands Applied Softly

Soft, sympathetic hands are easy to apply from a correct seat or half-seat, supported by strong legs. Ideally, the reins are held either side of the left-hand index finger, with the two snaffle reins above and the two gag or pelham reins below (see Figure 5). In addition to the four reins, a polo player must also hold a whip in the left hand. As most of the

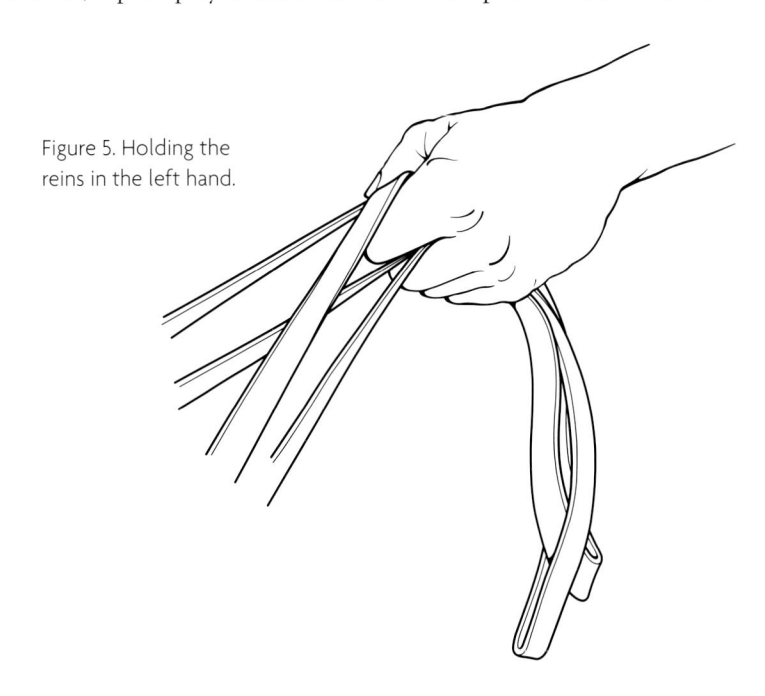

Figure 5. Holding the reins in the left hand.

Light hands. Pite Merlos seen here balancing himself on his legs, not the reins: the pony's mouth remains closed.

steering should be done by the indirect rein, any direct pull by your hands must be minimized to a light contact at all times. Two reins, and sometimes two hands, can be gentler than one. With no fear of pain in the mouth, a pony will follow you willingly. In a way similar to the brake in a car, the bit in a pony's mouth will cause progressive wear if overused, ending in destruction. During the initial damage, there may be no evidence of wear or the problem to come. But while, in due course, a car can be fitted with new brakes, a new mouth for a pony is unobtainable. By keeping your left hand low, neck-reining becomes extra effective for all lateral adjustments. The use of strong legs, before slowing or stopping, will lessen the amount of contact on the mouth by the hands. Halting can also be assisted by looking behind you, because it gives the pony a better and more pleasant warning than a pull on the mouth.

SUMMARY

In the heat of a polo match it is easy to forget, and to stop applying one or more of the SLOSH points. Between chukkas it must be helpful to hear a verbal reminder about these from someone, preferably a coach. For example, I have often simply asked a client one question: 'Are you using your legs?' At the end of the match, without fail, I would always be told that the result of this had been that controlling the pony had become much easier. Until players reach a high handicap, if they want their ponies to follow them obediently round the polo field, they must continually revise the five points covered by SLOSH when riding, schooling and practising. This should become simpler if the exercises, suggested in the ensuing chapters on riding, are carried out correctly and – even better – if they are supervised by a coach. If you include the *playmaker* dimension, as described, you will benefit doubly from riding and some tactical training.

REVISION

Seat should be
F — on the **F**ront of the saddle.
H — in the **H**alf-seat much of the time.
F — positioned with the rider's **F**ork **F**lush with the saddle.
C — maintaining balance and security with body's **C**entre of gravity forward.

Legs need to operate the feet
P — **P**arallel to the pony's flanks.
I — with the pressure on the **I**nstep.
S — to apply a **S**now-plough action.
A — applied **A**ll the time to provide first shock-absorber at knees and thighs, with second at ankle and feet.

Outside pony means
N — rider does **N**ot see pony.
P — **P**ony sees and reacts to rider/player.
S — rider can **S**ee all other players.
M — a rear-view **M**irror is simulated.

Steering is operated by
L — **L**ooking in the new direction first before turning.
N — **N**eck-reining positively while changing direction.
F — the pony **F**ollowing the rider when told, and not anticipating.
E — continual **E**ye focus in new direction throughout turn.

Hands should be applied
M — with **M**inimum force.
L — by a **L**ow left hand.
T — by **T**wo reins and **T**wo hands when necessary.
L — after and in combination with **L**egs.

7

PASSF for Striking

The PASSF Concept — Preparation — Approach — Swing Slowly — Sweet Spot — Follow Through

The PASSF Concept

The mnemonic PASSF describes five criteria – Preparation, Approach, Swing Slowly, Sweet Spot and Follow Through – which are essential elements in striking a polo ball. If you have amazing natural talent, you will quickly find a way to hit a polo ball without having to learn the details on PASSF expounded below and in the ensuing chapters on striking that explain further all the different shots. But if you are a normal mortal, you can only become a good striker by understanding the necessity for applying the five parts of PASSF to almost every shot you hit. Occasionally, you can get away with missing out one or more of the elements, but consistency will definitely be lost if any of them are frequently ignored.

I believe that a *slow swing* is the secret for perfecting the technique. This requires an acute awareness of how to apply economy, which will be explained and examined when relevant. Yet it is much easier to develop a regular slow stroke if the other four parts of PASSF are always incorporated in your style. Therefore, each element is, itself, essential and using all five of them necessitates a disciplined thought process, which, in time, should translate into valuable muscle memory, which can stay with you for life.

Five Circles

A perfect circle is the key to accuracy and power when striking a polo ball. Shots that are correctly hit should take the mallet head through an exact circle, or part of one. The mallet head can only stay in the required circle if the pivotal action by the hand is slow.

A polo player who has developed the ability to hit accurately in all directions, will have mastered the ten basic shots, by applying five different circles (see Figure 6). Each of the five circles relates to two shots, one of which turns clockwise and the other anticlockwise. For example, offside forehands and nearside backhands describe circles that rotate clockwise, and offside backhands and nearside forehands travel anticlockwise as follows:

Circle 1. The straight forehands on the offside and nearside of the pony (see Chapter 13).

Circle 2. The offside shots under the neck and the open backhand (see Chapter 16).

Circle 3. The offside shots, forehand cut and tail backhand (see Chapter 19).

Circle 4. The nearside shots under the neck and open backhand (see Chapter 22).

Circle 5. The nearside shots, forehand cut and tail backhand (see Chapter 25).

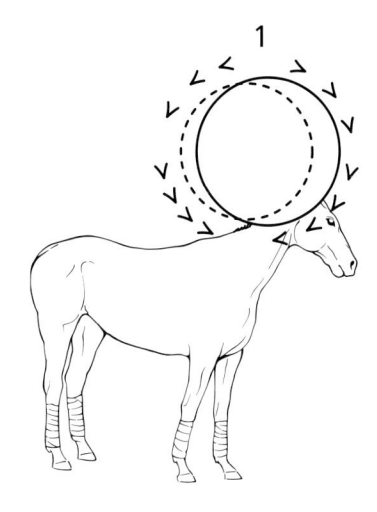

Figure 6. The five circles. These circles form the basis for the different shots explained in the chapters on striking; they should be referred to as appropriate and, ultimately, committed to memory.

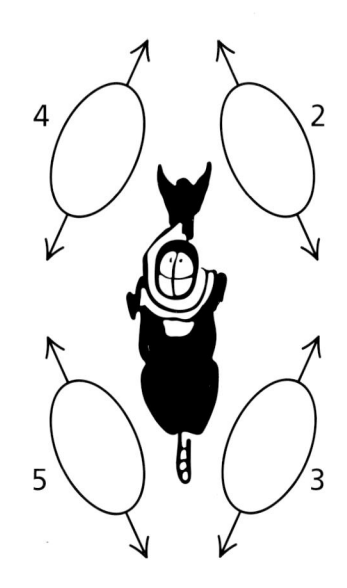

Avoiding Straight Backhands

Hitting straight backhands, on both sides of the pony, are the worst *mistakes* made by beginners. During a polo game they are universally regarded as bad shots. In the majority of situations they give the ball to an opponent, and they cannot be received as a pass by a team member. Also, straight backhands will, too often, hit a pony or player, thereby ruining the flow of the game and possibly causing an injury. However, although they occur seldom, there are two exceptional circumstances when a straight backhand could be required:

1. When the goal which you are attacking is close, directly behind you and not defended.

2. When all the other players are blocking every available angle on both sides of you and the only open ground is directly behind you.

Nevertheless, I firmly believe that to practise them will cultivate a bad habit and it is therefore not justified, and they are not included in the circles explanation.

Use of the Shoulder

Each circle rotates round the right hand of the striker, who should add support to it by turning the relevant shoulder towards the ball. This assists the eyes to focus on the ball and obviates using arm strength. For the forehands on the offside and the backhands on the nearside, the left shoulder couples with the chin. The right shoulder takes over the task for the nearside forehands and the offside backhands. It can help if you think of the chin and shoulder fighting each other (see Figure 7).

Preparation

In all the chapters on striking I have used this heading, preparation, to serve two purposes, each of which has three parts.

1. How to build the *construction* of each shot when learning and revising the *technique*.
   (a) Holding the mallet correctly.
   (b) Finding the relevant circle.
   (c) Developing the exact swing in the correct circle required for the shot.

2. Establishing a procedure before each individual shot when playing and practising.
   (a) Placing the mallet head at the bottom of the relevant circle for a half-shot and at the top for a full shot. One could say either on or directly above ground zero. (Some catchphrases that may help achieve this are suggested at the relevant points.)
   (b) Application of your legs to balance the pony and yourself.
   (c) Finding the relevant circle (if there is time), then returning to the bottom or top of the circle.

We should now look the elements of construction and procedure in more detail.

Figure 7. Use of shoulder for nearside forehand.

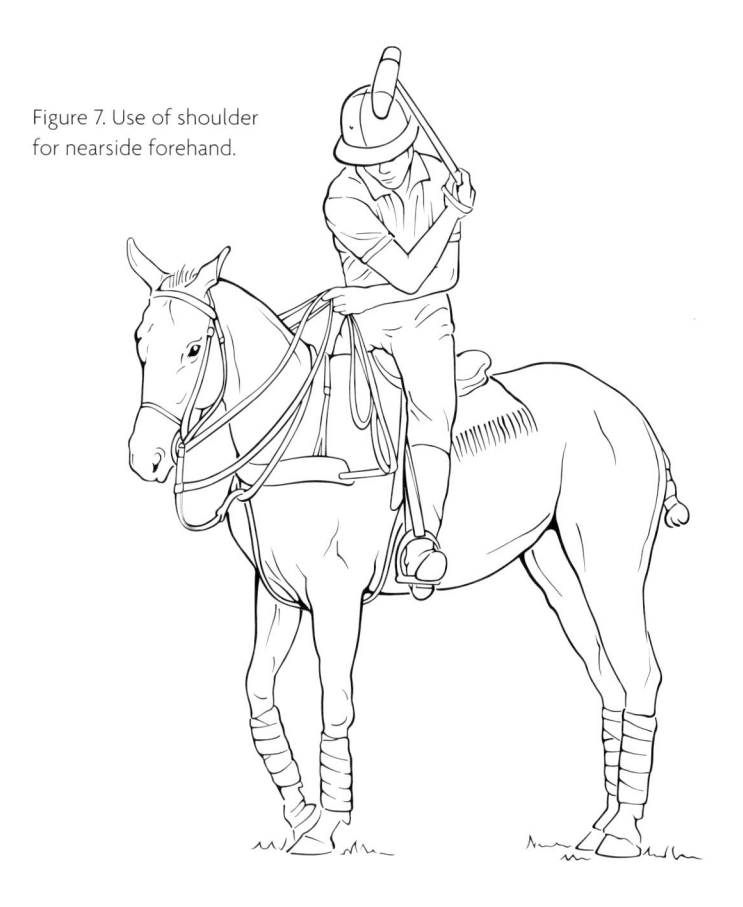

Construction of Shot

Holding the mallet correctly

1. The thumb and index finger take the majority of the weight while the other three fingers assist you to hold the mallet lightly. The thumb is placed in the sling, which supports the back of the hand, and the index finger operates like a pistol finger, in a way which avoids taking a hammer grip. The little finger is flush with the bottom of the handle (see Figure 8(a) and (b)).

2. Every time you sit on a pony, before hitting a ball, place the mallet head on ground zero for circle 1 on the offside and note where your right hand is in relation to your knee. Then you will know the correct height of your hand for the lowest part of the swing when striking the ball.

Finding the relevant circle

It is important to recognize that, during every shot, the mallet head should stay in a perfect circle. A golfer waiting to tee off often makes many practice swings in order to find the required circle. All the best polo players do something similar at intervals throughout a chukka. In every sport, the whole of your body – including the brain, which directs

PLAYMAKER POLO

the focus of your eyes – benefits from any action that makes the blood flow. There is an extra bonus if this can be combined with the preparation for a future action. When riding a horse it is not possible to run on the spot, like a tennis player waiting to receive a ball. But by revolving the polo mallet through 360 degrees fairly frequently you can produce a similar result, and by receiving a constant supply of blood, the right hand, plus all the fingers, will maintain total control of the mallet. With practice this becomes an effortless action because then the thumb and index finger merely allow the mallet head to fall and, with a small upward flick, maintain the momentum already induced. This can be done clockwise or anticlockwise when tactically in the 75% or the 25% (see Chapters 1 and 5).

Finding a circle will keep you warmed up and prepared for any shot you may suddenly have to take and, even when far from the ball, you can be practising a circle which might soon be required. While approaching the ball in the 25%, ideally, one circle should be made before starting the swing, but not if there is insufficient time. The better players, because they have developed the required timing, can afford to be extravagant

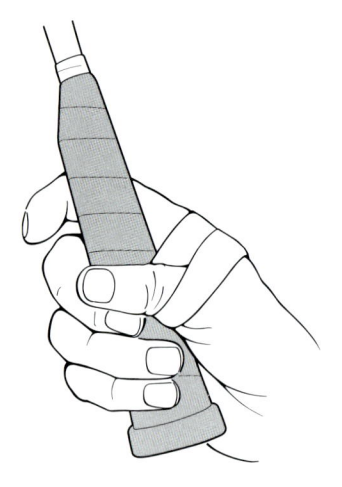

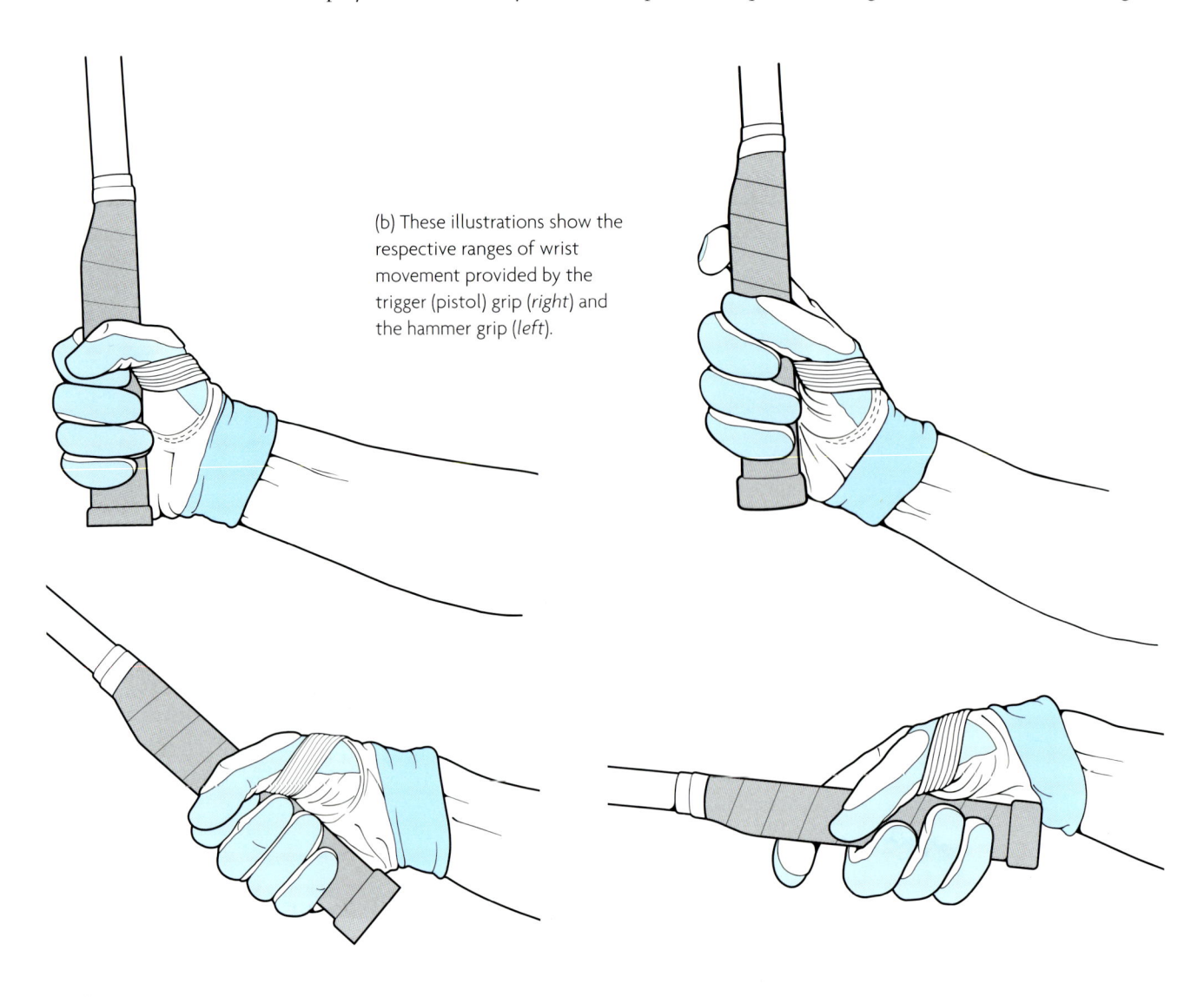

Figure 8. (a) Holding the mallet; taking the pistol grip.

(b) These illustrations show the respective ranges of wrist movement provided by the trigger (pistol) grip (*right*) and the hammer grip (*left*).

by incorporating finding a circle and the swing into one action. But the lower handicaps need more time to construct a shot from a defined mallet head position at the bottom or top of the circle, on or above ground zero. To achieve this necessitates separating the two actions by finding a circle earlier, or missing this out completely to move directly to the correct mallet head position. This induces economy by restricting the distance to be travelled by the mallet head during the actual shot.

There are added advantages from finding a circle (Figure 9):

1. It provides a preparatory swing.

2. The pony is also prepared for each shot and becomes so accustomed to a swinging mallet that the threat of shying away from the ball is reduced.

3. Your sense of timing and rhythm will be considerably improved so long as the preparation is not done late.

4. Your mind will be kept active, which should assist you to find ways of *playmaking* constructively, besides helping your powers of focus.

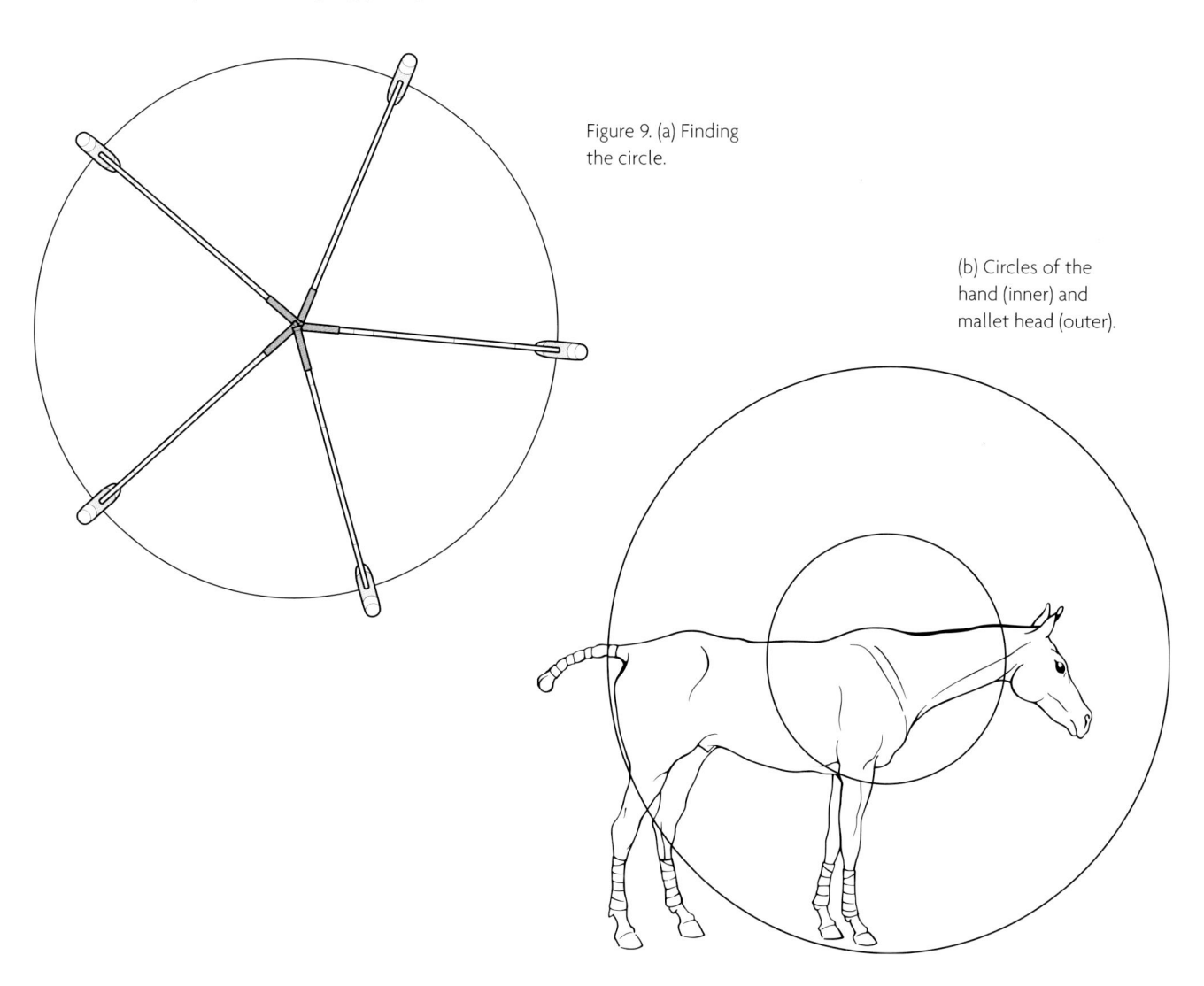

Figure 9. (a) Finding the circle.

(b) Circles of the hand (inner) and mallet head (outer).

Developing the exact swing for each shot

1. Before starting the swing, the mallet should be vertically down or vertically up, depending on whether a half- or full shot is intended and on how much time there is to make a full shot (see photographs). Again, a good, experienced player can, like a rich man, be extravagant and place the mallet down before a full shot, so that it has further to travel, thereby increasing the mallet head velocity. But the rest of us, like a poor man, need *economy* to avoid hitting late or missing and therefore need to have the mallet up before a full shot. In either case, your hand should be accurately placed, ready to start a swing from the centre of a perfect circle. For the ten shots, five on each side of the pony, I believe that the hand positions required for you to start from the centre of the circle can be limited to just four. These will be covered in detail when the shots are explained in later chapters. Watch for the catchphrase that each one has been given to help you memorize them.

2. From the correct mallet and hand starting position, several complete full or half swings should be made at an imaginary ball, until you are satisfied that the correct circle is being used, together with a slow enough swing. For the full swing, emphasis should be made on placing the mallet head exactly in the circle, so that during the swing it will point momentarily at the target. In order to achieve this, the thumb, for clockwise shots, and the V between the index finger and thumb, for anticlockwise ones, must take the weight of the mallet at the vital moment.

below and opposite page
Mallets being carried in action.

Establishing a Procedure Before Each Individual Shot

This is the equivalent of treating every strike as if it were the first shot and thus always achieving economy from the correct preparation.

Bottom or top of the circle

Immediately you decide which shot to take, you should place the mallet head at the bottom or top of the relevant circle. By doing this, you are ensuring economy of movement, which greatly assists you to maintain a slow swing. I have noticed that too many players carry their mallet like a spear or fishing rod, halfway between up and down, and this invariably makes them hit late, rushed and poorly. Whenever they allowed me to correct them, there was immediately a big improvement in their striking. Others are apt to begin correctly by placing the mallet in the circle, but then allow the mallet head to fall or swing forward or sideways, thereby delaying the first part of the swing and consequently causing the second part to be rushed.

Application of legs

The pony and the player should be balanced before a strike is commenced and this is done simply by a strong squeeze of your legs. This action will also greatly assist you to make an accurate approach to the ball.

Starting and finishing the circle

With the mallet head on or above ground zero, if there is time, you should find the circle and finish again at the bottom or top of that circle. The circle applied for the straight offside forehand can be adequate for all the shots because it makes the blood flow, bringing the mallet under control and creating a rhythm for any angle required. However, before an angled shot, a bonus is gained if you are able to find the circle using the required angle. For backhands, this will help to brief you not to hit straight back, as mentioned earlier.

Matias McDonagh (8) in mid-swing of the circle for the straight forehand.

Approach

Tennis players have to be fast and accurate with their two feet to make the correct approach before hitting a ball, especially if a shot has to be hit at an awkward angle. A polo player has to control the four legs of a pony, and any mistake during an approach to the ball will make the ensuing shot extra difficult and may cause a foul, or even an accident.

Two Dimensions

A good player en route to strike the ball makes a precise adjustment to deal with two dimensions:

1. To join the line of the ball as early as possible.

2. To place the pony to the ball accurately, in order to be able to hit through the required circle and aim in the exact direction of the chosen target.

A ball-chaser normally rushes to the ball without consideration of either dimension and adjusts much too late, with the last stride of the pony.

Two Clocks

Even hitting a difficult angle, without crossing the line of the ball, can be made easy if the approach is correct. For each shot, by first looking to see the exact location of the target, you will know where ground zero should be, which of the five circles is required and the spot, on the ball, that must be struck. The first element can be described by what we will call the *pony clock* (see Figure 10). The circles have already been explained and the required spot on the ball can be selected by using the *ball clock* (see Figure 11). You must then advance appropriately in a precise relationship to these two clocks. As examples, on the offside ideally:

1. The **pony clock** at **2** and the **ball clock** at **6** for a **straight** shot.

2. The **pony clock** at **1** and the **ball clock** at **4** for the average **neck** shot.

3. The **pony clock** at **4** and the **ball clock** at **2** for the average **tail** backhand.

Figure 10. The pony clock.

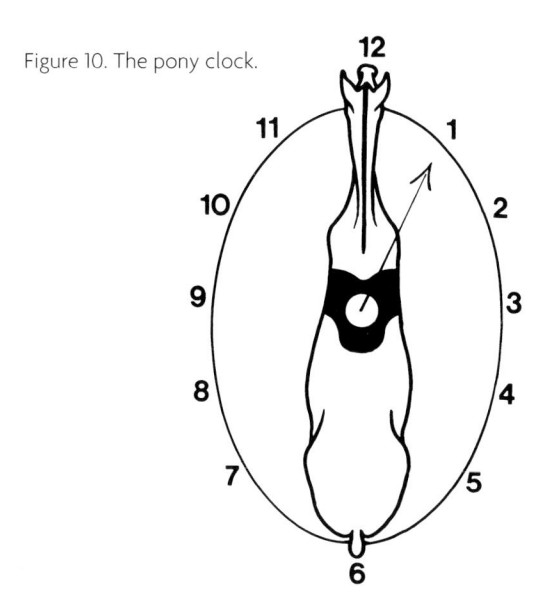

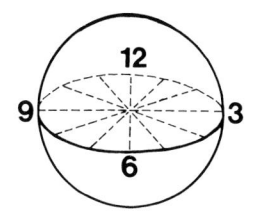

Figure 11. The ball clock.

These two figures form the basis for explanations on striking throughout the book, and should be referred to as appropriate and, ultimately, committed to memory.

Two Arcs

For any angled forehand and backhand shots, a slight arc, *which does not cross the line of the ball*, should be applied to the approach. This avoids hitting either the head or tail of the pony, as relevant, yet allows the mallet head to complete the required circle. Alternatively, the arc could be described as a very shallow curve. As examples:

1. The arc should be from **right** to **left** when applying **circles 2** and **5**.

2. The arc should be from **left** to **right** when applying **circle 3** and **4**.

More details of this will be covered in later chapters when the relevant shots are explained fully and the catchphrases given for the four different hand and mallet start positions; see also Figure 12.

Swing Slowly

Much thought and practice are needed to develop a slow swing, lest the subconscious should take over to control you. The mallet head will only describe a perfect circle if the swing is slow for both half- and full shots.

Economy

If your hand starts the swing from the centre of each circle that has to be described, this will induce economy, thereby making it easier to be slow and to stay in the perfect circle. Ideally, 50% of the swing occurs on each side of the ball – the downswing as one element and the follow through as other – because this is easy to control. Therefore, normally, a

Figure 12. Arcs for second, third, fourth and fifth circles.

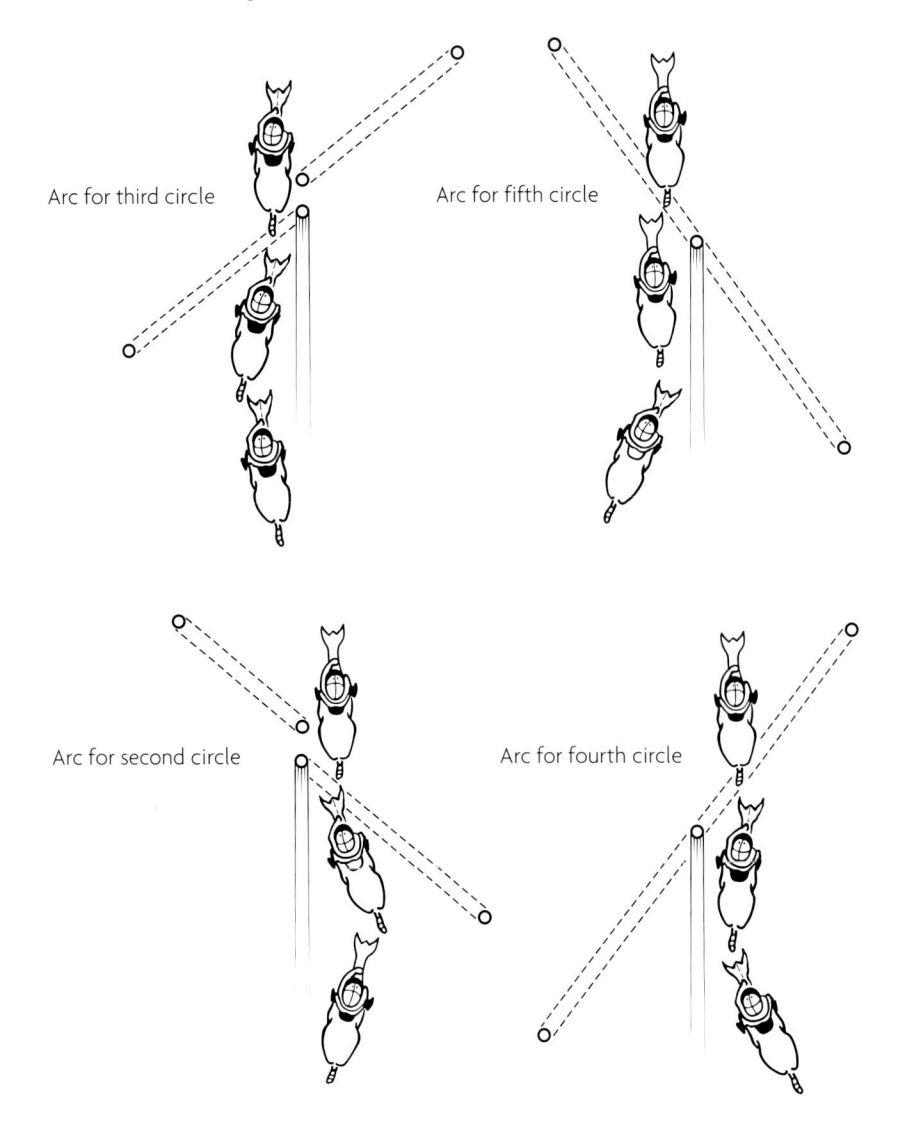

Arc for third circle

Arc for fifth circle

Arc for second circle

Arc for fourth circle

short swing back is followed by a short swing forward, and a long swing back by a long swing forward (see Figures 13, 14 and 15), but there are exceptions for specific shots or situations. One exception, which happens often, is when you know that you are about to hit late. Then, you should apply economy with a short first part of the swing so that the second half can be longer, can but still be slow (see Figure 16).

Shoulders

As in many other sports, including tennis and boxing, a turn of the shoulders will prevent the use of arm strength alone. The feet, thighs and hips can help by rotating under your shoulders, but be careful not to upset your riding seat. Also, by first looking at the ball before bringing the relevant shoulder to touch your chin, you can economize in body movement.

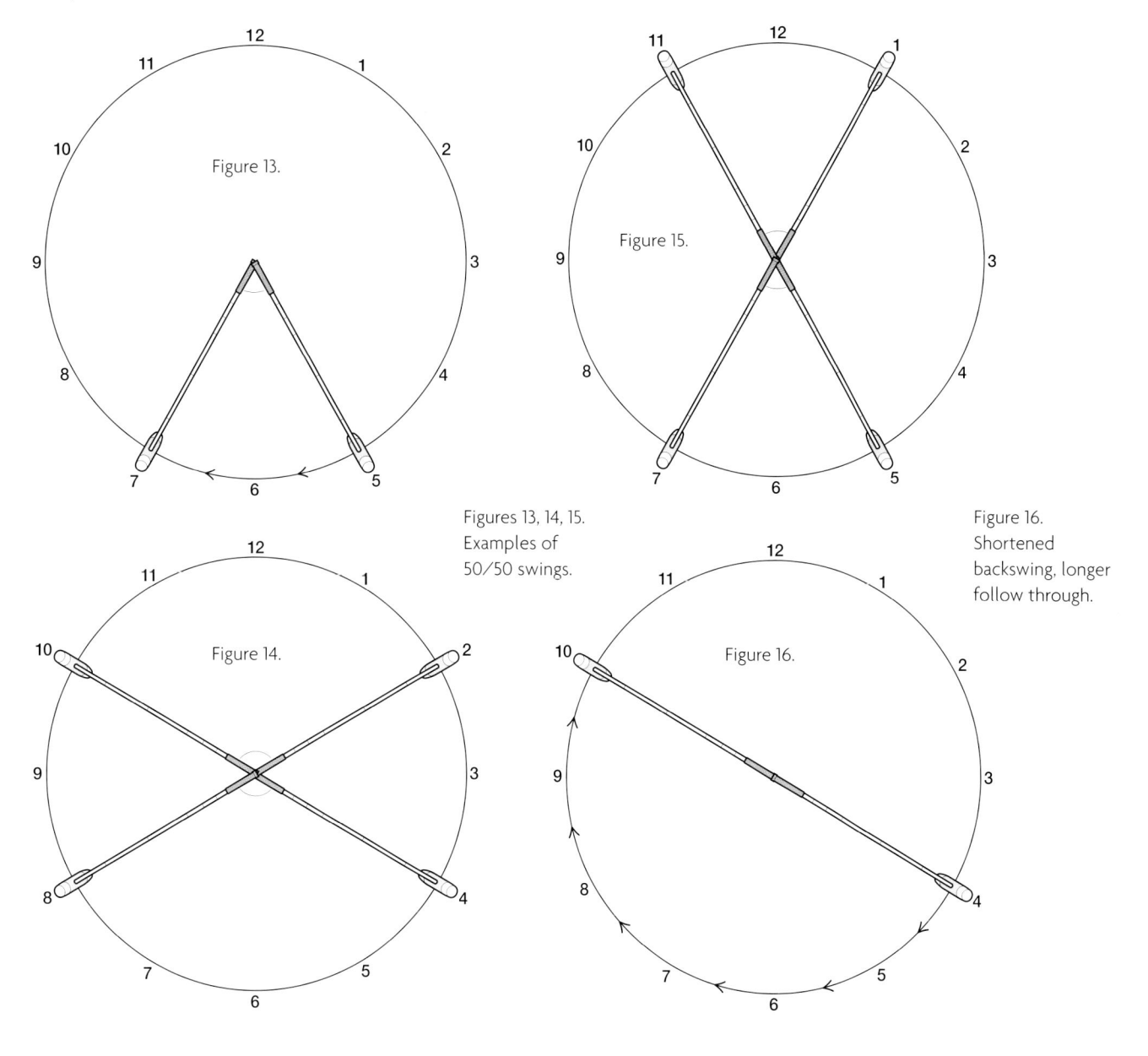

Figure 13.

Figure 15.

Figures 13, 14, 15. Examples of 50/50 swings.

Figure 14.

Figure 16.

Figure 16. Shortened backswing, longer follow through.

Effective use of shoulder – Charles Beresford.

Beware that too much shoulder movement causes the most common fault for a straight forehand, on both sides of the pony. This is allowing the backswing of the mallet to go above the pony's tail and out of the circle, thereby inducing a curve in the forward half of the swing. This can be controlled by thinking that you are riding parallel to a large pane of glass, which you wash with your hand while swinging. Alternatively take your hand and your mallet as for a half-shot, back to 5 on the pony clock on the offside and to 7 o'clock on the nearside and aim at 6 on the ball clock. Then learn to remember the feeling for future shots. Hence, for a moment, a straight line will always be formed between your hand, the required spot on the ball and the target.

Point at Target

For the majority of full shots, the shoulder turn supports the placing of the mallet head to point in the direction of the target. Thus, momentarily, the whole mallet is set as a pendulum which, if prevented from wavering, should stay in the perfect circle, although the mallet head accelerates to catch up with the hand, which continues to move slowly for the second part of the swing.

The classical swing of Tommy Morgan, pointing at the target.

Sweet Spot

There are three big advantages to be gained from aiming at a particular spot on the ball instead of trying to direct the whole ball:

1. Accuracy is increased.

2. The extra focus required to find the spot gives a better and more solid contact.

3. Your head has to stay down longer to pinpoint the spot.

If you have already, during the approach, clearly defined the spot on the ball which needs to be struck, this spot should be confirmed by you before contact is made. The combination of the early focus and confirmation increases the chance of hitting the exact spot.

When you select the spot on the ball clock you will probably focus on the middle of the ball. Yet, as you make contact, you should find the *bottom* of the ball with the middle of the mallet head, at ground zero, and adjust your focus accordingly

I suggest that you will find it easier to aim at the spot with your right hand, rather than the mallet head, so that you feel the hand go *through* the ball. In fact, you should aim your hand to travel along the line that goes through the spot and the ball. If the movement of the hand towards the selected spot is executed slowly, the mallet head will have time to complete the desired circle and reach the ball ahead of the hand. The pendulum will thus operate correctly, maximizing mallet head velocity. But if the hand moves too fast to the spot, there will not be time for the mallet head to accelerate sufficiently and it will leave the circle. Then you will have to resort (wrongly) to using too much arm strength.

Verbalizing initially will help to perfect the action, but the words must be your choice and they can be constructively varied to include, *'slow hand'*, *'hand to spot'*, *'slow spot'* or *'hand slow'*. The result can be startling, because not only does this make you concentrate at the time, but it also can give you useful muscle memory for the future.

Adolfo Cambiaso finding the sweet spot.

Follow Through

In all techniques for striking a ball in any sport, the follow through is the vital last part of the recognized style. It is used to confirm accuracy and to increase power.

Through Ball to Target

You should control the mallet head so as to take it through the ball and on, at least, to where it will be pointing directly at the target, while your eyes stay looking at where the ball was, when struck. In other words, your hand can be directed towards the target by the brain, which learnt where it was during the approach. If done correctly, this ensures accuracy and, since it promotes purity of strike, can add length to a shot.

Another Circle and Return to Vertical

After passing through the ball with a forehand, in order to point at the target, you ideally allow the mallet to continue rotating through another circle. Thereby it turns at least 360 degrees to reach ground zero again, and it can go much further. This action dissipates the mallet head velocity and prevents any lateral deviation away from the target, further assisting accuracy. All the best players apply this procedure and I recommend that you try to include it early on during training. It is not essential, and does not necessarily suit every player, but it must be to your advantage if you can acquire the habit quickly.

Finally, to complete the follow through you should allow the mallet to return to a vertical position ready for the next shot. By doing this you will be restarting the whole PASSF technique by making an early preparation for any ensuing shots, as well as continuing to apply economy.

SUMMARY

To apply all five points of PASSF consistently requires a detailed understanding of each of them. Then continual self-discipline and frequent revision are necessary in order to apply them to the ten shots within the five circles, as you learn these from the chapters on striking which follow, and when you practise them. It is easy to forget one or more of these elements from time to time, without realizing it – although you may be wondering why your striking has become less accurate than before. This problem can surely be reduced, or even avoided, if your style is regularly assessed to confirm the good points and to seek improvement in all dimensions. This will keep your muscle memory topped up and remind you of the significance of employing in your style:

1. A slow swing.

2. Accurate circles as relevant.

3. Shoulders towards the ball.

4. The principle of economy.

5. The concept that every strike is the first shot.

All this will be achieved through three key dimensions of *playmaking*: hard work, constant revision and seeking the help of a patient coach.

To simplify such a task and such commitment I have, in each chapter on striking, dealt with one circle and the two shots related to it by dividing the relevance of PASSF into two sections:

Construction of each shot in detail, as explained above, through experimenting while learning and applying the five-part technique.

Execution of shot, that gives you a brief for all the details required in order to use the circle and hit accurately in a specific direction.

REVISION

Preparation
C — bottom or top of **C**ircle.
L — application of **L**egs.
F — **F**ind the circle.

Approach
L — **L**ine of the ball.
T — **T**arget selected.
S — **S**weet **S**pot defined.
A — **A**rc to clear head or tail of pony.

Swing
S — **S**wing **S**lowly.
S — **S**tart in centre of circle.
S — **S**horten swing when late.
S — **S**houlders support mallet.

Sweet spot
B — **B**ottom of ball.
C — **C**onfirmed.
T — **T**hrough spot and ball.

Follow through
T — **T**arget reached.
C — **C**ircle completed.
N — mallet vertical for **N**ext shot with force dissipated.

8

Tactics 'A' — Playmaking Components

Three Essential Skills — Receiving a Pass — The Ride-off — Hooking Sticks — Leading Exponents

Three Essential Skills

To participate effectively in a team as a *playmaker*, you must develop three abilities:

1. To receive and give passes.

2. To compete successfully for the ball in the 25%.

3. To prevent opponents hitting the ball, from good anticipation, in the 75%.

All three dimensions of *playmaking* require you, at all times, to recognize instantly the exact situation that you are encountering. Each one may necessitate the employment of a ride-off, although the third can often be achieved by simply hooking a stick. Each of the three skills needs a thought process and a correct technique. The applied logic that follows should help you develop these attributes.

Receiving a Pass

Assessing Advantage and Disadvantage

When you find yourself in the 25% and the ball has been sent towards you, or to an area where you could go to receive it as a pass, you must assess whether, in relation to your opponents, you have an advantage or are at a disadvantage. You will be in one of the four different basic situations that can exist. In two of them you will have an *advantage* over the opponents and should be able to hit the ball, if you *playmake* early enough, and correctly. In the other two situations you are at a *disadvantage* and need surprise to outwit opponents and win the ball.

Four Situations

Obviously, you will benefit enormously if you quickly recognize which of the four situations you are encountering and then react correctly, positively and rapidly. Realizing the benefits or difficulties of each situation is crucial to your reactions. These are as follows.

Situation 1 – You are nearest to the ball and out of reach of a ride-off or a hook

Thus you have an advantage, and cannot be prevented from taking a shot. This appears to be the best of all situations, but beware – if you fail to look behind, you can easily commit a foul. Why? Because if you approach the ball by the direct route, experienced opponents are certain to join the line, behind and earlier than you, thereby causing you to cross them as you strike the ball and give away the advantage which you had.

Reaction
Go laterally before you go vertically – upfield may be the simplest way to describe it. In other words, use your advantage to join the line of the ball as early as possible, but look behind to ensure that an opponent has not reached the line first, to claim a foul. Then stay on the line until you have hit the ball and moved a few yards beyond where the ball was, thereby avoiding crossing the line of the ball after striking it.

Situation 2 – You are in front of an opponent who has already claimed the line

Again, you are the closest to the ball and have an advantage, but if you try to hit the ball, you are certain to foul.

Reaction
Go laterally, pause before winning a ride-off against the opponent and then hit the ball. To gain from the advantage of being in front, you must engage, in a safe and legal manner, by applying the five parts of a ride-off, as described in the next section.

Situation 3 – You are at a disadvantage behind an opponent, who is to the left or right, on the same side of the line as you

If you proceed down the line to the ball, the opponent can, without difficulty wait to win a ride-off against you. All ball-chasers make this error, because they only think about reaching the ball and fail to realize that they will be an easy target for the opponent to engage.

Reaction
To counter the disadvantage of your position, before a ride-off, go away from the line and the ball, moving directly towards the opponent. Against a weaker player, the surprise of this action should win the ride-off and the ball for you. You will probably still lose the ball against a stronger player, but if you can upset the timing of the next shot sufficiently to reduce its length or accuracy, this will be a help to your team.

Situation 4 – *You are at a disadvantage behind an opponent, who is to the left or right, on the other side the line*

If you join the line, any opposing player who thinks clearly can win the ball by striking a backhand, without crossing the line or making any contact. Alternatively, that player might be able to engage you early enough to control you, before hitting the ball on the other side of the pony.

Reaction
Cross the line before attempting a ride-off. As above, this reduces the disadvantage and is more effective against a weaker than a stronger player, but against any opponent, disruption of strike may be achieved even if the ride-off is lost.

Fallacy

It is a fallacy to say that crossing the line is a foul. When there is no other opponent behind you, if you engage sufficiently early before reaching the ball, you can legally cross the line and ride-off an opponent. However, be aware that, if the ball is suddenly directly between you and the opponent, before engaging you must first draw level and ensure that only a half-shot is about to be made.

The Ride-off

No other ball game has a right of way. A polo player frequently finds that an opponent has already claimed that right of way. To deal with this unique factor, you must know how to deprive an opponent of this right, by means of a legal ride-off.

Another unique dimensions of polo, referred to in my introduction, is that *at any time a player may obstruct an opponent with a ride-off, even if the ball is not in the vicinity and you are in the 75%*, so long as it is done in a legal manner and no other person is endangered. To take full advantage of this rule it is important that you know how to do this effectively without fouling.

The third unique polo dimension is the disparity of skills. This creates situations in which you have to compete one-on-one in a ride-off against an opponent who, with a higher handicap, has more ability and experience than you.

Normally, it is guaranteed that if two players with different handicaps engage in a series of ride-offs, the one with the higher rating will win most of them. This happens because the better player uses superior anticipation in the 75%, to get to a position from where the necessity for a ride-off can be seen early and the action begun, before an opponent has time to react.

Nevertheless this advantage can be reduced if you concentrate more on the opponent than the ball, thereby allowing yourself to be *taken* to the ball rather than *pushed away* from it. Also, dividing a ride-off into five parts and always applying all of them strictly will lessen your dominance by higher-handicapped opponents, and an advantage can be gained against players of similar experience and ability.

Five Elements of the Ride-off

Positioning

The best place to start from, before engaging in a ride-off, is ahead of an opponent. From there, you can come together with the opponent's knee behind yours. If you are catching up to engage, any adversary of ability will recognize the threat and do it first.

This advice holds good even for ball-chasers. Such people, who never look around, are vulnerable to being overpowered in any situation. Even so, playing safe by adjusting to be slightly in front before attempting a ride-off can help their cause.

Speed

Once in the correct position, your speed must be similar to that of the opponent whom you wish to engage. The most dangerous dimension of polo is when ponies, galloping at different speeds, make physical contact with each other. If one pony is going much faster or slower than the other, there will be an awkward moment of contact, which is certain to be called as a foul and may cause one or both of the ponies to fall. Thus, if you are the faster, slow down, and if you are the slower, accelerate appropriately.

In many situations, however, it is not possible to alter speed in time. Then, your adjustment must be either to hook a stick or allow the opponent one shot before engaging at a safe speed.

Angle

When the pace is slow, a wide angle of approach is necessary and safe. But when the game is fast, it is a dangerous movement, which could cause a pony to fall and should be blown as a foul. A narrow angle is sufficient to win a ride-off, when both of you are travelling with some velocity.

Hence when you have adjusted to be in the best position, then the required angle should be carefully selected, in relation to the speed of the opponent (see Figures 17, 18, and photographs in this chapter).

Figure 17. Good ride-off with minimum angle.

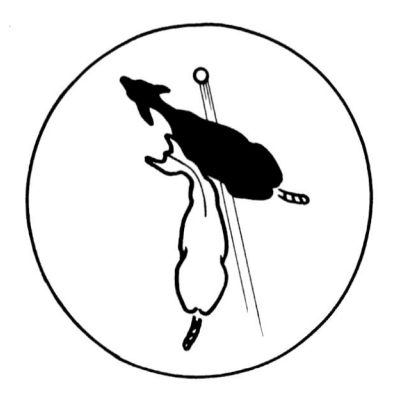

Figure 18. Bad ride-off with extreme angle.

Contact

At the moment of engaging, all the prior preparation described above could be wasted if you allow the opponent to play a trick. Many players, rather than lose a ride-off, will change pace, check and duck in behind you, to fabricate a foul. A good way to avoid this happening is to maintain focus on the eyes of the opponent until firm contact is clearly felt, and only then look for the ball.

Also, beware of any third party, from either team, who might appear at the last moment to cause a foul. They may not do it intentionally, but their appearance could render you dangerous, if you complete the ride-off.

If the ball is between the opponent and you the rule, introduced in the year 2000, allows you to engage provided you were level for at least one stride. Recently, this has been amended to apply only when half-shots are being taken, and therefore engaging is not now permitted against an opponent taking a full stroke.

Follow through

After firm contact is made, be prepared for counter-retaliation. A good player may suddenly reverse the advantage, by pushing you before you can hit the ball. To prevent this happening, contact must be maintained, while you take the opponent an extra yard

below left Sebastian Dawnay in a ride-off.

below right Sebastian Dawnay again, in a more extreme ride-off.

away from the ball. Then, under your control, return together, giving yourself enough space to make a shot.

Initially, you may find that by applying the follow through, as described, the timing does not work correctly and you are unable to return to the ball. Do not be perturbed because gradually, from experience, you will discover how to control the majority of opponents. There are no short cuts to this process of learning.

Hooking Sticks

A hook is necessary when you are in the 25% but it is clear that your relevant opponent has an advantage, in that it is too late for you to win a ride-off and not possible to look for a foul. Hence the priority is to prevent a shot being completed without committing a foul. This requires a good technique that can be applied when close to and behind an opponent.

Many players frequently miss opportunities to hook in the mistaken belief that they are too far away. But if the victim is taking a full swing for an offside forehand, with an extended right arm, you can hook from a distance of two mallet lengths. I suggest that, if you place two polo mallets end to end on the ground, you will be surprised to see how much ground is covered by them and will realize the possibilities of hooking from further away than expected.

Rules

The simplest explanation of the key rule is that, to hook a stick, the ball must be between the two ponies. Therefore, it has to be a foul to hook whenever a pony is between you and the ball. The six additional regulations that apply to hooking are:

1. Both forehands and backhands can be hooked, on the relevant side of the pony.

2. The opponent's mallet must have started the act of hitting the ball. A backhand is deemed to have started when and if the mallet is lowered. A forehand has to be swinging towards the ball.

3. A mallet above the shoulder level may not be hooked.

4. Excessive strength applied when hooking (umpire's interpretation) is a foul.

5. Allowing your pony's legs to be covering the ball while hooking is a foul.

6. To avoid a hook, a player may not change to hit the ball on the other side of the pony.

Further to point 6 above, when umpiring a final at Tidworth, in England, I witnessed for the first time an accident caused by a player changing sides to avoid a hook. The front legs of his pony tangled with the hind legs of the opponent's. Both ponies fell as if they had been shot. Ever since, I have never again doubted that this action is potentially dangerous and should be blown as a foul.

For the blue team, one player about to hook, the other player engaging in the 75%.

Technique

Focus on mallet not ball

By pointing the heel of the mallet head upwards, it is easier to make a firm contact on the other mallet as it swings down. Aim at a point on the cane of the opponent's mallet, two inches from the mallet head. To allow for an error of up to four inches, apply the hook with the same part of your mallet, thereby permitting four inches of inaccuracy. The real secret for a novice is to avoid looking at the ball, and focusing only on the part of the mallet you wish to hook.

Look – look – hook

When hooking the offside forehand, the following procedure could be used:

1. Look at the relevant part of the mallet (like a spot on the ball) when it is above the opponent's head.

2. Focus again on that spot as the mallet is extended behind the pony.

3. Make contact on the spot as the mallet reaches 5 or 4 o'clock on the pony clock of the opponent. Hence, you could be saying *'Look – Look – Hook'* as you apply the above.

Do not hang out your mallet like a fishing rod, because an opponent can hit through your attempted hook and still hit the ball. Instead, ensure that you make a firm movement in order to arrest the velocity of the swing by the opponent's mallet.

Leading Exponents

Gonzalo Pieres and Hector Barantes

While at Palm Beach, Florida, I watched many matches, in which the effective combination between Gonzalo Pieres (10) and Hector Barantes (7) was the outstanding feature. The art of receiving passes appeared to have been perfected by Gonzalo, who floated into open space to receive Hector's accurate deliveries. Thereby Gonzalo always seemed to have the advantage, which he used to join the line first or win a ride-off, before receiving a pass.

Michael Azzaro

The skill of winning ride-offs to receive passes by a No. 1 was brilliantly exhibited by Michael Azzaro, when he first burst onto the Palm Beach scene in 26-goal polo. He did this against highly experienced backs, who could normally control opposing No. 1s with ease. He went on to become a 10-goal player and still holds that rating.

Adolfo Cambiaso

The youngest-ever 10-goal player and currently the best in the world, Adolfo Cambiaso is also unique for another reason. Even though he is the strongest player in the team, he successfully plays in the No. 1 position in the Mecca of all polo, the Argentine Open. He is allowed to do this because of his ability to collect passes from any part of the field.

SUMMARY

The key to *playmaking* is anticipating what can or will happen, before it does. But that ability cannot be applied if you recklessly chase the ball, without applying the skills of receiving passes, riding-off and hooking. By inviting opponents to push you to the ball, and by recognizing the implications of every situation (including who has an advantage), you should be able to select the correct action that either gives you possession, prevents the opposing team from winning the ball or, at least, upsets the style of their shots.

REVISION

Playmaking components
P — receiving and giving **P**asses.
C — anticipating to **C**ompete in the 25%.
O — preventing **O**pponents hitting the ball.
U — effective **U**se of the 75%.

Skill requirements

S — recognizing **S**ituations encountered.
T — use of **T**hought processes and **T**echniques.
R — **R**iding-off in the 25% and when far from the ball in the 75%.
H — stick **H**ooking.

Receiving passes with advantage and disadvantage

L — advantage nearest to the ball; fouling danger minimized by going **L**aterally before vertically to line.
I — advantage **I**n front of opponent already on line maintained by first pausing to win ride-off.
S — if behind opponent on **S**ame side of line, disadvantage reduced by going away from ball directly to opponent.
O — if behind opponent on **O**ther side of line, disadvantage reduced by crossing line to engage opponent.

Ride-off relevance to unique factors of polo

O — opponent can be **O**bstructed by legal ride-off at any time without relation to ball.
D — **D**isparity of skills gives big advantage to better players, handicap indicates result in majority of ride-offs.
A — **A**nticipation of better players gives **A**dvantage of good position to win ride-offs.
T — weaker player can reduce disadvantage by concentrating on opponent to be **T**aken to ball, not pushed away.

Five distinct parts of a ride-off

P — initially **P**osition in front of opponent.
S — adjust **S**peed, faster or slower, to travel at almost same velocity as opponent.
A — select acceptable **A**ngle, narrow at speed, wide when slow, before making contact.
E — maintain focus on **E**yes of opponent, to counter tricks, until full contact made.
F — push opponent an extra yard from ball as a **F**ollow through to prevent a ride-off reverse.

Hooking a stick

M — can succeed from distance of two **M**allet lengths; many opportunities mistakenly missed.
P — ball must be between **P**onies; mallet in act of striking; below shoulder; no excess force.
F — select spot on mallet, **F**ocus on spot as mallet swings back, hook offside forehand at pony clock 5 or 4.
L — verbalize 'Look – Look – hook' not allowing pony to tread on, or be too close to ball.

9

Riding 'A' — Individual and Group Exercises

Turning and Halting Individually — Circling Individually — Copying Playmaker in One Horizontal Line — Conforming to Both Teams in Two Parallel Lines

In Chapter 6, SLOSH – Seat, Legs, Outside the Pony, Steering, Hands Applied Softly – was suggested as a way to remember the five principles of riding, so that you could use them as a thought process, to help you answer the question 'How to get there to be a *playmaker* or to defend effectively?' These five principles should be uppermost in your mind before playing polo and throughout each chukka. To assist you to achieve this and to get to know your ponies well, there are many exercises that can be done when schooling ponies, or while warming up before playing. Remember that you cannot play without a pony. You therefore need to develop a good understanding and healthy respect for all the ponies you play, in order that you never abuse them. I have devised some drills which can be done in groups, in pairs or individually, and each one simulates a movement that you will have to carry out during a polo game. By practising these drills, you should be helped to have quiet and effective control, which makes the pony *follow you*.

Depending on the weather, conditions and availability of facilities, you can perform these exercises in a riding school, a manège or any area with a suitable surface but, if possible, a polo field gives you more realistic practice.

All those participating on ponies in these exercises should, ideally, be dressed in riding boots and wear either a polo helmet or a hard hat with a chinstrap. Spurs are not recommended because they allow riders to be lazy with their legs and they can easily upset a pony if applied incorrectly. Of course, there are exceptions, for example when there is a very lazy pony on which the coach or person in charge knows that the addition of spurs is necessary – and the rider knows how to apply them correctly. On the other hand, everyone should carry a whip, if only to learn how to do so correctly along with four reins in the left hand. A good coach will choose suitable opportunities to include drills on how to handle a whip (see Chapter 21). The only exception here is when a pony is clearly whip-shy, or a rider is such a novice that the whip actually causes additional problems to his riding and control of the pony.

Turning and Halting Individually

Start, if possible, between two stationary ponies, before moving forward in the half-seat. The speed you move at and the ground covered between turns can be varied subject to many factors but, when in doubt, start slowly over a short distance and gradually increase both speed and distance.

After going a few yards, look behind you over the right shoulder (see Figure 19).

Focus on your vacated space between the two ponies, while applying strong legs.

Maintaining focus, neck-rein 180 degrees right, until opposite and facing the space left between ponies (see Figure 20).

Move forward between the two ponies and continue beyond them for a few yards.

Now look over your left shoulder to focus your vacated space and re-apply legs.

Holding focus, neck-rein 180 degrees left until opposite the vacated space (see Figure 21).

Move forward, look back and apply legs to halt exactly level with the two ponies.

Benefits

This exercise trains you to turn 180 degrees on your own axis, which is the most direct and accurate way of changing direction. It also coaches you to look behind before turning and stopping. This is important because it should activate muscle memory to make you do the same during chukkas, thereby allowing you to read the game during a turn or stop and, if necessary, to abort the change of direction or the halt.

Also, the pony will learn not to follow where you look, until told to do so. Using two other ponies simulates conditions of play but, if you are alone, you can start between any two objects – even two polo balls.

Circling Individually

Start by moving forward in the half-seat, using legs firmly to balance the pony. After a few yards, look over your right shoulder to focus on your pony's tail.

Simultaneously, your shoulders, hips and fork should turn to the right (see Figure 22).

Neck-rein to the right, maintaining focus on the tail, until a 360-degree turn is completed.

If required, your left hand can dip to your right knee and left foot can kick the pony.

Move forward again, balancing the pony with strong legs.

Look over your left shoulder to focus on pony's tail, conforming with your hips and fork.

Maintaining focus on the tail, neck-rein through 360 degrees.

If required, dip left hand to left knee and kick with right foot.

PLAYMAKER POLO

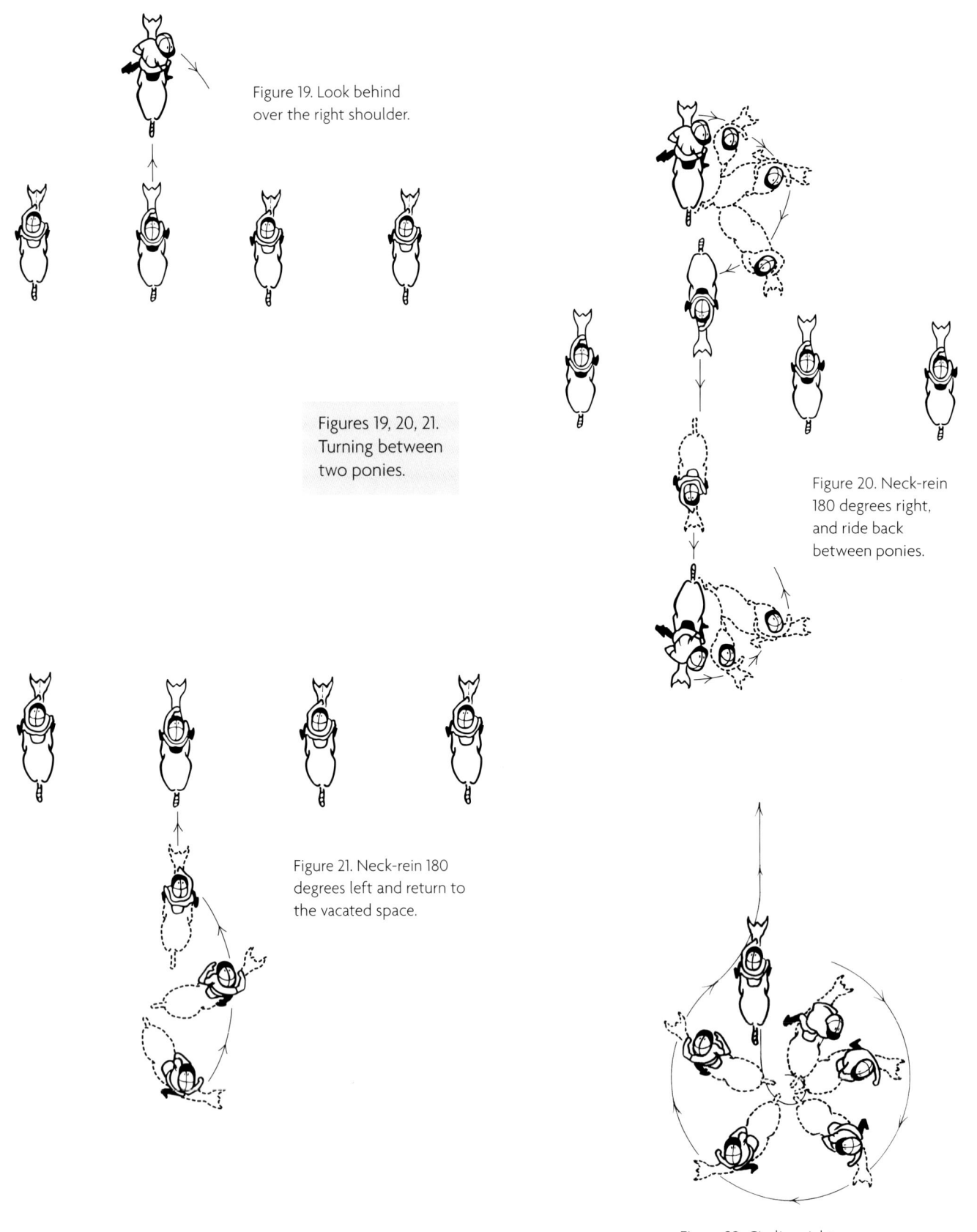

Figure 19. Look behind over the right shoulder.

Figures 19, 20, 21. Turning between two ponies.

Figure 20. Neck-rein 180 degrees right, and ride back between ponies.

Figure 21. Neck-rein 180 degrees left and return to the vacated space.

Figure 22. Circling right.

76

Tomás Fernandez making a spectacular turn in the air.

Benefits

This exercise exaggerates the action of the pony following you, without (since you are neck-reining) pulling it's mouth. It should teach you and the pony to find the shortest way through 360 degrees. If the pony loses momentum, comes to a standstill, or even starts to go backwards, adjust by slightly enlarging the circle. Also, be poised to kick, in order to regain sufficient momentum to complete the 360 degrees. Many people lift their heads early, enlarging the circle, and need to practise again and again until overcoming this problem.

Copying Playmaker in One Horizontal Line

Position riders alongside each other in a horizontal line in which they must stay level. Appoint a *playmaker*, who circles, turns, halts and 'finds the circle' with mallet swings. The rest of the group have to copy all the *playmaker* does and stay level in the line (see Figures 23–25). Change the leader regularly so that, if possible, all have an opportunity to *playmake*.

Benefits

This exercise adds to the riding skills the tactical dimension of watching and conforming to all your own team members, which is so important. It brings out clearly the necessity of applying legs from the half-seat, before halting or altering direction. The weak riders appears to benefit the most from being the leader *playmaker*, because they have to think what to do and thus make their pony follow them instead of themselves following others. At the same time it proves to everyone that they can be *playmakers* and thereby influence a game.

Conforming to Both Teams in Two Parallel Lines

Ask the even numbers in the original line to move forward and turn 180 degrees. They will now be each facing their vacated positions, through which they can pass at will. Both lines will now move in opposite directions, conforming to one *playmaker* (see Figures 26–28).

Circles, turns and halts are performed, while trying to maintain two parallel lines. Ideally, keep alternating the *playmaker* from one line to the other, using everyone.

Benefits

This introduces the dimension of adjusting to your own team, in relation to your opponents, when they are in front of and behind you. It also invites you to look around over 360 degrees, in order to watch everyone in the two lines and all the *playmakers*, located

Figure 23.

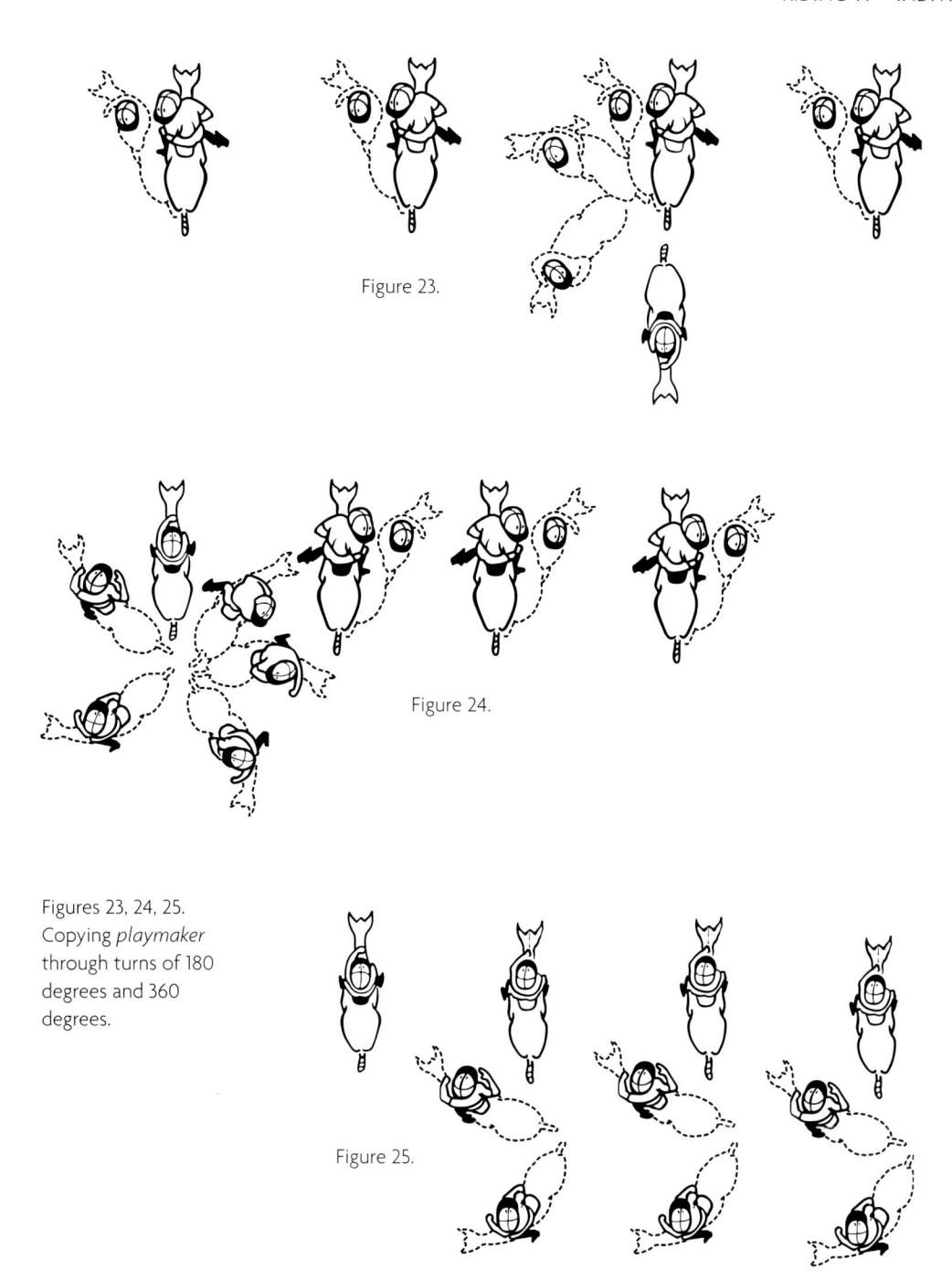

Figure 24.

Figures 23, 24, 25. Copying *playmaker* through turns of 180 degrees and 360 degrees.

Figure 25.

in different places. Controlling and balancing the pony with correct leg applications will be required, in order to conform to the actions of both teams, by making the pony follow you.

SUMMARY

The four exercises described above will help any individual to improve and maintain a good polo riding standard. Ideally, all ponies participate at some stage, so that pony/player relationships are maintained and enhanced. It is even better if the exercises

PLAYMAKER POLO

Figures 26, 27 and (*page 81*) 28. Conforming to *playmaker* in two parallel lines.

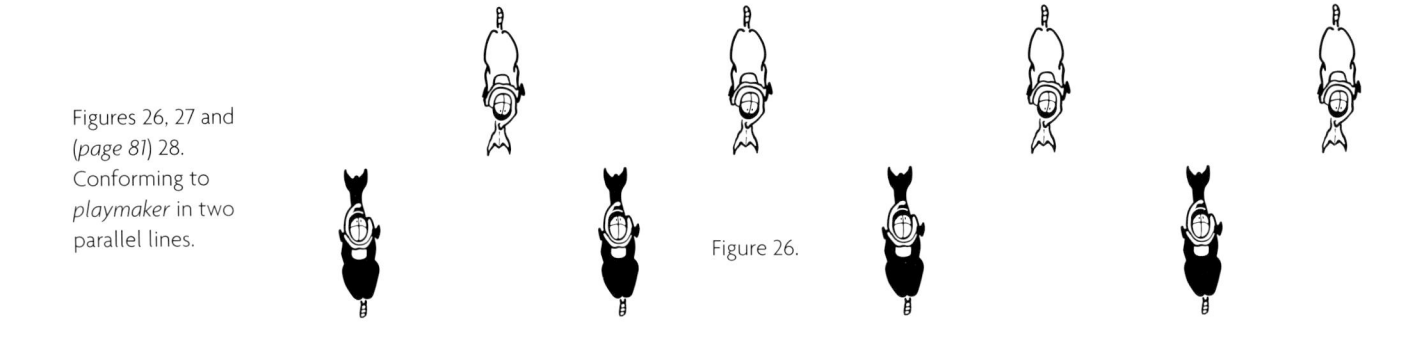

Figure 26.

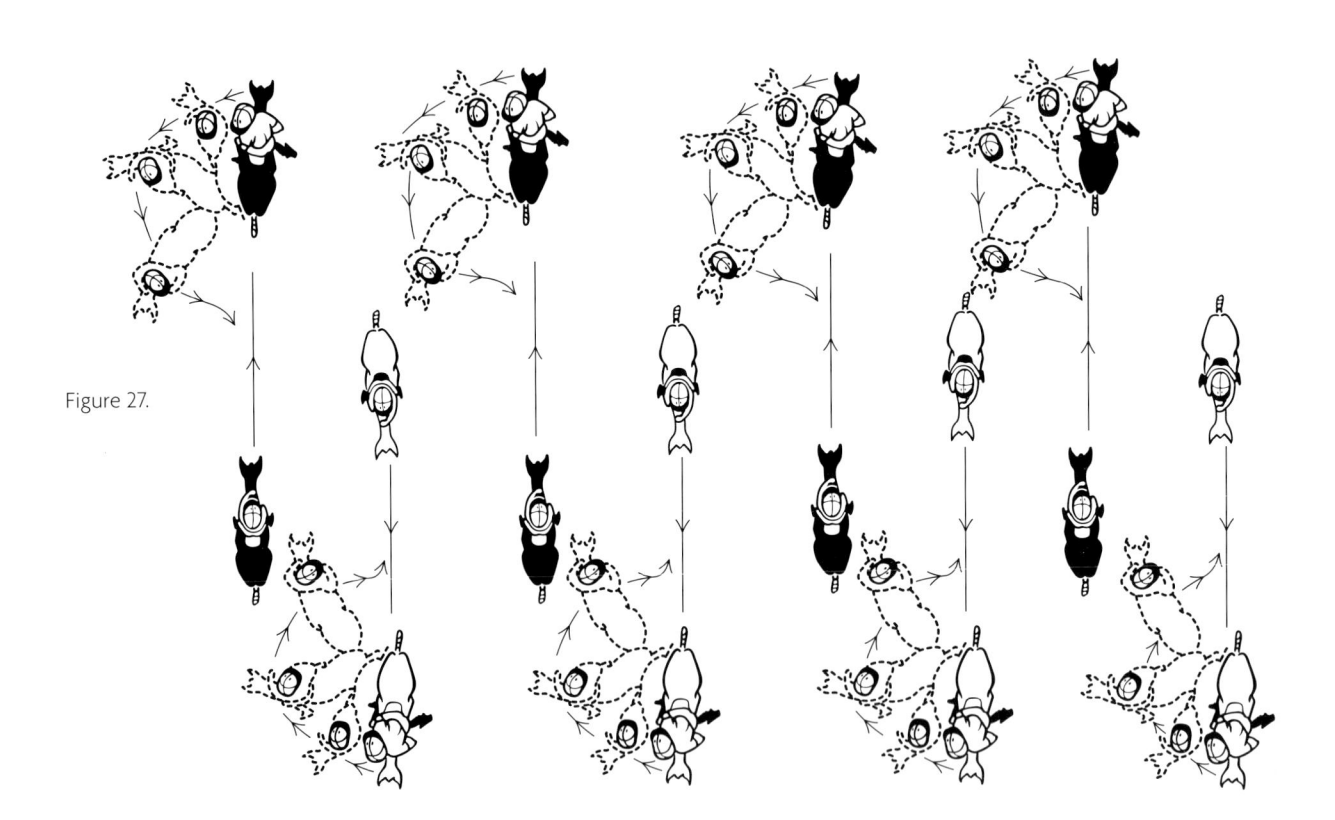

Figure 27.

are done with other people and include relating to a *playmaker*. Extra dimensions can be added as applicable to any riding or specific pony problems encountered. These could cover alertness, accuracy within a team, awareness of opponents' actions, speed and pressure of competition. But to achieve the full benefit for you and your ponies, you should look for constructive comments from a coach, as to how good you are at carrying out all these movements while you are playing. Then, if necessary, invite the coach to attend a training session, to give further assistance. Little details about the application of legs and hands, highlighted at a time of action, can only help your muscle memory to become established.

Figure 28.

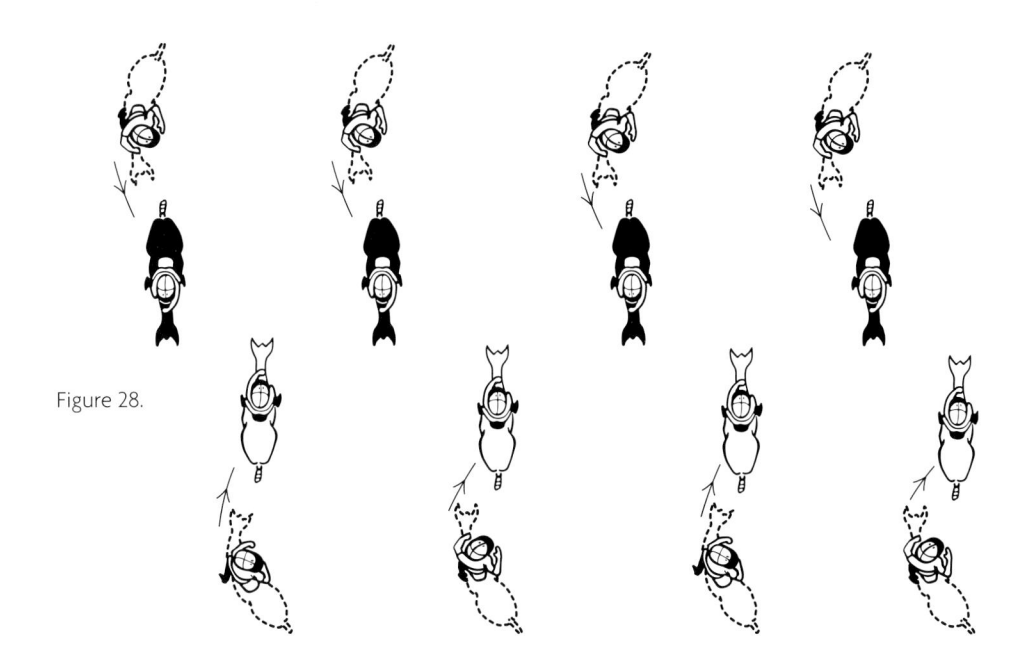

REVISION

Make a pony follow you by:

1. Turning with a consistent technique
L — **L**ook behind before turning.
H — **H**alf-seat.
A — on own **A**xis.
N — **N**o turn until pony clearly told.

2. Circling through shortest 360-degree route
F — **F**ocus on tail before circle.
M — **M**aintain focus throughout 360 degrees.
H — **H**alf-seat.
K — if necessary, left hand dips to relevant **K**nee, and opposite leg kicks.

3. Playmaking in a horizontal line
C — *playmaker* must be **C**opied when finding circle, turning, circling and halting.
A — **A**lternating *playmaker*.
W — **W**eaker players and riders gain extra benefit.
T — **T**actical awareness of own team's position and actions added.

4. Relating between two parallel horizontal lines
P — *P*laymaker alternates between the two lines.
L — **L**ines move in opposite directions and pass through each other.
A — extra dimension of **A**djusting to opponents from own-team awareness.
B — awareness **B**ehind of all action and players' positions.

10

Striking 'A' — Half-shots

Half-shot as Second Half of Full Shot — Constructing the Half-shot Forehand with PASSF — Constructing the Open Offside Backhand Half-shot with PASSF — Exercises

Half-shot as Second Half of Full Shot

The techniques for hitting ten full shots will be covered in Chapters 13, 16, 19, 22 and 25, together with suitable stick and ball exercises, which often finish with a shot at goal and make you face some form of pressure. Throughout any practice exercises and chukkas you should remember to apply PASSF as described in Chapter 7, that is Preparation, Approach, Swing Slowly, Sweet Spot, Follow Through.

Before attempting the ten shots, it is first advisable to become proficient with the half-shot, because it is the second half of a full shot. This will give you confidence in your ability to control the direction and speed of the ball and, at the same time, induce muscle memory, as to how to finish a full shot. In any case, it is important for a *playmaker* to be skilful with a half-shot, in many situations.

Constructing the Half-shot Forehand with PASSF

Preparation

Ensure that the mallet handle is held correctly across the palm of the right hand, with the thumb and index (pistol) finger taking most of the weight. Avoid the hammer grip (see illustrations of grip in Chapter 7). From your seat in the saddle, place the mallet head on the ground, while noting where your right hand is in relation to your knee. Now swing the mallet below you several times, with your hand going past that part of the knee, in order to memorize it for any future half- or full shot. Push the left shoulder to nudge your chin towards the ball. At the same time, check that your hand and mallet stay parallel to the side of the pony and do not go behind your back, towards the pony's tail – a common fault which takes the mallet head out of the circle. Next, find the circle by swinging the mallet forward and up into the vertical position with the mallet head above you and then allowing it to fall and complete the circle. At the same time, apply your legs to balance yourself and the pony, while alerting the pony to be ready to approach the ball. This procedure prepares you in every dimension, in that you make the blood flow from the hand up the arm, around the body and to the brain while the grip on the mallet is checked; the swing is rehearsed both in a line and in a circle and the pony has been controlled by your legs.

Approach

To take your first ever straight half-shot, use a wooden horse, if available, or hit from a static pony. Place the ball at 2 on the pony clock (see Figure 10, page 57) put your mallet head at 6 on the ball clock (see Figure 11, same page), and lean forward into the half-seat. Look ahead at where you wish to hit to, then identify 6 on the ball clock and (when you reach the stage of moving in the half-seat) control the pony very accurately with strong legs, along a line which brings you opposite 2 on the pony clock in relation to your axis.

Sebastian Dawnay approaching in the half-seat.

Eduardo Heguy (10), centre – straight swing.

Swing Slowly

If you imagine that there is a pane of glass connected to 6 on the ball and positioned parallel to your axis, then your swing back and forward should feel as if you are washing that glass but not breaking it. Only a slow swing can be guaranteed to be that accurate. Alternatively, some people relate better to the idea of swinging back to 5 on the pony clock and then forward to 6 on the ball clock (see Figure 29). Either way, remember to bring the left shoulder towards the ball and apply the 50/50 swing (see Chapter 7) unless you are late or have another reason not to. Use muscle memory to control the straight path of the mallet and ask a coach or friend to confirm that you succeed.

Figure 29. Using the 'pane of glass' image to swing from 5 to 2 on the pony clock and then forward to 6 on the ball clock.

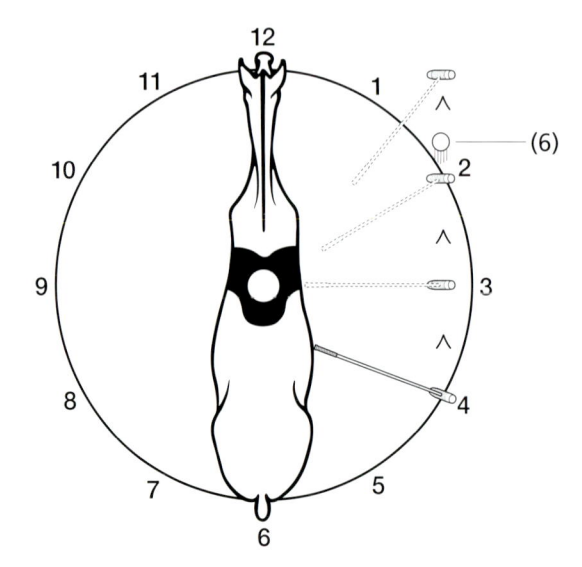

Sweet Spot

You have already located 6 on the ball clock so, as you swing forward, it should be relatively easy to confirm the sweet spot, or contact spot, and aim with the palm of your hand to go exactly *through* the bottom of the ball rather than *at* it. To overcome the temptation to look up too early, to see if you have succeeded, you could verbalize the contact as suggested in Chapter 7. Many people whom I have coached have been amazed how this co-ordination of voice and action has suddenly produced the best and most solid shot of their life. A large number of them were reluctant to try, but were highly impressed by the result when they finally did apply the idea.

Silvestre Donovan (8) shows perfect poise to find the sweet spot.

Follow Through

The motion through the ball should be continued towards the target to keep the swing straight until the mallet has passed the horizontal position or completed the second half of the 50/50 swing in order that accuracy is achieved. After that, it is ideal but not obligatory if your thumb and index finger can further project the mallet to complete the circle and ensure totally that the correct aim is maintained. Any form of follow through should add distance to the shot and the full circle will not only increase length but at the same time dissipate any force induced and thereby control the mallet so as to be prepared for the next shot, if this is required immediately.

Execution

All the above suggests a way to learn and practice a half-shot. Now let us look at how a *playmaker* can execute it in a practice chukka or a polo match.

Preparation
Apply legs and check grip on mallet before dropping it to the bottom of the circle and directly behind the ball. If there is time, find the circle and keep hand within it next to the right knee.

Approach
In the half-seat, re-apply the legs; while advancing look for the target and then register the required spot at 6 on the bottom of the ball, and the distance desired. Ride the pony exactly parallel to the line of the ball to bring you opposite 2 on the pony clock.

Swing
Start the 50/50 swing early enough to ensure a slow action, apply the left shoulder and use muscle memory to control the path of mallet and length of backswing.

Sweet spot
Aim with your hand to go through the spot at 6 on the bottom of the ball.

Follow through
Allow hand and mallet to complete second 50% of swing and then, as a bonus, employ thumb and index finger to continue through a full circle. Otherwise, stop swing as mallet head points at memorized target.

Constructing the Open Offside Backhand Half-shot with PASSF

Preparation

Check your grip on the mallet handle because ideally, for all shots directed with the back of the hand, it should be the same as described earlier for the palm of the hand. But if the bone structure of your hand interferes, making the grip uncomfortable for this shot, you will have to adjust the position of your thumb. From your seat in the saddle, place the mallet head down on the ground at 1 on the pony clock. Confirm that the right hand is in front of the right knee. Then swing the mallet in front of the pony's head to 12 and then back to 4 on the pony clock several times (see Figure 30). Feel the right shoulder nudge and fight your chin and sense that the swing is being guided by the back of the hand and/or your knuckles. Check that the swing goes consistently to 4 on the pony clock and that it is not following the normal instinct, which is to be pulled to 5 or even as far as 6. Try to memorize this as the basic swing for the open backhand. Next, find the circle by swinging again to 4 on the pony clock and allowing the mallet head to continue upward until it is vertical above you, before letting it fall to complete the circle. Again, apply legs to begin the approach, at which point, as previously described, every dimension of preparation has been covered.

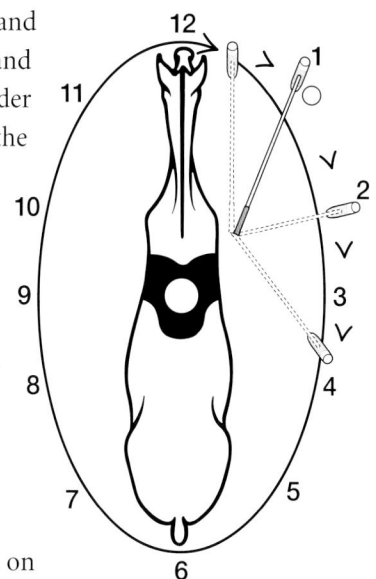

Figure 30. Open backhand swing.

Approach

If practising on the wooden horse, select the target by looking back. Place the ball at 1 on the pony clock, in line between 12 and 4. Put the mallet head barely touching 10 on the ball clock, and lean forward into the half-seat. On a moving pony, first look behind to see exactly where you wish to hit and then identify the spot on the ball clock (approximately 10). Advance in the half-seat along a line which brings you to the ball at 1 on the pony clock, in relation to your axis. With strong legs, without crossing the line, you can create a shallow arc to the left so that the pony's head does not interfere with the circle used for the swing (see Figure 12, page 58).

Swing Slowly

Let the right shoulder and your chin fight each other enough to rotate the hips and shoulders left, yet maintaining focus on the ball and the identified spot. Use muscle memory to swing from 12 towards 4 on the pony clock as slowly as possible in the 50/50 swing (unless late), with the shoulders and hips now gyrating to the right. This change of direction by the shoulders limits isolated use of arm strength and keeps the swing slow.

Sweet Spot

Your focus is already on the required contact spot and you confirm this as you swing towards 4 on the pony clock by aiming the back of the hand or knuckles approximately at 10 on the ball spot and *through* the bottom of the ball. Verbalization of 'spot' or 'knuckles' or '10', or any relevant word as contact is made should stop you lifting your head too early to see where the ball has gone.

Follow Through

As the hips and shoulders turn to the right, the mallet is projected through the second 50% of the swing towards the target. This will maintain accuracy of direction and add distance if the hand and mallet head stay in the circle around 12 and 4 on the pony clock.

Execution

Preparation
Apply legs and check grip on mallet before dropping it to the bottom of the circle. If there is time, find the circle and maintain hand within it, next to the right knee.

Approach
In the half-seat, advance in a shallow left arc, apply legs and look behind to identify a *playmaker* or target and to register desired distance and required spot.

Swing
Start a 50/50 swing from 12 to 4 on the pony clock early to ensure a slow action, using shoulders to rotate from left to right. Apply muscle memory to guide the mallet and control length of shot.

Sweet spot
Aim knuckles to go through the spot at approximately 10 on the bottom of the ball.

Follow through
Allow hand to complete the second 50% of swing, with shoulders and hips rotating to the right and the mallet pointing to the *playmaker* or target.

Exercises

Stick and ball practice is important, and will be extra effective as preparation for your first chukkas if done in combination with one or more other players. This allows you to experience the pressure of people relying on you, besides giving you practice in sending and receiving passes and thereby co-ordinating as *playmakers*. Once you are hitting off-side half-shot forehands and backhands reasonably solidly, *slowly* and accurately I suggest that you complete the following exercises.

1. (a) Individually hit half-shot forehands while travelling the length of the polo field and try to score a goal. Repeat many times, gradually increasing speed. If a coach or another player is available, ask them to pass to you if you ever miss. You can then practise looking behind before joining the line of a pass, as if *playmaking*.
   (b) Have a half-shot race with another player, or even with a coach. Handicap starts can be applied when race opponents are of different standards.

2. (a) Individually hit several half-shot offside open backhands in a clockwise circle (see Figure 31).
   (b) Work in pairs to hit alternate half-shot open backhands in a circle. This will give you an initiation into receiving as a *playmaker*, as well as hitting to another player (see Figure 32).

STRIKING 'A' – HALF-SHOTS

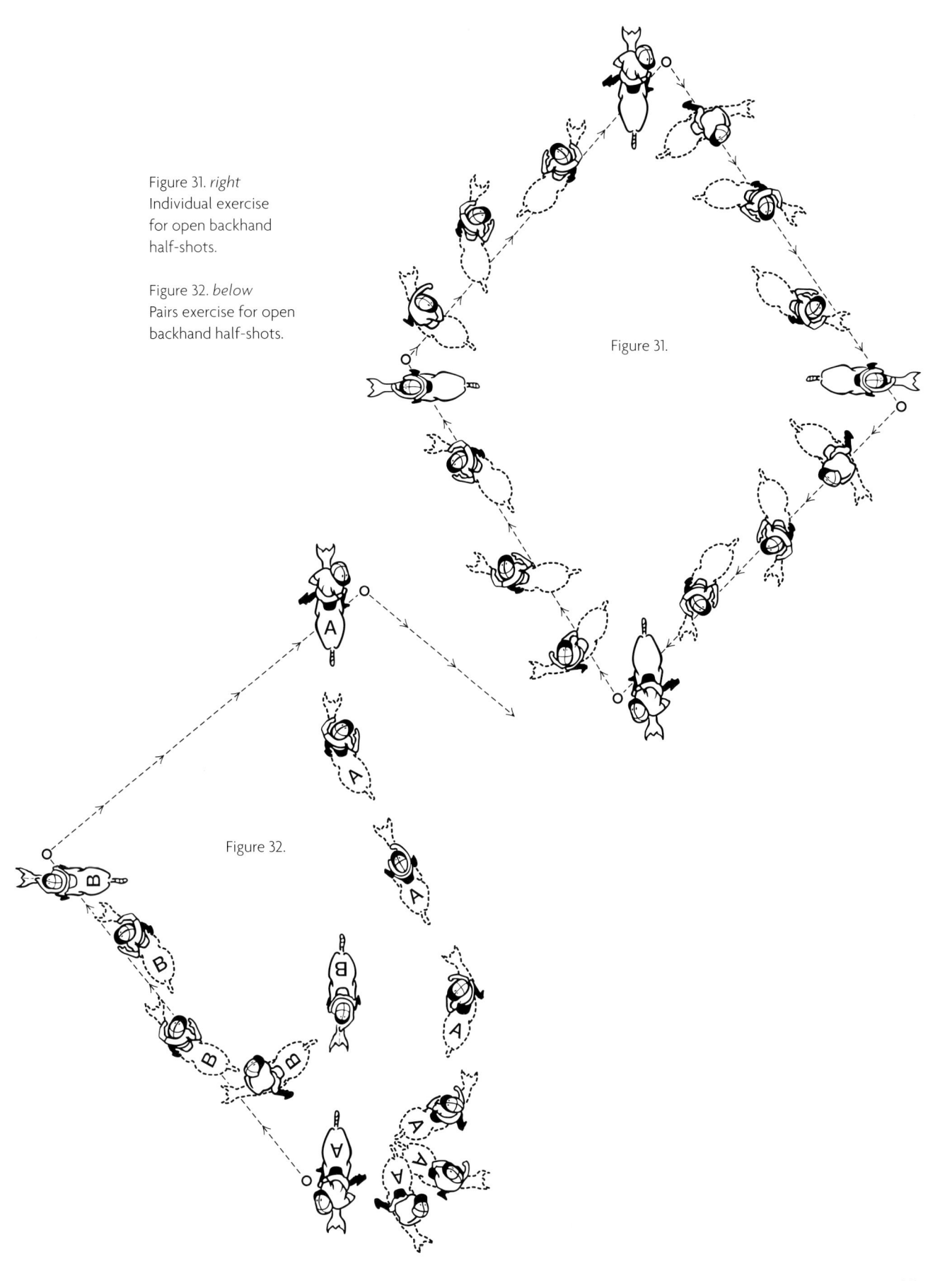

Figure 31. *right*
Individual exercise for open backhand half-shots.

Figure 32. *below*
Pairs exercise for open backhand half-shots.

Figure 31.

Figure 32.

89

SUMMARY

Once you are proficient at these exercises, you are ready to learn the full shots. Ideally, during these exercises, you should take advantage of the benefit of finding the circle and completing the follow through full circle whenever possible. But do not allow either of them to interfere with or prevent a slow swing, because once this is developed for the half-shot, it will assist your timing for all the rest of the shots. The more you apply the full technique to the half-shot, the greater the possibility that your muscle memory will take over and, in the future, assist you to strike all shots correctly.

You should now have an understanding of combining with others, and the beginning of a thought process of how to *playmake* and thus avoid ball-chasing. Also, it will be clear that the half-shot is useful and most effective because it takes less time to execute than a full shot. Therefore, it must be easier to swing slowly and every time you hit a half-shot you will be practising the second half of the full shot.

REVISION

Half-shot offside forehand
P — legs; grip mallet with thumb/index finger; find circle and **P**lace hand down in circle.
A — half-seat; on **A**pproach find target; focus on spot; apply legs to bring pony opposite 2 on pony clock.
S — left shoulder to ball; **S**wing back **S**lowly from 6 on ball clock to 5 on pony clock.
S — hand through **S**weet **S**pot at 6 on bottom of ball.
F — extend hand with mallet in **F**ollow through towards target and complete circle.

Open offside backhand half-shot
P — legs; grip mallet; find circle and **P**lace hand in front of knee in circle.
A — half-seat; look behind to **A**ssess target; focus on spot; legs to produce arc; pony to be opposite 1 on pony clock.
S — right shoulder to chin; **S**wing from 10 on ball clock to 12 on pony clock.
S — knuckles guide through 10 **S**pot on bottom of ball.
F — extend knuckles to **F**ollow through with mallet towards and then above target.

11

Tactics 'B' — Four Basic Tactics

Three Elements for Playmaking — The Rope —The Barrier — The Diamond — The Soft Diamond

Three Elements for Playmaking

Before you play in your first serious chukka or polo match, if you wish to have any possibility of being a *playmaker*, you must know and understand:

1. The *rules* of polo.

2. The *jobs* of all four positions in a team.

3. The *shape* of the game and how to contribute to it, with a thought process within a team formation.

The Rules

You should regularly read the rules of polo and also discuss them with an expert, preferably your coach. It is important to understand every type of foul, the penalties that can be awarded and the procedure for taking and defending them. Chapter 29 gives an elementary explanation for some of the rules and covers penalty procedures in detail. The Hurlingham Polo Association rules appear at the end of this book and, if you belong to another country or association, you will find only a few variations. By appreciating the many grey areas, which necessitate judgement calls by the officials, you will find it easier to be a *playmaker* who avoids fouling too much. Your understanding of the interpretation of the rules can be helped by watching the United States Polo Association's *Blue Book* video which gives excellent examples and explanations of many of the fouls and the ways in which they can be fabricated. It is important to understand the difference between a real foul and a fabricated one since, as in many sports, some players deliberately fabricate fouls while others, wrongly but genuinely, believe that they are being fouled in various situations.

The Jobs

Chapters 14, 17, 20 and 23 will cover in detail the jobs of each position. When you have absorbed this knowledge, you will not only know how to be a *playmaker* in any position, but you should also enjoy relating to everything done by the other three members of your team, having the confidence to interchange with them as required.

The Shape

By knowing how to apply LATET (see Chapter 5) to all set-piece and fluid situations, for attack and defence, you will be able to contribute to the shape and the tactics of a team at all times. This chapter explains four tactics, which help define that shape. I describe them as:

The Rope Exercise

The Barrier Concept

The Diamond Tactic (as a set piece and in fluid play)

The Soft Diamond

The Rope

Purpose

Deep down inside most of us, there is a desire to chase the ball, until suddenly one day a light comes on to show us that it is much better if the ball *chases us* as *playmakers*. Some people are serious ball-chasers and, when put on a horse and given a polo mallet, are a real danger to others. The majority of polo beginners, after doing some stick and ball work, go directly into chukkas without any further training, to become one of eight players who, overall, are competing in one team against another. I suggest that it would be better and more constructive if players first practised as a team, without opposition, to find out how to fit in correctly with their three other team members. For this purpose, and to control the dangerous elements, I developed the rope exercise, designed to help people apply LATET to a thought process.

This concept originated many years ago, when I encountered a player who was extremely difficult to control. This individual forced me to think up the idea of making a team hold a rope, while walking on foot down my mini polo ground. Hence, I used to invite all novice players to experience this extreme measure of being physically restrained by the rope. Later, I produced my instructional video, which includes a demonstration of four people doing the exercise holding the rope, and nowadays I generally find that showing this video is sufficient, if it is watched carefully a few times. For most people, it gives an understanding of the intended principle, without them actually having to hold a rope on the mini ground. After watching it, the majority of players find doing the rope exercise on ponies is easier, and it is a valuable piece of training. Nevertheless, if you have time, it may still be beneficial to walk through the exercise before riding it, and even consider doing it in its original form, holding a rope approximately twelve yards long, in order to emphasize the fact that a constant distance between each player is required throughout.

The crux of the exercise is that it teaches new players to stay correctly positioned away from the ball, within a team, in what I have already described as the 75%, until the ball arrives near them in the 25%.

The original rope exercise.

Set Up and Passing

I will now explain the rope exercise, as you should do it as a team on ponies. Place the ball on the back line, preferably on the left side of the goal. Team positions on ponies in relation to ball are:

No. 4 ten yards behind.

No. 3 ten yards in front.

No. 2 thirty yards in front (on the thirty-yard line).

No. 1 fifty yards in front (ten yards before sixty-yard line).

(These are suggested distances, which can be adjusted according to the standard of play.) All players should move at the same time as No. 4 approaches to make the first hit, so that there are three *playmakers* ready to accept the ball and give the second pass because:

A *long* strike of sixty yards or more can be received by No. 1.

An *average* shot of thirty to sixty yards may be collected by No. 2.

A *short* pass of ten to thirty yards should be picked up by No. 3.

The third shot on the rope is made by whoever receives the second pass, unless this was No. 1, in which case No. 1, after striking the ball, will then simulate losing possession, by continuing beyond the ball in order to receive a pass from No. 2.

Discipline and Completion

Those who, at any stage, are in front of the ball, must ensure that they never block the goal and instead adjust laterally to relate to one of the goalposts. As an exercise discipline, nobody may hit the ball twice in succession and No. 3 will check, after making a shot, to become last, allowing No. 4 to move ahead. In turn, if No. 4 misses or fails to reach Nos. 1 or 2, then No. 4 must quickly return to being last behind No. 3. Thus, during the exercise, except for the first hit, there should always be a back-up behind the striker.

If, at any time, there is doubt as to who hits next, No. 3 should direct by calling the relevant name. If possible, all four players should have at least one strike during a rope exercise, which ideally finishes with a shot through the goal. If necessary, one or more backhands may have to be played, to correct a bad approach shot and to enable a goal to be scored. From continual good passing, the ball should do more work than the ponies.

Extra Dimension

When this rope exercise has been completed smoothly and correctly, a team could then add the extra dimension of adjusting laterally behind the hitter in order to join the expected next line of the ball, which is intended to go towards the centre of the goal. Figures 33, 34 and 35 show the incorrect and correct way to support your team in attack. It is wrong to be parallel to the play in the 75%. By staying in a line which is close to vertical, all four players in the team can, at all times, count heads.

TACTICS 'B' – FOUR BASIC TACTICS

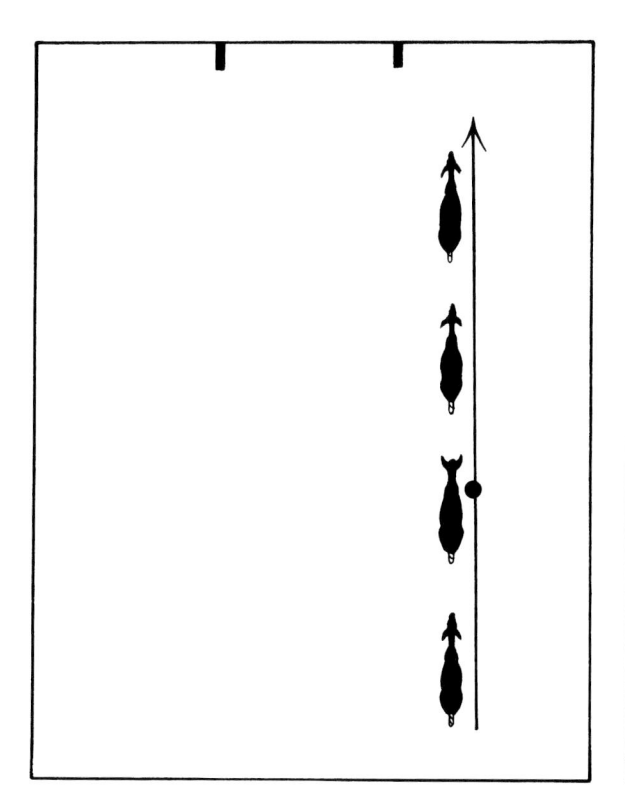

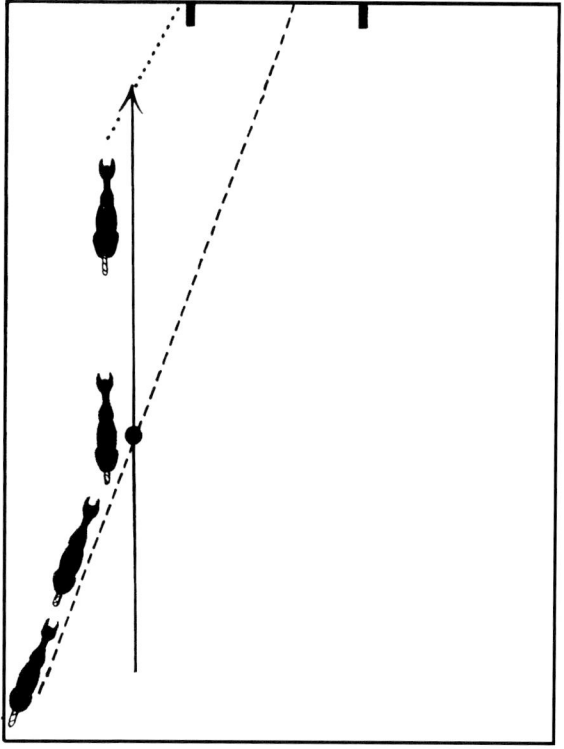

Figure 33.

Figure 34.

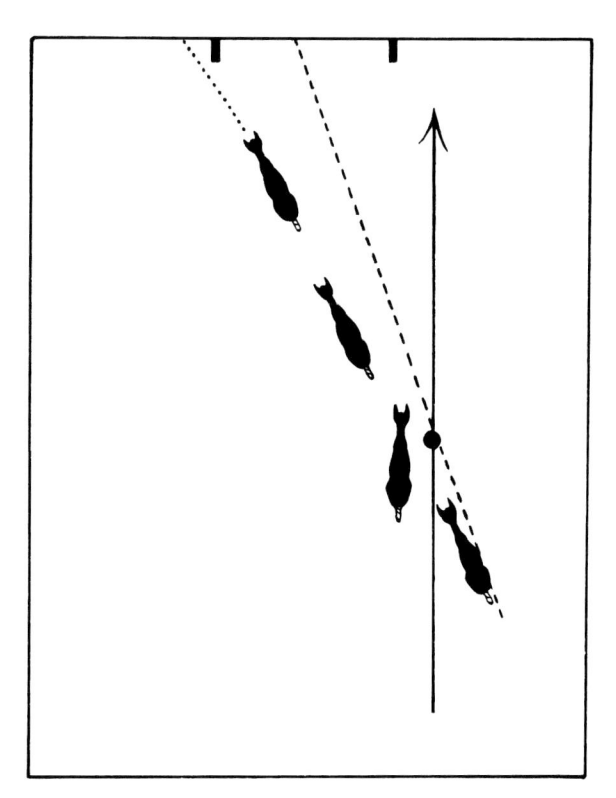

Figure 35.

Team support in attack.

Figure 33. Incorrect – blocking goal.

Figure 34. Correct approach from the left side of the field.

Figure 35. Correct approach from the right side of the field.

The Barrier

Two Players Each Side

We have just discussed the importance of four players maintaining distances between each other that cover three lengths of shot, (short – average – long). This enables them to fill the four team positions throughout a polo match and to *playmake* for one another. To achieve this is not so easy as it may sound, because there are so many distractions which can lead players into wrong positions. The ground is so large, the game can be very fast and the unexpected happens frequently. Therefore, the situation at all times must be simplified and this can be done by placing a *barrier* in the middle of the four players, insisting that there always are two players on each side of it, while giving different tactical criteria to the two playing in front of it and the two following behind it. This barrier will move up and down the polo field with the play, but *not necessarily* with the *ball*.

Two Fight in Front

In attack, the first two of the team, normally Nos. 1 and 2, should, if they have failed to gain possession by *playmaking*, deliberately speed up the play in front of the barrier and hurry the opposing defenders. To do this, they should compete and fight for every ball in their area of the field, during the 25%, even if their relevant opponent appears certain to make a backhand shot before they can stop him. Thereby, they hope to reduce the ability of those opponents to hit long and accurate passes. This will help their team to regain possession and, unless interchanging with Nos. 3 or 4, they themselves should stay in front of the barrier whatever happens. This process of harrying may be quick or take time, but it will still be valuable, even if it only becomes effective late in a match. However, even when a good backhand is struck by an opponent, it may not cause serious damage, because the other two members of the team should be waiting behind the barrier to receive it.

In Rugby Union, a similar barrier separates the eight forwards in the scrum from the seven backs. It is both a physical and mental barrier, which shapes their thought processes for positioning and responsibilities. Basically, the forwards stay in front of it and fight for the ball in all situations, while the backs play behind it and, in the main, receive the ball either by being given it through a pass from their own team, or an opponent's a kick. Thus the backs maintain a defensive line intact, yet are always ready to mount a dangerous attack. The scrum half stands just behind the barrier (as does the quarter back in American football), and both have a similar role to the No. 3 in polo. The roles of the rugby full back and the No. 4 in polo can also be compared.

Two Stay Behind

How do Nos. 3 and 4 stay, most of the time, behind the barrier? In defence, they normally stay close to the first two opponents. Then, in attack, they obey a rule not to commit themselves to make a forehand shot, unless they feel certain that they will make the strike successfully, or it is clear to them that another player will cover them by filling their position. A good shot will send the ball over the barrier as a pass to the No. 1 or No. 2, while the barrier remains in the middle of the four team players. If and when a forehand is missed, or is hit badly by a No. 3 or No. 4 then, as in the rope exercise, they should immediately reposition *behind* the ball and barrier, unless another player has covered them. This is called 'cutting out of the game'. To do this the best route, if available, is via the middle of the field.

Going to the Next Play

In attack, when they feel insecure about a forehand, those filling the Nos. 3 and 4 positions should stay behind the barrier, anticipate where the opponent's backhand will go and move there to compete for or receive the ball. Possession, temporarily lost, can then be regained and the ball once more sent over the barrier to a team member who should have applied LATET to be available in a reachable position as a *playmaker*.

In defence, whenever they realize that they are wrongly placed to cover either of the first two opponents, they cut a corner, normally by going straight down the middle of the field, to recover ground, before engaging and containing the escaped opponent.

Both situations will normally allow opponents to have one shot before they are intercepted. This is known as 'going to the next play', in order to be given the ball. Often this is a smoother and more effective ploy than fighting for the ball during the previous play.

Four Positions Filled

If the four members of a team are always aware of where the barrier is, and which side of it they should be, the likelihood that the four positions are always filled is greatly increased. Inevitably, mistakes will be made by someone crossing the barrier incorrectly, but the damage to the team can be minimal if the culprit realizes the error and adjusts quickly, by returning to the position wrongly vacated or going to the next play. How No. 4 and No. 3 carry out fully their jobs in relation to the barrier is explained in detail in Chapters 17 and 23. This is also very relevant to Nos. 1 and 2, because they need to know how to adjust to the actions of those behind the barrier, besides being prepared to take over their jobs, if necessary, thereby keeping the four positions filled.

The Diamond

Tactics and Team Motivation

Too many teams play a match without any pre-planned tactics. The best player normally has his own system and expects that the other three in the team will be able to support his actions. Surely, it is a wise policy to practice tactics, especially set-piece situations, and to give all the team a part as *playmakers* in them. This will create an advantage of surprise against unprepared opponents, and the excitement of trying to succeed with a plan should add to team motivation and enjoyment.

Opportunities

The hit-in (the equivalent of a goal kick in soccer), and penalty 5s from the centre or spot (see Chapter 29), provide the best opportunities to carry out pre-planned tactics. The same principles can also be applied for fundamental attacks, in fluid situations. There are many different ways to hit-in, but the majority of them are designed to apply lateral adjustment as a means of achieving effective team velocity. This principle is well demonstrated by the diamond, which is the first method that I teach.

Format

For simplicity's sake, we will assume that No. 4 takes the hit-in although, with the disparity of standards, some No. 4s are not confident enough and No. 3 is given the task. Ideally, the other team members all try to make themselves available, as mobile *playmakers*, so that No. 4 has three alternative places to hit to. The diamond (Figure 36) spreads these three to the left, to the right and straight in front, forcing the opposition to cover all of them. Yet it will be difficult for opponents to prevent the diamond from erupting into a rope formation quickly, after the ball reaches No. 1 and two passes have found a recipient. The wider apart they start, the faster they can move, but to be successful the following disciplines must also be observed:

1. Before the first hit is struck, all three team members are mobile *playmakers*.

2. No. 4 is accurate with the first hit.

3. No. 1 applies sufficient lateral adjustment.

4. Distances are maintained to make passing easy, yet allow the ball to be received at speed.

Execution

As No. 4 approaches the ball, everyone moves as follows. The first hit is often to the boards for No. 2, but can be across the goal to No. 3 or straight to No. 1, if it is safe to do so.

Nos. 2 and 3 initially move towards each other across field and then turn upfield, to accelerate into a rope as the ball flies past them.

No. 1 moves laterally in front of No. 2 or No. 3, whoever erupts to hit the second shot; No. 4 follows last, to back up the attack, but is ready, if necessary, to defend against a counter-attack.

Figure 36. Diamond hit-in.

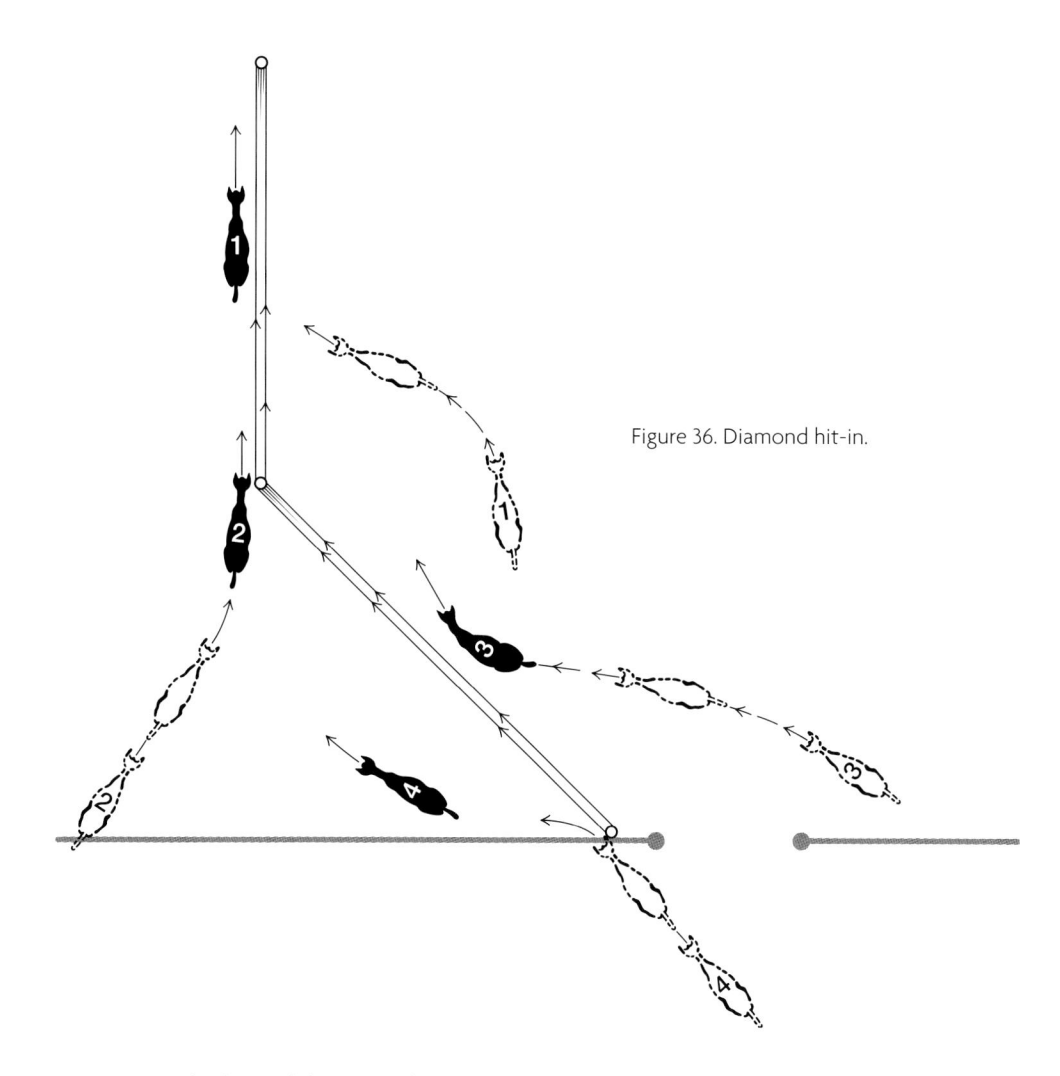

No. 1 joins the line of the second hit by No. 2 or 3, ready to accelerate to strike the third shot. At this moment the other three team members should be behind on the rope, backing up.

No. 3, unless receiving the first hit, moves across the ground and goal, prepared to back up Nos. 1 and 2, or to collect a weak hit – or even to defend, if something goes wrong.

Variation

Although, for safety, the majority of first hits go to No. 2, there is great scope for variation in that Nos. 2 and 3 can start from positions closer to or further from the ball, and then move faster or slower as required to let the ball reach them, but No. 1 must adjust to their actions to try to receive the second hit.

For hits across the goal, No. 3 becomes No. 2, while No. 4 takes over as No. 3, with No. 2 assuming the responsibilities of No. 4. This will be much more effective if No. 1 knows what is happening and changes direction, in time to receive from No. 3. It is safer to limit this tactic mostly to hit-ins from the left side, because those across the goal from the right carry a great risk of the receiver being hooked by an opponent.

If the first hit is long in any direction, No. 1 can take the second hit after early lateral movement to the line. When a shot is sent directly to No. 1, this gives No. 2 the alternative of moving in front to receive from No. 1 or staying behind to back up. In every situation, by looking behind, the receiver can spot any mishit early enough to attempt a major adjustment to join the new line.

No. 1 and Team Alertness are Key

A key to the success of the diamond is the anticipation required of No. 1, in order to receive a pass without fouling. Why? Because the effect is like a knife through butter, if No. 1 can *explode* to hit the third shot, after adjusting correctly to the two previous ones and thereby avoiding being marked. How so? Because the opponents will probably have conformed to the original line of the ball made by No. 4, while No. 1 moved to be one shot ahead of them, thereby allowing the *speed of the ball* to outpace even the fastest pony of the opponents. But should No. 2 or No. 3 fail to pass, and continue with the ball, their opponents should have little difficulty in marking them to stop the attack.

Another requirement for making the diamond work is alertness by all of the team, leading to quick reaction the moment the ball crosses the back line or the whistle goes to award the foul. By moving without delay to set up the diamond formation, you then allow your ponies to have a rest, while you watch, listen and prepare to be accurate *playmakers*.

Mistakes

Yet, if only one person makes a mistake or is casual, the whole drill can fail. The constructive observation of a coach can detect such faults. The following are possible mistakes, which ought to be easy to correct, for the next time, if seen from the sideline.

1. No. 2 starts too far upfield or infield, with the result that the ball does not reach him or, if it does, it finds him static and unable to speed to the line of the ball to give a pass.

2. No. 2 starts correctly, with mobility, but turns upfield *before* the ball arrives.

3. No. 1 stays too central or too far away and fails to accelerate to receive a pass.

4. No. 4 starts so close to the ball that the rest of the team cannot gather speed.

5. No. 4 taps the ball unexpectedly or is slow, giving opponents time to block the attack.

6. The first hit is inaccurate, or too straight, giving the ball to an opponent.

7. No. 3 blocks the ball or obstructs your team's mobility by being in the wrong place.

Practice

The same procedure as described earlier for the rope should be used to practice the diamond without opposition, except that obviously the initial team positions are spread out as shown in Figure 36, before lateral adjustment brings them back to the rope formation, as a line of *playmakers*.

Walking through the drill first will help to give a full understanding of the detailed actions of each player, including the maintenance of a continual back-up behind the hitter being ensured by Nos. 3 and 4 revolving behind the barrier when necessary, as previously described.

Then, on ponies, the first few hit-ins should be to the boards, so that No. 2 practises receiving from both the left and the right side of the field, with the rest of the team conforming. Later, hits across the goal to No. 3, and even a direct pass to No. 1, should be rehearsed. Whatever the route to goal, as for the rope drill, the aim is to make the *ball* do more work than the *ponies*.

In Actual Play

By the time the diamond is executed against opposition in a game, the combination between team members ought to be sufficiently fine-tuned to produce effective attacks from the majority of the set-piece plays, and from some fluid situations. Ideally, each *playmaker* finds freedom in space to receive the ball and accelerate down the line, but when opponents appear to be close enough to threaten possession, they should be engaged early. This should bring them under control *before the approach to the ball begins*, thus giving the *playmaker* the best possibility of retaining possession for the team.

The Soft Diamond

This tactic is designed to send the ball to the sideline or boards in the defending half of the polo field, and towards the centre field in the attacking half (see Figure 37). Thereby, there is less pressure on the defended goal and scoring goals becomes more feasible. Obviously, there are exceptions when a *playmaker* finds open ground that does not conform to the diamond.

For the majority of the game, the anticlockwise route, which takes the ball to the right-hand side of the field in attack, is best because:

1. It is easier to anticipate and receive the ball without crossing the line and fouling.

2. There is less likelihood that the receiver can be hooked by an opponent.

3. Defence can be quickly turned to attack.

4. The receiver initially controls the play.

However, it must be dangerous to be too dogmatic. So always consider alternative ways to initiate attacks by *playmaking* in a different direction, if and when there is a part of the field that is clearly not covered by any of the opponents.

Figure 37. Soft diamond.

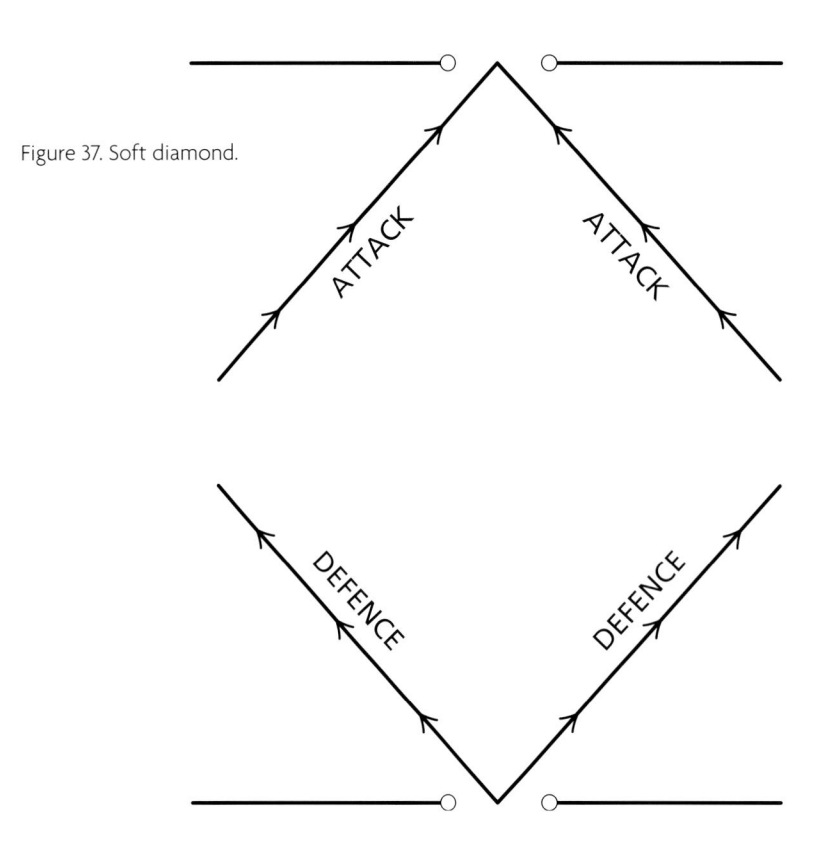

SUMMARY

I can not emphasize enough the value of a team practising the rope and both diamonds as exercises without opposition, before actually playing serious polo. The barrier concept can also be strictly applied to these exercises, if there is supervision from a coach. The experience should help you to develop a correct thought process for set pieces and fluid polo action. You should then have a big advantage, when learning the jobs of the four different positions in a team. All these factors will help you to understand how to *playmake* when the opportunity arises.

REVISION

Rope applied by

D — **D**istances between players being maintained consistently (approx. twenty yards).

M — all players **M**ove at same time as No. 4 approaches for first strike.

P — *Playmaking* by other three players to receive long, average and short strikes as a pass.

G — those in front of striker leave **G**oal open by relating to a goalpost.

L — when behind striker, anticipate line of next shot by using **L**ateral adjustment.

I — continual back-up to striker provided by **I**nterchanging between Nos. 3 and 4.

B — for exercise, no successive hits; good passing makes **B**all work more than pony.

Barrier is operated through

P — **P**lacing it in the middle of the four players and always having two on each side of it.

M — **M**oving with the play up and down field, but not necessarily with the ball.

I — **I**n front of barrier, aim is to diminish opponent's ability by fighting for every possible ball.

B — **B**ehind barrier, wait to be given ball unless a strike is certain, and go to next play if in doubt.

C — **C**utting out of game to reposition behind barrier by Nos. 3 and 4 when in front of the ball.

Diamond

P — **P**laymaking opportunity of all players through lateral adjustment.

E — all players **E**rupt into rope formation by being mobile at the beginning.

S — receive **S**econd hit through anticipating line of ball before it is struck.

A — **A**lternatives – recipients near sideline (mostly), across goal or direct to No. 1.

C — **C**over for weak shot given by player across goal.

B — aim to make **B**all work more than ponies.

Soft diamond

D — **D**efending half of field – ball delivered towards sideline.

A — **A**ttacking half of field – ball directed towards goal in centre.

B — **B**ackhands struck anticlockwise on majority of occasions.

F — **F**lexibility of all principles when situation requires.

P — **P**laymaking opportunity for every player through lateral adjustment.

12

Riding 'B' — Team Drills

Working in a Vertical Line — Parallel Vertical Lines — Joining in Pairs — Joining Vertical Lines

How to make the pony follow you, in relation to what others are doing, has been covered in Chapter 9, by a description of circling and turning exercises done individually and in groups while applying the SLOSH riding principles. The next stage continues with similar drills, which are carried out in a vertical rather than a horizontal line. Now the adjustments are more difficult, involving what is happening in front and behind each person, as well as the actions of those who are parallel to and alongside them. At the same time, if there are enough people, the tactical dimension of positioning within a team is included, without the distraction of a ball.

Working in a Vertical Line

Keeping Equidistant

If you are a group of four people or less, you should position yourselves in a vertical upfield line, equidistant one behind the other, five or six yards apart, or whatever distance is decided by you or your coach. Then, once again, each person takes a turn to be the leader *playmaker*, doing turns, circles, halts and any other variation of direction they decide upon.

This exercise requires even more looking than when in the horizontal line, and probably much more adjusting, especially if the *playmaker* is behind you. Even with only two people, this exercise is excellent for improving the skills required for accurate pony control when under pressure. Also, any pony that takes part will benefit from the schooling that is not related to the ball.

The leader *playmaker* should not allow the exercise to go out of control, and must slow down or even halt, if necessary, to permit others to regain their correct positions.

Sebastian Dawnay looking behind for a *playmaker*.

The tactical dimension of the vertical line is of extra significance, in that changes of direction and distances between people often alter outside your view, and must then be adjusted to quickly. Even so, better late than never. This requires constant use of legs and forces the weak riders to make the ponies follow them, while regaining lost ground.

Goalpost Dimension

Ideally, a polo field is used for these exercises. Then, when a group of four people, by keeping consistently equidistant, have clearly mastered the difficulties of the drills just described, it will be constructive to add a relationship to the goalposts. All those in front of the *playmaker*, at any time, going in either direction, have to relate to the left-hand goalpost ahead of them (see Figure 38). This is simulating a scenario wherein the current *playmaker* is always about to strike the ball, while those in front, not wishing to block the goal, remain as a link to it via the left goalpost. Once they do this well, there is

Figure 38.
(*pages 106 and 107*)
Team exercise in parallel lines.

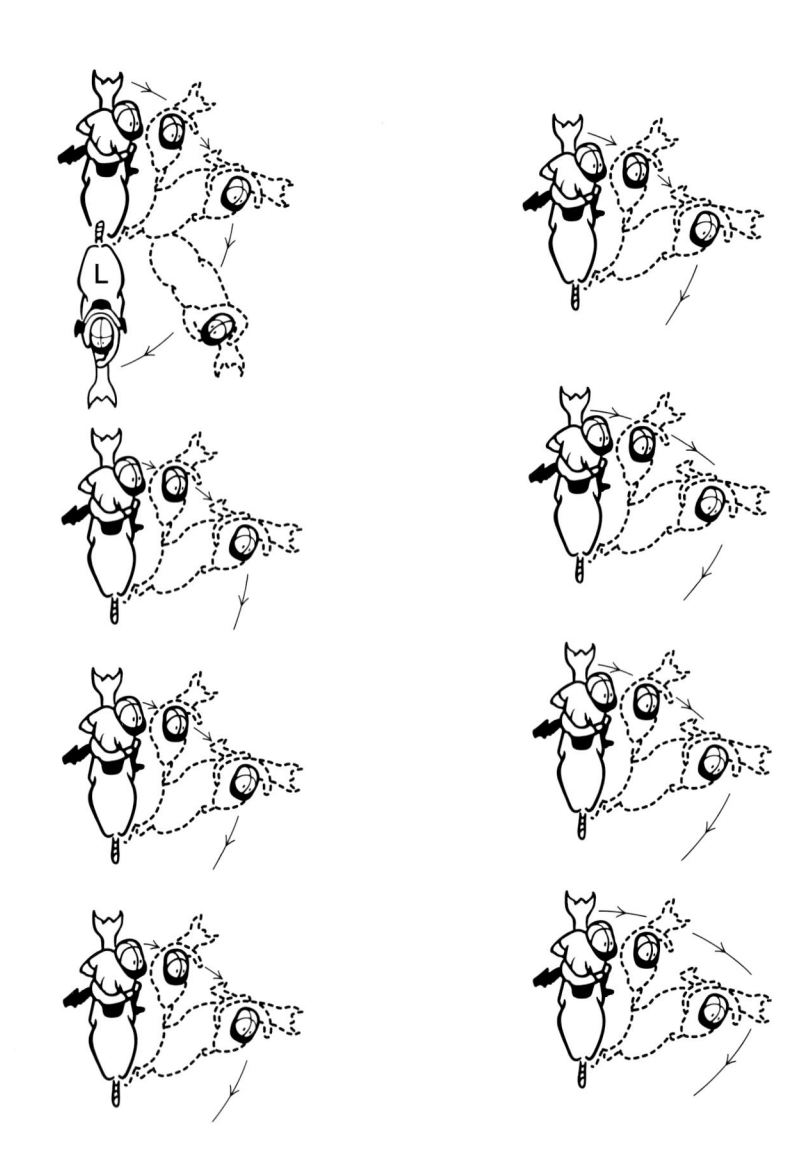

scope for the *playmaker* to deliberately exaggerate lateral movement. This will test the reactions of the others and improve their ability to leave an open goal and maintain the correct position despite unexpected plays.

Parallel Vertical Lines

Working in the Same Direction

Divide a group of people into two vertical lines, which form up as just described above. It will be more practical if each line has four people, simulating two or more teams, which are twenty yards apart, but any number can participate by adjusting the number in each line (team). Initially, the teams all move in the same direction, with each person trying to stay opposite their equivalent number in the other lines. Once again, everyone must conform to one *playmaker*, who circles, turns, halts and alters direction and speed continually (see Figure 38). This provides a most realistic tactical dimension, because the vertical lines will act and react to each other in a manner similar to much of what happens in a chukka. By changing the *playmaker* regularly to a different line, and with each person taking their turn, all will have the opportunity to adjust to something happening in almost every area around them.

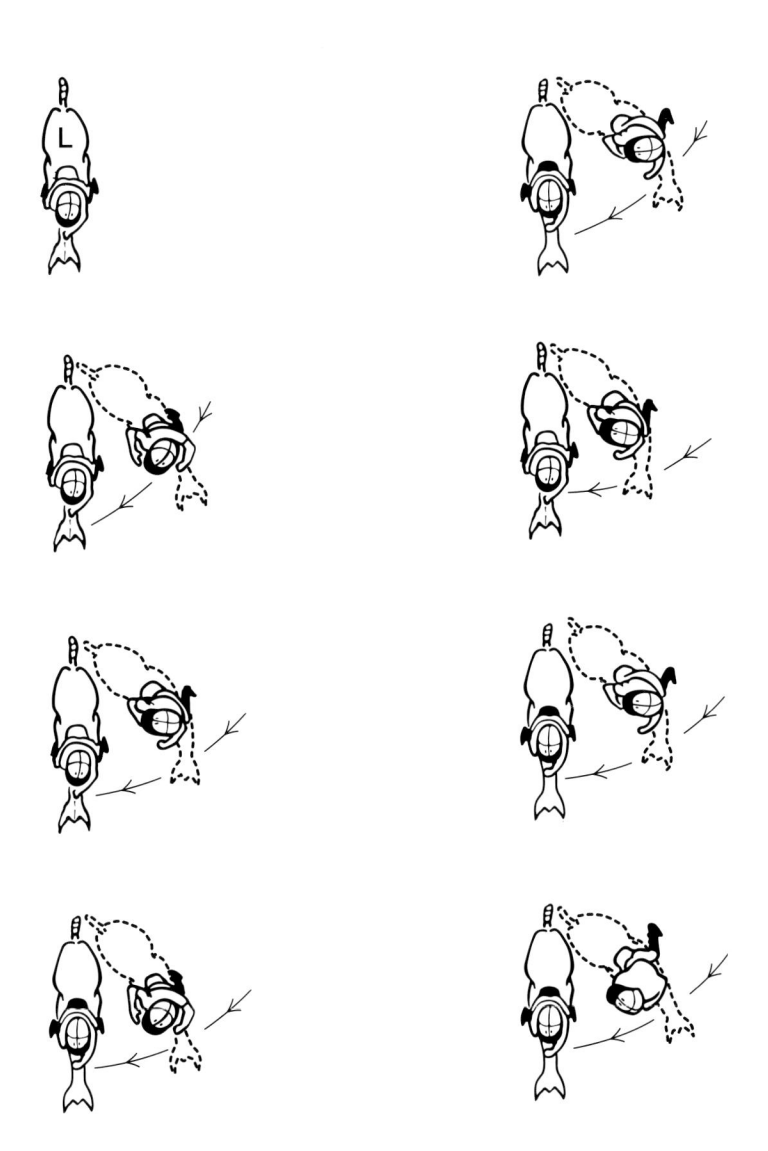

Working in Different Directions

Once the lines are conforming accurately to each other, the next step can be to make the teams move in opposite directions. Naturally, it is then important that the *playmaker*, by turning frequently, does not allow the teams to become too far apart. All participants will have the opportunity to learn how to watch and adjust to opponents, who are not close to them, while applying SLOSH during the exercise.

Joining in Pairs

Inward Half-circles

The ability to join another player, with precise accuracy, is the key to good marking. To build confidence in how to do this, I suggest you begin with a simple exercise that brings you together and level with another person several times (see Figure 39). You start together and then separate, A to the left and B to the right, each to ride an inward half-circle, (A clockwise and B anticlockwise). Watching each other carefully, you rejoin as a pair, before returning to halt on the spot from which you commenced, but facing in the opposite direction. You then repeat the exercise with A doing an anticlockwise and B a clockwise half-circle. To perfect the drill you can keep repeating it, with or without halting, until you rejoin in a very accurate manner.

The manoeuvre is similar to the U-turn, which is a tactical requirement in many set-piece situations, especially when facing the hit-in and spot penalties. As they join

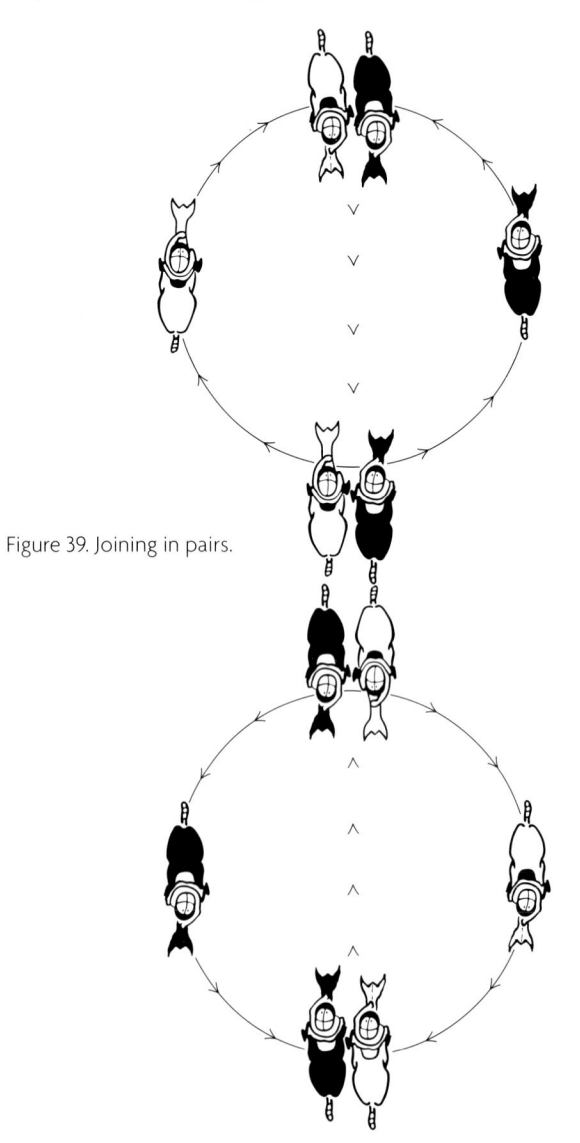

Figure 39. Joining in pairs.

together, *A* and *B* should look more at each other than at their ponies, by looking directly into each other's eyes. Strong legs and quiet hands must be applied throughout the half-circles, to help you stay together when stopping.

Joining Vertical Lines

With equal numbers in two parallel lines, joining in pairs can be done collectively. The two lines start together in pairs, following one behind the other, before they all separate at the same time. Next, they complete inward half-circles, which reunite them as pairs, now travelling in the opposite direction. They then continue, without halting, again separating before all make another inward half-circle to rejoin as pairs moving in the original order. If this is executed successfully, the double line can change direction, over and over again, with all the pairs remaining equidistant throughout.

This provides yet another way to practise conforming to your team and the opponents, at the same time. It also gives an opportunity to perfect the U-turn strategy.

SUMMARY

Working in pairs and vertical lines combines riding and tactical skills. Any opportunity to *playmake*, when not actually playing against opponents, is an excellent way of improving skills. Another advantage is that the difficulties that inevitably arise, as people school and play together, can be ironed out and overcome.

There are many factors that determine whether or not it is possible for you to participate, with your ponies, in the exercises described above. Time spent, distances to be travelled, and the availability of people plus facilities, are the key considerations. Overcoming the inevitable problems that appear to prevent you from getting together requires you to *playmake* away from the polo field. Determination to find the time, and a location suitable for several people, will have its reward when you next play in matches. The benefit must be further increased if your performance is assessed by a coach.

These drills can also create unison between rider and pony while specifically relating to other players. This is a vital requisite before *playmaking* on the polo field can be achieved.

REVISION

Working in a vertical line
E — stay **E**quidistant from each other all the time.
B — experience adjusting to actions **B**ehind, besides in front and alongside.
C — each *playmaker* must be prepared to slow or stop to keep **C**ontrol of the line.
G — relating to a **G**oalpost to learn to leave the goal clear for others to shoot.

Parallel vertical lines
P — when moving in the same direction, must remain **P**arallel to those alongside.
C — simulation of playing a **C**hukka by relating form of own team to opponents.
F — lines operating in different directions create relation to **F**ar-away players.
A — alternating *playmaker* provides necessity to see **A**ll **A**reas of the ground.

Joining in pairs
M — basic process of **M**arking an opponent.
C — start together, separate to make inward half-**C**ircles, reunite in opposite direction.
R — halt level together and then **R**epeat exercise, halt facing original direction.
E — similar to U-turn, look into **E**yes to see more of other person than their pony.

Joining vertical lines
F — pairs **F**ollow each other with the two lines moving together.
R — continual separating, inward half-circles changing direction, **R**euniting in pairs.
C — **C**onforming to own team and opponents throughout.
U — perfection of **U**-turn strategy.

13

Striking 'B' — Straight Full Shots (First Circle)

Introducing Full Shots — Constructing the Straight Offside Forehand with PASSF — Constructing the Straight Nearside Forehand with PASSF — Exercises

Introducing Full Shots

We have already examined the half-shots in detail for the offside forehand and open backhand. Now we move to the full shots, where the same application as used for the half-shot is required, for the second part of every stroke.

The Top of the Circle

Until you are an experienced, competent player, it is essential that you are highly aware of the main difference in the preparation for a full shot, as compared to a half-shot. This is the placing of the mallet head in the circle in a way which achieves economy. Instead of being below at ground zero, the mallet head should be above your head. Therefore, much concentration is needed to ensure that the swing does actually start at the top of the perfect circle. In this chapter, some catchphrases will be introduced to help with the technicalities of swinging and striking.

First of Five Circles

The full shot produces extra length which, at times, will be needed in order that you can be an effective *playmaker*. The application of PASSF is of extra importance in order to achieve consistent accuracy through the mallet head correctly turning a complete circle. The two straight forehand shots, on either side of the pony, require circles which are parallel and close to each other.

An accurate strike from either should hit a target only two yards wide and both shots can score from directly in front of goal. The forehand on the offside describes a

Chris Hyde hitting a straight forehand, applying full circle; left shoulder and mallet head pointing at the target.

clockwise circle and on the nearside, an anticlockwise one. Hence together they form the first of the five circles described in the introduction to PASSF in Chapter 7 (Figure 6).

Constructing the Straight Offside Forehand with PASSF

Preparation

As for the half shot (see Chapter 10) you should first prepare in every dimension including holding the mallet, applying the legs and making the blood flow. Until you are a skilled player, in order to find the circle (clockwise), it is better to start and finish with the mallet in the vertical position and the mallet head above you at the top of the circle. The right hand must be just outside the right knee, best remembered by thinking where you would *'hold a sword'*. This is the first catchphrase. From there, it can move straight

'Hold a sword'. A demonstration of this posture in action is given by Gonzalo Pieres in the first photograph in Chapter 1.

back and forward without deviation. Attention to these two points prevents wastage of movement, which in turn achieves economy of time for finding the circle and making the full swing. This, in turn, will help you to swing slowly at the ball.

When learning and practising any forehand you should first find the circle several times and then follow this by making many full swings through an imaginary ball at 2 on the pony clock. During these full swings you must check (or, even better, a coach could watch to see) two points, which normally need correction before you approach the ball. These are:

1. That, until the second part of the swing commences, the mallet head stays still at the top of the circle and, for a split second, points at the target, as the right hand is stretched behind it.

2. That your swing is *slow*. It will probably be necessary to continue swinging at the imaginary ball many times before it will become slow enough and look perfect.

above left Carlos Gracida, pointing at the target with classical use of shoulder prior to hitting an offside forehand.

above right Mallet head travelling back from top of circle – Sebastian Dawnay.

Approach

From a wooden horse, or on a static pony, place the ball at 2 on the pony clock. Then lean forward into the half-seat, ensuring that the mallet head above you, and the right hand below it, both stay still. First look ahead to the target, before identifying 6 on the ball clock. If you are on a moving pony, apply strong legs to advance in the half-seat. Move accurately along an axis parallel to the line of the ball, which brings you, 'holding a sword', to be exactly opposite 2 on the pony clock. When the goal is in reach, select a closer target, or a point halfway to it – see Responsibility (of No. 1) in Chapter 14.

Swing Slowly

Your right hand 'remembers' (muscle memory) that pane of glass and/or aims at 5 on the pony clock as it moves back, while the thumb now bears most of the mallet's weight. The left shoulder rotates so that it points at the ball while nudging your chin. This is a similar action to drawing a bow to shot an arrow. It can be assisted by the hips and legs turning underneath the shoulders while the thighs continue to secure the half-seat.

Ideally, the mallet head has stayed still at the top of the circle, pointing at the target until your right hand reverses direction to go forward towards the ball. Then, if you have good imagination, allow the hand to act exactly as if it were making a half-shot. This can help to slow down the swing which, without any overt use of strength, speeds up the mallet head – a paradox which is hard to believe. Also, the slow hand movement in the 50/50 swing assists the mallet head to stay in the perfect circle, despite gathering considerable velocity.

When you start a shot late, it might seem to be impossible to keep the swing slow. The solution in this situation is to forget the 50/50 swing and shorten the backswing. It is better to swing *short and slow* than *long and fast* (see Figure 16, page 59). However, the forward part of the swing can still be lengthened during the follow through and remain slow. In an extreme case of lateness, the ball can be hit effectively by what would otherwise have been the preparatory swing itself.

For every shot, whatever the situation, beware:

1. Not to allow your shoulder rotation to push the right hand above the pony's tail and out of the perfect circle.

2. That the mallet head does not move back too early and/or drop out of the circle.

Naturally, these faults can be easily detected for you by a coach or companion watching during practice and in matches.

Sebastian Dawnay – pony clock 2, ball clock 6.

Sweet Spot

This is exactly the same application as given for the half-shot. You will probably think that it is much harder to hit through the sweet spot with a full shot, but if you aim your hand, already vibrant from twirling the preparatory swing, to go directly through 6 on the bottom of the ball, you can simply repeat the half-shot action. If you have located 6 during the approach, it will assist you to confirm and then go through 6 on contact. Also, as you begin the swing, you can *'draw the bow'* with your hand back from 6 on the ball clock to 5 on the pony clock, and then return it through 6 on the ball. Verbalizing is suggested because it will help you enormously to maintain focus on 6, instead of looking up too soon, and will act as a recording in the brain for the future.

Follow Through

Because the mallet head started above you, the momentum gathered can easily take it to the left or right after passing through the ball. But if you have struck through the spot on the ball at 6 and have continued the motion towards the target with the thumb and index finger, the mallet head will not deviate. You are repeating the half-shot action, but the extra force induced by the bigger swing of a full shot will be totally dissipated if another circle is completed. It could also help you to regain the 'hold a sword' position Therefore, this action is ideal but not obligatory. However, using muscle memory, while keeping the head and eyes down until the mallet is through the ball, is essential.

Execution

Preparation
Lift the mallet to be vertical, and apply legs to pony. If there is time, find the circle by allowing the mallet head to fall and rotate through a circle then, assisted by your thumb and index finger, to return to the vertical; place hand outside right knee to 'hold a sword'.

Approach
In the half-seat, while preparing, register target and the distance to it before focusing on ball clock 6. If the goal is reachable, find a target closer to you, or halfway to the goal. Re-apply legs to bring pony parallel to line, arriving 'holding a sword', to hit the ball at pony clock 2.

Swing slowly
Draw right hand back slowly to pony clock 5, taking weight of mallet on thumb, while rotating left shoulder towards ball to nudge chin and keep mallet head still at top of circle. Muscle memory controls length of backswing and the slow path of the right hand as it goes to find the ball, which brings the mallet head round the circle to the ball.

Sweet spot
Guide the right hand to locate 6 on the bottom of the ball and go through it completely straight in conjunction with the mallet head, which continues the circle with gathering speed.

Follow through
Allow your hand and the mallet to complete the second 50% of the swing and then continue towards the target. Using muscle memory, keep your eyes and head down until the mallet head is through the ball and, if comfortable, employ your thumb and index finger to make another circle.

Constructing the Straight Nearside Forehand with PASSF

Preparation

Apply the legs and make the blood flow, by finding the circle in an anticlockwise direction on the nearside of the pony. Some clockwise circles on the offside could also be made, before switching to nearside. As explained for the offside forehand, it is important to start and finish from the vertical position in order to economize with time. For this shot, the hand and mallet should be held above the left knee. To remember to move there you could think about the superstitious action of *'throwing salt'* (another catchphrase), over the left shoulder after spilling it. Then it is constructive to hit some half-shots forward on the nearside, commencing with the mallet head down and behind the ball. The chin pushes against the right shoulder and the knuckles strike through the bottom off the ball in a similar manner to the half-shot for the offside open backhand, although this is on the nearside. This can be done on a wooden horse or a stationary pony and possibly on a walking pony. Next, you can do several full swings, from the 'throwing salt' position above the left knee, through an imaginary ball at 10 on the pony clock. Ideally, a coach or observer watches to see that:

1. The mallet head stays in the circle and, for a moment, points at the target.

2. Your swing is slow and creates a big circle.

3. You turn your right shoulder to the ball like a tennis shot, rather than a squash shot.

Approach

From a wooden horse, or on a static pony, place the ball at 10 on the pony clock. Then 'throw salt' with the right hand, holding the mallet vertical above the left knee. Lean forward into the half-seat, ensuring that the mallet head above you and the right hand both stay still. From a moving pony, look ahead to the target before identifying 6 on the ball clock. If the goal is reachable, find a target closer to you, or halfway to it. Apply strong legs from the half-seat to hold the pony straight on an axis that brings you to opposite 10 on the pony clock.

Swing Slowly

Your right hand reaches back towards your left shoulder and to 7 on the pony clock. The V between the thumb and index finger now takes the mallet's weight. The right shoulder rotates left to nudge your chin and point at the ball. This can be assisted by the hips and legs turning underneath the shoulders, while the thighs secure the body in the half-seat. The mallet head stays still, pointing at the target (see Figure 7, page 51) until the right hand reverses direction to move forward towards the ball as slowly as possible. Again, as for the offside forehand, if you can imagine that your hand is merely making a half-shot it will be easier to swing slowly. But you must ensure that the mallet head initially stays still in the circle above your head before revolving round your hand.

Sweet Spot

The earlier you focus on 6 at the bottom of the ball during the approach, the easier it will be to make an exact contact on the spot. Then, with the knuckles or back of the hand, you confirm that spot as you make the forward part of the swing. From the effects of the preparation, you should feel an active hand go through the spot with the mallet head. This sensation can be heightened by verbalizing 'knuckles' or 'spot', or something similar.

Follow Through

The right shoulder must be kept rotated to the left towards the ball and thence to where you know the target is. The hand should also continue in the direction of the target, to point at it momentarily, and possibly continue further, after passing through the ball. Your head and eyes stay down as muscle memory controls this second half of the swing. Lack of concentration will allow the mallet to go to the right and under the pony's neck. Poor application of the shoulder will produce a rushed 'squash shot' instead of the correct slow sweep, similar to a tennis backhand. The perfected follow through adds length to accuracy as long as the whole process of PASSF has been put into effect.

Execution

Preparation
Apply legs to pony and lift mallet into the vertical position, to 'throw salt' above your left knee. If you have time, find the circle to the left of the pony's head by allowing the mallet to fall and rotate through an anticlockwise circle. The back of the hand and the V should direct the mallet to return to the vertical position.

'Throwing salt'.

STRIKING 'B' – STRAIGHT FULL SHOTS (FIRST CIRCLE)

Carlos Gracida with classical use of shoulder in nearside forehand.

Approach

In the half-seat, register distance to target and then focus on exact spot at 6 on the ball clock. If goal is reachable, find target closer, or halfway to it. Re-apply legs to bring pony accurately parallel with and to the right of the line of the ball, to be placed to hit the ball at pony clock 10, with hand poised to 'throw salt' above left knee.

Swing slowly

Push right hand back, to brush left shoulder, and move towards pony clock 7, while rotating right shoulder towards the ball to nudge chin. Keep the mallet head in the circle and still by taking the weight on the V of the right hand. Change direction with hand to bring mallet head round the circle to the ball as slowly as possible.

Sweet spot

Guide back of hand or knuckles with muscle memory to locate 6 on the bottom of the ball and go straight through it in conjunction with the mallet head, which continues the circle with gathering speed.

Follow through

Allow hand and mallet to complete second 50% of swing and then continue the circle upward towards the target, controlled by thumb and index finger. Using muscle memory, keep head and eyes down until mallet head is through the ball.

Exercises

These are designed to make you practise being a *playmaker* by sending and receiving passes while making the shots described above. You have the opportunity to experience some pressure, similar to when playing, with rules to be obeyed. Although there is no opposition who can interfere with the result, you will be surprised how difficult it is to complete an exercise correctly, especially if a goal has to be scored.

1. Individually hit the ball down the polo field to try to score a goal.

2. Two players, working as a pair, alternate as *A* and *B*. Striking forehand passes to each other, from one end of a polo field to the other, they try to score a goal as follows. The ball is placed on the back line:
   A begins from ten yards behind the ball as a *playmaker* ready to send a pass.
   B positions fifteen yards in front of the ball as a *playmaker* ready to receive a pass.
   A and *B* move at the same time and *A* hits the ball as *B* approaches the thirty-yard line.
   B looks behind, joins the line, and hits quietly towards the far goal.
   B simulates being unable to hit again and *playmakes* as a link to the left goalpost.

    This sequence is repeated several times until one player, ideally *B*, has a shot at goal. It is important that *B* always makes it easy for *A* to pass by staying sufficiently close that it is unlikely that *A* ever has to hit twice in succession. If *B* always hits short, more opportunities to *playmake* will be created. When a mishit sends the ball towards the back line on the left or right side of the goal, one or more backhands may be necessary to complete the exercise with a goal.

3. Have races between two or more people, each taking a ball the length of the polo field to score a goal. Players will mainly hit with full shots, but should apply half-shots if necessary. Handicap starts can be used as relevant.

4. On the nearside only, starting from the centre of a polo field, individuals hit the ball in order to reach the goal and score.

5. *A* and *B* work together as in exercise 2 above, except that now *B* receives as a *playmaker* on the nearside and hits nearside forehands. As before, *A* sends passes as a *playmaker* by striking offside forehands. *B* stays close enough for it to be easy for *A* to be able to pass.

6. Similar races as in exercise 3, but now a designated number of shots must be hit on the nearside.

SUMMARY

With these two shots applied to the six exercises, you can practise how to hit straight down the middle of the field by yourself and when combining with others. As much as possible, try to use the full techniques for hitting in order to confirm your ability to find a circle before and follow through after a shot. To gain full benefit you should concentrate on applying the circles for both shots as precisely as possible, because this will give you consistent accuracy. Also, it will prepare you for the art of constructing the circles which are required for the angled forehands and backhands that are covered in the rest of the chapters on striking. Throughout the exercises, think as a *playmaker* who is enjoying helping another player to combine with you.

REVISION

Offside forehand

P — **P**repare with legs; mallet vertical; find circle (if time advantage).

A — **A**pproach in half-seat; register target (halfway to goal); focus on 6 on ball clock; apply legs to take ball at 2 on pony clock.

S — left shoulder to ball, **S**wing back with mallet, weight on thumb, **S**low hand forward towards ball.

S — re-focus on **S**weet spot (6 on ball clock), project hand through bottom of ball at 6.

F — **F**ollow through; continue circle upwards towards target allowing mallet (if possible) to circle again.

Nearside forehand

P — **P**repare; legs, mallet vertical, find circle (if time advantage).

A — **A**pproach in half-seat; register target (halfway to goal); focus on 6 on ball clock; apply legs to take ball at 10 on pony clock.

S — right shoulder to ball, **S**wing back with mallet weight on V, knees, **S**low forward toward ball.

S — Re-focus on **S**weet spot (6 on ball clock), project knuckles through bottom of ball at 6.

F — **F**ollow through – continue circle upward until pointing at target.

14

Tactics 'C' — No. 1 as Link Playmaker to Goal

Tasks Defined by PRST — PRST in Outline — PRST in Detail — Historical Examples

Tasks Defined By PRST

Experience has taught me that the simplest way to describe the jobs of the four positions is to give them each a title that describes the way in which they can be a *playmaker*. I then divide the jobs into four *tasks*, which are designed to produce a thought process that can be used in chukkas and matches. By employing a method for anticipating what will happen in the game, this makes all the team participate actively, instead of passively. To help you remember these tasks, there is a mnemonic PRST which stands for Position, Responsibility, Speed, Turn to defence:

Position – where to be in the 75% (not near the ball) as a *playmaker*.

Responsibility – what to do with the ball in the 25% to *playmake* for your team.

Speed – how to apply velocity and when to maximize it.

Turn to defence – when to turn to defend and what to do.

No. 1 as Link to Goal

Beginners are almost automatically put in the No. 1 position and then often left out of the game. This can happen because the rest of the team are selfish, or the No. 1 does not know how to *playmake*, or the opposing **No. 4** marks the No. 1 so tightly – or through a combination of all three. The result is that No. 1 becomes the most *difficult* position when it is intended to be the easiest. Basically, at No. 1 you are in the best situation to be a *playmaker*, if you know what you are doing and if you are *allowed* to do it. This is because three players can pass to you, using you as the link to goal, either with a short, average or long pass, as explained under LATET, in Chapter 5. But, for this to be effective, all three must recognize your job as the *link playmaker* to goal.

Adolfo Cambiaso, the supreme No. 1.

My belief is that, if your aim is to be a link, and your attitude is that scoring goals is a bonus, you are more likely to become a *playmaker* which, in turn, gives you an *increased opportunity* to score goals. This apparent paradox is rooted in the fact that No. 1 is actually the hardest position to score goals from, because No. 1 has three more problems than the other players:

1. The ball is nearly always received with little or no time to prepare or approach.

2. Shots at goal often have to be taken while the ball is bouncing.

3. Unless the ball passes directly under the right foot, it is difficult to collect a pass and shoot, without fouling, because it is easy for experienced opponents, following behind, to reach the line of the ball first.

Many professionals tell their No. 1 to spend the whole game with the opposing **No. 4** and, in doing so, are negatively relegating their No. 1 to defend only and never to attack or have any opportunity to be a *playmaker*.

When I played No. 4 in tournaments, I found that I preferred the opposing **No. 1** to stay with me all the time, so that I could always be in control, yet still choose my moments to *playmake*. When an opposing **No. 1** left me to attempt to *playmake*, I was worried, and my ability to assist my team in attack was more limited, by the fear that their **No. 1** could score a goal and put egg on my face.

Let us now look positively at how No. 1, as a link, can use PRST to *playmake* in attack and defence, yet still control the opposing **No. 4**, or whoever fills that position at any time. We will do this first in outline and then in detail.

PRST in Outline

Position (75%)
Always using two points of reference, one in front and one behind, relating:
In attack, from the next striker in your team to a goalpost.
In defence, from all your team to the opponent who is last in their attack.

Responsibility (25%)
When in possession, keep the ball in play:
In front of goal, aim at a point halfway to the middle of the goal.
Near a sideline, link to the goal with a backhand.
Prevent the ball from crossing the opponent's back line when possible.

Speed
In attack, apply controlled velocity to the two situations:
In the 25%, when in possession, by maximizing speed to help your team.
In the 75%, always be in reach as a link by continually adjusting speed.

Turn to defence
Turn before the game does, and act according to the situation determined by where the opposing **No. 4** or last player is at that moment:
If close to you, by engaging immediately.
If far behind, by watching closely, while maintaining the link to your team.

PRST in Detail

Position in the 75%

I believe that the primary skill required from a No. 1 is the ability to receive a pass, by making it very easy for anyone to find and reach him, and then being able to hit the ball without fouling. By *playmaking* in this manner, you can give the impression that your positioning is so good that *the ball is chasing you*. Second, you must be able to switch rapidly to mark the last opponent in defence. This necessitates a total application of LATET (see also Figure 40) as follows.

Looking

When in attack, it is important to look behind, in order to see all your team, and in front, to relate to one of the goalposts. This should give you a permanent awareness of the present and future line of the ball, helping you to move laterally, in order to be the first to the line of any pass which arrives. At the same time, you will be ready to switch into the correct No. 1 defensive position, in relation to your team and the opponents' **No. 4**, or whoever fills that position, as the game changes direction.

Adjusting

Changes in speed, distances and direction, in relation to your team and the last opponent, are continually required if, as No. 1, you wish to be a permanent link.

At times, to maintain an advantage over the last opponent (who from now on I will refer to as **No. 4**), you will need to alter orientation from one goalpost to the other. This ensures that you remain as a link and do not block the goal. The left goalpost gives you the easier offside shot at goal, but is more likely to trap you into a foul. The right post reduces the chance of crossing, but probably makes you take the harder nearside shot, which is illegal when an opponent faces you.

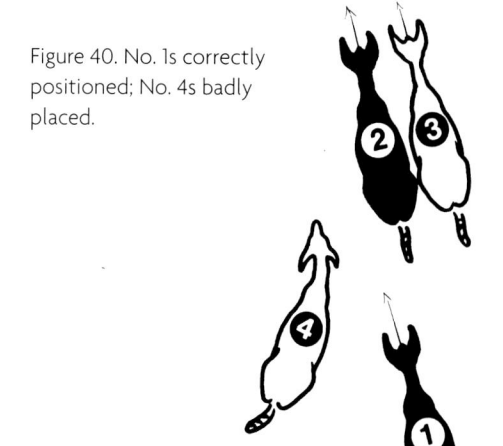

Figure 40. No. 1s correctly positioned; No. 4s badly placed.

Team

Watching other members of your team is essential, in order that you can frequently commentate to yourself, before the ball changes direction: 'Now in attack, now in defence', etc. This will make it easier for you to read the game and adjust laterally, to allow passes of different lengths to arrive. You can even receive mishits and unexpected shots. The superior anticipation of the best player will be imbibed.

Engaging

In defence, it is essential to control opponents with ride-offs, and this applies, throughout the 75%, to those who appear in your vicinity to threaten your ability to position yourself as a *playmaker* link. This dimension is also addressed by joining the line of any long pass sent in your direction quickly, before an opponent can claim it. If, at any time, this is not possible, the opponent must be ridden-off.

Turning

In order to *playmake*, you have to turn before the game does, by going into attack free, unmarked and facing goal to receive passes. Also, you must turn into defence early enough to ride-off or hook the last opponent.

Responsibility

To keep the ball in play means that it should not cross the back line unless it has been struck through the goal. Therefore, any long, angled or difficult shot at goal should be treated as an approach shot, which is a continuation of the job of linking.

Missing the goal with a wild, irresponsible shot will only discourage the rest of your team from passing to you in future. The three basic situations in which No. 1s find themselves in the 25% require very different precise actions.

In front of goal

It should be easy to hit towards goal, but instead the subconscious is affected by anxiety, to such a degree that the following mistakes happen:

1. Lifting the head before contact is made on the ball.

2. Rushing the shot.

3. Applying unnecessary strength.

These faults can be minimized by aiming at a point halfway between you and the goal. This should make you hit slower, help to keep your head down and allow you to catch up with any mishit before it goes out. Also, there may be a big bonus in that the perfect approach shot could go through the goal, because a slow, precise circle will add velocity to accuracy. Good anticipation as a *playmaker* will, of course, give you more time to be responsible and accurate.

Near the sideline

From a position close to the boards, the width of goal to shoot at is very narrow and, until you are a high handicap player, it is irresponsible to try with a forehand. A backhand link pass, directed so that another team member can score, is the better policy. Probably the worst thing that can happen to young No. 1s, in their first tournament, is that they score a goal, under the neck, from the sideline! Why? Because they will then continue to try this difficult shot in many polo matches, and will possibly never again succeed in scoring a goal with it.

At the back line

Once the ball crosses the back line, outside the goal, possession has been lost. No matter who in the team has made the mishit, No. 1s should do their utmost to prevent this happening, by stopping the ball with their mallet or pony, to keep the ball in play. Ideally, at the same time, they should try to *link playmake,* with a backhand pass, which can be converted into a goal by another *playmaker* who has anticipated this shot

Speed

In the 25%

In the 25%, many No. 1s maximize velocity to reach a pass sent to them because they are desperate to be there first. However, what is more important is the effect they will have on the velocity of their whole team, in the same way as the first car at a traffic light which has just turned green, controls the speed of all the vehicles behind it. If there are better players behind No. 1, they can only use their full skills if they are not delayed by the actions of those in front. Naturally, there is an exception and this is whenever No. 1 receives a pass, in isolation and completely clear of all opposition. Then accuracy would be lost by going fast when it is not necessary to do so.

In the 75%

The secret for a No. 1, in the 75%, is to go continually at the exact speed that permits you to *playmake*. This is very difficult, requiring constant alteration and adjustment, in order to remain in the perfect link position. Initially, you will be apt to go too fast and nobody can then reach you. Then, you may try to slow down a little and other players will run into you. The only solution is practical experience, by playing and learning from mistakes how to change from a gallop to a canter and vice versa in order to keep in a *playmaking* link position, while players behind you frequently speed up and slow down. Critical assessment, guidance and practice with a coach will help enormously.

Turn to Defence

It can seem to be impossible for No. 1s to *playmake* correctly, as the game rapidly alternates from attack to defence, and they find themselves marking when they should be free to receive, and waiting for a pass, when they should be defending. A skilful No. 1 combines both tasks effectively, by turning to defend early and deciding quickly which of the two scenarios, described in outline above and in detail below, exists at that moment.

Opposing No. 4 close

In the first situation, the **No. 4** is close and is such an immediate threat that a ride-off by you, the **No. 1**, is essential and should be maintained. Then, by controlling your opponent, you can cover all three of the alternatives which could follow:

1. Securing the defence link by preventing **No. 4** from helping the opponents' attack.

2. Holding a position from which you can *playmake* when a backhand arrives.

3. Changing direction with a sudden turn to *playmake* in anticipation of receiving a pass if you see one of your team about to gain possession.

*Opposing **No. 4** far behind*

In the second situation, the **No. 4** is waiting defensively, some distance behind the rest of the opposition, and should be watched carefully, but not joined by you, because by doing so you will have to vacate your *link playmaker* role. But if that **No. 4** suddenly moves closer and the opposition still retains possession, a ride-off is again important. Hence once more you are poised to:

1. Defend at a crucial moment.

2. Make a *playmaking* backhand.

3. Leap into attack as a *playmaker* by receiving the ball.

However, beware that **No. 4** can easily join the line before you to draw a foul, if you strike a backhand, and also, if you cross the right of way, while you are turning to attack. Only continual looking and adjusting can avoid this and you will nearly always be safer to take the backhand on the nearside. You may even have to allow that opposing **No. 4** to take one shot before you decide to hit the ball, or ride-off, or hook a stick – whichever suits the situation.

Exceptions

Polo requires such flexibility that every rule and principle which I give you has some exceptions and, for No. 1, there are two that must be mentioned.

Interchange

At any time in a chukka, you may interchange positions within your team and then, temporarily, you will cease to be the link to goal, as another player takes over the job. But this means that you must carry out other team duties, including marking a different opponent in defence.

Stronger players

Your team captain may decide that you should not be exposed to compete with the stronger players of the opposition, because they would probably use the disparity of standards to make a complete fool of you, to the detriment of the team and yourself. Hence, it could be pre-planned that you always mark the opposing **No. 4** in defence, regardless of where that **No. 4** goes. This will not prevent you from being the *playmaker link* most of the time in attack but, in defence, you will deliberately shadow that **No. 4** wherever he goes in the field.

Historical Examples

Hitchcock

In his book, *Tommy Hitchcock*, Nelson Aldrich describes how Eric Pedley, as No. 1 for the USA against England in the first match of the 1930 Westchester Cup, was the *star*, although scoring only four goals. He wrote 'He seemed to do things with wild passes which most players could not have done with good passes'. In the second game of the series, Pedley was credited with nine out of the fourteen American goals, yet this time the author commented 'Hitchcock was recognized as the genius of the team and earned the chief laurels.' What better proof can we have that vital *playmaking* may be done by a link receiver or the ball provider, rather than the actual goal scorer?

Army team

When I went with an army team to play at Sotogrande, in Spain, I had pre-trained our No. 1 in how to make every shot, hit upfield, look as if it was a good pass to him. I knew this was important, because our No. 2 was a thrusting, fast, big hitter, who was not very accurate and often overtook his No. 1 instead of passing to him. The result was outstanding, in that we had a link for everything, even for shots that went as far astray as the corner flag, and we won the two matches played there. Obviously, we all enjoyed the polo and I will never forget the surprise on our big hitter's face, when he found that he never hit a ball twice in succession. In a minor way Our No. 1 had repeated the feat of Eric Pedley, described above.

Young team

In my early days as a coach, I helped a team of four young players, who all had a zero handicap, to win a tournament. Previously, their No. 1 was always too far away, expecting impossible long passes, while the others were happy just to hit the ball, without any concept of reaching him. As a result, the No. 1 had never before been involved in attacks. With a little training, including set-piece practices, he learnt to be a link, who could adjust laterally to receive more passes than the others. The team was transformed and many goals were scored in each round of the tournament.

26-goal polo

At the other end of the handicap scale, when at Palm Beach I watched a 26-goal team, with a 7-goal No. 1, who seldom received a pass, lose several matches. Before their last game, I had a chance conversation with the team patron and asked him if he was enjoying Palm Beach polo. He replied 'Yes, but it would be more fun if my team could win a match.' I commented that no team could avoid defeat if they left a 7-goal player out of their tactical plans. The next day his team concentrated on passing to that player and won by 8 goals, defeating opponents who, in their previous encounter, had beaten them by 6 goals. The 7-goal player had only scored a few times himself in this match, but this staggering difference of 14 goals surely proves the point that *playmaking* is required by both the link and those who play behind it. *I rest my case.*

SUMMARY

There is a surprising similarity between a rugby winger and a polo No. 1, in that both are often wasted, because they take little part with the ball. There is a difference in that the winger is one of the fastest in the team, while the No. 1 may be the slowest, but the former is one of fifteen players and the latter only one of four, so which is the bigger loss?

The worst scenario for a No. 1 is when there is no coach, and communications within the team are so bad that the disparity of standards factor is exacerbated. Then the No. 1 is disgracefully abused, being sent passes which cannot be linked to, and, when one does eventually arrive in the right place, is called to leave it. Not only will that No. 1 lose all confidence, but any opportunity to develop ability under pressure will also be denied. People forget that the best way to learn to take pressure is live practice in tournaments, so that misses at goal are a good experience and not totally negative.

A logical summary of the job for No. 1 is that, if he receives the ball regularly, this indicates that the rest of the team has to be playing well and, before long, if not immediately, the No. 1 will contribute constructively to the team performance as a valuable link. To achieve this, No. 1s must apply both PRST and LATET, as described above, with strict discipline, plus a touch of flare in anticipation, which makes the ball *chase them*.

The perfect link:

1. Continually improves position in the 75%.

2. Is responsible in the 25% for keeping the ball in play.

3. Uses speed to help the attacks, yet always stays in reach of the team.

4. Turns to defend when required, but maintains the link.

If you have understood my ideas of how to be a *link playmaking* No. 1, I suggest that, before the next or first time you play that position, you practise with another person, ideally a coach, how to carry out all the PRST points and especially the way to receive a pass without fouling. Then, before the chukkas start, talk with your team and strongly request that they should try to send you passes, because you are prepared to receive them in a responsible way. That conversation will be your first act of *playmaking* on that day, and may give you the opportunity to take the second step of practising it in the heat of a match. The quickest way to learn to play No. 1 is to be allowed to participate, while facing the pressure of coping with the three unique dimensions of polo.

REVISION

Job of No. 1 Link playmaker to goal for the team

P — **P**osition; use LATET to receive WAS passes in attack and defence from all team members: Weak from No. 2, Average from No. 3, Strong from No. 4.

R — **R**esponsibility for keeping the ball in play for ISB: I – In front; aim halfway to goal, S – Side of field link with backhand, B – Back line; stop ball from crossing and link if possible.

S — **S**peed varied for the two situations:
25% – maximize to assist team velocity and skills.
75% – continual adjustment from fast to slow, staying in reach as *playmaker* link.

T — Continual awareness, relating **T**urning as to whether first or second scenario exists, and if it changes:
1. **No. 4** opponent is close and must be physically marked while *link playmaking*.
2. **No. 4** opponent is too far behind to be marked, but is watched, while *link playmaking*.

Exceptions for changing position and countering disparity of standards

CP — **C**easing to be the link when covering another **P**osition.

CDS — **C**ountering **D**isparity of **S**tandards; regardless of events, always staying with opposing **No. 4** to avoid any strong opponents.

15

Polo Riding 'C' — Control Within a Pair

Opponents as Partners — Turning in Pairs – Turning Inside an Opponent — Pairs Joining as Foursome — Coaching Assistance

Opponents as Partners

A good polo player spends most of the time close to or alongside a member of the other team. To be able to control that opponent, while at the same time looking to see what everybody else is doing, requires considerable skill. In Chapters 9 and 12 we have covered exercises which demanded a disciplined application of SLOSH, in order to ride accurately enough to stay in one team, in the correct relation to another. The next stage is to perform similar exercises, working in pairs. Although this simulates being with an opponent, you should treat each other more like partners.

Feel Where Your Partner Is

Some people find it difficult to be consistently 'outside the pony', in order to look with all-round vision. So how can you be 'outside' a *pair* and yet keep control of an opponent? The riding drills, suggested below, provide an opportunity to practise this. Initially, you continually swing your eyes from your partner to the other people and then gradually replace the looking with a sense of *feeling* where the other half of your pair is. But, whenever in doubt, re-establish visually that the partner is under your control.

These exercises can be carried out at the gaits appropriate to the participants' level of skill, as determined by a coach, or whoever is supervising them.

Turning in Pairs

These introductory exercises can be done by only one pair, or by a group of people making up any number of pairs, with an appointed *playmaker*, who should be copied as described in Chapters 9 and 12. For example, let us imagine that you are in a group of eight, who have been working as two teams in two vertical lines, as described in Chapter 12. Now, the two lines join together to make four pairs, as if on a rope. The *playmaker* has the scope to go anywhere on the field, changing direction and speed, while the others conform to all movements made.

During turns, ideally the inside partner should not leave the outside one behind, but if they are separated, he must then wait until they are firmly together again. If any pair is left behind, the *playmaker* should slow down and even stop in order to prevent the rope formation totally losing shape.

When a group seem to have perfected the art of staying in pairs, throughout all movements of the above drill, the next stage can be to add a relationship to the goalposts, as in Chapter 12. Then, when any of the other three pairs are in front of the *playmaker*, they head for the left-hand goalpost in order to simulate leaving the goal open and not blocked by either of the partners.

Turning Inside an Opponent

In a match, during a ride-off, when the direction of play suddenly changes, how can you turn in the same direction as the opponent, yet not be left behind? The answer is by turning *inside* the opponent (see Figure 41). To do this, you have to slow down or even stop, waiting with your eyes focused on the tail of the other pony, until it reaches the nose of your pony, before neck-reining. Strong leg application will be essential if you are to succeed. With good timing, despite starting the turn after the opponent, you can find yourself going in the new direction slightly ahead and therefore in control of a ride-off.

Developing the ability to turn inside other players will help you to compensate for the disparity of standards when marking a better player (see Personal Experience, page 135). Therefore this skill should be introduced and added, in due course, to the exercises in pairs. Ideally, begin by working in pairs only, to master the technique before including it collectively on the rope. Then, if the *playmaker*, for example, turns twice to the right followed by twice to the left, each person will have practised being on the inside and outside of a turn, in a match scenario. Partners must help each other to make it work, until the turns are smooth and accurate.

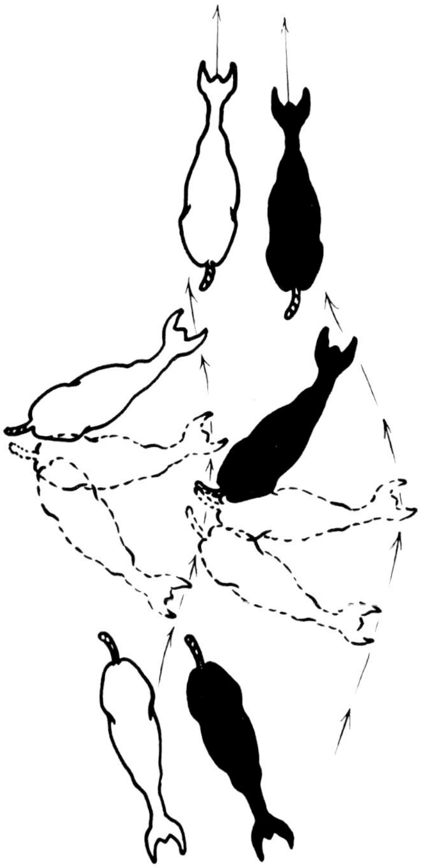

Pairs Joining as Foursome

The good timing and accurate riding required for two individual people to join together, as in Chapter 9, will be further improved if two pairs can succeed in joining as a foursome. Each person must bring their partner with them and, at the same time, shadow the movement of the other pair so that they join as four smoothly and in a horizontal

Figure 41. Turning inside an opponent.

line. This bares no relation to what happens when playing polo – in fact the manoeuvres would be deemed illegal – but the action described should help you to be more effective in a pair scenario.

Half-Circle and Rejoin

In the exercise in Figure 42, you can start as a four together and, as you move forward, the right-hand pair half-circle to the right clockwise and the left-hand pair to the left anticlockwise. On completion of their half-circles the pairs should come together again as a four, but now with the outside riders in the middle. Then they stay together for several strides, before restarting another half-circle, to rejoin in the original formation.

Full Circle and Rejoin

When the drill above has been done accurately and smoothly several times, the pairs should take a short pause. When restarting, they can now separate to complete a full circle before rejoining, travelling a few yards and then making another similar circle (Figure 43). Once satisfied with the harmony in one line up, the pairs should keep changing positions and direction, until each individual has experienced going clockwise and anticlockwise, as well as being on the inside and the outside of the foursome who are performing the circles.

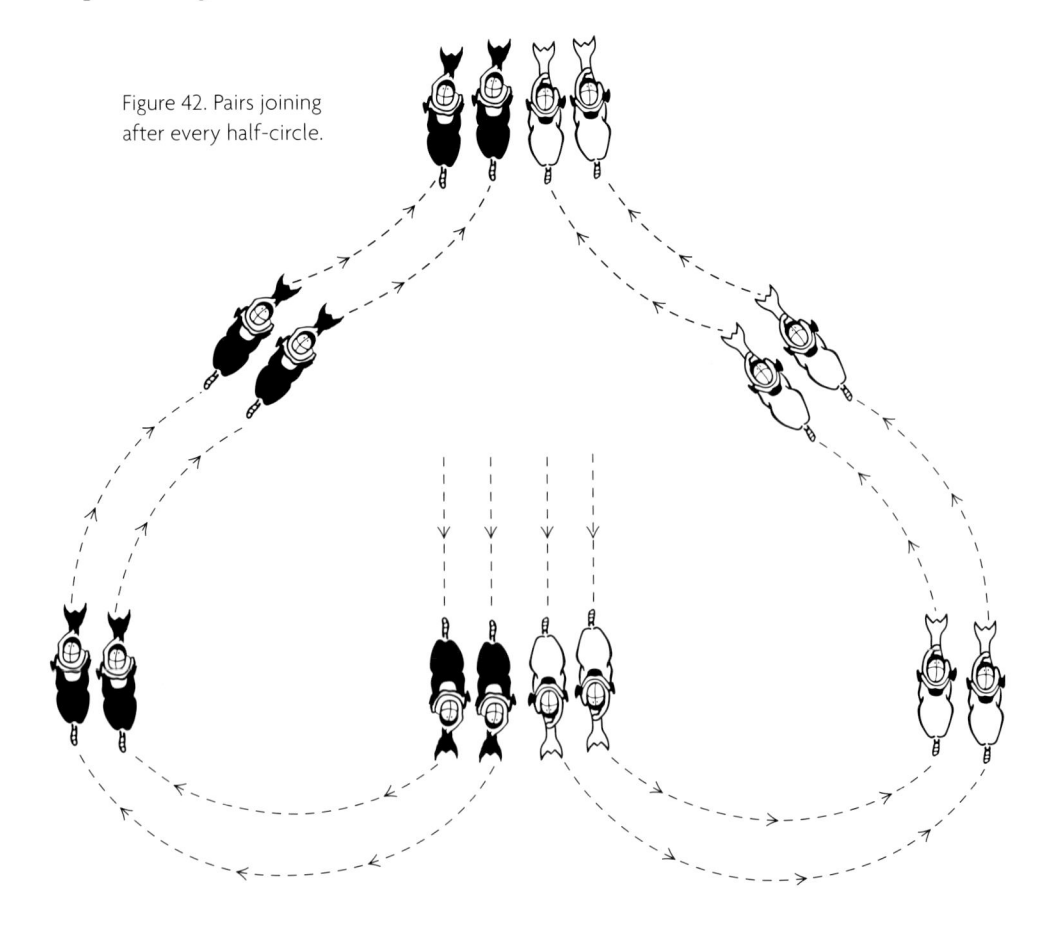

Figure 42. Pairs joining after every half-circle.

Figure 43. Pairs joining after full circles.

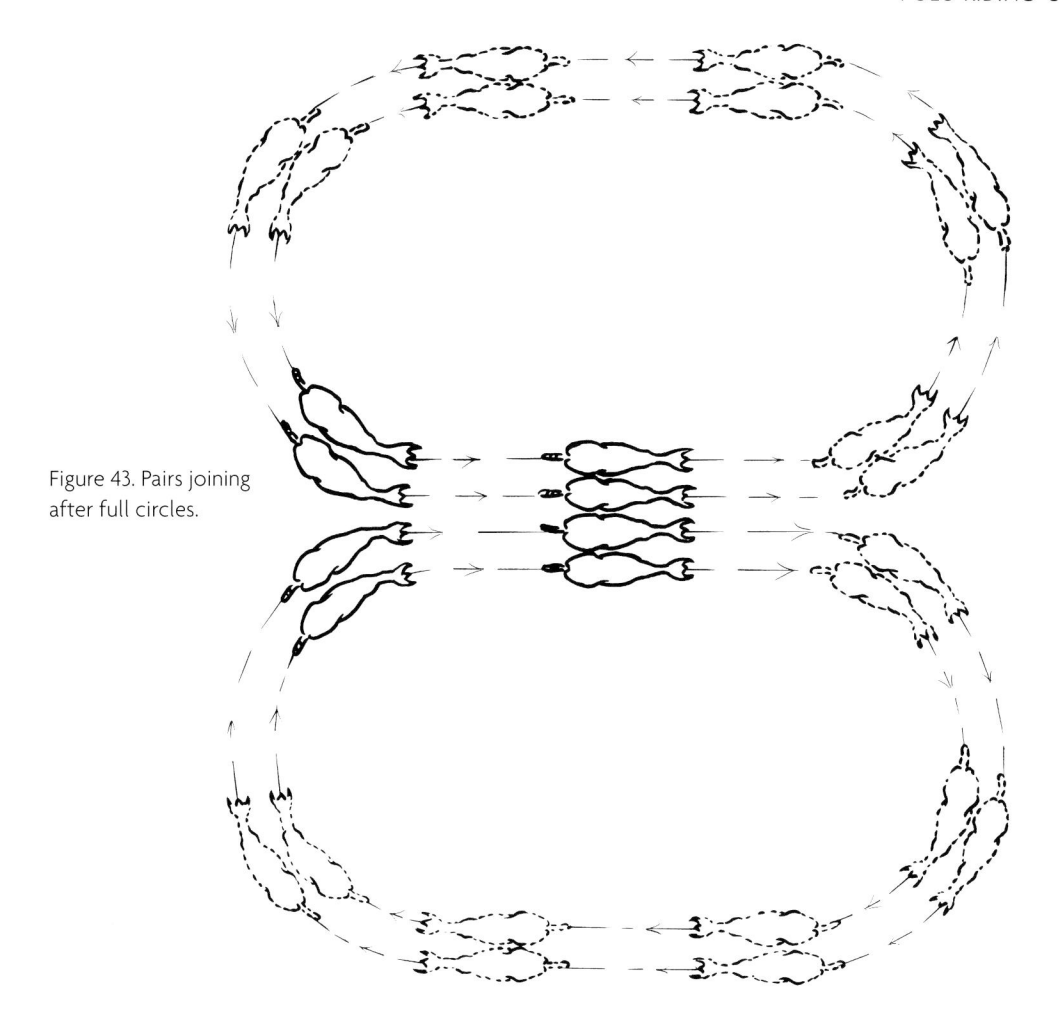

Coaching Assistance

These exercises for pairs require much application and attention to detail, before they can be perfected. The correct timing of when to use your legs, move your body in a new direction and then neck-rein, is essential. A coach can detect any slight faults which, if corrected, will assist you enormously to stay with an opponent and to turn inside one, where necessary, to win a ride-off.

Personal Experience

On the best pony I ever owned, I once did the above, throughout a medium-goal match, to a 7-goal player with spectacular results. But on many other occasions, I failed to restrict better players and afterwards realized that I had not tried to employ the 'looking at the tail' trick, to turn inside them. In those days there were no sideline coaches, who, of course, could have helped me so much with reminders about such details. Nowadays, from the sidelines, I frequently bring these points to mind and find that they are much appreciated by the attentive players. Also, I now derive great personal benefit from applying them against opponents who are younger and quicker than me, but do not know these tricks.

SUMMARY

For the majority of players, the only practice for riding with and controlling an opponent is when actually playing. The exercises described in this chapter are designed to make you experience most of the situations, relevant to being together with an opponent, which can be expected in a polo match. The first covers the art of staying together and the second should help you stay in control of an opponent after a turn. The third, although strictly unrelated to a game, will add much to your accuracy of positioning alongside an opponent. However, doing these drills without supervision could do more harm than good and the observations of a coach during practice and play should bring about improvements and good results.

REVISION

Opponents as partners
- **P** — treat each other as **P**artners, although both should feel as if in control of the other.
- **E** — continually swing **E**yes from partner to being 'outside pony' and back to partner.
- **F** — gradually replace visual control with **F**eel of partner, with only an occasional look.
- **V** — re-establish **V**isual control when in doubt of partner's position.

Turning in pairs
- **E** — keeping **E**quidistant, pairs move in a vertical line as if on a rope.
- **P** — alternating *Playmaker* uses whole field to change speed and direction.
- **B** — partners concentrate on not leaving each other **B**ehind.
- **G** — progress to relating to **G**oalpost and leaving **G**oal open.

Turning inside an opponent
- **I** — turn **I**nside opponent to avoid being left behind.
- **T** — focus on **T**ail of opponent's pony, wait until it reaches your pony's nose, then neck-rein.
- **A** — finish turn just **A**head of opponent through timing and strong legs.
- **S** — all situations practised by a pair through two **S**uccessive turns in each direction.

Pairs joining as foursome
- **B** — start as four, separate to left and right, **B**ring partner with you, watching other pair.
- **H** — complete **H**alf-circle before rejoining in opposite direction.
- **R** — move short distance again as a foursome before commencing **R**everse half-circle.
- **F** — progress to making **F**ull circles and rejoining, change direction and positions.

Coaching assistance
- **F** — detecting **F**aults that can be corrected.
- **I** — to stay with and turn **I**nside opponent.
- **R** — to give **R**eminders of important details.
- **A** — much **A**ppreciated by attentive players.

16

Striking 'C' — Offside Front Circle (Second Circle)

Second of the Five Circles — Constructing the Offside Neck Shot with PASSF — Constructing the Offside Open Backhand with PASSF — Exercises

Second of the Five Circles

For both the neck shot and the open backhand on the offside, the same circle is used to hit the ball, but in opposite directions. This circle is the second of the five circles referred to in Chapter 7 under the PASSF heading. Regularly practising these two shots together will assist you to find the best approach and perfect the application for this circle in both directions.

Avoid Hitting the Pony

The neck shot is probably the easiest shot to learn on a wooden horse or when going *slowly* on a pony, but at speed it becomes the most difficult to perform accurately. This is because it has to be struck across the front of the pony's moving legs and you have to hit very early, to avoid striking them. Hence players often miss the goal or give a bad pass, because they do not swing precisely and slowly with a neck shot.

With the open backhand, you must avoid hitting the head of the pony, while striking the ball very early in order to complete the correct circle. Failure to apply the required circle can result in a straight backhand, which gives the ball to the opposition, because an opponent should be able to meet the ball and gain possession.

Constructing the Offside Neck Shot with PASSF

Preparation

For the neck shot, it is more important than any other to hit early and to achieve this, economy of movement is essential. Good preparation will assist you to be early, and it is helpful to hold the mallet vertical before and after finding the circle. This must be done well before reaching the ball, or not at all. Then, I suggest that the right arm should be straightened, with the hand pointing at the ball. This establishes the hand in the circle of the neck shot, so that it can swing sideways when required and there is no delay, thus achieving optimum economy. A catchphrase that may help you to remember this is to think *'reach into the fridge'*.

'Reaching into the fridge'.

Begin with some half-shots under the neck, with a sideways half-swing, after placing the mallet head down and behind the spot at 4 on the ball clock. This should prepare you to find the path of the second half of the full swing and the follow through. Then practise a number of full swings, starting with a vertical mallet that slowly sweeps sideways and then returns towards an imaginary ball as if passing through it.

Approach

From a wooden horse or static pony place the ball at 1 on the pony clock. In the half-seat, straighten your right arm above the ball. On a moving pony, look forward to identify the target and then the relevant spot close to four on the ball clock. Apply strong legs to advance in the half-seat parallel to the line of the ball and, maintaining the right arm straight, 'reach into the fridge'. Then bend the pony's head to arc a little from right to left and arrive opposite 1 on the pony clock (see Figure 12, page 58). For a reachable goal, pick a halfway target.

Swing Slowly

Deliberately swing your hand sideways to the right. This has already been practised as described above with some half-shots and full swings at an imaginary ball. Allow the weight of the mallet to be supported by the thumb as the mallet head points at the target. The left shoulder nudges the chin to point at the ball, supported by the left hip above the left knee on the saddle. Then, as slowly as possible, sweep the hand towards the ball and the target, using imagination to suggest to yourself that you are making a half-shot.

Sweet Spot

During the approach, you should already have focused on the relevant spot and now, as the swing brings the mallet head to the ball, you confirm it by aiming your hand to pass through that exact spot on the bottom of the ball, close to ball clock 4. It is even better if you initially draw the first half of the swing sideways from the spot, in order to return in the same plane to make the contact. Verbalizing will help you to concentrate on the spot as contact occurs.

Follow Through

As for the straight offside forehand, the momentum gathered can deflect the mallet head away from the target. Therefore, your hand must continue to be guided exactly to the target by muscle memory and, if the swing path avoids the pony's head and neck, allow the mallet to turn another circle to dissipate the force and maintain direction. The head and eyes must stay down until the mallet head has passed fully through the ball. The left shoulder, hip knee and leg act as support for the whole action.

Completion of the neck shot – Sebastian Dawnay.

Execution

Preparation
Apply legs, while holding the mallet vertical. Straighten right arm and 'reach into the fridge' to point hand at the ball after finding the circle (if you have time).

Approach
Register exact location of target, and distance to it. Then find and focus on relevant spot close to ball clock 4. In the half-seat re-apply legs to bring pony parallel to line of ball before making shallow arc to left in relation to pony clock 1. Continue to 'reach into fridge'. Pick halfway target to reachable goal.

Swing slowly
Bring left shoulder to nudge chin and swing sideways from spot to take mallet weight on thumb. Return swinging slowly on the same plane through the ball.

Sweet spot
Aim palm of hand to pass through and confirm spot (ball clock 4) on bottom of the ball in conjunction with the mallet head.

Follow through
Allow your hand and mallet to complete second 50% of swing and continue in the target direction to make another circle if this avoids pony's head and neck. Use muscle memory to keep head and eyes down until mallet head is through ball.

Tom Berney about to strike a neck shot.

Constructing the Offside Open Backhand with PASSF

Preparation

First, you could repeat much of the initial forehand preparation, because this shot should also be commenced with the mallet in the same vertical position and the right arm straight. Economy of time is equally important and obtained by the 'reach into the fridge'. Hitting in the opposite direction from which you are moving adds extra scope for the error of a late contact on the ball. Second, you could revise some half-swings between 12 and 4 on the pony clock to brief the muscle memory as to exactly where the second half of the swing should travel.

I suggest that the swing to find the circle should also made between 12 and 4 on the pony clock to remind you where the actual swing should be and help you to remember not to hit the ball straight back to the opposition. You could do several of these preliminary swings when learning and practising the open backhand and then make many full swings through an imaginary ball close to 1 on the pony clock. A coach or observer could check that:

1. The mallet head points at the target when above the right shoulder, halfway through the swing, and again at the end of the swing.

2. Your swing is slow enough.

Approach

On a wooden horse or a static pony, place the ball close to 1 on the pony clock. Lean forward into the half-seat and look behind to find the exact target, before focusing on the relevant spot between 10 and 11 on the ball clock. On a moving pony, while preparing, look behind to locate the target and follow this by identifying the relative spot on the ball clock. As for the half-shot, create a shallow arc from right to left, without crossing the line (see Figure 12, page 58), apply strong legs to hold the pony's head away from the swing path, then 'reach into the fridge' with a straight arm.

Swing Slowly

When your right hand moves forward, the V between your thumb and index finger should accept the mallet's weight. The right shoulder fights your chin so that focus on the sweet spot is maintained although the hips rotate left as the right hand now stops at 12 on the pony clock, as the V directs the mallet head to point at the target. From this position, apply muscle memory for the second half of the swing from 12 to 4, which should be as slow as possible, with the shoulders and hips now gyrating to the right. Try to imagine that you are bringing your knuckles to execute a half-shot. If you are starting late with a backhand, shorten the first half of the swing towards 12. A watching coach or colleague can assess the shape of your circle and the correctness of technique.

Sweet Spot

You have focused on this spot, since beginning the approach, and you know where to hit the ball, having already looked there. Now confirm the spot by aiming the back of the hand or knuckles at it so that the mallet head passes through the bottom of the ball and on in the direction of the target. Try to pinpoint the spot by verbalizing.

Follow Through

Although this is the same action as for the half-shot, there is greater scope with the full swing to rotate the shoulders and hips more in both directions and to extend the mallet further in the direction of the target. Use muscle memory to keep the head and eyes down while continuing to send your hand and mallet head towards the target. Be aware that, if there is a lack of concentration, both will be drawn wrongly towards the pony's tail, which results in a the dreaded straight backhand giving the ball to the opposition.

opposite page Ground zero, second circle, after an arc approach to the offside open backhand – Gonzalo Pieres.

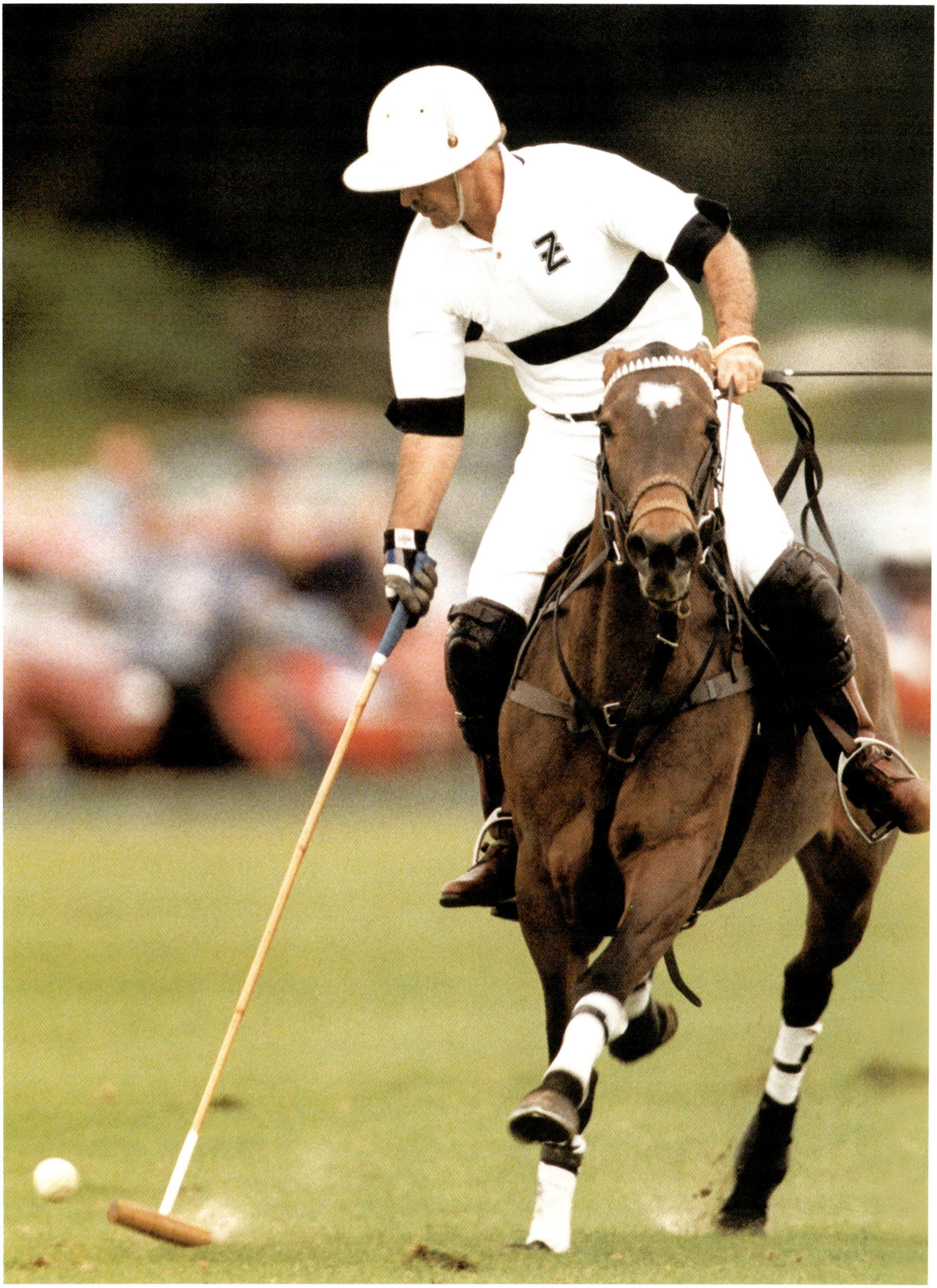

Execution

Preparation
Apply legs to pony and lift mallet into the vertical position. If you have time, find an anticlockwise circle from 12 to 4 on the pony clock by allowing the mallet to fall forward and, assisted by your thumb and index finger, rotate to return to the vertical. Then 'reach into fridge'.

Approach
In the half-seat, before or while preparing, look behind to register exact location of target and distance to it. Look forward to focus on precise spot at, or close to, ball clock 10. Re-apply legs to bring pony parallel to the line of the ball and then create a shallow arc to the left, before you 'reach into the fridge', to strike the ball near pony clock 1 without hitting the pony's head.

Swing slowly
Extend the right hand forward, rotating the right shoulder to the left against your chin. Take mallet's weight on the V of your right hand as it goes towards pony clock 12. Change direction to the right with hand, shoulder and hips and use muscle memory to guide knuckles slowly towards the ball and on to the target.

Sweet spot
Guide right hand to find and go through the bottom of the ball at the required spot, close to ball clock 10, in conjunction with the mallet head, which then continues the circle with gathering speed.

Follow through
Allow hand and mallet to complete second 50% of swing and then continue the circle upwards, controlled by thumb and index finger. Use muscle memory to keep head and eyes down until mallet is through the ball.

Exercises

The two shots learnt in this chapter can be usefully combined in exercises, working individually and in pairs, or in a larger group. The format of the exercises demands attention to detail, which provides an excellent method of revision. Combining with others gives a player a useful preparation for *playmaking* in a team and taking pressure.

1. Individually, hit the ball round the shape of a star (see Figure 44a) on the offside by alternately striking a neck shot and then an open backhand.

2. As a pair, work together on the offside in the following sequence (see Figure 44b):
   A hits a neck shot and then approaches the ball to make an open backhand to B.
   B *playmakes* to receive the backhand from A and then hits a neck shot.
   B then sends an open backhand to A, who *playmakes* to hit a neck shot.

3. Individually, on the offside, hit open backhands in a clockwise circle.

STRIKING 'C' – OFFSIDE FRONT CIRCLE (SECOND CIRCLE)

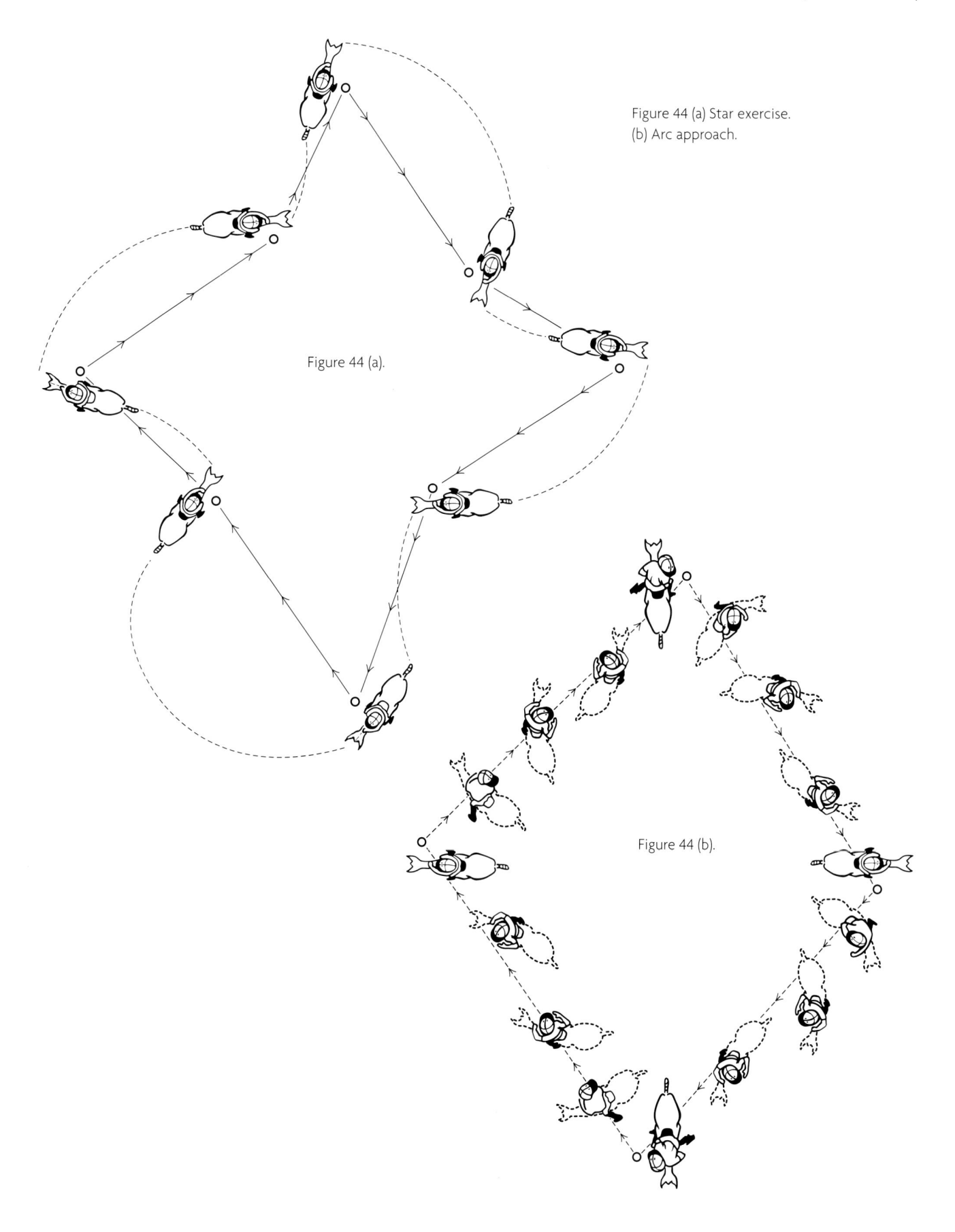

Figure 44 (a) Star exercise.
(b) Arc approach.

Figure 44 (a).

Figure 44 (b).

145

4. Working in pairs on the offside, hit alternate open backhands in a circle (see Figure 32, page 89).

5. In pairs, work with *A* to the right of *B*, travelling parallel down the field:
A strikes a neck shot on the offside across the field and in front of *B*, who approaches the ball laterally across the field, without respect to the line, to hit an open backhand on the offside across the field and in front of *A*. These alternate shots are continued until the ball is close to goal, when one of them attempts to score. Then *A* and *B* change roles.

SUMMARY

Being able to complete the exercises in this chapter successfully should give you confidence that you can control, with accuracy, any shot in this second circle, across the front of a pony on the offside. Then you will know that you can regularly give good passes, and score goals under the neck of the pony, which will add much to the attacking powers off your team. At the same time, defence will be constructively strengthened by consistent open backhands of length, which can not only alleviate the pressure on your goal, but may often initiate a counter-attack, if there is a *playmaker* in your team, positioned to receive as in exercises 2 and 3 above.

REVISION

Offside neck shot

P — **P**repare; legs; mallet vertical; find circle and straighten right arm.

A — **A**pproach in half-seat; register target (halfway to goal); focus on 4 on ball clock; apply legs to arc left and place pony to ball at 1 on pony clock.

S — left shoulder to ball; **S**wing **S**lowly sideways; point mallet head at target; weight on thumb, hand toward ball.

S — aim right hand to pass through **S**weet **S**pot at bottom of ball, at or close to 4 on ball clock as required.

F — control mallet head to continue **F**ollow through exactly toward target and, if practical, make another circle.

Offside open backhand

P — **P**repare; legs; mallet vertical; find the circle.

A — **A**pproach in half-seat; register target; focus on 10 on ball clock; legs to arc left and place pony to ball near 1 on pony clock.

S — right shoulder to left against chin; right hand to 12 on pony clock; mallet weight on V; knuckles toward ball; **S**wing **S**lowly.

S — aim right hand to pass through **S**weet **S**pot on bottom of ball, at or close to 10 on ball clock as required.

F — control mallet head to **F**ollow through exactly toward target and extend as far as possible.

17

Tactics 'D' — No. 4 Shuts the Back Door

Principal Roles of No. 4 — PRST Outline for Shutting the Back Door — Shutting the Back Door in Detail — The Reverse Rope — Historical Examples

Principal Roles of No. 4

No. 4 should be the easiest position to play, if you understand what you are intended to do and if your No. 3 is helpful. From behind all the other players, you have more time than them to watch what is happening, in order to anticipate the next play. With good self-discipline, it is relatively simple to defend and to *keep the back door shut*, by stopping the first opponent. If this is achieved, you should then be able to find some secure opportunities to leap into attack as a *playmaker*.

Despite this logic, many teams do not let beginners play at No. 4, because they think that they are unlikely to hit good backhands, which might cause disaster. I believe that, with this attitude, they miss the significance of the disparity of standards, in that No. 4 will probably be marking the weakest player in the opposing team. This can be a much simpler task than carrying out the duties of No. 1, as described in Chapter 14 – and taking backhands should initially be a second priority. Notwithstanding this, some people actually find the offside backhand *easier* than the forehand and, at No. 4, by engaging opponents frequently, you can have more opportunities to practise it, under pressure, than at No. 1. If and when you do miss a backhand, provided you apply LATET and your No. 3 stays close enough to cover you, any damage should be minimized. Also, it is better to miss than to hit a straight backhand, which goes directly to the opposition. For this reason, in the chapters that address striking, I began with angled backhands and emphasized that there are only very few situations when a straight one might be required (see Chapter 7).

When, at the front of the game, from any place in the field, No. 1 links to goal effectively, a door is being *opened* for the team. In the same team, No. 4, at the back, must *close* the door to the other goal at all times, except when someone else temporarily takes over that task. Therefore, I say the job of No. 4 is to *shut the back door* and this is best described through the PRST concept (see Chapter 14). We will look at this first in outline and then in detail.

PRST Outline for Shutting the Back Door

Position in the 75%
Be the last of the eight players on the field in both defence and attack.

Responsibility in the 25%
Receive the ball through making players *give* it to you by:
1. Staying behind the barrier to intercept an opponent and/or the ball.
2. *Playmaking* only when a secure chance arises to hit the ball.

Speed
Maximize velocity to:
1. Engage in defence the first opponent or the *line of the ball*.
2. *Playmake* in attack, especially before your own No. 3 hits a backhand.

Turn to defence
1. When your team's attack is about to fail.
2. In attack when the ball is behind you.

Shutting the Back Door in Detail

Position in the 75%

It should be very easy to be the last player at your end of the field (see Figure 45), but distractions and temptations can complicate good intentions. I have watched many No. 4s who simply could not comply. In attack, as in defence, it is equally important to be last most of the time because, at any moment, one backhand by an opponent can put your goal in danger. In defence, it is impossible to protect your goal from any place other than being the last on the field. Only by continually looking to see where the other seven players are, can you adjust to all that is happening and ensure that you remain last.

Of course there are exceptions to this principle, the two main ones being:

1. If the opposing **No. 1** is of no value, or is often in the wrong place, too far upfield.
2. When another team member is clearly covering the No. 4 position for you.

Taking these points into consideration, we might say that No. 4 should be *operationally last*. To be behind an opponent of no value, or one who is too far forward, in a place where passes cannot reach, takes away the advantage gained from that player's inability or mistakes. The only result will be that you take a very small part in the game. In the

No. 4 position in general, great patience will be required at times when it appears that you may never become involved with the ball. But you must remember that *all* players should expect 75% of play to be away from the ball and, while shutting the door, you could suddenly be given a chance to *playmake*.

An observant coach can monitor the consistency of the positioning of a No. 4. During matches I have often told No. 4s, between chukkas, that they were playing too far up or too far back and this immediately helped them to be more effective.

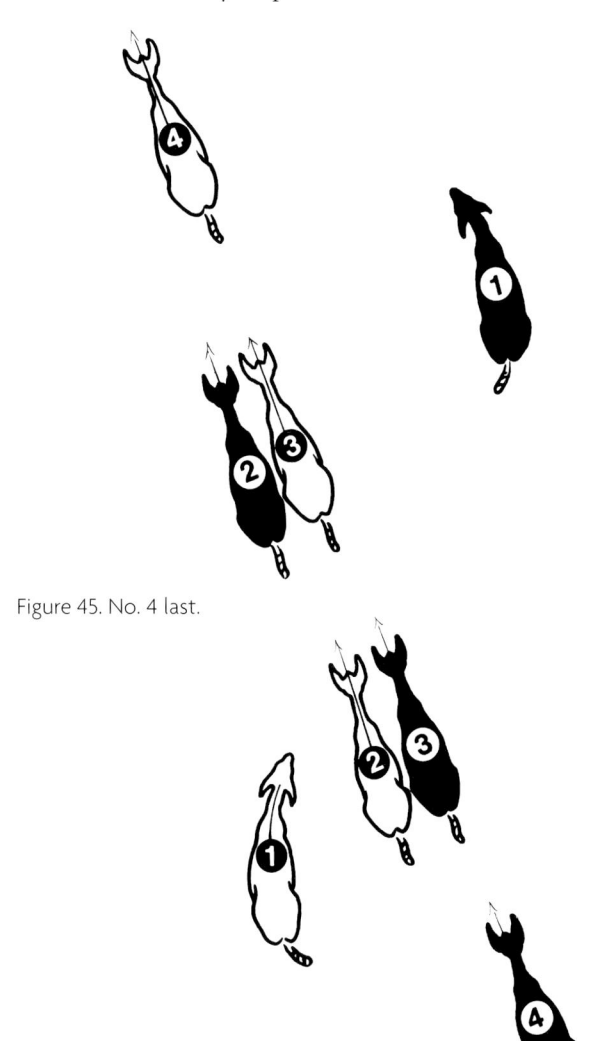

Figure 45. No. 4 last.

Responsibility

When given the ball

The thought process required for a No. 4 to play safely has already been described in the section about the barrier in Chapter 11. The polo field is so long that it is often preferable to lose a few yards rather than to risk leaving the back door open. Hence, when in doubt, a No. 4 should go to the next play, instead of allowing the possibility of being left behind there and then. In both attack and defence this means allowing an opponent at least one shot, in order that the ball will then be *given* to you. In attack you must *stop* rather than compete for a doubtful ball or, in other words, *only go for certainties*. In defence, you should cut a corner to be in front of the opponent, so that after one shot you have regained the advantage. How do these actions *give you* the ball?

Attacking opponent's alternatives are:	**Your reply when you stop is:**
1. Attempts, but misses, a backhand.	The ball has been *given* to me to hit.
2. Strikes a straight backhand.	I can meet and hit the ball or turn to join the line.
3. Strikes an angled backhand.	I can engage the line or an opponent.
4. Turns the ball towards goal. the ball.	I can engage the opponent to win.

In defence, from in front of an opponent, two alternative actions will give you the ball:

1. Waiting for and then engaging the opponent before hitting the ball.
2. Engaging the line of the ball without fouling, before hitting the ball.

Secure playmaking

Good anticipation will create opportunities for you as a No. 4 to be a *playmaker* – see Figures 34 and 35 (page 95), where lateral adjustment places No. 4 on the line of the next shot before it is taken. This action enables you to back up in attack, if the ball is over-ridden by those in front of you, and possibly to meet an opponent's angled backhand, instead of having to go to the next play as a defender. By continually watching and adjusting to your No. 3's actions, you should be able to make well-timed sudden accelerations, or engage opponents early, to ensure that, when you reach the ball, you are either first to arrive or you have won a ride-off. Thereby, you can assert your authority while being responsible. But if, in the middle of any *playmaking*, you are surprised by a quicker opponent, you can always adjust to the next play.

Sideline input

From the sideline, it easy for a coach to see whether a No. 4 is being responsible or not. It will be important to distinguish between recklessly committing to plays that are unsafe, misjudging the situation and mishitting in what should have been a no-risk play. Highlighting all behaviour patterns will be constructive, in that both encouragement and correction help No. 4s to learn from good play and mistakes.

Speed

Engaging in defence

Bursts of acceleration are useful at any time in a game, but for No. 4 the most important moment has to be when the door urgently requires shutting. It will be essential to apply velocity when you adjust from attack to defence, because the change of direction may put you temporarily at a disadvantage. Your thought process and action should be governed by whether you are in the 75% or the 25 %.

In the 75%, the ball is not near you, but if an opponent is correctly positioned as a link in **No. 1**, you must use speed to engage and win a ride-off. Thereby, the back door is not only shut, but is also locked against the opponents' link, who cannot then receive a pass while their attack lasts. Someone else may score a goal, but that will not be your fault. If the ball then arrives, you should stay engaged in a ride-off and try to hit a backhand, if that is constructive for your team.

In the 25% there are two alternative scenarios:

1. You are in direct competition with an opponent for the ball. Your first priority is to prevent that opponent scoring. Your second priority is to hit the ball away from the goal and your third is to *playmake* by delivering a good pass. Therefore, depending on the exact situation, you should use speed to do one of the following:
   (a) Engage and ride-off the opponent before hitting an angled backhand.
   (b) Engage and ride-off only.
   (c) Hook the mallet as the opponent attempts to hit.

2. You are alone with no opponents close to you. The priority is to hit a backhand and not to foul. Therefore, you must join the line with speed, so that you clearly claim the right of way, because better players have the ability to jump on to the line when a long way from the ball, to claim a foul. By engaging with speed, beginners will not be left alone in defence, and they can avoid fouling or giving the ball to experienced opponents.

Erupting in attack

If you wish to *playmake* in attack as No. 4, it will also be important to apply velocity at the crucial moment when you see the opportunity arise. By watching your own team, especially your No. 3, you will increase the possibilities. The best of these will be presented as defence changes to attack, a situation that will be analysed shortly under Reverse Rope. This can happen as a result of either 1(b) or (c), – just mentioned under Engaging in Defence – being carried out satisfactorily, if this clearly gives your No. 3 a backhand. Also, when attacks start down a sideline, a No. 4 can erupt down the middle to receive.

Being trusted

When playing No. 4, in all situations where you need to produce speed, you must remember to apply SLOSH and PASSF with extra emphasis on *legs* and *preparation*. To keep the back door shut you must be ready, at a moment's notice, to act with controlled velocity and you cannot do this unless your training equips you to react correctly and instantly. Sometimes the opponent could be the other team's best player, who has temporarily become the **No. 1** and can easily fool you, unless you are quick. Working with a coach in practice should help you to find the best technique for developing such control. Then, in a match, I suggest that a No. 4 should always be trusted to stop the first opponent and seldom helped, in order to develop confidence and to be able to learn from mistakes. The exception to this is when it has been decided before a match that the No. 4 must not be exposed to the skill and tricks of the best opponent. Then, when that player becomes **No. 1**, someone else will shut the door.

Turn to Defence

When attack could fail

When an attack made by your team is about to fail, you, the No. 4 could be in many different situations such as:

1. Last, and following behind your team in the 75% when you see that an opponent is about to hit the ball.

2. In the 25%, but realizing rather late that you are losing a ride-off or that an opponent will hit the ball before you can.

3. In front of one of your team, who has just missed the ball.

In each case, you should be beginning to defend before any opponent can hit the ball. This, initially, may only require you to stop while you watch what unfolds, because you can shut the door from that position. But in the third example, and many other situations, you must turn and retreat rapidly directly towards the goal, to reach a position where you are last and are able to shut the door again. The clear exception to this rule is if you see that one of your team has taken over your position and job of No. 4. But it is better to start this defensive action and then check to see if the exception exists, before making the necessary adjustment, because turning to defence requires minimum delay. Even then, you may have to move some distance to fill No. 3 or another position, in order to mark an opponent who is free to attack.

When ball is behind

In attack, the ball may suddenly be *behind* No. 4. This can come about for a variety of reasons, but normally it happens because you have missed a shot, or you have lost a ride-off, or you have been hooked. Any of the above can occur in one of the following three situations:

1. When none of your team is behind you and the back door is wide open. Then your turn to defence should take you towards the goal, to be behind the ball. Normally, an

opponent will reach the ball before you, or claim a foul from you, if you return direct to the ball and so it is safer to go to the next play, as explained earlier under Responsibility.

2. When one of your team is behind you. Then the barrier is still in front of you and, regardless of whether possession is being held or lost, you should turn to defence to become the last player again. This action adds depth to both attack and defence for your team and hopefully the ball will reach a player who is in front of the barrier.

   The exception to this rule is when the player behind you calls the intention to pass the ball to you, probably because the other two players in your team are badly positioned and too far away.

3. When two or even all of your team are behind you. Then your initial action is again to return to be last as No. 4, by moving directly towards goal down the middle of the field. By doing this you will be achieving the following:
   (a) Shutting the door.
   (b) Allowing your No. 3 to retain that position.
   (c) Minimizing confusion as to whom is marking the opponents' link to goal.
   The exception is when, en route, you see that your job is being done for you.

Before change

The key to turning to defence is to do it *before* there is a change in direction, so that you can re-establish your position as last player and then engage an opponent or hit the ball. However, even if you are late with the turn, by heading directly to goal you may do enough to distract an opponent from being accurate and scoring.

The Reverse Rope

General Basis

The reverse rope tactic provides the greatest scope for a No. 4 to *playmake*, while changing defence into attack. It is a manoeuvre which the opposition find difficult to control, especially if the whole rope changes direction in a few seconds, and No. 4 is unmarked for at least one shot. This tactic can be initiated from any part of the rope but I believe that No. 4 should have the most opportunities. It is based on the principle, espoused by Gonzalo Pieres, the best No. 3 of his era, that, when taking a backhand, No. 3, is effectively the No. 4. However, No. 4 must turn and move into space early enough to *receive* that backhand, and Nos. 1 and 2 can assist enormously by *playmaking* to accept the next pass.

   By discovering this tactic, I learnt an extra dimension about *playmaking* to receive a pass. I only realized the complete significance of it after Dickie Cernadas' interpretation gave me such pleasure in Dublin. This incident is described in detail in Chapters 23 and 26.

Sebastian Dawnay at No.4 attacking from the reverse rope, watched by Mike Azzaro (10).

Method

As a No. 4, shutting the door in defence, you suddenly see that your No. 3 is approaching the ball to strike a backhand. Ideally, your action defines where the ball should be sent (see Figures 46 and 47). The tail shot is easier than the open backhand for you to receive a pass without fouling or being stopped by an opponent and, if there is room for you to fit in with that, it will normally be the best decision. But if the only area available for you to receive a pass requires an open backhand, you should *playmake* by going there. Whichever way you go, it is important that you move in time for No. 3 to see and to be able to hit the required angle to reach you.

If the whole team is involved in the tactic, Nos. 1 and 2, by closely watching their own players behind the barrier, can conform to left or right as necessary and can even be able to receive directly from No. 3 if the backhand is sufficiently long. Hence three members of your team could be *playmaking* at the same time, but probably No. 4, having interchanged positions with No. 3, is the least likely to be marked, and it is better if the other two are going on to the next play.

In any event, the principle is that, in between changing directions, the rope disintegrates temporarily into a shape similar to the diamond, and then reforms after some accurate lateral adjustment. Therefore, the ball might reach No. 1 after one, two or three shots in the same way as happens in both the rope and diamond exercises, described earlier in Chapter 11.

TACTICS 'D' – NO. 4 SHUTS THE BACK DOOR

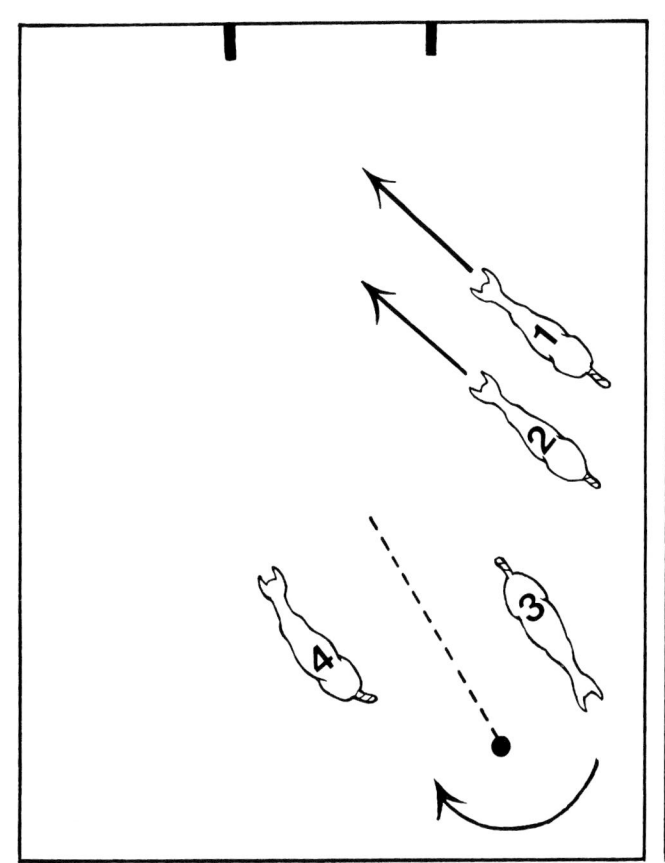

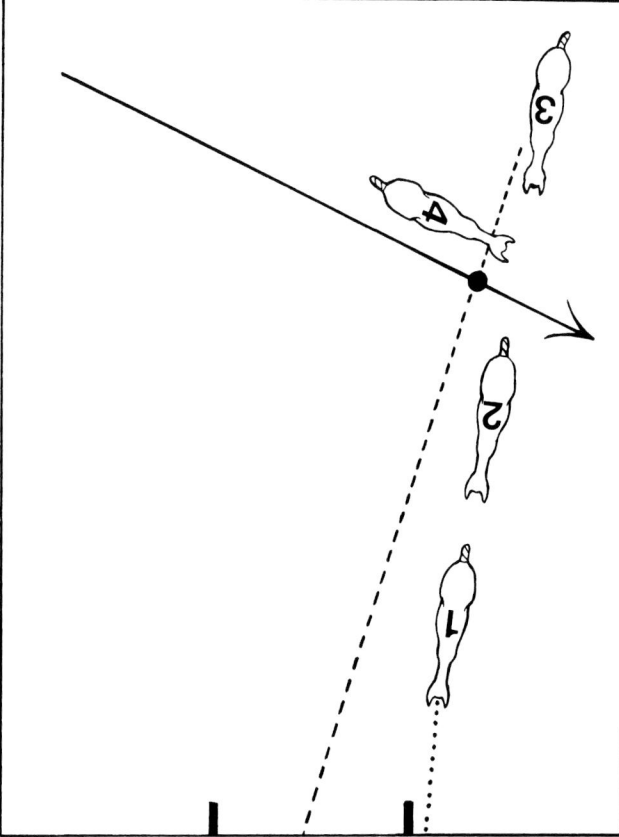

Figure 46. Stage one of the reverse rope.

Figure 47. Stage two of the reverse rope.

Practice

Figures 46 and 47 show a reverse rope being enacted from an open backhand by a team. By practising this as an exercise, without opposition, and then repeating using a tail backhand, the four players are more likely to succeed with this tactic in a match. For novice players it will be even better if they first walk through it, to understand the detailed application. The exercise is carried out as follows.

The whole team is moving in defence in the normal order of 4, 3, 2, 1 and the ball is situated between Nos. 3 and 4.

No. 4 turns left or right to *playmake*; Nos. 2 and 1 turn the same way.

No. 3 strikes the appropriate backhand to No. 4.

No. 4 joins the line while No. 2 adjusts to be in reach of a short pass.

No. 1 adjusts for the two alternatives: a long pass from No. 4 or a short pass by No. 2.

No. 4 strikes a forehand and either No. 2 or No. 1 joins the line to take the next shot. (When No. 2 receives a pass, the ball should be sent on to No. 1.)

No. 1 strikes the ball whenever it arrives and then simulates losing possession.

Ideally, the exercise continues in similar manner to the rope exercise, until a goal is scored, with all team members having at least one shot and nobody hitting twice in succession. Nos. 3 and 4 alternate positions behind the barrier so that there is always a player behind the hitter. This should happen automatically if either of them miss, or mishit, the ball. Otherwise, it can be practised when a good pass has been delivered over the barrier. When repeated, No. 4 *playmakes* in a different direction. The exercise also provides great scope for beginners to practise changing positions, and they can benefit significantly if everyone calls out (verbalizes) their new numbered place on the rope as they fill it.

Promoting Success

If eight or more players are practising together, some races between teams can be highly productive. To win, the drill, as above, must be completed with a goal scored. This is good fun, besides adding the vital dimension of experiencing pressure.

In an actual match or chukka, the success of the tactic depends on the other three players watching their No. 3, so as to interpret the best times to *playmake*, before a backhand can be hit. The receiver could be any of the three, according to the length of the backhand, but No. 4 should *playmake* into the No. 3 position, regardless of where the ball goes. By always having someone very close in front, a novice No. 4 will only need to take one shot each time, and will thus be more likely to avoid being dispossessed. If the opponents intercept the ball, it is then essential that No. 4 rapidly obeys the rule of turning to defence.

It is also essential that the unexpected must be covered. For example, if No. 3 anticipates an interception by an opponent in one place and therefore calls out a different direction from that expected for the intended backhand, all must react quickly. On occasions, No. 4 may have to move into No. 2 or even No. 1 to receive, because the others have been marked, or have failed to *playmake*. Also, if and when this tactic is initiated by No. 2, or even No. 1, then No. 4 has to be prepared to participate in any role, so long as the result does not bring a charge of irresponsibility.

Historical Examples

USA team

Devereux Milburn, who was the greatest American polo player early in the 20th century, in the period immediately before Tommy Hitchcock's ascendancy, always filled the No. 4 position. When Hitchcock began playing for the American team, he loved to play No. 2 when Milburn was No. 4, because with the security provided by the older man, he could roam freely to *playmake*. But after Devereux retired, Tommy soon had to become the international No. 3 in order to help defend behind the barrier. This demonstrates that, at every level, there is a necessity to keep the back door shut.

Argentinian greats

In the 1960s and '70s, Francisco Dorignac and Alfredo Harriott were the two outstanding 10-goal backs. I saw them both many times play in Palermo, Buenos Aires, exhibiting an air of total authority. Their respective doors were kept tightly shut and they joined attacks, via the reverse rope or otherwise, so early that it was hard to tell that they had come from the No. 4 position.

Defending against a prince

I played No. 4 in a number of tournaments and learnt many points from my mistakes. In a final at Cowdray, in England, the opposing **No. 1** was HRH Prince Charles. For a moment, all my team were crowded together, in the goalmouth, trying to score, when a backhand to the boards allowed Prince Charles to escape with the ball. Instead of crossing the field towards the Prince, I set sail down the middle of the ground towards the other goal. He hit two shots along the sideline and then a struck a glorious cut, which reached the sixty-yard line in front of the goal. I arrived, on my pony Dora, in time to ride-off the Prince and hit a backhand, just before the chukka ended. The man from whom I had bought Dora came running onto the field and shouted 'Hugh, you bastard, I sold you that pony too cheap'. I had made a bad error in the goalmouth, by leaving the door open, but I had compensated when turning to defend correctly. By recovering ground and going a shorter route than the Prince, I had made Dora look *much* faster than she actually was.

Beginner shuts door

In the early days of my club in Waterford, Ireland, I trained four beginners for a special match against a team of rather more experienced players from Dublin. Our No. 4 shut the door so well that the novices surprised themselves and the visitors by winning.

Reminded to be last

In a Pony Club Championship Final I could not believe my eyes, when Jason Dixon, who had recently completed a scholarship with me, frequently failed to stay last and his team looked like losing. Between chukkas I remonstrated with him, with the result that he became disciplined, scored a goal, and his team duly won. After the match I asked him why he had forgotten the rule 'to be last' and he replied 'It helps to be reminded.' Jason is now a 6-goal player and in 1998, he captained the British team in the 14-goal World Championship.

SUMMARY

A bad No. 4 is seldom last (see Figure 40, page 125), joins the attack recklessly, fouls often and, when in the wrong position, fails to return to shut the door.

A good No. 4 has the patience to *wait* as last player until given the ball (see Figure 45), avoids fouling, controls the opposing No. 1 and automatically returns to shut the door after losing possession.

I have trained many No. 4s to apply all the points of PRST in order to shut the door in low-goal teams during tournaments. The result has been that their Nos. 2 and 3 have been able to concentrate on dominating the midfield, in the knowledge that the first opponent would be stopped, when attempting to attack.

I have seen many teams who lost opportunities to create the reverse rope move. Either their No. 3 was always turning the ball, or their No. 4 was over-defensive and never ready to enjoy the fruits of secure *playmaking*.

Surprise has to be the most effective way of breaching the opposition's defence and this is best achieved by No. 4 quickly converting your own defence into an attack. This requires the full application of LATET together with PRST and excellent team play, all of which can be helped by the constructive comments of a coach.

REVISION

No. 4

J — **J**ob is to shut the back door through PRST.
P — **P**osition as last of the eight players.
R — **R**esponsibility to ensure no risk by going on to the next play.
    In attack, stop behind barrier to make them give you the ball.
    In defence, cut the corner to be in front of opponent before engaging.
S — **S**peed used to mark first opponent in defence, with or without the ball.
    To join the line before backhanding.
    To *playmake* in attack by interchanging with No. 3.
T — **T**urn to be Last when:
    The ball is behind you.
    Your team's attack is finished or clearly about to fail.

Reverse rope

P — best scope for No. 4 to **P**laymake and change defence into an attack.
C — difficult for opposition to **C**ontrol while your No. 4 is unmarked for one shot.
I — can be **I**nitiated by Nos. 4, 3 or 2, but ideally by No. 4 when No. 3 becomes No. 4.
R — No. 4 in space early to **R**eceive, with Nos. 1 and 2 positioning to accept next pass.

Method

B — ideally, *playmaker's* action defines where **B**ackhand should deliver the ball.
T — **T**ail backhand preferred as more effective, unless only free ground requires an open backhand.
E — *receiver playmaker* must move **E**arly to allow backhand to be hit with perfect angle.

D — rope changes to **D**iamond and back to rope and three of team can *playmake* at same time.

Practice

B — beneficial to practise without opposition, using all players to make **B**all do the work.

W — detailed application best learnt by **W**alking through exercise.

G — ideal if Nos. 3 and 4 alternate positions behind barrier and exercise finishes with a **G**oal.

V — good opportunity to practise interchange and **V**erbalize new positions when reached.

Promoting success

P — with eight or more players, reverse rope races between teams effective to simulate **P**ressure.

W — No. 3 being **W**atched by other players is key to co-ordination of receiving passes.

R — any player can **R**eceive from short or long backhand; No. 4 can be No. 3 without ball.

F — great **F**lexibility with receiver close to hitter and No. 4 always ready to turn to defence.

18

Riding 'D' — Movements at Speed

Progressing from Previous Exercises — Figure of Eight — Ripple Turns — Cavalry Charge

Progressing from Previous Exercises

In the previous chapters on riding, we covered ideas for schooling people and ponies in various exercises that relate to what happens on the polo field. Drills for individuals, pairs and in a team framework were suggested. There was no ball to cause confusion, as teams adjusted to each other, in horizontal and vertical lines, to simulate all the different situations which you might meet while playing.

Now, we will look at three more exercises, designed to bring out the advantages of working together with many people, if they are available. These drills should push you to seek the additional accuracy that is required for co-ordinating complicated movements by big numbers. Then, I will suggest how a large group can carry weaker riders along at speed, and give them the confidence to encouner fast polo. However, all three exercises can also be constructive for small groups.

Figure of Eight

For the purposes of illustrating this exercise, I will use as an example a group of six people. They should form up in a horizontal line, with the appointed *playmaker* positioned in one of the middle spots. If numbered from the left, No. 6 will be on the far right and No. 3 or No. 4 can be the *playmaker*, who is responsible for setting the speed and the direction for the figure of eight, to which the rest must conform.

Once formed up, the group canter down the middle of the polo field and, on arrival at the centre of the field, commence a figure of eight, which takes them close to the goals at both ends and finishes at the centre field (see Figure 48).

This begins with the *playmaker* bringing the line towards the corner flag, to the left of the goal in front of them, until reaching the sixty-yard line. Then, the line of six starts to wheel to the right, to go past that goal, at right angles to the back line, before continuing to wheel and returning to the centre. On the outside of the line, No. 1 will have to move the fastest and, on the inside, No. 6 must go the slowest. The remainder have to adjust precisely, to remain in the horizontal line.

Then, after crossing the centre field, the *playmaker* heads for the corner flag to the right of the other goal, until reaching the sixty-yard line. A wheel to the left then commences, in order to pass the other goal at right angles and return to halt at the centre field, applying strong legs. For this part of the exercise, No. 6, on the outside, moves fastest and No. 1, on the inside, moves slowest, the remainder adjusting accordingly.

This drill provides the best possible training, for being *outside the pony* and for making the *pony follow you*, while applying the other four points of SLOSH (see Chapter 6). The secret to maintaining a perfectly level line, the whole way, is that all the riders swing their vision,to see the other five people throughout, and avoid looking at their own ponies. Ideally, the ponies will canter leading on the inside leg and hence at least one flying change will be necessary during the figure of eight. Most trained ponies should change lead automatically at the appropriate point, but riders must assist them as necessary.

At high level, polo demands speed, accuracy and rapid reactions.

Figure 48.
Figure of eight.

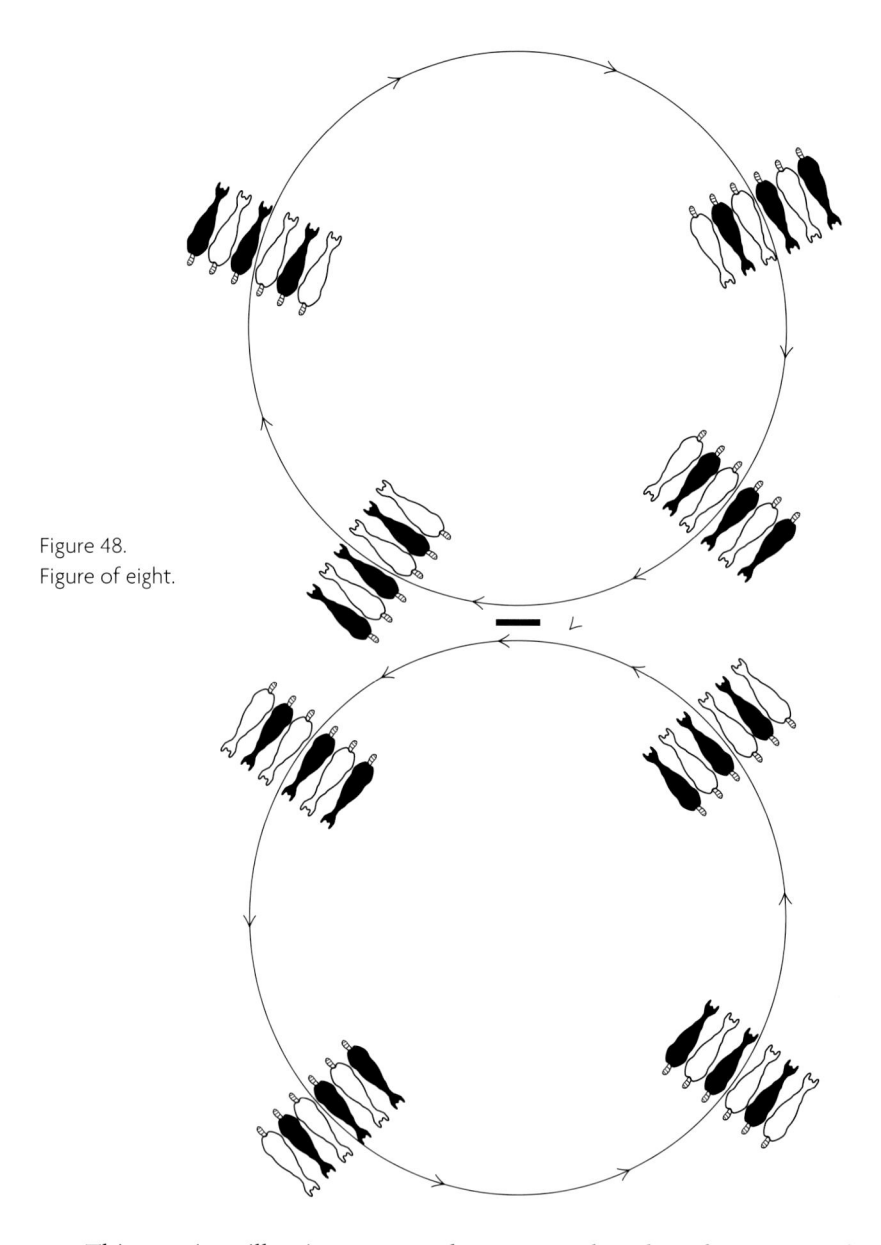

This exercise will assist you, as a player, to watch and conform primarily to *playmakers* and secondarily to everyone else on the field of play. Anyone who has the opportunity to be the *playmaker* for this drill will clearly broaden their experience of relating to others while playing constructively. Larger groups of twelve or more will provide even better training.

Ripple Turns

The next stage is for the whole line of six (or twelve) making what I call ripple turns, before, during or after the figure of eight. This is essentially a repeat of the technique of Turning in Pairs, as explained in Chapter 15, but now each person, in a line, must wait for the exact moment to make their turn in correct order. For example, if the *playmaker* signals or calls for a turn (not a wheel) to the left, No. 1 turns first, followed by No. 2 and then No. 3, etc. All must wait for the tail of the pony on their left to reach the nose of their own pony, before starting to turn (see Figure 49).

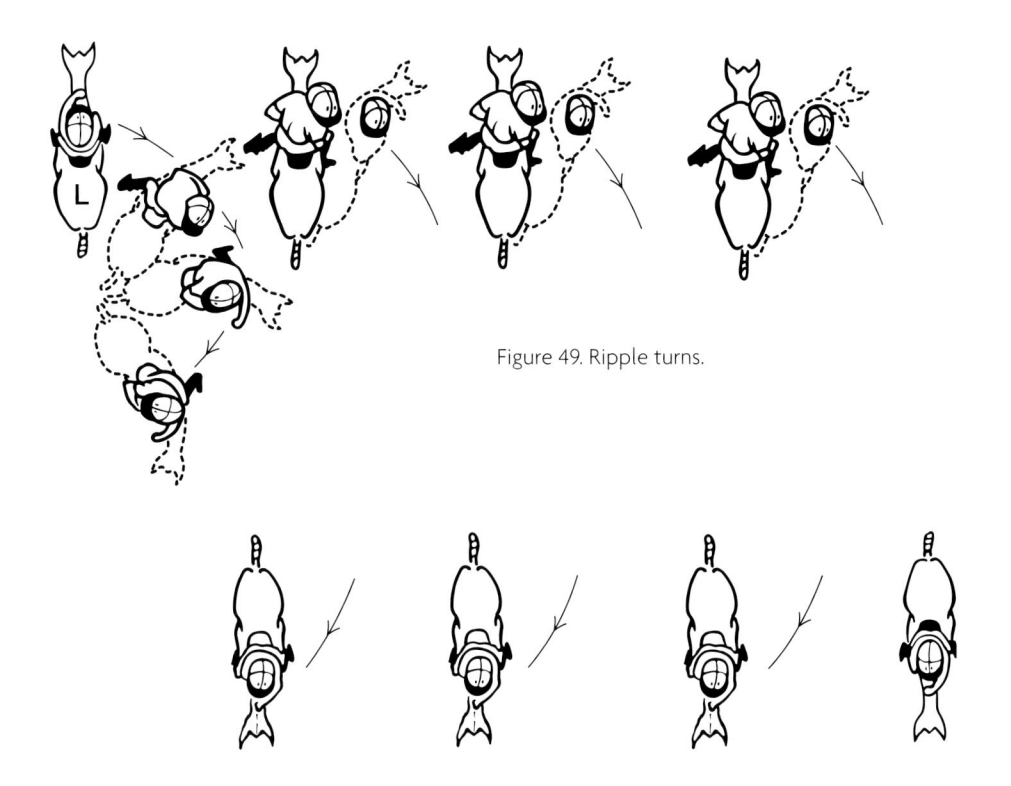

Figure 49. Ripple turns.

On completion, they should check, and adjust enough to allow all those turning after them to catch up and rejoin the horizontal line. Then, for the turn to the right, No. 12 turns first, followed by No. 11 and then No. 10, etc., each successively waiting for the adjacent pony's tail to reach their pony's nose. When several ripple turns to left and right have been carried out smoothly and successfully, an extra lesson on accurate pony control in combination with others will have been experienced.

Cavalry Charge

Many people will have ancestors who took part in a ferocious cavalry charge, on a battlefield. The following exercise provides an opportunity to feel a little of the thrill that those heroes must have experienced. I have performed this exercise with groups of various sizes, the largest consisting of twenty-four people at the Nairobi Polo Club, in Kenya. There, to simulate a charge, we used the length of two polo fields to build up the speed of such a long horizontal line. Obviously, a number of twelve or less is easier to manage and better for providing assistance, with the courage factor, for beginners and weak riders. To be able to finish going up a hill or a small incline is also helpful, if there is one close to the end of the polo field.

Having completed some figures of eight, and a few ripple turns, confidence will be suitably bolstered and the participants prepared for a cavalry charge. A good starting point could be after a wheel at one end of the field, allowing the *playmaker* scope for imparting to the horizontal line a gradual increase of speed, until a gallop is achieved, well before reaching the other end of the field. Staying level in the line, throughout the build up of velocity, is not easy, but not so difficult as some people think. It is equally a fault to get ahead of the others, as it is to be left behind. Once again, being totally *outside the pony*, in order to watch others, is the simplest way for all the riders to stay together, as the *playmaker* accelerates and the pace reaches a crescendo.

The actual speed reached will depend on everyone being able to keep up, and the *playmaker* must use judgement and encouragement to achieve the maximum that is possible from a group, rather than cause chaos by going too fast. Then, at a suitable moment, the cries should go out 'Look behind'; 'Legs' followed by 'Halt'. Ideally, everyone should stop in line and level, but if they manage to be reasonably close to the horizontal line, this will be satisfactory in that control at speed and effective use of legs will have been applied.

Cavalry Charge as a Finale and Lessons Learnt

Every group which I have taken on a cavalry charge has appeared to be highly elated afterwards and normally requested a repeat. I use it on the last day of my courses and clinics, as a finale to the riding sessions. The exercises described in previous chapters, done on earlier days, help enormously as a preparation for a cavalry charge. Trying to perform a charge earlier will probably do more harm than good. Normally, at least one person in every group will initially upset the line, by looking at their pony instead of at other people. Only after some exhortations are they persuaded to stop doing this, and then the charge is allowed to succeed. The participants will always need frequent reminders to apply legs and to look at each other. These points are so basic, yet it is vitally important that they are included in the coaching and are carried on, from the schooling sessions, to the field of play. Hopefully, muscle memory will take over to make you apply these skills in a game, but a sideline coach, giving timely reminders, provides the best solution.

SUMMARY

To acquire the ability to see, and adjust to, a large number of people at the same time, will greatly assist any polo player. However the ball is such a big distraction that many people do not succeed in mastering this skill during play, because they have never participated in any kind of relevant practice. The Figure of Eight, Ripple Turns in a long line and the Cavalry Charge provide useful rehearsals of the riding and tactical dimensions required, and a subtle preparation for when the ball is introduced. To participate in such exercises necessitates joining a clinic which includes them, or alternatively inviting a coach to supervise their implementation amongst a group, small or large, of willing learners.

REVISION

Figure of eight
C — line abreast canter to centre field, *playmaker* directs line to left **C**orner flag.
W — **W**heel right to pass goal at right angles, again **W**heel right to return to centre field.
O — *playmaker* to right corner flag at **O**ther end, wheel left to pass **O**ther goal at right angles.
M — wheel left again to return to centre field; outside of line **M**oves fastest, inside slowest.

Ripple turns
T — repeat pair turning **T**echnique, starting from either left or right end of line.
E — turn one after another, each at **E**xact moment and in correct order.
A — when tail of **A**djacent pony reaches nose of own pony.
C — check and wait for next one to **C**atch up to maintain level line.

Cavalry charge
C — numbers in line can be large or small, figure of eight and ripple turns build **C**onfidence before charge.
S — best **S**tarting point at end of field after a level wheel, for gradual acceleration of line.
P — *playmaker* careful to control crescendo of **P**ace as manageable for all.
H — finish with look behind, legs and **H**alt; line to stop as level as possible.

19

Striking 'D' Offside Rear Circle (Third Circle)

Constructing the Offside Forehand Cut Shot with PASSF — Constructing the Offside Tail Backhand with PASSF — Exercises

The two shots discussed in this chapter employ the third of the five circles originally mentioned in Chapter 7. These shots are regarded as difficult angles by people who are unaware of the significance of the circles. Too many players strike a cut shot in the belief that only luck, not skill, obtains accuracy. Others mishit the tail shot because they can not wait for the ball to be at ground zero of this circle near the rear of the pony.

But if PASSF is applied correctly and the exact location of the circle is fully grasped, the offside cut is found to be relatively simple, and deadly accuracy can be achieved. Also, the tail backhand becomes easier than the open backhand when it is understood that it must be taken late.

For both shots, however, an accurate approach is important, as is meticulous use of the two clocks. Therefore, strong legs are a necessity for giving you the ability to apply the clocks around the pony and the ball to the exact location of the target. This will help you enormously to perfect the other parts of the techniques.

Constructing the Offside Forehand Cut Shot with PASSF

Preparation – 'Catch a Bus'

As for all the forehand shots, the pre-swing to find the circle will create a helpful rhythm for the cut shot. It will assist even more if it finishes with your hand and mallet behind the right knee and level with your right shoulder. This not only places the mallet head at the top of the cut shot circle, but it is also economical, because time is saved, enabling you to start the swing early and thereby make a slow stroke. If it suits you, try remembering this with the catchphrase *'catch a bus'* while thinking where you put your hand to stop a bus!

STRIKING 'D' OFFSIDE REAR CIRCLE (THIRD CIRCLE)

'Catching a bus'.

Using the same principle already applied to other shots, in order to find the exact path of the second half of the full swing, a few cut half-shots should be made. These start with the mallet head down and end with a follow through. Then, before a full shot is attempted, with the mallet vertical, some practice full swings through an imaginary ball will further help to find the cut shot circle.

Approach

On a wooden horse or a static pony, place the ball wide from you and adjust it in the area of 3 on the pony clock, until it is clearly in the circle of the cut shot, and then sit in the half-seat. On a moving pony, locate the target (halfway to a reachable goal) before finding the spot close to 8 on the ball clock. In the half-seat, apply strong legs to advance parallel to the line of the ball. Then make a shallow arc from left to right, without crossing the line, to arrive opposite 3 on the pony clock, with your right hand still level with your right shoulder (to 'catch a bus'). Hence the two clocks define your route.

Swing Slowly

The left shoulder must push the chin well to the right, so that your right hand can swing back towards the pony's tail. This allows the mallet head to point directly at the target while the left leg and hip turn to support the action. The right thumb can take most of the mallet's weight before the hand sweeps slowly through the ball towards the target, as if hitting a half-shot.

Sweet Spot

You should already have found the sweet spot, during the approach, and now you confirm it by aiming your hand to pass through the exact spot close to 8 on the bottom of the ball. Verbalizing will help you to concentrate on the spot as contact by the mallet

Offside forehand cut shot: Carlos Gracida follows the correct arc of approach to find the sweet spot.

Ignacio Novillo Astrada – cut shot with a bouncing ball.

head, in conjunction with your hand, happens. Therefore, the earlier you locate the spot, the easier it will be to hit it accurately.

Follow Through

It is difficult not to divert the mallet towards the pony's head and away from the target after you hit the ball because, unless properly controlled, your shoulders will rotate to the left. Hence it is important that the left leg, hip and shoulder are all securely held to the right and in the target direction, while your hand and the mallet head continue from the spot through the ball and on to complete another circle, or stop when pointing at the target. Using muscle memory, your head and eyes should stay down, at least until the mallet is horizontal, and ideally the follow through completes the third circle (after the two made by the preparation and the swing) in order to dissipate the power induced and to ensure total accuracy.

Execution

Preparation
Apply legs with mallet vertical and (if there is time) find the circle by making a preparatory swing, which finishes with the mallet vertical and opposite your right shoulder ('catch a bus').

Approach
Locate exact position of target and distance to it (halfway to goal). Focus on the relevant spot close to 8 on the ball clock. In the half-seat, re-apply legs to join the line of the ball and bring pony in a shallow arc to the right opposite to 3 on the pony clock (still 'catching bus').

Swing slowly
Rotate left leg, hip and shoulder strongly to the right while your right hand swings back towards the pony's tail. Point mallet head at the target by supporting weight with thumb and then swing slowly through the ball (imagine half-shot).

Sweet spot
Aim palm of hand to pass through and confirm spot (close to 8) on the bottom of the ball in conjunction with the mallet head.

Follow through
Allow hand and mallet head to continue through ball to point at the target and, if possible, to turn another circle. Use muscle memory to keep head and eyes down until mallet is horizontal.

Constructing the Offside Tail Backhand with PASSF

Preparation – 'Catch a Bus'

Constructing the perfect circle behind the tail of the pony only becomes easy after a careful preparation. Several preparatory swings will help you to be sufficiently supple to turn the shoulders, hips and legs so that the mallet can swing past the tail to 7 on the pony clock, or even further. The flow of blood round the body and into the right hand should supple the muscles and override any stiffness. Then 'catching a bus' with the mallet held by the hand opposite the right shoulder will once more assist an economical swing.

On a wooden horse or a stationary pony, you should practise some half-shots by placing the ball at 4 on the pony clock and the mallet head at 2 on the ball clock before making a 50/50 swing through the ball. After that, some full swings should be made at an imaginary ball, while a coach or observer checks on the exactness of the circle behind the pony's tail.

Approach

You use the two clocks, for the pony and the ball, to define the route required. For the average tail shot, the pony clock is at 4 and the ball clock at 2. But if the ball is too close to you, either because of a ride-off or because of it is bouncing, you may have to wait until 5 on the pony clock and have to hit close to 3 on the ball. After looking behind to locate where there might be a *playmaker*, who can receive your pass, you focus on the selected spot on the ball. You mildly adjust the route by creating a shallow arc from left to right, without crossing the line, to ensure that the swing misses the rear end of the pony, and apply strong legs to hold the pony's quarters away from the ball. Remember the 'bus'.

Sebastian Dawnay – correct approach for the offside tail backhand while pointing mallet head at target.

Swing Slowly

Your right hand now moves upwards while the V between the thumb and index finger accepts the mallet's weight to point the mallet head in the direction of the target behind your back. Your right shoulder quietly fights the chin but gives way to turn towards the target. Beneath the shoulders, the hips, helped by your legs, gyrate to the right to initiate the second half of the swing through the ball. Try to imagine you are now doing a half-shot with your knuckles directed slowly towards the ball. If you find yourself poised with the mallet head pointing at the target, before the ball is behind you, then that position must be retained (even tell yourself to wait) until starting the second half of the swing at the correct moment – that is, a moment that still allows a slow swing.

Sweet Spot

Even if you have correctly focused on the spot at, or close to, 2 on the ball clock during the approach, beware that your subconscious does not deflect you to look at 12. Instead, confirm the selected spot by aiming the back of your hand or knuckles to pass through it on the bottom of the ball and proceed in the target direction. Once again, verbalizing will help you to maintain concentration.

Follow Through

Let your right hand continue the swing towards the target, after contact through the ball. Keep your head down and your eyes where the ball was, with muscle memory directing the mallet. The left leg can act as a counterweight to allow the hips and shoulders to follow the swing. An optional, extreme, way of doing this is by raising the heel to take the weight on the knee.

Execution

Preparation
Apply legs and ensure that mallet is in the vertical position. According to time available, find the circle with one or more anticlockwise preparatory swings and 'catch a bus'.

Approach
Look behind to register exact location of target and distance to it. Then look forward to focus on exact spot at or close to 2 on the ball clock. Re-apply legs to bring pony parallel to the line of the ball and then make a shallow arc to the right in order to strike the ball at or around 4 on the pony clock, with the pony's quarters a little to the left. 'Catch a bus'.

Swing slowly
Right hand swings a little upwards to take mallet's weight on V and point mallet head behind your back at the target. Right shoulder nudges chin, and then knuckles or back of hand sweep slowly through the ball and on towards target. Left leg supports gyration of hips and shoulders to the right.

Sweet spot
Guide right hand (knuckles) to go through bottom of the ball at the required spot, close to 2 on the ball clock, in conjunction with the mallet head, which continues with gathering speed to complete a circle.

Follow through
Allow hand and mallet to complete second 50% of swing and then continue the circle upwards, controlled by thumb and index finger. Use muscle memory to keep head and eyes down until mallet is through the ball.

above An offside tail backhand struck accurately by Sebastian Dawnay.

Following through after the offside tail backhand.

Exercises

1. Individually go the length of the polo field alternately striking offside cut shots and neck shots, trying to finish with a goal.

2. In pairs, ride parallel the length of the field passing to each other with *A* striking offside cut shots and *B* offside neck shots. Return the other way, with *A* striking neck shots and *B*, cut shots. Ideally, finish with a goal. When satisfied with the standard of shots, repeat the exercise using two balls, which are exchanged each time they are hit. Finish by scoring two goals.

3. *A* is parallel to and left of *B*, in order to hit an offside cut shot across to, and in front of, *B*, who *playmakes* laterally towards the sideline without respect to the line of the ball, in order to strike a tail backhand across to and in front of *A*, who receives it to repeat an offside cut shot to *B*. They aim to finish with a goal. *A* and *B* then change roles.

4. As a pair, practise the reverse rope tactic as follows:
   A canters past the ball and then *playmakes* by turning to receive a backhand from *B*.
   B observes the direction in which *A* turns, and either opens or tails a backhand to find *A*.
   A hits the ball forward to a suitable place and canters past the ball to restart the exercise.
   This continues until *B* has struck successfully several open and tail backhands. Both of the pair should participate in the roles of *A* and *B*.

SUMMARY

The slow swing through this third circle should be simple to apply to both the cut and tail offside shots, if the suggested preparation, shallow arc approach and the two clocks are put meticulously into effect. Then, such accuracy must be confirmed by a premeditated correct follow through. The exercises are designed to employ a practical way of improving these shots that is relevant to actual play, with an added dimension of pressure. If you can complete them satisfactorily, you will gain important confidence that you can participate effectively in many of the team plans for attack and defence.

REVISION

Offside cut shot
P — **P**repare – legs; mallet vertical; find circle; hand and mallet opposite right shoulder.
A — on **A**pproach; register target (halfway to goal); focus on spot ball clock 8; half-seat; arc right to join line to be opposite pony clock 3.
S — rotate shoulder right; swing right hand to pony's tail; mallet weight on thumb; point at target; **S**wing **S**lowly through ball.

S — hand confirms **S**weet **S**pot ball clock 8 on bottom of ball, in conjunction with mallet head.

F — hand and mallet **F**ollow through ball to point at target, then complete circle with head and eyes down.

Offside tail backhand

P — **P**repare – legs; mallet vertical; find anticlockwise circle; hand and mallet opposite right shoulder.

A — on **A**pproach look behind; register target; focus on spot ball clock 2; half-seat; join line in shallow arc to right to be opposite pony clock 4.

S — right hand sideways; mallet weight on V, mallet head points at target; right shoulder fights chin; shoulders gyrate towards ball; **S**wing **S**lowly.

S — knuckles confirm **S**weet **S**pot ball clock 2 on bottom of ball in conjunction with mallet head.

F — knuckles and mallet **F**ollow through ball to point at target, supported by shoulders.

20

Tactics 'E' — No. 2 as Link Playmaker from Barrier to No. 1

Demands of a Difficult Position — No. 2's Role Explained by PRST — Goalpost Drill — Historical Examples

Demands of a Difficult Position

This position is the most difficult to play well, because No. 2 normally has to mark the best opponent and, at the same time, set up attacks by *playmaking*. Also, there are times when the team's No. 3 needs covering and other occasions that require No. 2 to do the job of No. 1. Hence, frequently, with little warning, No. 2 has to switch between attack and defence while interchanging positions.

Ideally, the second best player in the team fills No. 2, but if the two strongest in a team both prefer being behind the barrier, an inexperienced player may have to do the job. Therefore everyone must know the responsibilities and priorities for playing behind a No. 1. These will be explained through PRST, first in outline and then in detail. The relative strengths of the two No. 3s and the No. 2s are important factors.

No. 2's Role Explained by PRST

In outline, the role of No. 2 can be expressed in these terms:

Position	Normally stays a short distance in front of the barrier.
Responsibility	Keep the ball *in front of the barrier* and to pass to No. 1.
Speed	Maximize velocity to switch between *playmaking* and marking.
Turn to defence	*Before* opponents start attacks, and to cover own No. 3 taking risks.

We will now look at these functions in more detail.

Position

Most of the time, as No. 2, you should be placed so that your No. 3 can reach you easily, with a forehand or a backhand pass. This means being in front of, but close to, the barrier, so that your No. 1 can receive an average strike from No. 3 and a long shot from No. 4, without interference from you (see Figure 50).

At the same time, to be a vital link to No. 1, you must position close enough to be able to:

1. Send the ball on with a short pass.

2. Back up the attacks.

3. Interchange when necessary to be the link to goal.

Too many players position as No. 2½ or 1½ and thereby muddle their No. 3 or No. 1, instead of helping them by being a useful link between these two positions, from in front of the barrier. To maintain this position correctly requires continual looking and adjusting, especially after turning to *playmake* in both attack and defence.

Responsibility in the 25%

Keeping ball in front of barrier

No. 2 should be a constructive *playmaker* with the ball, every time a pass is received, in order to keep possession of it for the team. Normally, the best solution is to send the ball on to No. 1, but if that player is not available for any reason, then No. 2 ought to act like a No. 1, to keep the ball in play in front of the barrier. Alternatively, by changing the direction of play, an interchange with No. 3 can be very effective. Deciding which to do will become very much easier if you always watch your own No. 3 as prescribed by LATET (see Chapter 5). Too many No. 2s frequently lose possession of the ball because of:

1. Trying to score a goal individually, instead of combining with other *playmakers*.

2. Ball-chasing, thereby allowing the opposing **No. 3** to be unmarked and free to win the ball.

Passing to No. 1

To be highly responsible, No. 2 must have the ability to control opponents in ride-offs and hit accurately, with angled shots, as a *playmaker*, so that the ball can be sent to another team member, or a goal can be scored. If you abuse the disparity of skills factor and belittle your No. 1 by always yelling 'leave it' and never passing to him, you will deny No. 1 the opportunity to learn and improve besides doing the following damage:

1. Reducing your team to three in attack.

2. Taking away confidence from No. 1 on the day, and for future matches.

Figure 50. No. 2s in good positions; No. 3s badly placed.

Cody Forsyth wins the ball against Memo Gracida.

3. Putting extra pressure on yourself, which will probably result in loss of accuracy.

4. Making it easier for the opponents to defend their goal.

Speed

Switching between attack and defence

More than any other position, a No. 2 needs to be quick nearly all the time, because endless adjusting is required to cover the midfield in front of the barrier. Even so, the most important emphasis upon speed should be at the moments when the game is about to change direction, that is, when switching from attack to defence and vice versa. At other times, where possible, any chance to preserve a pony's energy should be taken, for the benefit of the pony, both on that day and in the long term.

Related to other players' strengths

You will be more effective as a No. 2 if, when deciding on tactics, you take into account the relative strengths of other players. You should especially consider the two No. 3s in relation to yourself. If the opposing **No. 3** is the best of all eight players, then there is extra urgency for you to defend, but when your No. 3 is the strongest on the field, *playmaking* takes priority in the need for speed. Also, if you happen to feel that you can outplay their **No. 3**, you should move into any attack very early. In every situation suggested above, you can increase speed when turning by employing the tail trick as explained in Chapter 15.

Marking exceptions

For all tactical planning there are exceptions. Therefore, when the disparity of skills factor shows that the opposing **No. 3** is far too strong for you to mark, the sensible solution is that the task is taken on by your own No. 3. Then, you should also compare your strengths with the opposing **No. 2** before deciding how to play, but it will still be necessary to maximize velocity when changing directions between marking and *playmaking*.

Turn to Defence

From attack to defence

The most dangerous time for No. 2 to forget about defence, is when an attack is flying down the field. A sudden burst of acceleration by an opponent, to win a ride-off and hit a surprise backhand, can start an opposing attack instantly. Hence the necessity for No. 2 to watch for this possibility at all times, and be ready to counter it, by turning to defend, before that backhand is actually struck. This keeps a tight defence in front of the barrier.

Covering your own No. 3

Another perilous moment is when your own No. 3 takes a risk in attack and, as No. 2, you see that you should cover this attack from behind the barrier. Then, if that attack fails, you will be positioned temporarily to carry out the defensive job of No. 3. There are many times when this becomes necessary, for example, when your No. 3:

1. Is losing a ride-off or is clearly going to be hooked.

2. Is following a bouncing ball and will probably miss it.

3. Is forced to compete for a 50/50 ball.

4. Deliberately moves in front of the barrier to interchange with you, the No. 2.

Although this action will initially be done to cover the No. 3 defensively, it will also provide a very effective back-up to an attack, through which possession can be retained. But it is important that you do not interfere with the basic rope formation of the team by covering your No. 3 when this is not required.

Goalpost Drill

The Underlying Situation

When the ball is in the possession of a player who is in attack behind the barrier, and quite close to the goal, those in front of the barrier can find that their situation becomes difficult. To comply with the tactical rule of four players in four positions, and to stay on the field of play, in front of the barrier, is impossible. Maybe they have just been neutralized in a ride-off, or one of them has just missed the ball, or they have galloped forward in the hope of receiving a pass. Whatever the reason, what should they do? Can they be *playmakers*?

The Wrong Solution

In low-goal polo, a No. 1 normally turns left or right and then attempts to rejoin the game by means of a full circle. This means that the team is minus one player for an interval and, at the end of the circle, No. 1 will probably muddle another member of the team by being alongside and could easily commit a foul by not knowing where the line of the ball is and thus crossing it. Alternatively, No. 1 circles wide to become No. 4 at the back of the team, which is then down to three effective players for an even longer time. Also, the barrier will have been crossed, probably upsetting the tactical balance of the team for both attack and defence.

In such a situation, some players lose their heads and continue straight through the goal before returning to be in a goalmouth mêlée. Here, they are almost certain to prevent a goal being scored by deflecting the ball with their pony, or by fouling.

The Best Action

Players with high handicaps can adjust with great agility and anticipation to *playmake* and not hinder their team, but I believe that less experienced forwards need a drill in mind, to apply as necessary.

No. 2s must always bear in mind their duty to turn to defence, if their No. 3 requires to be covered, and must be ready to cross behind the barrier. But if they see clearly that possession is being safely maintained from behind the barrier by the combination of Nos. 3 and 4, then they can join No. 1 so that both forwards do the same drill, one on each goalpost.

Playmaking from Behind a Goalpost

Instead of circling or being in a goalmouth mêlée, a forward can head for the outside of the nearest goalpost. Depending on the speed at which he is travelling, he can either stop at the goalpost or go beyond it, to turn sharply and return to hide behind the goalpost (see Figure 51). Normally, there is only time for one forward to do this drill, but if circumstances allow for both forwards to do it, they obviously should head for different goalposts. What can you do from behind a goalpost? Depending on what you see

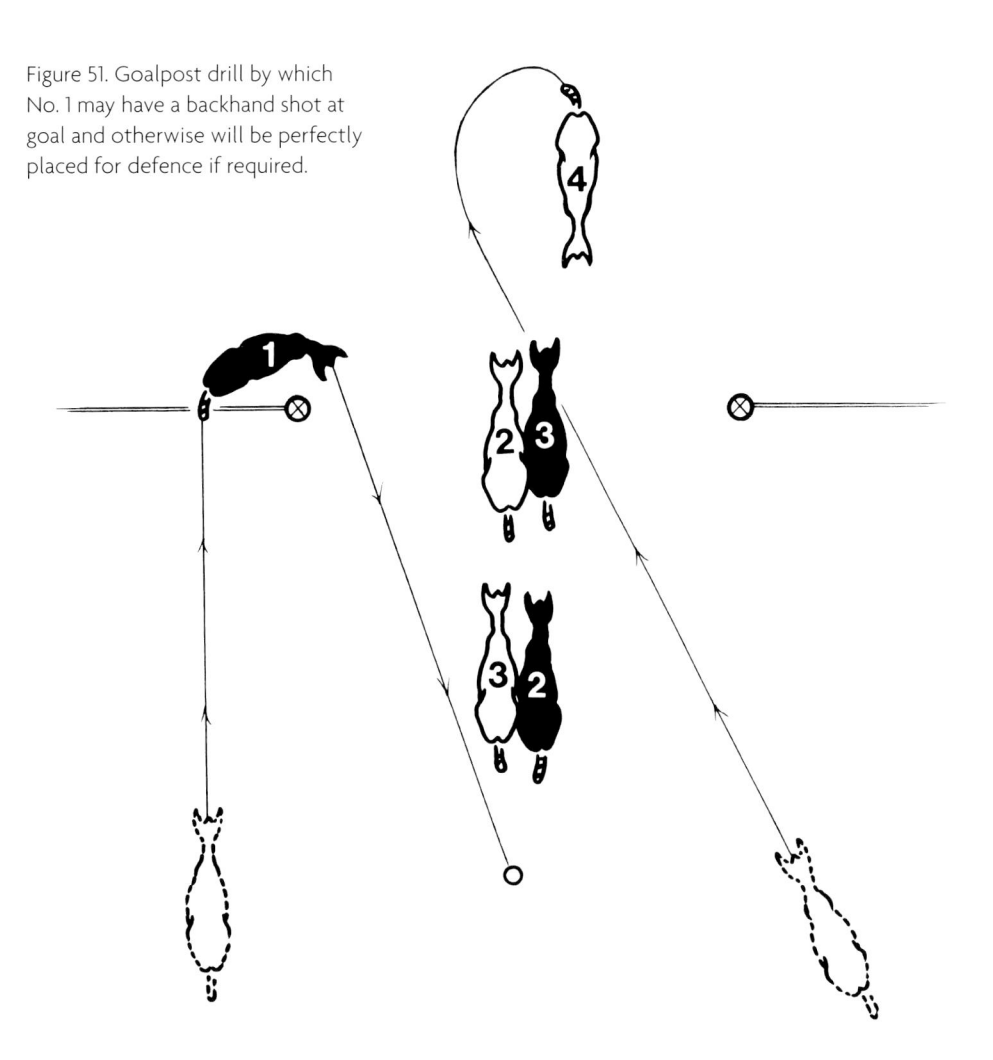

Figure 51. Goalpost drill by which No. 1 may have a backhand shot at goal and otherwise will be perfectly placed for defence if required.

happening, after you arrive at the goalpost, one of the following four adjustments will be required of you:

1. Allow the attack to continue by staying still and out of the way until a goal is scored.

2. If possession has been lost, *playmake* in defence, by going to mark a relevant opponent.

3. If the ball will miss the goal, *playmake* by trying to stop the ball in order to link to goal.

4. If the ball has stopped close to the goal, *playmake* in attack by backhanding at the goal.

The Result of the Drill

Every possible situation is covered by the above and, as applicable, each of the four adjustments will keep you in the game, to assist your team constructively in both attack and defence, in the following ways:

1. By drawing an opponent to mark you while not blocking the goal or risking a foul.

2. Because you can go down the middle of the field from the goal, using the quickest route for finding and intercepting a relevant opponent.

3. Instead of having to overtake the ball to stop it you are already placed to block the back line with pony and mallet.

4. After a small lateral movement you should be able to go through the goal to hit a backhand without fouling. But, if and when you do have a chance, you must try to take it on the offside to eliminate the possibility of meeting an opponent on the nearside.

Patience and Clear Thinking

The opportunity to score in this way does not arise too often, but eventually it will happen and it is worth waiting for. Anyway, you are covering all other possible scenarios from behind the goalpost. Yet it is important not to let the drill confuse you and there are occasions when this can happen. First, when your team unexpectedly loses possession and you feel left behind at the goalpost. Then simply remember that you are better off placed centrally than being out to the side. Second, beware that you do not apply this drill at the wrong end of the field when defending your own goal, as I once did – see next page.

Historical Examples

Tommy Hitchcock

Between the two World Wars, Tommy Hitchcock became the most famous American polo player ever, as a No. 2. He was gifted with the ability to play for his team, in all the ways described above and, at the same time, he gave individual displays of brilliance.

Horacio Heguy

Horacio Heguy was outstanding as No. 2, playing at incredible speed in the famous Coronel Suarez team, which won the Argentine Open so many times in the 1960s and 70s. I had the privilege to watch that team several times and observed Horacio be a brilliant link between his brother Alberto and the incredible Juan Carlos Harriott, besides scoring many goals. His four sons have since made history by being the first-ever team of brothers to win that coveted championship, and all of them have been distinguished No. 2s in other teams.

Julian Hipwood

Post-war, in the annual international Coronation Cup, Julian Hipwood gave many great displays at No. 2 for the British team. He always worked hard and unselfishly to cover his No. 3 and pass to the No. 1. As the first Englishman to be invited post-war to play in the Argentine Open at Palermo, in Buenos Aires (1971), he was duly rewarded. The following year his ability was fully established when, in the same tournament, the renowned Mar de Plata team picked him to be their No. 2, in front of the famous No. 3, Gonzalo Tanoira.

8-Goal tournament

Long ago, as the No. 3 in an 8-goal tournament final, I found that my No. 2 was playing too close to me and was often behind the barrier, when not required to cover me. We approached the last chukka 2 goals behind and, in desperation, I told him to change positions with me. From then on I watched to allow him freedom to play where he wished, so that I could adjust to him, instead of the other way round. To my surprise, he then spent too much time in front of the barrier and I covered him from behind it, resuming most of the role of No. 3. He was suddenly doing the job of linking to No. 1 correctly, with the result that we took control of the game to score 3 goals and win. This experience gave me valuable confirmation that a team with a No. 2 correctly positioned between the barrier and No. 1 can dominate the play.

Goalpost drill win – and loss

Years ago, a regimental team, which I had coached before a tournament in Germany, sent me a welcome telegram 'Won the final; winning goal from Goal Post Drill.' Many other people have told me that the drill has helped them enormously because, prior to learning it, they were lost, when near to the goal, and in front of the ball.

Once, in a 14-goal semi-final, I caused chaos to my team and infuriated a 7-goal player, by doing the drill at the wrong end of the polo field. The result was that I gave away a penalty in the goalmouth, which caused us to lose the match.

SUMMARY

The perfect No. 2 makes both the No. 1 and the No. 3 look good, by being the link between them from in front of the barrier, while *playmaking* for and covering the No. 3 when required, and marking the opposing **No. 3** in defence. The bad No. 2 chases the ball, seldom passes to No. 1, does not help No. 3 in vital situations and allows the opposing **No. 3** too much freedom.

The goalpost drill can be extremely helpful for novice players, to fit in with better players, while not interfering with them.

REVISION

No. 2

J — **J**ob is to be a *link playmaker* between the barrier and No. 1 through PRST.
RS — **R**elative **S**trengths of own and opposing No. 2s and 3s a big factor for tactics.
P — **P**osition in front of barrier and close enough to receive easily from No. 3.
IA — **I**nterfering with No. 1 **A**voided by continual adjustment in attack and defence.
R — **R**esponsibility to pass to No. 1 or, if not possible, to keep ball in play.
AA — hit **A**ccurate **A**ngles while controlling opponents.
S — rapid **S**witch between *playmaking* and marking opposing **No. 3** or relevant opponent.

D — when changing **D**irection, quickly control the midfield in front of barrier.
T — **T**urn to defend before ball changes direction and when own No. 3 requires covering.
C — **C**over No. 3 who commits to a failing attack or wishes to interchange.

Goalpost drill

N — team in attack **N**ear goal with Nos. 3 or 4 in possession behind the barrier.
I — normal low-goal Nos. 1 and 2, **I**n front of barrier, circle left or right, block goal or cause foul.
B — unless required to cover No. 3, better if Nos. 1 or 2 (or both) hide **B**ehind goalpost for goalpost drill.
A — they must stay behind posts until one of four alternatives dictates a positive *playmaking* **A**ction.
  1. **S** – goal **S**cored; blocking goal and fouling avoided while possibly opponents drawn to mark.
  2. **M** – opponents win ball so Nos. 1 and 2 *playmake* via centre of field to **M**ark relevant opponent.
  3. **S** – ball about to miss goal but Nos. 1 and 2 can *playmake* by trying to **S**top ball crossing back line.
  4. **B** – ball stops in front of goal, so goal could be scored by **B**ackhand giving best *playmaker* chance.

21

Riding 'E' — Short Races

Maintaining Riding Skills Under Pressure — Races Between Two Individuals — Team Relay Races

Maintaining Riding Skills Under Pressure

By doing all the drills and exercises explained in the earlier riding chapters, you will become confident with your application of all the SLOSH points as explained in Chapter 6 – correct seat and use of legs, being 'outside' the pony, looking before turning and soft use of hands. These attributes will make the pony follow you consistently, thereby giving you the necessary mobility to be a *playmaker*.

Now, I suggest, is the time to find out whether you can continue to maintain a high standard of riding at speed and under pressure. Besides playing polo, the best way to test yourself is in the shortest of short races. Basically, it is bad for a polo pony to race but, if the distance is extremely short, the pony will not relate the experience to that of racing, and will benefit from it, rather than suffering any damage.

Use of the Whip

The whip is a necessity, without which even the best of ponies could start to lose respect for the rider. However, if the whip is handled badly, a pony's confidence will suffer. Therefore, before people compete in any races, an examination of their use of the whip should be made, and an opportunity taken to practise correct technique. A polo player can apply the whip in three ways.

1. Slapping the pony's neck on the nearside without altering the position of the reins in the left hand. This requires being careful not to hold on to the pony's mouth at the same time as slapping the neck, because this would give contradictory orders to the pony to both move and stop. A good analogy would be to consider what would happen if a car driver applied the accelerator and brake together.

Javier Novillo Astrada at full stretch in half-seat.

2. Tickling the pony behind the saddle with the end of the whip while still holding the reins in the left hand. This may necessitate slipping the fingers backwards through the reins in order to apply the whip without having contact on the pony's mouth.

3. Hitting the pony firmly behind the girth with the left hand after taking the reins in the right hand, together with the mallet. The best way to learn how to do this is to practise a drill of the following five movements:
   (a) Throw the reins from left to right hand.
   (b) Lift the whip above and behind your left shoulder.
   (c) Make a dummy hit with the whip, without actually touching the pony's flank.
   (d) Retake the reins in the left hand.
   (e) With the mallet in the right hand, either find the circle or make a dummy shot.

   This drill must be repeated many times until it can be done effortlessly.

Races Between Two Individuals

The First Race

Ideally, you should start by taking on just one opponent, so that it is easy for a coach or any observer to watch the results constructively, without being distracted by the actions of many people. Two riders, *A* and *B*, carrying polo mallets, form up on a horizontal line (H) with markers placed to represent two parallel lines, one (P) five yards in front of the ponies and another (R) five yards behind the ponies.

The first race must be simple and should include only one turn, as follows:
Start at H – cross P – turn 90 degrees right – return to halt on H facing R. The winner is the first to halt exactly on H. You can be disqualified for:

1. Failing to reach the line at P.

2. Overrunning the line at H when halting.

Next Two Races

Second race – Start at H – cross R – turn 90 degrees left – halt at H.
Third race – Start at H – cross P – turn 90 degrees right – cross H and R – turn 90 degrees left – halt on H.

Being quicker than your opponent, while maintaining total control of your pony, has to be the key to finding open space or to winning a ride-off, in order to *playmake*. The short races described provide excellent practice for this, especially for the correct use of legs for both starting and halting.

Number participating

If there are more than two people present, the others can also compete against each other, in these three race formats. For example, *C* versus *D* and *E* versus *F*, etc. Obviously there can be any number in a race, but when it is limited to two people, a constructive critique of riding skills will be easier for the coach/observer. However, even with races of two people, the competitors can still be changed around, so that the line-up for the next series could, for example, be *A* versus *D*, *B* versus *E* and *C* versus *F*.

Fourth Race Includes a Circle

A circle can then be introduced for the fourth race, as follows:
Start at H – before reaching P, circle right – turn left at P, cross H and before R circle left – turn right at R to halt at H.

The dual use of the left hand should be emphasized here, so that it is used strongly for neck-reining, but very smoothly and sympathetically for the stops and turns.

Team Relay Races

The Hand-over

A relay provides a good way of having a team race, while still having only two people in action at any one time. The excitement, together with the pressure of competing for a team, will be added to the proceedings. The hand-over can be done by touching mallets, or simply by one rider starting as the previous rider halts. The split-second timing required could be compared to *playmaking* and the performance of each rider, while on the move, should reflect the importance of maximizing pony control to contribute to a team effort.

Team Numbers and Race Contents

Teams can consist of any number from two upwards. Let us imagine that you have eight people to form two teams with *A*, *B*, *C*, *D* in one and *W*, *X*, *Y*, *Z* in the other. They line up on H in the given order with five yards between *D* in one team and *W* in the other. *A* and *W* start, then hand over to *B* and *X*, succeeded by *C* and *Y*, with *D* and *Z* to finish.

The number of relay races between the teams, and their precise content on any particular day, depend on the time available and on the amount of exercise already done by the ponies.

1. To give the riders the concept of the hand-over and the halt within their team, I suggest that the first relay race contains only contains one turn.

2. The final relay race ideally includes two circles and two turns, as described above in the fourth race between two individuals.

Rules and Special Points

Either team can be disqualified if any rider fouls by:

1. Starting too soon.

2. Failing to reach the line at P and not adjusting to correct the mistake.

3. Overrunning the line at H and not circling to stop correctly before the next rider leaves.

If the eight riders do not belong to different teams, I always try to find some form of demarcation, such as older and younger or male and female for dividing them. This creates a competitive rationale for them to try to win, thereby pushing them to learn and apply the required skills.

Emphasis must be placed on the technique of looking behind before turning and circling. Apply an exaggerated twist of the body to turn 90 degrees at P and R and return on the same axis, at speed, directly to your own place in the team. This will enable your eyes to focus on the axis behind before asking for the turn.

SUMMARY

Controlled speed, fast turns and accurate halts done under the pressure of an individual race, and then in the team dimension of a relay race, have to be an excellent way of preparing for match polo. There will be a small percentage of ponies that, for reasons of temperament, would dislike the competition and be negatively affected by it. Obviously, such ponies should not take part, but the rest will benefit and I suggest that polo players should try to involve all their ponies at some stage in these shortest of short races. From the experience, player and pony should learn constructively together how to give their best joint performance. Teams will also gain a feeling of togetherness, which will help in future polo matches.

REVISION

Individual short races

- **H** — first race line up **H**orizontally on H, race five yards to turn right at P, return to halt at H.
- **T** — second race start H to **T**urn left at R, halt at H; third race start H to **T**urn right at P, left at R to halt at H.
- **C** — fourth race start H to **C**ircle right, at P turn left, cross H to **C**ircle left, at R turn right, halt at H.
- **D** — **D**ual use of legs to speed up and halt, correct use of hand to neck-rein strongly and halt smoothly.

Team relay racing

- **H** — ideally team of four, but can be any number; **H**and over by touching mallets or halt then next rider starts.
- **P** — start with race of only one turn, **P**rogress to race with two turns and two circles.
- **B** — emphasize looking **B**ehind at own team before turning and circling.
- **T** — exaggerate **T**wist of body to look and focus behind on own axis for return to H.

22

Striking 'E' — Nearside Front Circle (Fourth Circle)

The Value of Nearside Shots, and When to Avoid Them — Constructing the Nearside Neck Shot with PASSF — Constructing the Nearside Open Backhand with PASSF — Exercises

The Value of Nearside Shots, and When to Avoid Them

Playing with the left hand was banned because too many serious accidents, including head-on collisions, had been experienced. Hence skills on the nearside are valuable, but you must always remember that they only give you the secondary right of way, which can never be ridden when meeting an opponent who has legally claimed the primary one from the offside of their pony.

The connection between the two shots examined in this chapter is the support required by the right leg during the follow through, in order to apply with exactness the fourth circle (see Figure 12, page 58), which we will discuss shortly in terms of PASSF. Once again, for both shots, it is necessary to be deadly accurate with the pony clock and the ball clock.

Despite their value in the right circumstances, nearside shots should be avoided in the following situations:

1. When locked in a ride-off with an opponent on your right, hitting a neck shot is a necessary skill, but it is difficult, when shooting at goal or giving a pass, to be pin-point accurate. Therefore, when alone near the left side of the field, with a *playmaker* waiting to collect your pass, a wide-angled offside open backhand, or a cut forehand, will provide a better alternative than a nearside neck shot, because the line of the ball will be more accessible to the *playmaker*.

2. When competing with a parallel opponent for a nearside backhand, beware that an open shot could hit the opponent's pony and that a straight shot will more than likely be met by another member of the opposing team, who is following behind.

3. NEVER attempt any nearside stroke when an opponent is facing you and coming in the opposite direction, with the ball on the offside.

Constructing the Nearside Neck Shot with PASSF

Preparation

The key is to be ready to hit early and this is best achieved by placing the mallet vertically above your left knee, ready to 'throw salt' (see Chapter 13) immediately there is a necessity for this shot. Then, if there is time, a preparatory swing can help the blood to flow, but forget it if there is any rush to hit. When learning this stroke, the construction process will be greatly assisted by practising half-shots, followed by full swings through an imaginary ball at 11 on the pony clock.

Approach

From a wooden horse or a static pony, place the ball at 11 on the pony clock and be in the half-seat. On a moving pony, look forward to identify the target and then the relevant spot close to 8 on the ball clock. Apply strong legs to advance in the half-seat parallel to the line of the ball, before making a shallow arc from left to right to arrive opposite 11 on the pony clock, ready to 'throw salt'.

Swing Slowly

Deliberately extend the right hand and arm further to the left. Allow the V of the right hand to support the weight of the mallet so that the mallet head points at the target. The right shoulder rotates even further left than when applied to the straight nearside forehand, while nudging the chin towards the ball. This can be assisted by the right hip and leg turning underneath the shoulders, while the thighs secure the body in the half- seat as the hand is raised to complete the first half of the swing. Then, as slowly as possible, in the second half, the knuckles sweep through the ball and towards the target. If possible, imagine that you are making a half-shot.

Sweet Spot

Hitting the exact spot is extremely important for this shot and, even if you have focused on it early, you should reconfirm it on the bottom of the ball during the swing, and as the knuckles pass the mallet head through the ball. It is a bonus if the extended right hand initially draws away from the spot in the same plane as the line to the target. Verbalizing, as before, will maximize your concentration.

Follow Through

To prevent any deflection, the right shoulder must be kept rotated to the left and the mallet head should continue towards the target after passing through the ball. Muscle memory has to guide the direction of your hand and knuckles while your head and eyes stay down. To dissipate any force, the mallet head should be extended as far as possible.

Execution

Preparation
Apply legs and lift mallet (to 'throw salt') into a vertical position above your left knee. Make a preparatory swing only if there is time. Return mallet and hand to vertical.

Approach
Register exact location of target and distance to it. Find and focus on spot, close to ball clock 8. In the half-seat, apply legs to bring pony parallel to the line of the ball. Arc right to be opposite pony clock 11, ready to 'throw salt'.

Swing slowly
Extend right hand and arm to the left while nudging the chin with the right shoulder. Allow the V of the right hand to point mallet head at target. Aim knuckles as slow as possible to pass through the ball in the target direction and complete a circle.

Sweet spot
Guide the knuckles to the exact spot, close to ball clock 8, to pass through the bottom of the ball in conjunction with the mallet head, which completes a circle with gathering speed.

Follow through
Keep head and eyes down while completing second 50% of swing. Then let muscle memory take your knuckles and the mallet head in the exact direction of the target.

Constructing the Nearside Open Backhand with PASSF

Preparation

To hit this backhand early, you can save time by starting with the mallet vertical on the offside, above the right knee, as if to 'hold a sword' (see Chapter 13), even though it is a nearside stroke. Also, the preparatory swing must not be done if it delays the start of the technique but, as for all shots, if there is time, sending blood round the body is a bonus. Therefore, any offside preparatory swings in the 75% will be very beneficial. Alternatively, some quiet twiddles of the mallet head above your head can be effective, and this is done by most high-goal players. When learning or practising, you should first make some half-shots from 12 to 8 on the pony clock. Then, add many full swings through an imaginary ball at 11 to finish at 8 on the pony clock, thereby finding where the required circle is for the open backhand.

Approach

On a wooden horse or a static pony, place the ball at 11 on the pony clock. Look behind to find the exact target, lean forward into the half-seat and focus on the relevant spot –

STRIKING 'E' – NEARSIDE FRONT CIRCLE (FOURTH CIRCLE)

The fourth circle: nearside backhand in mid-swing.

normally between 1 and 2 on the ball clock. On a moving pony, apply strong legs to start the approach before looking behind to locate the target, and then forward to identify the spot, close to 2 on the ball clock. Create a shallow arc from left to right, without crossing the line; while advancing 'hold a sword' in the half-seat, keeping the pony's head away from the swing path.

Swing Slowly

Your right hand moves upward, above the right shoulder, to place the mallet head above your helmet in the circle as the left shoulder fights your chin. Focus on the spot is maintained, although initially the hips and shoulders turn away from the ball to the right. For the second half of the swing, the hips and shoulders change direction to gyrate to the left. Try to imagine you are making only a half-shot. The right leg can release its weight by lifting the heel and thereby securing your thighs on the saddle to prevent loss of balance as the mallet completes the swing out at 8 on the pony clock. This is optional, depending on how supple you are, because some people can rotate the body perfectly without such assistance. However, I have seen players fall off by following the mallet and others who never attempt the shot through lack of confidence, because they do not know this method of securing themselves. If you know you are late with the shot, minimize lift of the right hand to save time.

Sweet Spot

The spot which you identified during the approach as being between 1 and 2 on the ball clock (depending on exact location of the target) must now be focused upon strongly. Then confirm the spot by aiming the palm of your hand to pass through it on the bottom of the ball and go on in the direction of the target, in conjunction with the mallet head. Verbalizing will help more than ever with this shot, because your instinct will bring this slightly awkward swing to the wrong spot at 12 if you do not control it.

Follow Through

Let your hand and the mallet head continue towards the target, using muscle memory to direct them while your head and eyes stay down. This action can be supported by your right leg, which will counter the weight of your head and prevent the mallet from taking the path of least resistance towards the pony's tail. A deliberate change of weight and shoulder direction in the middle of the swing will help enormously to allow you to extend the follow through fully.

Execution

Preparation
If there is plenty of time, make a preparatory swing, assisted by thumb and index finger. Apply legs and 'hold a sword' by placing mallet vertically above right knee.

Approach
Look behind to locate target and the distance to it, and then look in front at relevant spot close to 2 on ball clock. Take half-seat and reapply legs to bring pony to the right of, and parallel to, the line of ball. Create a shallow arc to the right in order to strike the ball at pony clock 11, with the pony's head a little to the right.

Swing slowly
Bring the left shoulder to nudge the chin while lifting mallet head above your helmet. Release all weight from the right side to swing hand and mallet towards ball.

Sweet spot
Aim palm of hand, in conjunction with mallet head, to pass through the spot near ball clock 2, low on the ball.

Follow through
Allow hand and mallet to complete second 50% of swing and then continue the circle towards the target, using muscle memory to keep head and eyes down.

Ernesto Trotz (ex-10); nearside open backhand.

Exercises

Good anticipation is required before receiving a pass delivered by a nearside open backhand. Practising with others should be helpful for developing the way to *playmake* when doing so. Furthermore, *playmaking* by striking this shot can quickly turn defence into attack. But first, players should individually fine-tune this shot and, in order to do so, you can combine both shots learnt in this chapter in exercises similar to those in Chapter 19.

1. Individually, hit the ball on the nearside in the shape of a star by alternately striking a neck shot followed by an open backhand.

2. As a pair, work together on the nearside in the following sequence:
   A hits a neck shot and then approaches the ball, after locating B, before making an *open backhand*.
   B *playmakes* to receive from A before hitting a neck shot.
   B approaches to send an open backhand to A, who *playmakes* to receive and to hit a neck shot.

3. As a pair, practise the reverse rope tactic using backhands as follows:
   A canters past the ball before *playmaking* by turning to receive a backhand from B.
   B observes the direction in which A turns and hits an open backhand on either the offside or nearside to find A.
   A hits the ball forward to a suitable place and canters past the ball to restart the exercise.
   This continues until B has struck several open backhands on both sides. Obviously, players participate in both roles of A and B.

4. Individually hit nearside open backhands in an anticlockwise circle.

5. Work in pairs to hit alternate nearside open backhands in a circle.

SUMMARY

Efficient application of this fourth circle can assist in both defence and attack equally. Crucial goals can be scored by neck shots and set up by backhands from the nearside, while pressure from opponents is often relieved by wide-angled open backhands. For each shot, care must be taken that there is no opponent meeting the ball with the priority right of way on the offside. A detailed critique of any strike within this fourth circle, whether in play or practice, will achieve consistency and accuracy, but to benefit fully, a coach should be involved.

REVISION

Nearside neck shot

P — **P**repare; use legs; keep blood flowing; mallet above left knee.

A — on **A**pproach, register target, focus on ball clock 8; half seat; arc to right to relate to pony clock 11.

S — extend right arm leftwards, right shoulder to chin; mallet weight on V; knuckles **S**low through ball.

S — confirm **S**weet **S**pot on ball clock 8, knuckles through bottom of ball; verbalize action.

F — hand and mallet head **F**ollow through to point at target; head and eyes stay down.

Nearside open backhand

P — **P**repare: use legs; keep blood flowing; mallet vertical above right knee on offside.

A — on **A**pproach, register target behind; focus on ball clock 2; half-seat; arc to right to relate to pony clock 11.

S — mallet head in circle, left shoulder fights chin, bodyweight released by right leg, gyrate left to **S**wing through ball.

S — reconfirm **S**weet **S**pot on ball clock 2; palm of hand through bottom of ball; verbalize action.

F — hand and mallet head **F**ollow through to point at target, supported by right leg; continue circle, head and eyes down.

23

Tactics 'F' — No. 3 the Pivot Playmaker from Behind the Barrier

Understanding an Important Role — No. 3 Role Defined by PRST — Historical Examples

Understanding an Important Role

The most important position in a polo team has to be No. 3. The majority of teams put their best player there. It is only practical for the strongest member of a team to play in a different position if there is someone else good enough to fill the pivotal *playmaker* role.

Because of the disparity of skills factor in polo, the role of the pivot is even more important than in other sports. The necessity for the rest of a team to understand the job of their pivot, to watch it being done and to know how to adjust to each action, is crucial to success. Many low-goal players seldom see their pivot, because they are ball-chasing and not looking behind to see what No. 3 is doing, as prescribed by LATET.

The pivot should play the game for the benefit of the team and not to monopolize the ball, to look for all the glory. A good No. 3, in a well-trained team, will hit the ball a similar amount to the other players but, when striking, will initiate attacks and control the defence, as a creative *playmaker*. The method of doing this is through PRST, as explained below.

No. 3's Role Defined by PRST

In outline, the PRST roles of the No. 3 are as follows:

Position   Behind and close to the barrier.

Responsibility   To distribute the ball over the barrier.

Speed   To engage the correct opponent in defence and to create attacks.

Turn to Defence When attacks fail, or No. 3 is in front of ball, reposition behind the barrier, or as No. 4.

Let us now examine these roles in more detail.

Position

It is impossible to pivot properly from in front of the barrier, or from too far behind it. Many No. 3s are apt to be at No. 3½ for much of the time, with the result that they often interfere with, and muddle, their No. 4.

However, from behind, but close to, the barrier, No. 3s can launch effective attacks and back up the forwards. From the same place they can co-ordinate the defence, by marking the relevant opponent rapidly, or covering behind No. 4 if necessary (see Figure 52).

England No. 3, Henry Brett (8), in action.

Responsibility

Distributing the ball to other players in a reliable manner requires a No. 3 who avoids taking risks, which can give away possession. *Playmakers* in a team move to receive passes and the ball should be delivered to them, over the barrier, by accurately angled backhands and forehands, that are easy to receive and difficult for opponents to intercept. Also, the ball sent to the forwards via a *playmaking* No. 4 through the reverse rope is very effective.

Added to this, as a No. 3 you must only commit to a play that seems certain to succeed, and does not leave you in front of the barrier, having lost possession. In other situations it is more responsible to go to the next play, behind the barrier, where possession can easily be regained or where the ball will literally be given to you, as previously described with reference to No. 4, in Chapter 17. The exceptions to this apply when you see that, by neutralizing an opponent:

1. Your action will give the ball to your No. 4, who is free and could then pass to you.

2. You can quickly reposition behind your No. 4, who then becomes No. 3 in possession.

3. Your No. 2 (or even No. 1) can and will interchange with you to become No. 3.

Speed

Part of being a pivot is to mark a relevant opponent so decisively in defence, that the rest of your team can see clearly which opponents belongs to them. This is best achieved through engaging as swiftly as possible. But beware that too much speed does not take you to do the job of No. 4, who then contributes nothing to your team. For No. 3, the relevant opponent is normally the one who is second in attack – unless, before the match, something different was decided upon to compensate for the disparity of skills factor.

Not only does rapid engaging clarify the situation for others, but it also improves the defence. The use of the tail trick, covered in Chapter 15, will help on occasions, as attack switches to defence.

The other side of this coin is that, through *playmaking* with velocity, the pivot can change defence to attack, by creating an opening that can be taken advantage of by the team.

An apparent paradox to these uses of speed is that, sometimes, the other team are clearly quicker overall than the rest of your players and, by *slowing the pace of the game* at significant moments you, the pivot, can *playmake* in a subtle way. Hopefully, this is not detected and allows your players to *playmake* themselves.

Turn to Defence

Reposition early

Staying behind the barrier makes it easy to switch to defence as the game changes, but it is even better when No. 3 anticipates the loss of possession, before it happens, and

Figure 52. No. 3s in good position; No. 2s badly placed.

repositions early to a place of advantage. Often, this means temporarily becoming No. 4, but at other times it involves slowing or stopping to be firmly established as the pivot, behind the barrier. These actions not only improve the ability to defend, but can also help the positioning for backing up an attack.

Return after mistake

Inevitably, as No. 3, you will sometimes find yourself making a mistake, perhaps by merely missing the ball or losing a ride-off unexpectedly, or simply finding yourself in front of the ball, before discovering that there is nobody available to cover you in defence. This produces an emergency, which is exacerbated if your No. 4 is out of position, or is being tightly marked. But all is not lost, if you keep your head, to turn and move rapidly behind the ball and barrier. En route, you should see exactly where your No. 4 is located and make a decision whether to re-establish as No. 3 or interchange to take the No. 4 position.

Cutting out of the game

Most of the above drill has previously been covered in Chapter 11, in the text about the players behind the barrier, and in Chapter 17, about the job of No. 4. Here, I must also repeat that the best route for No. 3 to take, when repositioning in defence, is down the middle of the field, regardless of where the ball is. There will be exceptions, but the opponents have to finish any attack in the direction of the goal and, by doing this act of *cutting out of the game*, you can be waiting for them. This is also an exaggerated way of going to the next play and of *playmaking*, especially if you can regain possession and restart an attack for your team.

Historical Examples

Gonzalo Pieres

I have watched Gonzalo Pieres, for years the best player in the world, play No. 3 in many matches in England, Palm Beach, Florida and Argentina. He was the perfect pivot and never crossed the barrier, unless he was *playmaking*, either with the ball or by moving to receive it from another player. With incredible control of brilliant ponies, he pushed and checked against opponents, normally outwitting them to keep possession, but never proceeding forward without the ball, and he turned to defend in a flash. Hence he maintained control of the area behind the barrier and picked the right moments to *playmake* and initiate attacks.

At Palm Beach, I was frequently surprised to see some No. 3s, in high-goal teams, fail to pivot correctly, because they tried to do too much, with the inevitable result that other players could not contribute much and their team duly lost the match. There was no coach to correct the situation, but often there was Gonzalo Pieres, or Memo, or Carlos

The formidable Gonzalo Pieres, a truly pivotal No. 3.

Gracida in the opposing teams, and these players took full advantage, as firm pivots, to win by *playmaking*.

Dickie Cernadas

The best example of a good No. 3, with whom I had the privilege of playing, was Dickie Cernadas (7) from Argentina. In a 14-goal tournament in Dublin, as we dismounted between chukkas, I always noticed that his pony still looked fresh, although he had dominated the game against other 7-goal players. He appeared only to canter around the field, but never failed to stop his relevant opponent, while giving many passes to us, his three grateful team members. From a field of eight teams, we easily won the cup, because we had in our team the perfect *pivot playmaker*.

Personal experience, bad and good

I have played No. 3 in medium- and low-goal polo teams with mixed results. I found that the hardest games to play were those in which my team-mates had no conception of how No. 3 should play and therefore no idea of how to adjust to my tactics and *playmaking*. For example, I once came on as a substitute No. 3 in a match at Windsor, in England. There was no time to discuss tactics and I found that I had to ask my No. 2 to hurry and rush the opposing **No. 3** a bit more, instead of watching him hit backhands. Later in the game I stopped, to avoid crossing the barrier without the ball, and heard No. 2 shout that I was a hypocrite, with a certain expletive attached.

I had a better experience as No. 3 in the British Army team, touring Kenya. There, my No. 2, Roland Notley, a 3-goal player, worked liked a Trojan in front of the barrier. But I had to pivot and employ speed in an unusual way, to cover the erratic behaviour of our No. 4 when he was backhanding. He could hit prodigious, big backhands, but liked to gallop to take them on his own, giving the opposing **No. 1** an easy chance to claim a foul. All kinds of pleading, ordering and threatening had no effect. After losing two matches I adjusted my play, so that every time he had a backhand, I accelerated to ride-off the opposing **No. 1**, or whoever came looking for the foul. The result was unbelievably successful, because his backhands duly sailed down the ground, as long passes to our forwards, who quite often scored. We did not lose another match. With hindsight, for the team's benefit, I was constructively combining the three unique dimensions of polo:

1. The *disparity of skills*, which brought out the best and the worst from our No. 4.

2. Preventing ignorance of the *right of way* from destroying our team.

3. Using obstruction at any time, indirectly to set up long passes.

Thus I was *playmaking* without touching the ball. I believe our No. 4 never understood what was really happening!

SUMMARY

A good No. 3 co-ordinates team tactics behind the barrier by being a secure pivot, who distributes the ball, with angled shots, and selects appropriate moments to *playmake*. As pivot, he rapidly engages the second opponent when defending, and turns to defence if in front of the ball or the barrier, and whenever required to cover No. 4.

A bad No. 3 monopolizes the ball, fails to defend in a disciplined manner and expects the rest of the team to remove stronger opponents, in order to clear the way.

By using the barrier strategically, No. 3s can control both attack and defence throughout a match.

REVISION

No. 3

- **J** — **J**ob of *pivot playmaker* from behind barrier through PRST.
- **W** — must be continually **W**atched by others while initiating attacks and controlling defence.
- **P** — **P**osition behind and close to barrier, to back up attacks and co-ordinate defence.
- **AI** — **A**void **I**nterfering with No. 4 by being too far behind barrier.
- **R** — distribute the ball over the barrier with minimum **R**isk of losing possession.
- **NP** — only commit to certain plays, otherwise go to the **N**ext **P**lay behind barrier.
- **S** — in defence, engage relative opponent with **S**peed, and *playmake* rapidly in attack.
- **DS** — relative opponent can be determined through **D**isparity of **S**kills factor.
- **T** — when attacks fail, or ball is behind No. 3, **T**urn to reposition behind ball and barrier.
- **AP** — best route is via centre field to **A**lternative **P**osition of No. 3 or 4.

24

Riding 'F' — Playing Ponies

Considerations Before and During Play — Number of Chukkas Played — Additional Match Considerations — Post-match — Schooling Between Matches

In the previous chapters we have discussed many ideas and exercises, which can be used to improve and sharpen up your polo riding sufficiently to enable you to become a *playmaker*. I also suggested that these would all be beneficial for your ponies, besides giving you the opportunity to develop a better relationship and understanding with them.

The next stage is the actual *playing* of the ponies, when all of the above can bear fruit – but it can also be wasted if due thought is not applied. You must realize that both you and the pony can only give of your best if both the preparation is correct and the application on the day is good. The key has to be frequent revision of basics.

Coupled to this, plans for the day of play, at times between games and matches, should be flexible, to accommodate any surprise factors and unexpected occurrences. Importantly, it should also be remembered that a pony is not a machine, and each one requires individual attention.

Considerations Before and During Play

Before Play

On the day of a game, the precise form of preparation varies, depending on the standard and handicap of the players, and factors pertaining to the ponies. The fitness requirement for high-goal ponies is so great, that the routine for them is normally quite different from other levels. For an average standard, the ponies should at least be walked earlier in the day and, to curb excessive exuberance, some need more extensive exercise. At the polo field, there should always be a last-minute check on the pony's tack, to see that everything fits correctly and nothing is too loose or too tight. Apart from the necessity for both player and pony to be warmed up before play, the priority then is for both to become harmonized. Some turns, circles and halts can create mutual confidence between them and clearly establish that the rider is in control. A common mistake is to rush onto the field, only to hit the ball, without ensuring that the pony is disciplined and balanced, before the play commences.

During Match Play

Depending on whether the polo is only chukkas, a practice game, or a match, the competitive attitude of all players should vary considerably. In all situations, however, there should be some attempt to save the ponies where possible. In a match, this will be governed by the depth of the pony string, because if there are spare ponies to change to in mid-chukka, then all plays can be contested. But if there is no such luxury, it will be essential, during the 75% of play, for all ponies to be eased deliberately from time to time, so that when a chance comes to *playmake*, you have the pony power to take it.

Practice Days

On a practice day, a player should consider what is required for each pony before every chukka. Some may be short of work and need as much fast play as possible, while others may already be very fit and require light work only, in order to be kept fresh. Normally, unless there is a reason for doing otherwise, most practice chukkas should be played in third gear, with a burst of speed injected occasionally. This not only saves the ponies from unnecessary exhaustion and injuries, but also allows the players to keep an extra gear in reserve for upcoming matches.

Practice days are a good time to improve any schooling deficiencies in the ponies by working through them, rather than circumventing them. For example, some ponies turn better to the left than the right (or vice versa) and, in practice, it can be beneficial to concentrate on turns to the difficult side when possible. A similar philosophy can be applied to other faults. Also, players should consider their own weaknesses and look for opportunities to work on them. For example, you could hook sticks whenever feasible, and take nearside shots, even when it is not necessary to do so. Additionally, set-piece tactics can be practised and interchanges during fluid play could be tried, even in risky situations, in order to experiment with different ways of *playmaking*.

Number of Chukkas Played

On a Given Day

The number of chukkas played by each pony should be planned for the good of the pony more than the benefit of the player. In club chukkas, many people automatically book two chukkas for all their ponies, in pursuit of enjoying the maximum playing time, without realizing that they are indulging in a false economy. It is easy to overplay a pony but, after doing so, it is difficult to bring about a quick recovery. Another common mistake is always to double your best pony, instead of any of the others, and then suddenly find that that pony is lame or tired and unable to finish the season. However, there are ponies that play better in their second chukka than the first, and others that need two chukkas regularly to keep them fit, and obviously these should be played more than the rest.

Over a Period

How much polo should a pony play in one week, one month and one season? These questions cannot be given a general answer, because there are enormous variations in the physical ability and endurance of different ponies. But it must be wrong to ask any pony to play every polo day, in order to justify the costs of upkeep. On the other hand, it is also a mistake to give a pony only an odd practice chukka, and then expect a fabulous performance in a match or a tournament. Therefore a compromise between over- and under-playing should be planned, that is relevant to the characteristics of each pony. If a player has only two ponies, they will both have to play two chukkas in every match and, if there are always tournaments at the weekends then, in mid-season, mid-week practice chukkas should be very limited, if not avoided completely.

Additional Match Considerations

In a match, consideration must be given both to helping a pony to compete effectively, for the whole length of a chukka, and to protecting its long-term welfare. When simple exhaustion sets in, this is similar to a car running out of petrol, and although the problem is significant, it is only temporary. But if the legs, heart and lungs take too much strain, this has an effect similar to a car being driven without oil, and the damage is lasting and serious. Therefore, knowledge about the stamina of each pony will help a player to conserve their energy, in order to prevent injury and save them for important moments of *playmaking*.

Also remember that the mouth of a pony can be compared to the brakes of a car. New brakes can be bought for the car but a fresh mouth can never be obtained for the pony.

In order to compete effectively, and to assist the pony in respect of improved balance and understanding of the aids, riding standards must be maintained at optimum level. I have helped many people to achieve better pony control simply by asking 'Are you using your legs?' as they changed ponies between chukkas. Often the reply was 'Not enough' and later they have acknowledged that, in the chukkas that followed, they had better results from applying their legs more consciously. During a match, the presence of a coach who, besides suggesting improvements where relevant, confirms any good part of your riding, can encourage and assist you to find that extra gear essential at moments in defence and for *playmaking* opportunities.

Attention to detail in all aspects of training, care and preparation will promote smooth, fast play.

Post-match

Physical Inspections

When a game is over, all ponies ought to be given a brief inspection for injuries or any damage that requires treatment. Even more important, on the following day, a thorough examination should be done, because swellings and filled tendons normally do not appear until several hours after playing. All ponies should be trotted up, even if their legs appear to be perfect, because there can be problems which would not otherwise be found. It can be disastrous if an injury is not detected and treated early. Other places which must be looked at are the mouth, back and under the belly to check that the bit, saddle and girth are not beginning to cause injury. It is also advisable to note the general demeanour of a pony and confirm that it has eaten all of its feed.

Performance Diagnosis

Quite separately from checking the condition of the ponies, an analysis could be made of their *performance* in each game. Then, from discussions with anyone who helps you to look after a pony – including the vet, if relevant – you may be able to form a diagnosis for any deterioration in the way a pony plays. A change of bridle, a visit by a horse dentist or the farrier, can return a pony to its best. The aim must be to find any reason for pain being suffered and to rectify it. In some cases, the rider himself can be the cause of a pony's problem, and chiropracters say that a muscular problem experienced by a player may have a negative affect on a pony, in which case both could be treated constructively together.

Schooling Between Matches

I have, on a few occasions, met people who could not understand why their ponies started the season playing so well, and then ended it playing badly. From asking some questions, it became clear that they thought that one should only school a pony because an obvious fault required correcting, or as ongoing training for a green pony. In fact, it is important to refresh ponies even when they are playing well. Therefore schooling should take place regularly between matches, in order to maintain a standard of performance which can otherwise deteriorate slowly, without anyone realizing that it is happening. Then, suddenly, the damage is found to be beyond repair, unless the pony is given a long rest. The reason for this is that ponies can be hurt in a minor way, which is not noticed, during any match or even in practice chukkas. The mouth may be bruised by the bit, the face by a strap, the chin by a chain or noseband and the legs by a tread or a careless swing of the mallet. Pony collisions and direct hits by the ball may appear not to trouble your mount, but it is impossible to tell whether pain is suffered or not. But clearly, if ponies remember experiencing some or all of the above in one match and their next strenuous exercise is another match, they will be subconsciously building a defence mechanism to avoid suffering in a similar way. On the other hand, a lively school, which they enjoy, will take the place of that last match in their memory, besides helping them to be balanced and feel confident about their ability. The long-term result of regular schooling is the continued willingness of the ponies to compete as required, with courage and speed, enabling you to *playmake* as opportunities arise. Thereby, also, the ponies are kept content throughout a season.

In between days of play, the method of schooling can be flexible. The exercises suggested in the previous chapters on riding are an excellent way of keeping the pony and player in unison, besides refreshing the former, as just mentioned. Alternatively, any basic schooling in which the pony can enjoy a mixture of stretching out at speed and some slower work, without being hurt, can serve to regain confidence and may well suffice. A common mistake is to do stick and ball practice only, and to forget the requirements of the pony. Then, if the pony is hit by a mallet or struck by a ball during the schooling session, any existing problems will be exacerbated instead of corrected.

If any pony has developed a clear fault, the schooling should attempt to correct this. But if the performance was simply not as good as usual, the schooling may provide a chance to find the reason. An observant rider has more time in a school, than in a game, to examine what is upsetting the pony, and he may be able to rectify it during a session. It could involve anything from a small alteration of tack to a complete change of bridle and bit. It might be discovered that a particular pony requires slightly different riding aids from the others, in one or more situations. But, if it is noticed that there is resistance to making any manoeuvre, or avoidance of taking weight on any limb, this information will assist with the diagnosis of any problem. Also, if relevant, attention can be paid to increasing the general strength and fitness of a pony by varying the routine and making it more demanding. For example, extra hill work or longer spells of cantering could be added.

SUMMARY

I hope all the above shows clearly that, to play a pony requires much thought and planning before, during and after any game and that, at no time, should any of these four-legged friends be regarded or treated like a machine, if you want to *playmake* on them. Any polo player who wants to have ponies which play consistently well throughout a season needs to plan carefully. A programme of tournaments, chukkas, schooling and exercise should be made and kept to as far as possible, but with a degree of flexibility to cover changes of weather, injuries and other unexpected happenings. The joint performance given by the rider and pony provides the link which connects tactics to striking. On the day of any big match, the achievement will be limited if the preparation during previous weeks has not been properly thought out. Yet, in the game, the best planning can be totally wasted by poor application of riding skills. To be a successful *playmaker*, you require all your ponies to be constructively and sympathetically looked after, so that they are correctly prepared for each match. Ideally, you should often allow a coach to watch and assess you in order to confirm that you are applying SLOSH consistently, and to remind you about essential details.

REVISION

Before and during play

T — walk, or do more, at field; check **T**ack not loose or tight before warm-up to confirm control.

A — decide competitive **A**ttitude from many factors; save ponies to take *playmaker* chances.

G — in practice, put consideration for pony first and use third **G**ear, reserving top gear for matches.

W — work on pony's and player's **W**eak points in chukkas; experiment with set and fluid plays bravely.

Number of chukkas a pony plays per day and per period

E — priority is pony over player; false **E**conomy to play two chukkas per pony each time.

T — distinguish **T**ypes – some thrive on two chukkas, those with less endurance better on one.

A — **A**void tough pony playing too often, thus getting stale, and softer one too little, thus getting unfit.

M — maximum match play countered by no **M**id-week chukkas when season under way.

Match considerations

V — commitment in chukkas **V**aried as relevant to short- and long-term pony welfare.

S — knowledge of pony's **S**tamina applied to avoid lasting damage to legs, heart and lungs.

L — control and stamina improved by coach's reminder of strong **L**egs, etc. being used continually.

C — extra gear for *playmaking* and defending inspired by **C**oach's **C**ritique during match.

After match

I — brief **I**nspection to spot injuries and damage – treatment given if and when necessary.

T — next day **T**rot up; thorough inspection of tendons, back, mouth and all parts of ponies.

D — ponies' performances analysed and reasons for any **D**eterioration diagnosed.

C — investigate requirements for **C**hanges of tack or service from farrier, dentist, vet, etc.

Schooling between matches

R — prevent pony deterioration and damage beyond repair by **R**efreshing through light schooling.

E — overcome defence mechanism to avoid pain with **E**njoyable lively schooling.

F — drills to correct known **F**aults; also be flexible between given exercises and general work.

D — time used to **D**iagnose problems and discover whether tack or riding change produces remedy.

25

Striking 'F' — Nearside Rear Circle (Fifth Circle)

Constructing the Nearside Cut Shot with PASSF — Constructing the Nearside Tail Shot with PASSF — Exercises

The two shots detailed in this chapter are the nearside forehand cut and the nearside tail backhand. To perfect these shots the application of the fifth and final circle (see Figure 12, page 58) is most helpful, and this is easier for those blessed with supple hips and shoulders.

Many players mishit the nearside forehand cut and thus give away possession but others, when being strongly marked by an opponent on their right-hand side, score vital goals with it. The tail backhand can provide a useful pass and should also be struck, to avoid hitting ponies, when an opponent is parallel on your left competing for the ball.

When approaching the ball for either of these shots *it is imperative to be constantly aware that you are in the secondary right of way on the nearside*. Therefore, it may suddenly be necessary to abort the shot because an opponent has turned to face you.

Constructing the Nearside Cut Shot with PASSF

Preparation

Although you do not need to hit this shot early, it is important to be ready well in advance of reaching the ball, in order to be able to turn your body fully to the left. The mallet should be vertical and held by the hand close to your left hip, as if to 'throw salt'. Before this, a preparatory swing to find the circle will be beneficial (if there is time). A few half-shots will help you to feel how and where the full shot must finish and then some full swings, at an imaginary ball, will confirm the required circle for an accurate, powerful cut shot.

Approach

From a wooden horse or static pony, place the ball at pony clock 9 and be in the half-seat. When moving, seek the relevant spot close to ball clock 4, by first identifying the target. Apply legs to be parallel to and on the right side of the line of the ball. Then arc slightly left so that you arrive to 'throw salt', with the ball close to pony clock 9.

The nearside cut shot sweet spot.

Swing Slowly

Push the right shoulder hard to the left while your right hand swings back towards the tail of the pony. Take the weight of the mallet in the V between thumb and index finger in order to point the mallet head directly at the target. Turn your right leg and hip to support the action before slowly sweeping the knuckles of the right hand through the ball and on towards the target.

Sweet Spot

Reconfirm the exact spot, close to ball clock 4, before aiming your knuckles to go through that spot on the bottom of the ball, coinciding with the centre of the mallet head. Concentration on the correct spot will be assisted by finding it early and verbalizing the moment of contact.

Follow Through

Using muscle memory, after passing through the ball, the mallet head must be extended in the exact direction of the target, while the head and eyes stay down. The shoulders, hips and right leg continue to give support to the swing, to help obtain accuracy. This will ensure that the mallet head describes a perfect circle to give a shot of required length in the direction of the target.

Execution

Preparation
Hold the mallet vertical with the right hand close to your left hip to 'throw salt'.

Approach
Apply legs strongly to come parallel to the line, then arc slightly left and 'throw salt' ready to hit ball close to ball clock 4 when it is in the area of pony clock 9.

Swing slowly
Turn right shoulder firmly to the left while using the V of the fingers to support mallet's weight and point mallet head at target. Your right hand swings back towards the pony's tail before slowly sweeping the knuckles through the ball towards the target. The right leg and hip assist this precise action.

Sweet spot
Aim knuckles to pass through the exact spot in conjunction with mallet head, close to ball clock 4 on bottom of ball.

Follow through
Extend mallet head with right arm fully in target direction, using muscle memory, with head and eyes down.

Constructing the Nearside Tail Shot with PASSF

Because you must hit the ball when it is behind you, there is no requirement to start as early as for the open backhand. Yet a lack of suppleness can make you hit late, or even miss the ball. Thus any action which keeps the blood flowing around the body, supples the muscles and overrides stiffness, is beneficial. Therefore, staying prepared during the 75% of the game is of extra importance for this shot. Also, the 'hold a sword' position, as for the open backhand, is desirable. Only if there is ample time, after looking where to hit behind you, can you afford a full preparatory swing immediately before making the shot. Alternatively, make small rotations of the mallet head above you.

When learning and practising on a wooden horse or a static pony, some half-shots can be constructive. Place the ball at pony clock 8 and the mallet head at ball clock 10 before making a 50/50 swing through the ball. Then, some full swings through an imaginary ball can be assessed to check the exactness of your circle behind the pony's tail.

Mike Azzaro (10) on left, hoping and preparing for a nearside tail backhand.

Approach

For the average shot, the pony clock marker is probably 8.30 and the ball clock, 10. But if you are in a ride-off, the ball may have to be hit earlier or later depending on whether you are wide from or close to it, and these factors define your route before striking. After locating a *playmaker*, or the best place to hit to, you select the necessary spot on the ball and focus on it. 'Hold a sword' and make shallow arc to the left, without crossing the line, in order to make the perfect swing that clears the rear of the pony. Strong legs must be applied, first to hold the pony's quarters away from the ball and second, so as not to cross the line after the shot (see Figure 12, page 58).

Swing Slowly

To be economical, you can start the swing in exactly the same way as for the nearside open backhand. But, as the left shoulder fights the chin, further time can be saved by minimizing the action of turning the hips and shoulders away to the right while focusing on the spot on the outside of the ball at ball clock 10. As it moves upwards, your right hand can allow the mallet head, above your helmet, to move a little to the left to find the circle that will pass behind the pony's tail. Your right thumb must take most of the mallet's weight. The hips and shoulders start the second half of the swing by gyrating to the left to help your right hand and the mallet head reach the outside of the ball. Your thighs are secured on the saddle by releasing all weight from the right leg as you lift the right heel to maintain balance during a relatively slow movement.

Sweet Spot

On the outside of the ball, confirm the spot upon which you focused earlier and aim the palm of the right hand to pass through it in conjunction with the mallet head, while continuing in the direction of the target. Beware that your subconscious will try to make you take the easy route to ball clock 12, for a straight hit, and therefore exert an extra effort to reach ball clock 10, in order to counter this. As for other shots, verbalizing will assist you to concentrate and thereby find the correct spot, which in turn makes you describe the required circle, which passes behind the pony's tail.

Follow Through

Keeping your head and eyes down, let your hand and the mallet head continue towards the target. Support this posture with your right leg and use muscle memory to guide the mallet behind the pony's tail. You could have recorded this action for muscle memory earlier, when making those full swings through an imaginary ball.

Execution

Preparation
Ensure that the mallet is vertical to 'hold a sword' while applying legs to pony. Rotate mallet above you, or make full preparatory swing if there is time.

Approach
Look behind to register a *playmaker*, or the target and distance to it. Then, look at the ball to focus on exact spot close to ball clock 10. Reapply legs, 'hold a sword' and bring the pony in a shallow arc to the left to enable you to hit the ball between pony clock 8 and 9 and clear the tail.

Swing slowly
Left shoulder nudges chin as you raise right hand and allow mallet head to move left into required circle. Shoulders and hips gyrate to left as you sweep your hand through the ball towards target. The right leg supports this action.

Adolfo Cambiaso – incredible reach for a backhand.

Sweet spot

Guide right hand to the outside of the ball to confirm and go through the required spot close to ball clock 10 in conjunction with the mallet head, which should continue in a circle.

Follow through

Keep head and eyes down while allowing mallet head to go as far as possible towards the target, using muscle memory.

Exercises

1. Individually, go the length of the polo field, striking alternate offside cut shots and neck shots, trying to finish with a goal. Repeat using nearside cut and neck shots. Then employ a programme that mixes these four shots.

2. In pairs, ride parallel the length of the field passing to each other, with A striking offside cut shots and B nearside cut shots. Try to finish with a goal. Then A and B swap roles.

    When satisfied with the standard of shots, repeat the exercise using two balls, which are exchanged each time they are hit. Try to finish by scoring two goals.

3. A passes to B with a nearside neck shot. B strikes a nearside cut shot and *playmakes* to receive the next nearside neck shot from A. They aim to finish with a goal. Then A and B swap roles.

4. As a pair, practise the reverse rope tactic (see Chapter 17), using only nearside backhands as follows:

   A canters past the ball before playmaking *by turning to receive a backhand from B.*

   B observes the direction in which A turns and hits either an open or tail nearside backhand to find A.

   A hits the ball forward to a suitable place and canters past the ball to restart the exercise.

   This continues until *B* has struck several open and tail backhands. Both players should participate in both roles.

SUMMARY

The ten shots described by the five circles have now all been covered and you could have used all of them in the suggested exercises. The details demanded by the PASSF headings are many, and it is easy to forget one or more at any time. Yet, through constant revision of all the techniques and practice of the strokes, both individually and combined during the exercises, mistakes can be minimized. Carrying out the exercises in rotation will ensure that regular attention is given to all of the strokes. Naturally, the likelihood of good technique being confirmed and faults being detected is far greater when playing or practising in the presence of an observant coach.

REVISION

Nearside forehand cut

P — **P**repare by applying legs; mallet vertical by left hip; body ready for violent left turn; find circle.

A — on **A**pproach register target; focus on spot at ball clock 4; join line; arc left; half-seat; relate to pony clock as appropriate.

S — right shoulder hard left; right hand toward pony's tail, mallet weight on V, knuckles **S**lowly through ball.

S — confirm **S**weet spot at ball clock 4; knuckles through bottom of ball; verbalize spot on contact.

F — hand and mallet head **F**ollow through to point at target; head and eyes stay down.

Nearside tail backhand

P — **P**repare by applying legs; blood kept flowing by circle; mallet vertical.

A — on **A**pproach, register target behind; focus on spot at ball clock 10; shallow left arc; relate to ball at pony clock 8/9.

S — left shoulder to chin; mallet head into circle; gyrate shoulders left to sweep hand **S**lowly through ball.

S — confirm **S**weet spot at ball clock 10; strike outside of ball; keep hand and mallet head in circle.

F — mallet head **F**ollows through toward target; head and eyes kept down.

26

Tactics 'G' — Going to the Next Play

The Throw-in — Interchanging Positions — Recovering Ground — Historical Examples

We have, up to this point, already examined a number of tactics. LATET connected to PRST has been discussed, as a joint thought process required by all members of a team to co-ordinate the actions and the jobs of the four positions. Also, the use of the diamond and its variations for the hit-in, penalties from the spot and during fluid play, has already been explained, as a way to *playmake* by using lateral adjustment.

All this knowledge will become even more useful when you add to it the extra abilities to *playmake* freely by interchanging in attack and recovering ground in defence. These will further assist your tactical awareness and muscle memory to take you to the next play before it happens.

Yet all of the above will be of little use if your opponents win most of the throw-ins, with the result that they dominate possession for too much of the time. This happens if there is no thought process for winning the ball and for how to get to the next play. Therefore, the players must apply such a thought process while they are waiting for the ball to be thrown.

The Throw-in

This set piece happens, more than any other set piece, and at the following times:

1. To start a polo match.

2. To restart after every goal is scored.

3. When the ball goes out over the boards or sideline.

4. After stoppages caused by injury, broken tack, buried or broken balls and overruled fouls.

Rules

1. The two teams line up, individual players one behind the other (see Figure 53), in a manner similar to a rugby line out.

2. To start a match, or to restart after a goal, the players form up on a T, which is marked out at the centre of the field.

3. If the ball has gone out over the boards or sideline, the umpire must throw-in from the side, towards the middle.

4. For all stoppages, the ball is thrown from where it stopped, *towards* the nearest sideline.

5. The players cannot touch each other until the ball has left the umpire's hand.

6. The throw creates the first line of the ball and an immediate right of way.

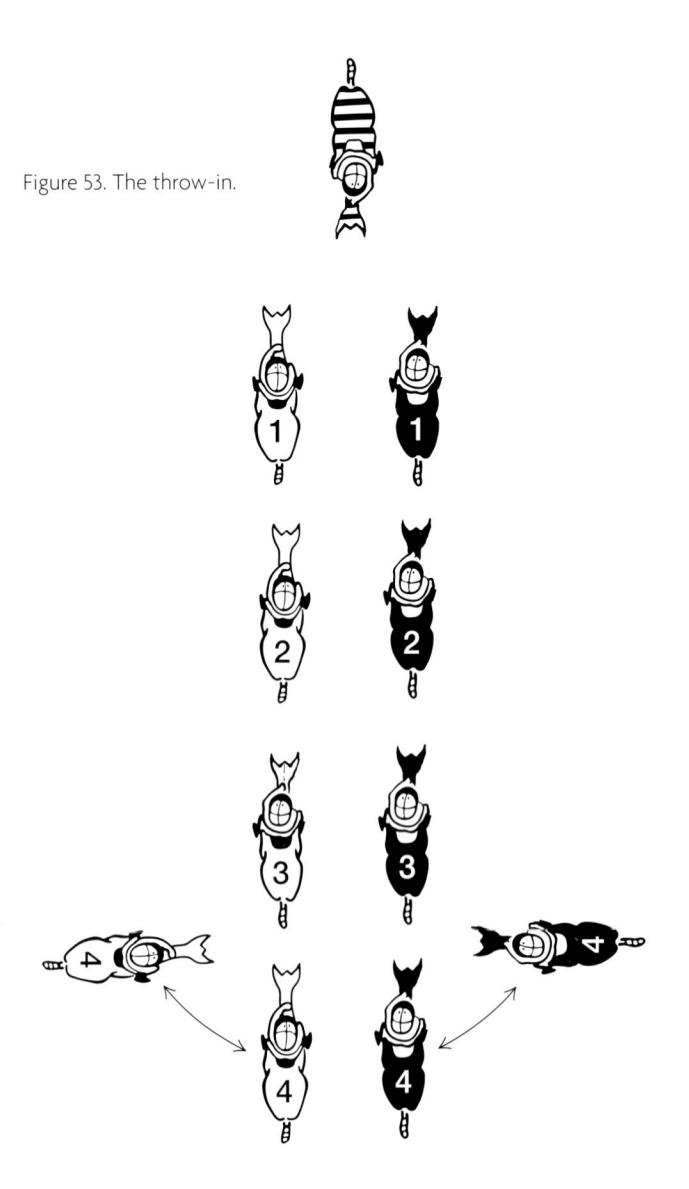

Figure 53. The throw-in.

Problems

Ugly scrum

Despite the rules, throw-ins cause far too many chaotic moments. Sometimes, all eight players become locked together in an ugly scrum. This is caused by poor discipline, no consideration of the line made by the throw and no prior thought of how to act in the line-up. The result is that the amount of flowing polo is severely limited, the spectacle is appalling and injuries to players and ponies occur more often.

Because of these problems, I prefer to teach beginners the rope and hit-in, before the throw-in, so that they know how to spread out, before being embroiled in a scrum.

Negative instructions

Many professionals tell novice No. 1s to stay at the front of the line-up, blocking an opponent, after the ball has gone by. I believe these instructions are negative and probably selfish. It adds to the chaos and cruelly denies the No. 1 the chance to learn, from the experience of receiving an early pass, how to be the link to goal. The principle of making the ball do more work than the ponies, is discarded, without any realization of the consequences.

Line-up Order

Traditionally, the majority of teams position themselves in numerical order, with No. 1 at the front, although there is no regulation regarding this.

One difference that applies commonly to low-goal and high-goal polo is that, in the former, No. 4 normally stands behind the line but, in high-goal, is generally last in the line. The reason for this difference is that high-goal players have much greater mobility than those in low-goal, who therefore need to compensate by positioning last, from the beginning, in order to shut the door immediately.

In some cases, teams will change the order in a variety of ways, to counter known tactics and abilities of their opponents. Two alternative line-ups are:

Reverse order
This is a one-on-one formation in that:
No. 4 lines up at the front against the opposing **No. 1**.
No. 3 is second in the line against the opposing **No. 2**.
No. 2 positions third to be against the opposing **No. 3**.
No. 1 is last and moves forward from the back of the line to be the link.

The advantage of the reverse order is that all the players are immediately with their respective opponents. But a problem can arise if No. 4 is late coming back in defence.

No. 3 separate
No. 3 stands separate from the line-up, while the other three players only try to stop the opponents gaining possession of the ball immediately after it has been thrown. The

order of the other players can be adjusted for each game, in relation to the disparity of skills factor. This will increase the blocking effectiveness of the team and maximize the opportunities for No. 3 to pounce on the ball.

Strategy

Depending on the relative strengths of both teams, the strategy at the throw-in should be varied. The first priority must be to stop the opponents hitting the ball and, if all four of your team do this, one of them should gain possession a high percentage of times. Various strategic manoeuvres can follow on from this initial aim.

Team rope

The second priority is to spread out quickly into a team rope formation to gain a tactical advantage for attack and defence. This is the equivalent of going to the next play. Remember that all players start alongside No. 3, who can and must be related to, there and then. As the ball lands in the line-up it can be diverted in any direction, but normally the ball stops in the middle of the players. Then, the key to the first priority lies with the middle two players, and for the second, to Nos. 1 and 4.

No. 1 to link

If and when the ball has gone by, No. 1 must cease to block, and should quickly evade the opposite opponent, ideally by pushing past in front but, if necessary, by going behind.

The aim should be to move upfield through two positions to become an instant link to the goal. If this is achieved regularly, the rest of the team will know that they have a *playmaker* link who can receive a pass. At the same time, the last opponent can be marked by No. 1 if a defensive situation arises.

If the opponents get first possession, the initial aim is still to reach an area to link from, because after one ride-off and/or backhand an attack may ensue. Therefore it is important to avoid:

1. A useless battle and being stuck in the line-up.

2. Being distracted or diverted before reaching the link position.

In order that arrival at the correct position for both attack and defence is quickly achieved.

No. 4 ready for defence and attack

No. 4 canters in defence, watching the game by looking over his shoulder, ready to shut the door or turn up to join the attack. The latter could involve *playmaking* through initiating the reverse rope or striking any ball that comes out of the back of the line-up, which is a certainty without creating a foul. It is important:

1. Not to follow an attack which will clearly not succeed.
2. Not to allow an opponent to move in front of you.
3. Not to muddle your own No. 3.
4. If *playmaking*, that you are covered by another player.

Hence the back door will initially remain shut for both attack and defence.

Nos. 2 and 3 fit in

It should be relatively easy for Nos. 2 and 3 to fit in to the team between Nos. 1 and 4, in order to control the relevant opponents and be ready to move rapidly to *playmake*. This could include covering No. 4 or filling a vacant link to goal position. However, they must not confuse each other or ignore their relationship to the barrier.

Interchanging Positions

Changing positions with another team member is the most effective way of surprising your opponents, especially if you are *playmaking* to initiate the next play. Not only can you evade your normal marker, but you also will confuse the other opponents if, undetected, you suddenly get possession of the ball in a new position.

The scope for *playmaking* is greatly increased for the receiver of a pass when positions are exchanged. But, to make a success of this tactic, all the components of LATET must be applied as follows:

Look
1. To *locate a team member* who has possession and can pass the ball to you.
2. To *locate open ground* where the pass can be received.
3. To see any *opponents* who could interfere, in order to avoid or engage them.

Adjust
1. By altering *speed* to conform to the length of the pass.
2. By finessing your *distance* from the striker.
3. By changing *direction* towards the open ground well before the ball is struck.

Team
1. Ensuring *no muddle* from another team member doing the same as you are.
2. Checking that you will have *someone behind you to defend* if needed.
3. Identifying to *whom you could pass*, when the ball reaches you.

Engage
1. Any *opponent* who threatens your possession or could be fouled by you.
2. The *line of the ball*, if opponents, while not close, are converging from any direction.
3. Whoever becomes your *next opponent* after the interchange is completed.

Looking to see where the ball is going. Bartolomé Castagnola (10).

Turn
1. To initiate the interchange and to reach the open ground *early and unmarked*.
2. To adjust to any mishit, or to an *unexpected* action.
3. When relevant, to *return behind the barrier*.

Examples of Interchange

In Chapter 17, the reverse rope was explained and specifically related to No. 4 changing positions. In Chapter 11 an alternative version of the diamond demonstrated how Nos. 3 or 4 can cross the barrier, to become No. 2 or even No. 1, whenever the ball is hit across the goal at a hit-in. These two examples cover the two principal forms of interchange as follows:

1. When defence switches to attack, the striker changes places with any player who turns.

2. When in attack, a team member overtakes another in order to receive a pass.

Looking for a possible chance to interchange and playmake. Ellerston v. C.S. Brooks in Cowdray Gold Cup final.

Identifying the playmaker and striker

In both the situations just described, the temporary change from the conventional team line-up should create surprise, which will enable your team to retain possession and increase the goal-scoring possibilities. To describe how these come about and can be executed successfully, we will identify the *playmaker* as P and the striker of the pass as S. P can be No. 2, 3 or 4. S will always be one number lower than P, as relevant, thus either No. 1, 2 or 3.

Defence to attack

When travelling in defence, *P* sees that *S* has won, or is obviously about to win, possession of the ball. *P* then clearly indicates the open ground to where the most desirable pass should be sent. To do this, *P* will normally turn left, in order to be level with or have moved past *S*, who should then hit a pass to *P* with a tail backhand (see Figure 54). *P* has thereby interchanged with *S* to receive the ball with little chance of being hooked, because the opponents should be to the left. Also, if *P* turns left very early, there will be no danger of crossing the line, because the ball will arrive on the offside. But, when the only open ground is to the right, *P* should probably turn right to receive an open backhand from *S*. In this case, *P* must be extra quick, in order to avoid fouling or being hooked.

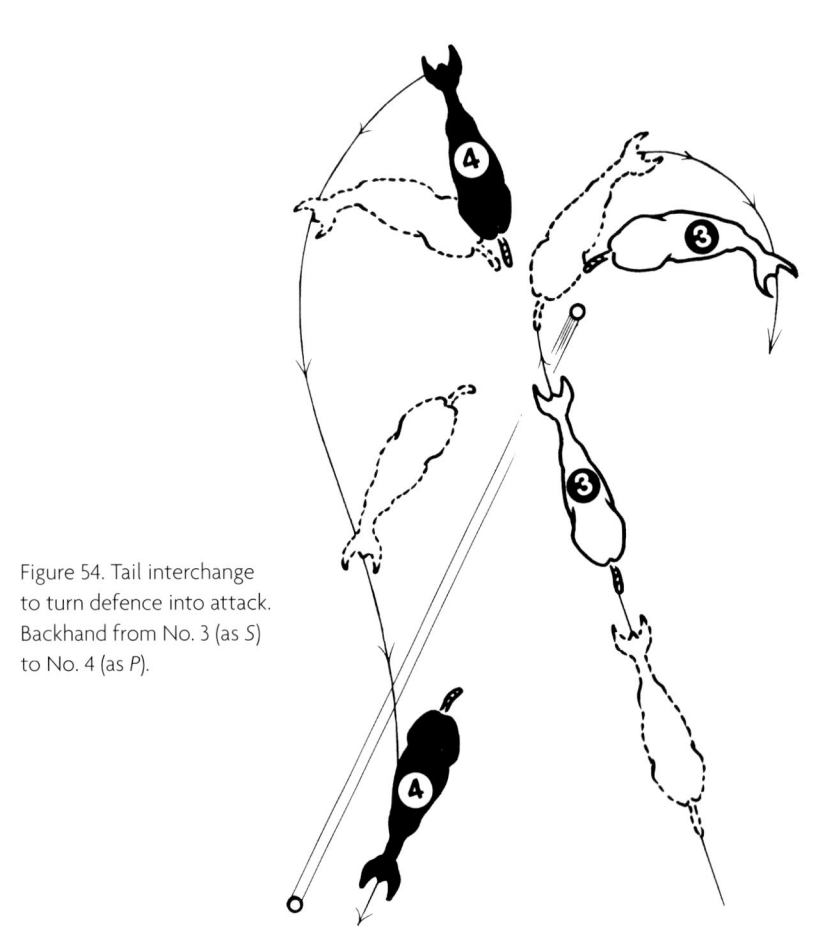

Figure 54. Tail interchange to turn defence into attack. Backhand from No. 3 (as *S*) to No. 4 (as *P*).

Advantage maximized by other team members

To maximize any advantage gained by the interchange, the other two team members (who we shall call *X* and *Y*), must adjust to the actions of *P* and *S*. Ideally, *X* should become the next *playmaker* by moving to a link position, where a pass could be received from *P*. *Y* backs up the attack, on the rope, as described in Chapter 11. Alternatively, both of them back up the attack on the rope, but are prepared to turn to defence when necessary.

Overtaking in attack

When both *P* and *S* are moving in the same direction, the most economical route for *P* to overtake *S* and thus arrive where a pass can be received, is achieved by cutting a corner. Alternatively, it can be achieved by rapid acceleration, but this requires a pony with sufficient speed. However, after too much exertion, even a fast pony can tire before the end of a chukka, and then becomes difficult to control.

In fact, this tactic is simpler to carry out if *S* is moving partly horizontally across the polo field, or is close to the side of the field. Then *P*, going directly towards goal, can overtake without haste, down the middle of the field, to *playmake* clearly, so that *S* knows where to send a pass (see Figure 55). It is important that *P* avoids committing a foul, and this may necessitate engaging in a ride-off or taking a nearside shot. *S* can assist by striking the ball with precision, to give *P* a pass which is easy to receive.

By overtaking your own player, you should confuse the opponents as to whom they have to mark. The actions of *X* and *Y* can add to this, if they adjust to fill the vacant team positions on either side of the barrier. They also have the responsibility to cover defensively, if possession of the ball is lost.

Exercises in Interchanging

When coaching beginners and inexperienced players, I strongly encourage them to verbalize their actions while interchanging. The simplest way to master this is to practise each type of interchange as an exercise, without opposition. As players move to different positions they should call their new number. For example:

No. 2, when *playmaking* to receive from No. 1, shouts 'I'm one'.

No. 3, if cutting a corner to be in front of No. 2, calls 'I'm two'.

No. 4, while moving to interchange with No. 3, says 'I'm three'.

Whether interchanging from defence to attack, or overtaking in attack, commentating on your actions loudly will clearly indicate that you are *playmaking*, while also enabling the rest of your team to understand where they are, in relation to you and the opponents.

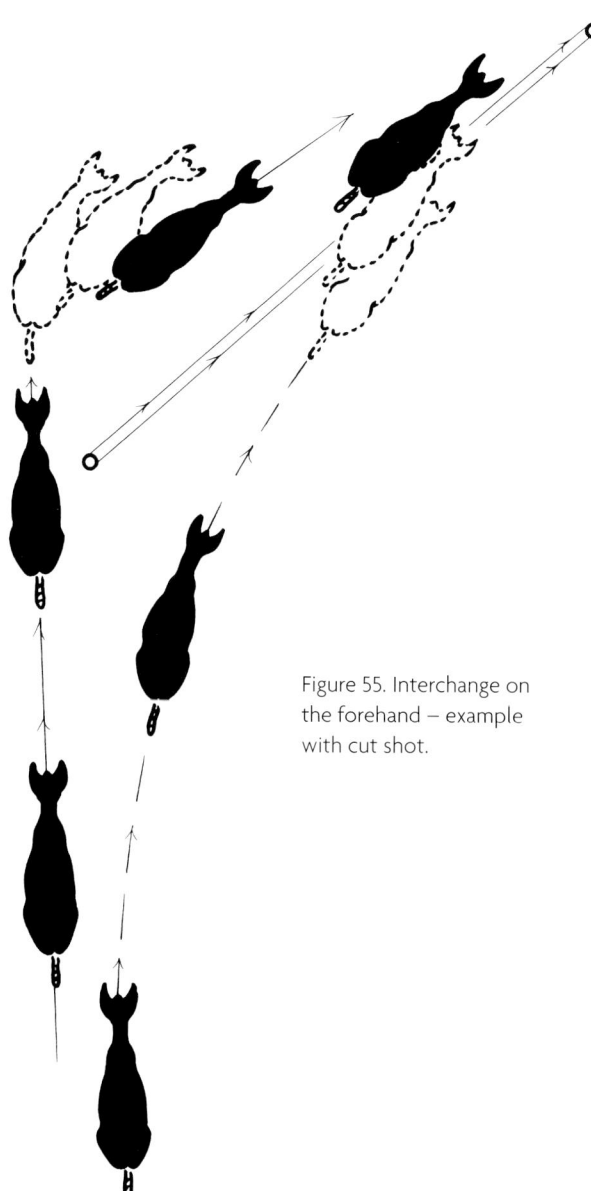

Figure 55. Interchange on the forehand – example with cut shot.

Continual application of LATET will not only help you to see extra opportunities to interchange, but will also assist you to complete the tactic successfully. The more your team interchanges, the harder it will be for the opponents to maintain a secure defence, as long as all the four positions are continually filled by your players.

Recovering Ground

Most people may think that *playmaking* is not related to defence. However, we have already seen that one form of interchange results from a defensive situation that releases a *playmaker* into attack. But, to make this happen, a defender first has to gain possession from opponents in attack, before sending the vital pass. This can be a straightforward action, arising from good anticipation, and may merely involve a backhand, either with or without a ride-off.

But a far more subtle tactic is when the defender, beginning from a disadvantage, *playmakes* via the middle of the field, by going goalward, to regain the initiative at the next play and win the ball with a backhand.

It is even better if this also produces a pass for a second *playmaker*, who has similarly adjusted to receive and be put into attack. Then two of the team will have combined through two acts of *playmaking*.

Sadly, this rarely happens, because of the disparity of standards in most polo teams, which causes the speed of thought to be so varied. Hence, learning the art of recovering ground is essential for all members of a team, both to strengthen defence and to combine when changing defence into attack.

It has to be said that inexperienced players seem to have a problem assimilating the reason for this tactic and putting it into practice. The main reason for this is their desire to chase the ball regardless of all other considerations. Unless strongly disciplined, the influence of the subconscious will overrule the logic of moving to the next play. Hence this is another area in which coaching can prove invaluable.

No. 4 Moves Goalward

In Chapter 17 I explained that, when No. 4s have to turn to defence, in some situations they should retreat directly towards goal, in order to become last again and re-shut the door. This described recovering ground as an action which any No. 4 (who, for the purposes of the following illustrations, we shall call *P*), frequently has to do. Even when moving in defence, as the last player, an opponent *(A)* who is **No. 1**, or who is interchanging to become **No. 1**, can suddenly produce a burst of acceleration to get beyond *P*, before the door can be shut. Then, instead of panicking, *P* should go directly towards goal and *not* anywhere near *A*. No matter how many times *A* hits the ball, *P* must not be distracted from going goalward, until being re-established as last on the field. Then, and only then, the ground has been recovered, and *P* should now change direction to engage *A* as quickly as possible.

If *A* happens to score while *P* is heading for the goal, there is no reason for criticism, because the mistake happened when *A* passed *P*. However, *A* will have felt under pressure and may have rushed, while *P* was recovering ground, and this could have upset *A's* concentration and accuracy. Also, there is a good possibility that the ball will hit *P's* pony instead of going through the goal.

Receiving Pass to Regain Control

This correct method of recovering ground is definitely a form of *playmaking* because, as previously explained, while preventing a goal, an attack can be set in motion by a backhand pass, to threaten the goal at the other end. But a second *playmaker* must, at the same time, be recovering ground in order to be well positioned to receive that pass.

Just as No. 4 applies this tactic to regain control of the opposing No. 1, so:

No. 3 can do the same to the opposing **No. 2**.

No. 2 should use it against the opposing **No. 3**.

No. 1 must do it to mark the opposing **No. 4** after attack changes to defence.

In fact, it can be used by all players at any time. Thereby pony energy can be conserved by going to the next play, instead of arriving negatively at where the ball *had been*.

Historical Examples

Throw-in experiment

In the 1970s, when he played in the Argentine Open, I saw Sinclair Hill, the only resident Australian post-war 10-goal player (since Bob Skene lived in the USA), introduce and experiment with the reverse order line-up for the throw-in. Later, the four famous Heguy brothers also used this when winning the Open and, since then, many teams have at times copied it.

Lucky me

As No. 4 in our family team, for the biggest Dublin tournament, I lined up alongside the opposing **No. 1**. Most of the time it helped me to keep the door shut and only once did I forget to retreat early enough. Luckily for me, an instant attack on our goal missed by inches.

Control

Once, in Dublin, when asked to umpire a friendly game after a tournament final, I agreed on condition that I could control the throw-ins, because I had personally experienced chaos in Dublin chukka throw-ins. After much arguing and one attempt by me to leave the location, my request was acceded to. Hence, at every throw-in, I told the No. 1s to avoid each other, by deciding who went in front and who turned behind the other. They duly did this and always flew upfield quickly, while the No. 4s retreated rapidly. The result was unbelievable, with much flowing polo, and both No. 1s scored three times, shortly after throw-ins, during the four chukkas. *I rest my case.*

Dickie Cernadas

I concluded Chapter 23, about the role of No. 3, by praising the *pivotal playmaking*, in a Dublin tournament, of Dickie Cernadas. I mentioned how his ponies never looked tired. This was clearly because he was supreme at recovering ground and *playmaking* early. As No. 4 behind him, I learnt how effective this interchange could be. In the first game he *playmade* by calling me to receive and in the semi-final we became joint *playmakers*, as I would be approximately level with him as he backhanded. In the final I was so confident in his unselfish play, that I had gone past him well before he hit the ball. The disparity factor had been overcome allowing me, a weaker team member, to *playmake* and interchange with our best player.

Versus Prince Charles

In Chapter 17 I told how, when playing No. 4 against HRH Prince Charles, I turned to defence to compensate for allowing him to escape. I was also describing a good example of recovering ground, but I had applied it to remedy a mistake, whereas a high-goal player controls a game by frequently doing this so early that no one can escape.

Sporting analogies

Good analogies can be taken from other sports. In Rugby, a full back who has been tackled will normally reposition at the back of the game, in the same way described above. The famous Welsh full back, J.P.R. Williams, was outstanding at doing this and was largely responsible for the long era of success that was enjoyed by Wales in international rugby.

Bobby Moore, the soccer captain of England's 1966 World Cup winning team, was described by Pele, the most famous Brazilian player, as being the best defender he ever met. According to Sir Alf Ramsey, the England manager, Bobby Moore was not a fast runner, yet he could appear from nowhere, to take the ball from someone about to shoot at goal. He must have been supreme at recovering ground.

SUMMARY

To be victorious in a polo match, it is necessary to gain possession from most of the throw-ins and set-piece plays, before going to the next play early to control the ball by passing it, with or without using the interchange tactic. Mistakes will happen, but they will not be fatal if the correct adjustment is quickly applied – and this often necessitates recovering ground. Whether in attack or defence, it is more important to calculate *where the next play will take the ball*, than knowing the exact location of the ball at any one moment.

REVISION

Throw-in

When

- **S** — to **S**tart all polo matches.
- **G** — restarting from the centre after a **G**oal is scored.
- **O** — after the ball goes **O**ut over the sideline or the boards.
- **S** — after **S**toppages from injuries, broken tack, buried or broken balls, overruled fouls.

Rules

- **CT** — match started from **C**entre **T** line-up, one behind another, similar to a rugby line out.
- **M** — after going out, ball thrown from sideline into field towards the **M**iddle.
- **S** — after stoppage, ball thrown from where it stopped towards nearest **S**ideline.
- **T** — opposing players may not **T**ouch each other until ball is thrown by umpire.

Format

- **N** — teams traditionally line up in **N**umerical order, but this can and is changed.
- **A** — teams can **A**dapt order to counter known tactics and abilities of opponents.
- **R** — one alternative reverses order to put each player opposite **R**espective opponent.
- **S** — in another alternative, No. 3 stands **S**eparate, while other players block opponents.

Strategy

- **P** — first priority to **P**revent opponents hitting the ball.
- **S** — second priority to **S**pread out quickly in a team rope formation.
- **M** — No.1 **M**oves directly to be link to goal; No. 4 Moves back to shut door ready to *playmake*.
- **B** — Nos. 2 and 3 fit in **B**etween link and the back, controlling relevant opponents.

Interchange

Surprise

- **P** — changing positions to receive the ball is the most surprising way to **P**laymake.

LATET applied

- **L** — **L**ook to ensure possession obtained; find open ground and avoid or control opponents.
- **A** — **A**djust direction, speed and distance from striker to improve possibility of receiving pass.
- **T** — check no duplication of **T**eam positions; *playmaker* covered and second receiver possible.
- **E** — **E**ngage any opponent threatening before or after interchange and be early to line of ball.
- **T** — **T**urn to initiate interchange, to cover mistake or to return behind barrier in defence.

Defence to attack

- **T** — best plan is *playmaker* turns left to receive offside **T**ail backhand from lower number – no line to cross.

O — alternative plan is right turn receiving offside **O**pen backhand – must be quick to avoid fouling or being hooked.

R — most effective with No. 4 *playmaking* as in **R**everse rope tactic, giving depth of all players.

P — can be operated by Nos. 3 and 2 being ***P**laymaker*, but less depth of attack.

Overtaking in attack

C — rapid acceleration or **C**orner cutting by *playmaker* to overtake current team striker.

A — precise **A**ccuracy by striker helps *playmaker* to receive ball to complete attack.

M — aim is to confuse opponents about who **M**arks whom, thereby leaving the *playmaker* free.

V — other two players fill **V**acant positions as required to help attack and keep defence ready.

Execution

C — players verbalize interchanges by **C**alling out new positions, e.g. 'I'm one'.

I — commentating on actions **I**ndicates clearly that *playmaking* is occurring.

T — rest of the **T**eam made aware of where *playmaker* is in relation to them.

O — the more interchanges that occur the more difficult for the **O**pponents to defend.

Recovering ground

D — in defence player compensates for disadvantage by going **D**irect to goal to gain advantage at next play.

R — ideal if another player anticipates this action by adjusting to **R**eceive a backhand.

S — No. 4 should always recover ground if unexpectedly out of position to keep door **S**hut.

G — when opponent keeps possession, defender must continue towards **G**oal until ready to engage.

27

Striking 'G' — Hitting the Ball Further

Striking Principles — Adapting PASSF for Greater Length

Striking Principles

In all the previous chapters on striking, we have discussed the application of PASSF in relation to accuracy for a shot of average length. In those chapters, I emphasized the importance of a slow swing, while explaining that it was easier to achieve this if the correct details of the preparation, approach, finding the spot and following through were applied. To hit the ball further, no change to these *principles* is necessary, but some *details* of PASSF must be altered in order to increase mallet head velocity.

To add length, many people think wrongly that the key is physical strength, and that they should try to hit harder. Instead, you must remember the paradox which explains that, the slower the swing, the faster the mallet head will travel within the circle.

Adapting PASSF for Greater Length

Below, I have outlined how each of the five headings of PASSF may be modified to achieve longer hitting, without employing overt force. Remember, also, that there is no necessity to rush a big hit and, furthermore, a hasty swing upsets the timing of the shot or disturbs the circle. This can be avoided either by preparing *really early*, or never attempting to hit further if it feels wrong to do so during the approach.

Preparation

Lubrication

The thumb and index finger should start a process which 'lubricates' the whole body. Initially, this might only involve rotating the mallet head in a tiny circle above your head. Then, for an offside forehand, the full circle should be described with extra intensity, and more times than usual. For other shots this can be optional.

Height of mallet head

Mentally, you should plan where your hand will place the mallet head in the circle:

1. Before starting the swing.

2. In the middle of the swing.

There is a wide choice between the extreme and minimum modifications, which are explained fully below under the heading Swing.

Time limit

For the moving ball, in fluid play, there is little time to make extra preparation and it is better not to attempt a long strike unless you feel confident that you are ready. At the same time, be aware that extra pony speed, together with correct technique will, themselves, add distance.

Recap

For the dead ball, in a set-piece situation, there is always time for a recap of all the points required to reach the target, especially if it is far away. Doing this will assist muscle memory for moving-ball shots during the rest of the game.

Approach

Pony position

As the ball is struck, the exactness of the pony's position is essential in order that the correct technique for a big hit can be executed. Being too close to, or wide from, the ball will make the execution of the circle and follow through extra difficult and these faults are almost certain to prevent the combination of accuracy and distance.

No deviation

Extra effort to increase distance can cause the pony to deviate before and after the stroke. Hence strong legs must be applied some distance from the ball and then maintained to ensure that the pony does not deviate from the required line. This should also assist in avoiding a change of course after completing the shot in a manner dangerous to others.

Initial hand position

The correct early placing of the hand and mallet is essential, and using the appropriate catchphrase should be helpful. This will give maximum scope for applying any swing modification. For the dead ball, when taking a penalty or in a set-piece play, it will be more effective if you start a good distance from the ball to give yourself time for clarity of thought.

Gonzalito Pieres (8) – mallet head below horizontal.

below Circle and action for hitting the ball further with an open backhand – Adolfo Cambiaso.

Swing

When looking for an increased length of swing, the mallet head should be made to travel further and faster than usual, while the slow hand action is maintained. Much depends on how extravagant your ability allows you to be without upsetting the timing.

The *extreme* technique, which throws economy to the wind, would be:

1. Start the swing, after finding the circle, with the mallet head by your foot.

2. In mid-swing, allow the thumb to drop the mallet head below the horizontal as it points at the target while reaching behind as far as possible with the hand.

The *minimum* increase that might be applied to gain length would be:

1. Start the swing, after finding the circle, with the mallet head above you, but a little in front of the vertical.

2. In the mid-swing, let the thumb drop the mallet head a fraction more than usual as it points at the target, but remaining above the horizontal, while reaching only a couple of inches further behind with the hand than for a normal economical shot.

Thus all players should find and apply a compromise between the extreme and minimum increase, as related to details of both and what suits them, depending on their individual skill. This must be well supported by a strong turn of the shoulders. Thereby, although extra length is obtained, control of accuracy can also be maintained.

Sweet Spot

When the mallet head velocity has been increased, any error in hitting the sweet spot will be magnified. Hence, attention to the exact spot on the ball becomes even more important. Use of the ball clock to pick a precise spot must help. The earlier the spot is selected, the better. This should help you to focus on it at the vital moment of contact, despite the extra mallet head velocity.

Whenever you want to hit further, the subconscious tendency to look up is increased and must be overcome by:

1. Aiming at a point closer than the actual target.

2. Deliberately keeping the head down, with the eyes staying where the spot *was* after contact is made.

3. Verbalizing your actions, especially spot contact.

Follow Through

In all sports, the correct follow through adds distance to any shot and at the same time assists in the maintenance of accuracy.

Control of an extra long polo mallet can easily be lost when seeking a big hit unless the striking technique is correctly completed. By ensuring that it does rotate another 360 degrees after contact, the mallet head velocity will be dissipated. Thus control of accuracy and preparation for the next shot will be achieved.

If the circumference of swing has been considerably increased, then the hand should travel that much higher, after contact through the ball is made, to obtain even further distance. This could be at least to the level of your head, before the thumb and index finger initiate the finishing circle.

Be aware that this extra hand elevation adds to the temptation to look up too soon, which must be avoided. Not only will that effect your focus on the ball but it will also interfere with the thought process for shot completion. Instead, the exactness of the follow through should be controlled by prior briefing and the resultant muscle memory.

SUMMARY

It is more important to strike accurately than far, but if big hitting is achieved through application of the correct technique, it is useful and effective against opponents. This requires a disciplined thought process, which should be based on the ability and experience of each player. Intensive preparation, a careful approach, emphasis on the sweet spot and a full follow through will help. However, the key to success with long shots is the thoughtful control of the mallet head in all parts of the swing, in relation to the standard of each player. Inevitably, problems will be encountered, confidence lost and mistakes made from time to time. The sensible *playmaker* will frequently reassess and look to a good coach to locate any faults, diagnose the reasons for them and rebuild self-confidence. Then, it is essential that ongoing critique is available and that confirmation of the right style, together with praise and encouragement, are received when relevant. The end product should be the confidence to hit further, which is maintained and built upon.

REVISION

Striking principles
W — **W**rong concept that strength is the key.
P — **P**aradox that the slower the swing the faster the mallet head.
D — adaptation of PASSF without **D**isturbing timing or shape of the circle.
R — avoid **R**ushed shot by preparing early or aborting big hit.

Adapting PASSF
Preparation
L — extra intensity of action to **L**ubricate body.
P — think where mallet head will be **P**laced at start and middle of swing.
F — for moving ball in **F**luid play, beware of lack of time.
R — for set-piece dead ball, **R**ebrief to assist muscle memory.
Approach
P — exactness of placing **P**ony to ball is essential.
L — strong **L**egs to prevent pony deviation.

E — **E**arly placing of initial hand and mallet position helped by use of catchphrase.

D — for set piece, start some **D**istance from dead ball to give time for briefing.

Swing

S — **S**low hand still applied in conjunction with faster mallet head.

E — **E**xtreme mallet head arc starts by foot and drops below horizontal in mid-swing.

M — **M**inimum mallet head swing starts just in front of vertical and drops in mid-swing above horizontal.

C — each player must find **C**ompromise of extreme/minimum to suit them.

Sweet spot

E — looking for exact spot avoids **E**xaggerating error.

S — early **S**pot selection improves length and accuracy.

U — prevent looking **U**p before ball contact by using three details of technique.

T — aim at point closer than **T**arget – head down longer – verbalizing.

Follow through

D — correct action adds **D**istance and controls accuracy.

C — **C**ontrol of mallet increased by dissipation through 360 degree rotation.

H — distance added by hand and mallet head extending **H**igher before 360 degree rotation.

U — control temptation to look **U**p by carrying out full brief and implementing muscle memory.

28

Tactics 'H' — Facing the Hit-In

Opponents' Strategy — One on One — The Box — Meeting the Ball — Historical Examples

Opponents' Strategy

We have examined the principle of the rope and the diamond in Chapter 11 and elsewhere. For their hit-in and spot penalties, during matches or chukkas, opponents are likely to employ a similar two-phase strategy, by first spreading out and then converging rapidly to be on a vertical line, like the rope.

Therefore, when facing the hit-in, your team must be able to *cover* phase one and *counter* phase two. Pivoted by No. 3, the aim should be that one of your players gains possession, while at least one other *playmakes*, to receive a pass. There are many different methods of achieving this, and the decision about which one to apply should depend on the quality of the opposition and on their expected tactics. Governed by the disparity of skills factor, the objective should be that, within the capabilities of each person, some part is played by all the team. Defence can be changed to attack by one of these three systems:

1. One on one close marking.

2. The box shape, to put two against one.

3. A formation for meeting the ball.

Whichever system is applied, immediately after the ball has crossed the back line, the players should move *early and quickly* to the pre-planned locations. They can then rest themselves and their ponies, while observing the actions of both teams. Thereby, any surprise is minimized and necessary reactions are prepared for the upcoming hit-in.

One on One

This is the simplest method of countering the opponents' strategy and it is initially explained on the presumption that the opposing **No. 4** takes the hit. Later, variations to this are examined.

In this system, each player of your team is responsible for marking one member of the opposition. Normally, this will be your opposite number so that:

Their		Your
No. 1	is against	No. 4, who waits behind the opponent, ready to ride-off or hook.
No. 2	is against	No. 3, who stands behind the opponent ready to defend or attack.
No. 3	is against	No. 2, who waits behind the thirty-yard line opposite the opponent.
No. 4	is against	No. 1, who waits behind the thirty-yard line opposite the ball.

No. 1 U-turns

The most difficult task, possibly, belongs to your No. 1, who will be thirty yards away from the opponent when the ball is struck, but an advantage can be derived from this situation. Moving forward initially, ready to make a U-turn, will place No. 1 on the inside of the opponent, who is thereby pushed towards the sideline, so No. 1's job of link to goal can be carried out perfectly (see Figure 56). Initially, after a U-turn, the opponent will be marked in defence correctly and then, if your team wins possession, No. 1 can *playmake* in attack to receive a pass near the centre of the field, from where a strike could

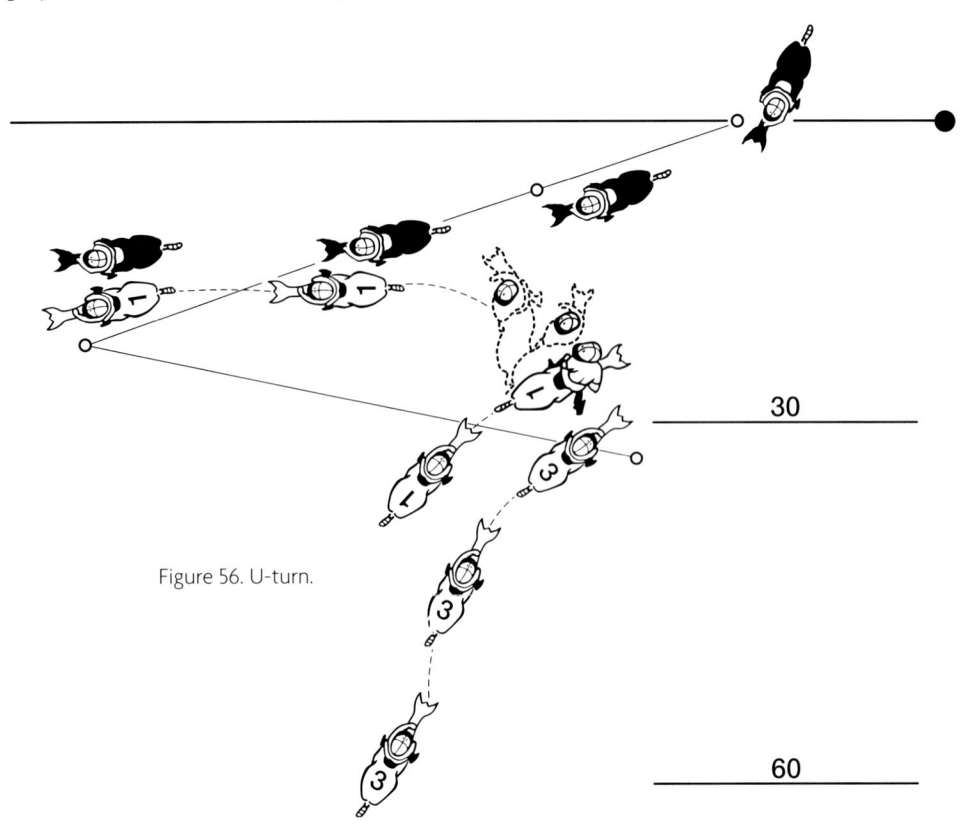

Figure 56. U-turn.

link towards, or shoot at, goal. Also, No. 1 should be well positioned to *playmake* in any of the following different situations:

1. The opposing **No. 4** tries a solo run from the back line. Then No. 1 can *playmake* by riding-off **No. 4**, before striking an angled backhand to another team member, who receives it and shoots at goal (see Figure 56).

2. All the other players compete for and leave the ball loose behind them, after neutralizing each other. Then No. 1 also hits an angled backhand.

3. The opposing **No. 4** hits straight at No. 1, who can *playmake* by meeting the ball, instead of making a U-turn. If No. 1 fails to meet by missing the ball, it might still be possible to make the U-turn, as described above, and then try to hook a stick, or ride-off, as relevant.

Advantage on Inside

Ideally, by waiting behind their relevant opponents, all four players in your team can adjust to be on the inside of them, to gain an advantage, even against stronger opposition. Then, if one of your team strikes a backhand, one of the other players will have a good chance to *playmake* and score from the centre of the field.

Variations

If the opposing **No. 3** takes the hit-in, there are three alternative variations:

1. Your Nos. 1 and 2 stay positioned as above and temporarily No. 1 marks the opposing **No. 3** and your No. 2 is against their **No. 4**.

2. Your Nos. 1 and 2 exchange positions to be still marking their opposite numbers.

3. A three-way change of position, to face the hit-in:
   Their **No. 3** against your No. 3.
   Their **No. 2** against your No. 2.
   Their **No. 4** against your No. 1, but your No. 1 stays marking their No. 4.
   This could be the marking arrangement for the whole game.

The Box

System

This system (see Figure 57) is devised to put two players (*A* and *P*) momentarily against one opponent. Any of the opposition, who try to receive the ball, will have to compete with *A* while *P playmakes*.

The other two team members (*L* and *D*) can move to cover both ends of the *rope*. *L* will become the link to goal, looking for the opportunity to *playmake*: *D* will defend by shutting the door, ready to *playmake* through the *reverse rope*.

Figure 57. Facing the hit-in from the box.

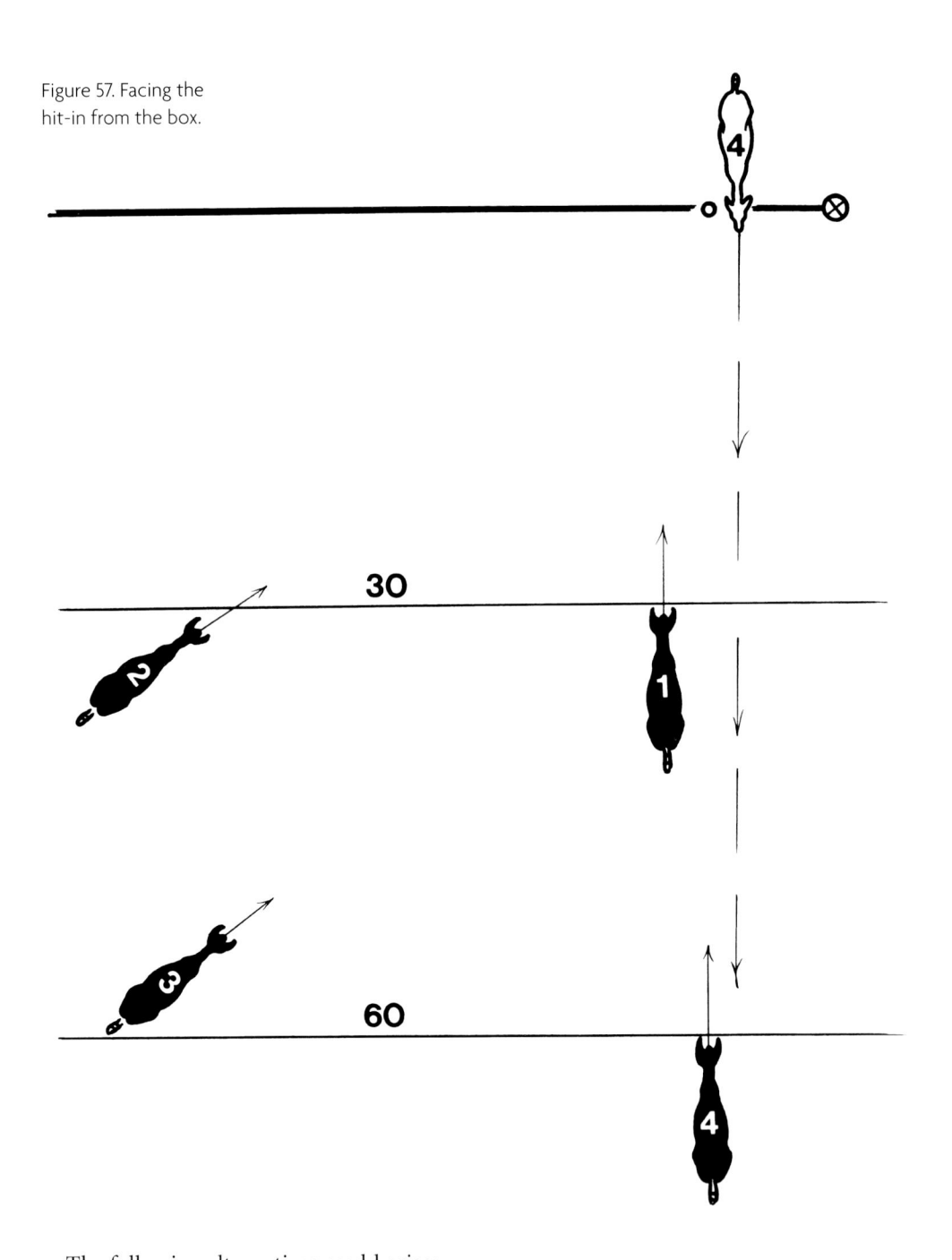

The following alternatives could arise:

1. *A* neutralizes the opponent with a hook or ride-off, while *P* hits the ball towards the goal.

2. *A* rides-off the opponent and backhands to *P*, who hits the ball towards the goal.

Starting Positions

The exact positions of your team will depend on the expected length of strike by the opponent who takes the hit-in. Normally they stand as follows:

No. 1 at the thirty-yard line, near the centre of the field and opposite the ball.

No. 4 should be thirty to forty yards behind No. 1, and a little closer to the centre.

No. 2 can be somewhere between the thirty- and forty-yard lines, near the boards.

No. 3 should be on or near the sixty-yard line, close to the boards.

A, P, L and D Identified

This arrangement is highly flexible and can be adjusted to suit the disparity of skills and other factors. If we assume that the opposing team are in the diamond, as in Figure 36 (page 99), or a similar formation, then each opponent can be covered by *A* and *P* from your players as follows:

When the hit-in is *short*, the lower No. should be *A* and the higher No. should be *P*.

When the hit-in is *long*, the higher No. should be *A* and the lower No. should be *P*.

On the boards side of the box, Nos. 2 and 3 are *A* and *P*, with No. 1 as *L* and No. 4 as *D*.

The side of the box in front of goal, Nos. 1 and 4 are *A* and *P*, with No. 2 as *L* and No. 3 as *D*.

At the back of the box, Nos. 3 and 4 are *A* and *P*, with No. 1 as *L* and No. 2 as *D*.

At the front of the box, Nos. 1 and 2 are *A* and *P*, with No. 4 as *D* and No. 3 a possible *L*.

Discipline

The success of the box depends on good discipline and the application of LATET, to prevent or minimize any muddling as to who is *A*, *P*, *L* and *D*. A definite advantage can be gained, if the team watch and allow No. 3 to exert a pivotal influence. In this way, the question of who takes the role of *A* can be clarified early, while the others complete the rope formation correctly on each occasion. This provides the opportunity for possession to be won from the opponents in either phase of their hit-in, with the possibility of a goal being scored. A sideline coach will be able to assess whether all the players are conforming properly and spot the occasions, if and when they occur, that the tactic is destroyed by a player ball-chasing instead of *playmaking*.

Meeting the Ball

Box Modification

With a small modification to the positioning of each player in the box, the possibilities of your team becoming aggressive when the ball is hit-in can be considerably increased. This adjustment involves No. 3 moving forward and inwards, to be between, and an equal distance from, Nos. 2 and 4, thereby forming an arc (see Figure 58).

PLAYMAKER POLO

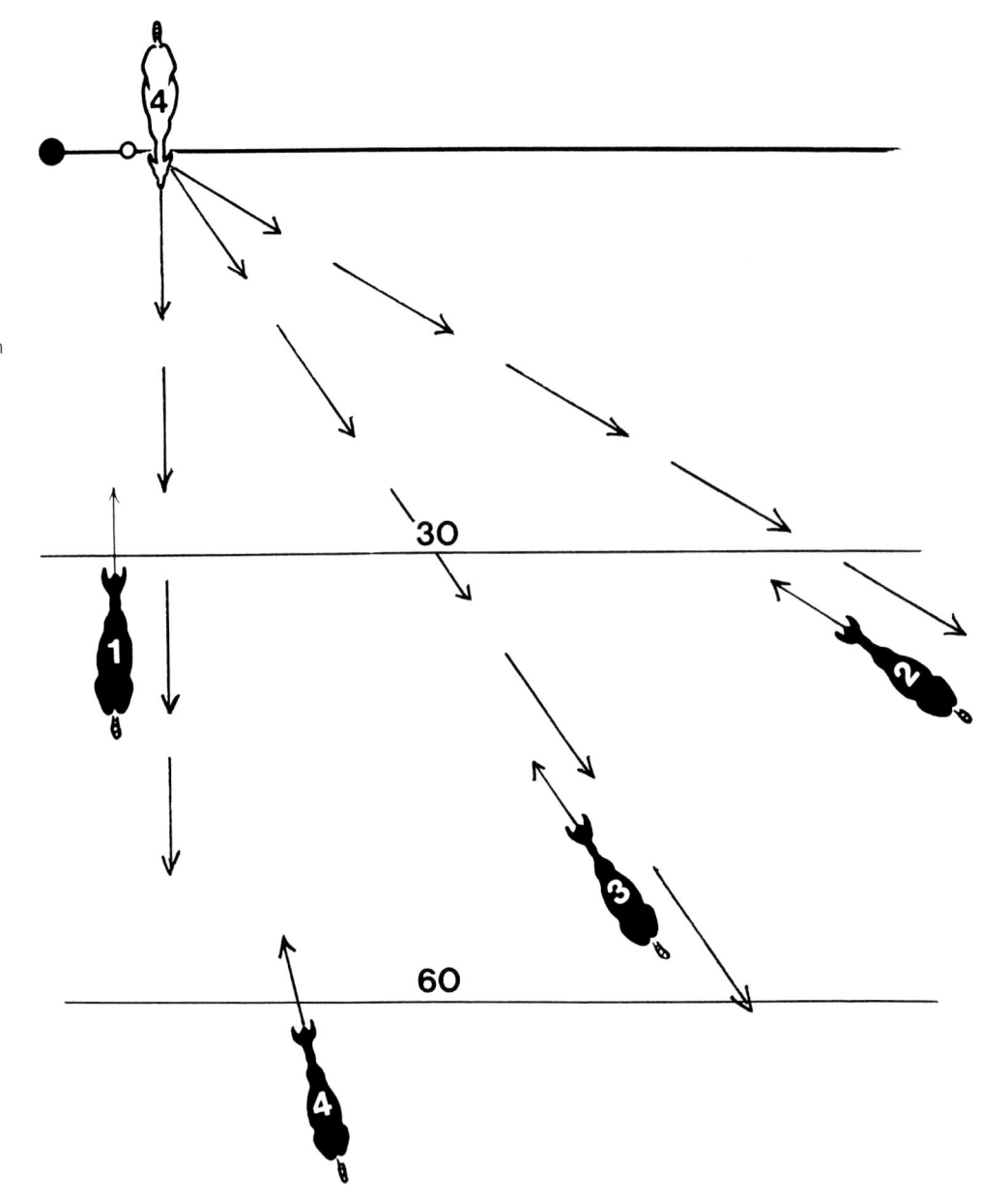

Figure 58. Facing the hit-in with the modification of the box in order to meet the ball when possible.

This produces a system by which all of your team may be able to *playmake* by meeting any hit-in that is travelling in their direction and, at the same time, being covered by at least two other players.

All of your team must watch and adjust to each other continually, to avoid offering an obvious hole through which the ball could be hit.

This tactic is more likely to succeed if the opponents are unaware of the threat.

Lateral Adjustment

A hit-in will seldom come directly to any of your team. But if one of the players moves sideways a small distance, the ball will often come straight to them.

Gonzalito Pieres meeting the ball.

It is important not to advance until you see that the ball can be met without fouling, and it may be better to wait longer or only advance slowly, so that the pace of the ball has reduced when you meet it.

If the ball reaches the arc where Nos. 2, 3 and 4 are placed there will only be a few feet between them, where the ball can arrive and not be met by anyone.

M, X and Y Alternatives

The drill for one of the team (*M*) to meet the ball, with another (*X*) immediately behind to cover *M* and a third player (*Y*) further back, acting as secondary cover behind the barrier, could be any of the following alternatives:

1. *M* is No. 2—*X* is No. 3—*Y* is No. 4.

2. *M* is No. 3—*X* is No. 2—*Y* is No. 4.

3. *M* is No. 4—*X* is No. 3—*Y* is No. 2.

4. *M* is No. 1—*X* is No. 3—*Y* is No. 4.

In examples 1, 2 and 3, normally No. 1 will assist *M*, in front of the barrier, as a link to goal.

In example 4, probably No. 2 will stay in front of the barrier, to back up and assist *M* (No. 1).

The moment that any of your team decide to be *M*, I believe that it will be helpful if they call out loudly 'MEETING' because then:

1. *X* and *Y* receive early warning to cover *M* by moving behind him.

2. The warning does not assist the opponents, who have no time to react, before the meet.

3. An opponent is made aware of a possible collision in time to pull out.

Danger or Threat?

A danger of the meeting tactic is that one or more players may try to do it too often, at inappropriate moments. The result can cause fouls, or the defensive rope to be incomplete.

Also, a team with poor discipline will often move away from their correct positions, leaving holes through which the ball can be hit, giving an advantage to the opponents.

The big advantage is that a well-organized team will directly threaten all opponents at every hit-in and, when a meet is not attempted by anyone, the players can immediately switch to the box or the one on one system.

Historical Examples

Pony Club

Over the years, I have attempted to train individuals and teams in all three of these methods of facing a hit-in. If they are to succeed, they all need consistent discipline by the whole team, and it is difficult to extract this from four people at the same time. The exception was with the Heythrop Pony Club team, who sent me a letter saying how much these and other tactics had helped them to win the British Championships.

Regimental team

In one tournament in Germany, the 10th Hussars team won quite easily, because our No. 1 carried out the U-turn drill to perfection and caused chaos at all the hit-ins taken by our opponents. But this was a rare example of such good application of a tactic, in low-goal polo.

SUMMARY

It is important that your team have a plan for facing the hit-in and that all the players are confident about how to operate it. It could be your own plan, gleaned from watching other teams play. It might be one of, or a mixture of, one on one, the box and meeting the ball. In all cases, it must be flexible, in that the team is prepared to change from one system to another during a match, depending on the tactics used by the opponents. Any of the above plans can also be usefully employed to oppose penalty hits from the spot or the centre.

The moment the ball crosses the back line, or the whistle goes for a penalty, you should keep mobile, because no tactic will work unless your players have moved to their correct positions, to be ready to react quickly to the hit as it happens.

The experience gained from operating all the systems will be reflected beneficially in many fluid moments of play. Opportunities to gain an advantage, or to win a battle for possession, by positioning ahead and on the inside of an opponent, will become more obvious. The ability to meet an oncoming ball will be useful in various situations.

REVISION

General
- **C** — opponents likely to spread out before converging into rope, both phases **C**overed by team.
- **P** — one player gains **P**ossession, another receives pass; method based on quality of opponents.
- **S** — when possible, one of three alternative **S**ystems (one on one, box, meeting) changes defence into attack.
- **O** — as ball crosses back line, players move rapidly into positions to **O**bserve and react quickly.

One on one
- **M** — normal **M**arking No. 4 > opposing **No. 1**; No. 3 > opposing **No. 2**; No. 2 > opposing **No. 3**; No. 1 > opposing **No. 4**.
- **U** — No. 1 starts **U**-turn to find inside of opposing **No. 4**, providing three *playmaking* alternatives.
- **R** — **R**eceiving a pass; **R**iding-off opposing **No. 4** to give a pass; meeting the ball instead of turning.
- **V** — if opposing **No. 3** takes hit-in, **V**ariations could put Nos. 1, 2 or 3 > opposing **No. 3**.

The box
- **S** — No. 2 in front of No. 3 form **S**ide of box next to boards; No. 1 and No. 4 form Side in centre.
- **P** — Nos. 1 and 2 in front with Nos. 3 and 4 at back of box; exact **P**ositions depend on expected strike length.
- **E** — any opponent receiving ball **E**ngaged by two players (*A* and *B*); other two cover link to goal and back door.
- **C** — *A* to ride-off and/or hit backhand; *B* **C**ollects ball to approach goal, pass to link or score.

Meeting

A — box shape **A**djusted by No. 3 moving between Nos. 2 and 4 to form an Arc, leaving no hole.

L — players move **L**aterally if required before going forward to meet ball without fouling.

C — **C**all of 'MEETING' to tell two other adjacent players to go behind as **C**over in case meet fails.

B — team switches to **B**ox system of two marking opponents when it is clear that a meet is not possible.

29

Tactics 'I' — Rules and Penalties

Learning the Rules — Penalties and Tactics — Historical Examples

Learning the Rules

In Chapter 11, I advised you to do the following:

1. Read and discuss the rules.

2. Watch the United States *Blue Book* video.

From these you can gain an understanding of all the rules, fouls and penalties. Yet only after playing under match conditions, and learning from mistakes, will you be able to comply with all these regulations, without having to be guided by other people. The following tips and pointers may help to shorten the time needed to assimilate the necessary knowledge, while you experience the pressure of competing amongst players who have such a disparity of skills.

Ponies and Equipment

The basic requirement is that nobody is put in danger by the behaviour of the pony. Safety must be achieved from good training and the use of correct tack. Sharp edges on shoes or on any equipment are not allowed.

Timing and Duration of Game

The whistle stops the clock when fouls are blown or when it is necessary to cease playing because of injury, broken tack or an unusable ball. The game is restarted by either by a penalty hit or a throw-in.

When the ball goes over the back or sideline, and when there is a goal, the whistle should *not* be blown unless there is a valid reason for a delay of more than a few seconds. A chukka lasts for seven and a half minutes, or finishes at the first stoppage after the seven-minute bell. The length of a match can be four, five, or six chukkas depending on the tournament rules.

Right of Way

Primary and secondary

Remember that the offside has the primary right of way and the nearside only holds the secondary right of way. Therefore, in a match, beware of striking nearside shots against any opponent meeting you from the opposite direction, because you never have the right of way in that situation. But when taking a backhand, with all the opponents behind you, if in any doubt, hit a nearside. This lessens the probability of fouling any opponent who has used superior skill to claim the primary right of way on the offside, before you did.

A quandary for the umpire produced by Sebastian Dawnay's long reach.

TACTICS 'I' – RULES AND PENALTIES

The line of the ball

Every time you play or practise, or even watch a game, you could commentate to yourself, where the line of the ball is. As the ball is struck by a mallet or bounces off a pony you, simply say 'there is the line' while your index finger describes the exact path across the ground. Basically, you will be countering the normal instinct that makes people think that the line runs up and down the field between the goals, or that they can join the line without making a detailed adjustment. Also, any time a pass is sent to you in play and practice, actually say to yourself 'lateral before vertical' and go laterally until you are behind the ball.

Dangerous Play and Fouls

Playing polo is similar to driving a car in the UK, when the right of way is on the left side of the road. This is even better illustrated when there is a solid white line in the middle of the road. If a car either crosses the white line, or threatens to do that, or any other act, which endangers other traffic, the driver can be guilty of breaking the law. On the polo field, the exact route of the ball (line of the ball) is that white line and, in exactly the same way, the players foul if they endanger or threaten opponents with their pony or mallet. The rules list many ways in which riding-off (engaging) and other actions, such as sandwiching (see photograph), can be dangerous. To these rules, umpires have to add common sense and judgement to determine acceptable and unacceptable play.

In the preceding chapters on tactics, I have explained where you should be and what alternative actions you could make at the set-piece plays: the throw-in and the hit-in. Now, we must cover your position and tactics when your team is taking penalties and defending against them.

Brian Mullins in a classic Wexford sandwich, watched by young umpire George Kennedy.

Penalties and Tactics

Penalties can be awarded from the spot, the centre, the sixty-, forty- and thirty-yard lines, or take the form of a penalty goal, followed by a throw-in ten yards from the goal. The umpires decide which one to award using three criteria:

1. Where the foul took place.

2. The direction of play.

3. The severity of the infringement.

Penalty 5

Positioning of players

These penalties are taken from a spot anywhere on the ground, or from the centre of the field. In either case, the rules to be obeyed are the same. The team taking the penalty can be positioned where they wish to be without any restrictions. The team defending has to be at least thirty yards from the ball.

Tactics

The team taking the penalty should be highly flexible with their tactics. They could employ any of their normal hit-in plays, or use one or more other pre-planned ways of gaining surprise, in order to keep possession and try to score a goal. In the majority of polo matches that I have watched, the players have been boringly unenterprising, (see Historical Examples, this chapter), probably excusing themselves with the fact that, as a team, they had had no time to practise anything different.

The team defending must also use flexibility to adjust to:

1. How close the spot is to the goal.

2. The relative strengths of all members of both teams.

3. The expected tactic of the other team.

Probably one of their regular methods of facing the hit-in will be the most effective, because it is well known to them. But, again, a switch to any form of surprise which will wrest possession from the opponents, if pre-planned and suitable to the situation, should be contemplated. Any system must clarify who is marking whom and avoid any confusion over individual responsibilities.

Penalty 4

Positioning of players

This has to be taken from the sixty-yard line in front of the goal. After the first strike, until the ball makes contact with a pony or mallet of the other team, the attackers can

TACTICS 'I' – RULES AND PENALTIES

only use half-shots. This rule was recently introduced to prevent injury to any players in the area of the goalmouth. The team taking the penalty may position anywhere they wish. The defending team has to be not only at least thirty yards from the ball but also behind the thirty-yard line (see Figure 59).

Tactics

The team taking the penalty normally conform to the barrier, in that two players stand either side of the goal, like wings on a jump, and the other two start behind the ball and the barrier. Those at the goalposts are there to try to prevent any ball going wide, and to hit it through the goal. Alternatively, if there is a save and a counter-attack is mounted, they are well placed to mark and defend against the last two opponents. Those behind the ball have the choice of letting one of them try to score with a big hit, or to combine to dribble the ball through the goal. In either case, if they fail to score, they must be ready to defend from behind the barrier against a counter-attack.

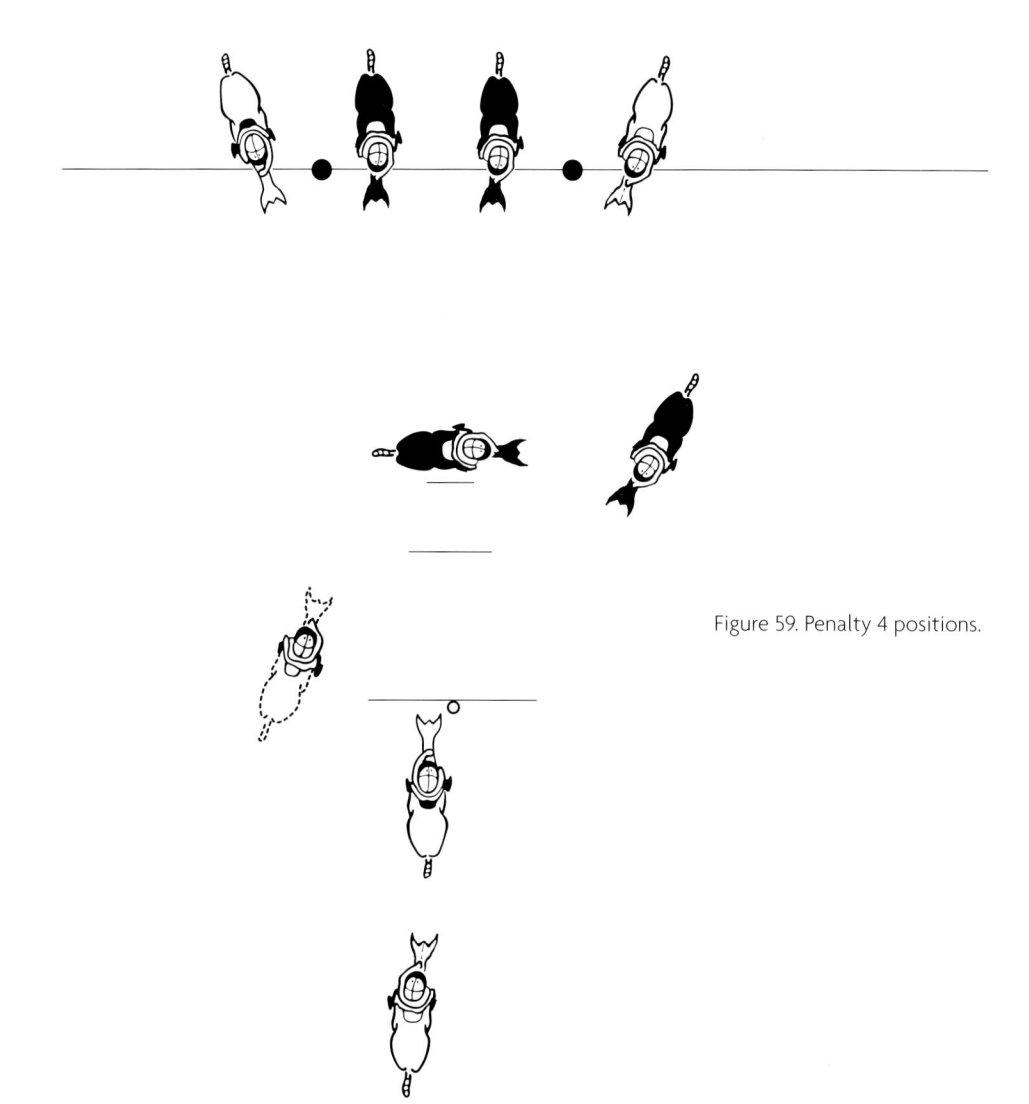

Figure 59. Penalty 4 positions.

Most teams defending the sixty-yard line also apply the barrier, placing two players close to the thirty-yard line, with the other two in the goal. The former have to decide which task to attempt: (a) blocking the big hit, or (b) trying to meet or deal with the deliberate tap. These tasks can be addressed as follows:

(a) By standing nose to tail so that, if the ball deviates to either side, it will give one of them the right of way. But they must move out of the way quickly and only attempt to hit the ball if there is no possibility of crossing the line.

(b) By one of them (X) positioning centrally and the other (Y) about ten yards to the left. Y has the best chance of a meet, and then X can back up the resulting attack. If the tap cannot be met, Y must turn to take on the penalty striker while X goes to mark the opponent who backs up the striker.

Whatever they do, it is important that those near the thirty-yard line do not commit another foul, giving the opponents a thirty-yard penalty, especially if the sixty-yard shot is mishit.

The other team members act like two goalkeepers, either one behind the other, or taking one side of the goal each. I believe that the two goalkeepers are most effective if they take half a goal each and do not move out until there is some clear action for them to take, or they have to move to avoid giving away a penalty goal. I have often seen a defender leave the goalmouth to go towards a ball that is out of reach, and then be stranded and unable to stop the next shot, which scores the goal.

Conversion technique

There is much skill, discipline and practice required to convert a sixty-yard penalty regularly. The whole of PASSF should be applied, and this requires the striker to repeat a set brief every time. At all levels, I have seen players miss because they approached carelessly. Others have ignored the priority of hitting slowly or have forgotten to concentrate on keeping the mallet head in the circle. Also, details like focusing on the exact spot on the ball and aiming at a point much closer to you than the goal itself, such as an opponent on the thirty-yard line, will be very helpful.

Penalties 3 and 2 from Forty and Thirty Yards

Rules and players' positions

The rules for these two penalties are the same, but there are two differences in their application.

1. The placement of the ball (ten yards difference).

2. Only for the thirty, when the foul occurs closer to the goal than thirty yards, can the umpire offer the choice of the penalty being taken from the thirty-yard line, or from where the foul took place.

Adolfo Cambiaso (10) taking a sixty-yard penalty.

All the players of the team taking either of these penalties have to be behind the ball when it is hit. If any player is in front of the ball, a goal scored will be disallowed and the defenders can be given a free hit from the centre of the goal. The team defending has to be behind the goal line, before and until the ball is struck, and the players may not come through the goal at any stage (see Figure 60). The rules explain what happens if a defender crosses the line early. A summary of them is as follows:

If a goal is scored it stands; if the goal is missed the penalty is taken again.

If the ball is blocked on its way to go through the goal, it counts as a goal.

Under HPA rules, as for the sixty-yard penalty, after the first strike only half-shots can be used. Under USPA rules, the striker has only *one shot* against an undefended goal. If the

Figure 60. Positions for penalties 3 and 2.

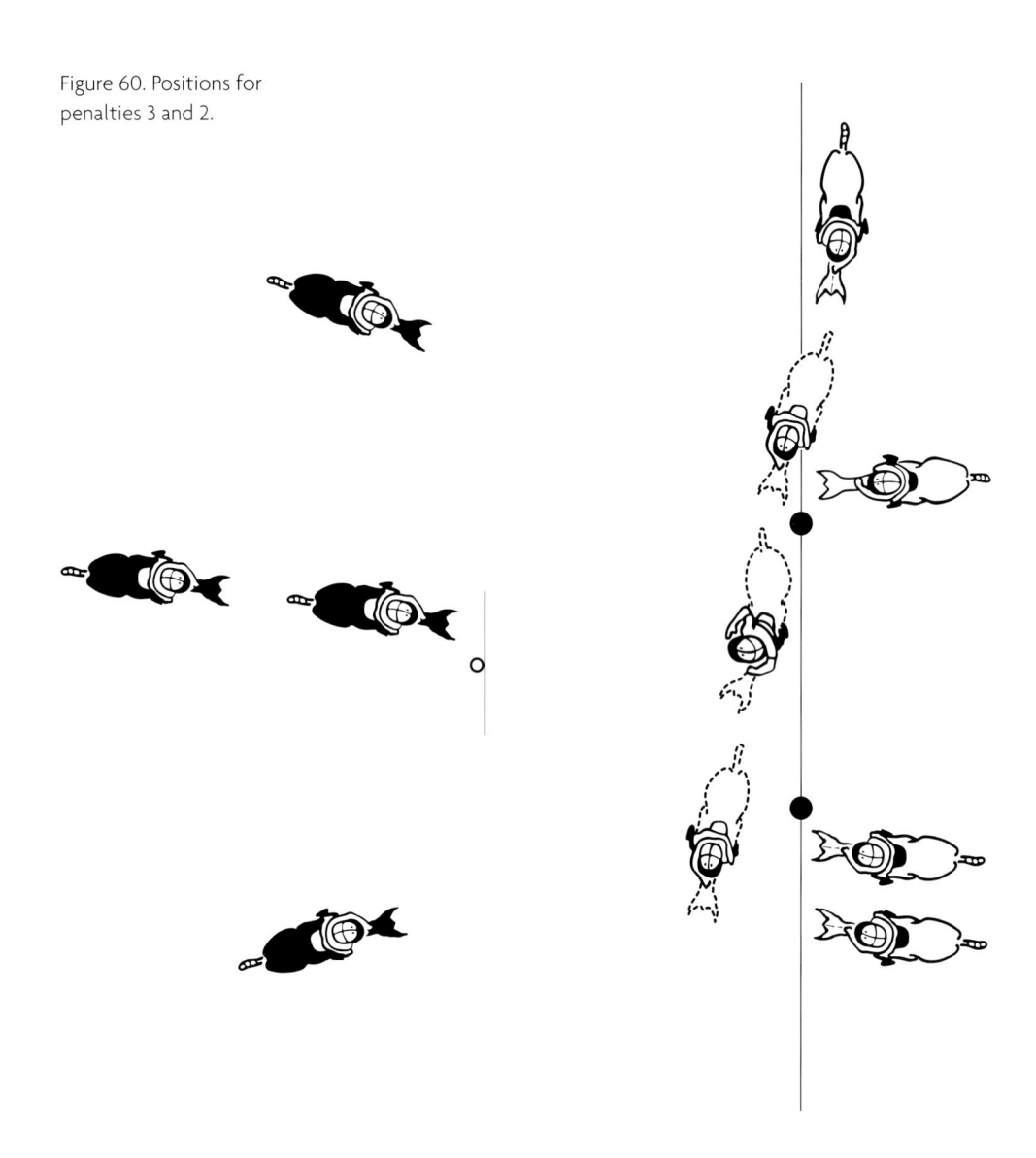

ball fails to reach the goal or goal line, the defenders have a free hit from the spot where the ball stopped.

Tactics

When the goal is defended, the penalty takers should plan and cover for defence as well as attack. I have seen a well struck thirty-yard penalty intercepted, to be followed by a goal being scored at the far end. Therefore, the barrier should again be applied, with the striker and the player backing up taking over the responsibilities of Nos. 1 and 2. Then the other two players stand still, behind and on either side of the ball, temporarily becoming Nos. 3 and 4, ready to cut off the counter-attack after an interception.

The defending team's aim is to attempt to block the ball from crossing the goal line. There are many alternative ways of doing this, which can vary from all crossing the back line outside the goal at the same time, to the conventional method, using two players converging at right angles to each other. Any of these methods is dangerous if not well co-ordinated and highly disciplined because, besides the possibility of colliding with any opponent following the ball, there is a bigger likelihood of knocking each other down.

Conventional defence

Whichever defence plan you operate, a quick team briefing before the game will help to prevent muddles, unless you decide on the conventional method. In this case, all the players should know the exact drill and the only instruction required from the team captain is who fills which place around the goal. The four places and their jobs are:

A, who stands outside the right goalpost with the task of calling 'Missing', if relevant.

B, who is the second of two players outside the left goalpost, also calling 'Missing'.

M, who is between *B* and the left goalpost, can try to meet the ball but only as stage 2.

I, who tries in stage 1 to intercept by crossing the goal at right angles to *B*.

Depending on how far from the ball the striker's approach starts, I initially positions between ten and thirty yards from the right goalpost, before moving behind the goal line in order to cross it as the ball is hit.

M's motto should be 'It is better to let them score than to risk death' (see personal experience in Historical Examples, later this chapter). To abide by this, *M* must watch *I's* movements carefully, and only start to put stage 2 into action:

(a) After *I* has crossed the goal, or if *I* has stopped before passing the right goalpost.

(b) If there is no possibility of endangering an opponent who has the right of way.

If either *I* or *M* is successful and achieves possession, *A* and *B* must back up the resulting counter-attack, but stay behind the barrier ready to adjust to defend again.

Conversion technique

The striker of a thirty-yard penalty has to beware of overconfidence, because this should be easy to convert – yet many of the better players, including some with a 10 handicap, have been known to miss the goal. The cause can be hitting too hard, or a bad approach. I believe that both of these faults should be minimized by two actions:

1. Starting from a long way behind the ball, even if the approach is taken slowly.

2. Reinforcing every detail of PASSF, especially the slow swing, in the brief to yourself, to ensure that you apply them during the shot.

For a forty-yard penalty, the extra ten yards obviously makes an interception that much easier, and this increases the pressure and, with it, the temptation to over-hit. To overcome this, your brief should remind you to include a full follow through after the slow swing. Without upsetting accuracy this thought tends to add extra velocity, that is harder to stop.

I have watched in dismay as opponents using this conventional method have saved my penalty shots on a few occasions. But, even more times, I have enjoyed being the interceptor despite one experience of being knocked down (see Historical Examples, later this chapter).

Penalty 1

This consists of a penalty goal followed by a throw-in ten yards in front of goal. It should be awarded when, in the area close to the goal, a defender deliberately or dangerously fouls to prevent a goal from being scored.

Too many umpires are reticent about awarding a penalty 1. This is unfortunate because, without this deterrent, there is an extra dimension of danger.

This is the only time in outdoor polo, played on grass, that teams do not change ends after a goal. Instead, they line up for a throw-in ten yards from the centre of the goal, with the attacking team on the right and the defenders on the left.

It is important that the umpires ensure that the goal has been added onto the scoreboard, before throwing-in, so that there is no possibility of confusion amongst the players, officials and spectators.

The players should always be aware that a penalty 1 can give the opponents two goals and, instead of risking this, it must be preferable to pull out of a foul, to allow a goal to be scored. Then, they can return to the centre field, where they will be half a polo field closer to scoring a goal themselves.

Historical Examples

Joe Barry

Once, in Palm Beach, Florida, in a Sunday 22-goal polo match, I saw Joe Barry, possibly the highest hitting player of all time, have a day when, for some strange reason, every shot he made stayed at ground level (otherwise described as 'worm-burners' by some American commentators). From three penalty 5s struck by Joe, the ball went via two other players through the goal. On previous days, his high-soaring penalty 5s seldom scored because, by the time the ball landed, his team members had lost all velocity and were easy to mark and dispossess. The next time Joe's team played, I was fascinated to see if the point had been taken or lost, but sadly the high explosive shells were again landing harmlessly near the goal. Ironically, Joe later became a very successful coach, and must have learnt much from that experience.

Video lesson

Also at Palm Beach one winter, during each week of my polo clinics, I showed the same video of a high-goal game. After seven weeks of watching it, I realized that one of the goals scored in that match came about after two drastic mishits, which ended with the ball going towards the corner flag. It was then backhanded to the goalmouth, from where it was tapped through the goal. I thought 'That would be a fantastic tactic if it was done on purpose', and I took the idea to a team I was helping. Sadly, they were frightened of trying it and, in the next game, all the penalty 5s were hit high and long and failed to score. They lost the match.

Personal experience

When defending a thirty-yard penalty, I have been crashed into by a team-mate who, in the excitement, had lost his head and I was lucky not to be badly injured. I have also seen many near misses, and have been told about one death from a similar accident in American polo.

As an umpire in Rome, I once separated two opposing players who were hitting each other with polo mallets after a similar incident, but they then dismounted and continued the fight with fists.

SUMMARY

You will feel more comfortable and have greater enjoyment from polo matches, once you no longer need to be guided by other players when a penalty is awarded. You must therefore learn where to be and what to do for all the penalties, in the many different situations. Added to this, if you understand everything that constitutes a foul and how to avoid committing them, you will cease to be the cause of many penalties against your team.

If you want to remain sane throughout your polo career, you have to accept that there are different interpretations of the rules, and of what is deemed to be a foul. Sometimes these interpretations work in your favour and, on other occasions, they work against you. It is also important to realize that an umpire who is correctly positioned can see where the line of the ball is very much better than can a player who is competing for the ball. At the same time, it not possible for an umpire who does not keep up with the game to see the line, or any dirty tricks that are used.

REVISION

General rules

L — learn to distinguish exact line of ball, then go **L**ateral to line before vertical behind it.

G — counter instinctive idea that line is from **G**oal to **G**oal or directly from you to where ball is.

W — line of ball same as **W**hite line on road, where it is mandatory to drive on left.

O — primary right of way on pony's **O**ffside and secondary right of way on pony's nearside.

M — do not **M**eet opponent on nearside but, if doubtful, take nearside backhands so as not to foul.

Penalty 5

R — under penalty 5 there are no **R**estrictions for attackers; defenders to be at least thirty yards from ball.

H — attackers employ a **H**it-in drill or a rehearsed tactic as a surprise.

F — defenders **F**lexible to cover close to goal, depending on opponent's tactic and players' relative strengths.

P — always clarify who marks whom and try to see suitable situation for **P**re-planned surprise.

Penalty 4

R — penalty 4, from sixty yards; defenders must be behind thirty-yard line and attackers have no **R**estrictions.

D — two **D**efenders in goalmouth and two near thirty-yard line, head to tail or one meeting a tap.

A — two **A**ttackers like wings on the goal and two behind ball and barrier for big hit or dribble.

H — after first shot only **H**alf-shots allowed, disciplined skill by applying PASSF required.

Penalties 2 and 3

A — penalties 2 and 3 from thirty and forty yards, all **A**ttackers behind ball, two behind barrier.

O — defenders from behind and **O**utside goal can cross line as ball is struck to intimidate opponents.

R — penalty **R**etaken if defender crosses early, and goal awarded if ball would have scored.

D — two attackers strike and back up penalty hit and two stay behind barrier to **D**efend.

Penalty 1

D — penalty 1 given for a **D**eliberate or **D**angerous foul committed close to goalmouth.

T — goal given, followed by **T**hrow-in ten yards in front of goal; attackers receive ball on right.

E — only occasion in outdoor polo when **E**nds are not changed after a goal is scored.

C — better to pull out of fouling to allow goal and return to **C**entre halfway from a goal.

30

Tactics 'J' — Team Play

General Concepts — Pre-match Preparation — Patron's Role — Position and Marking — Team Discipline — Historical Examples

The best results in polo matches are achieved by teams that have a special understanding between all their players. Not only do they all know what is expected of them in their own positions, for set-piece situations and when covering each other while interchanging during fluid play, but they also combine well through *playmaking* in many different ways.

A good relationship between players can be improved by constructive planning. Pre-match preparation, in which all relevant details are discussed, has to help a team. This is even more effective if coaching is extended into team practice sessions. An attempt to remove, or at least reduce, team weaknesses ought to be made and, if there is a team patron, he will normally have a role in these matters. Furthermore, respect for the man paying the bills can help to instil good discipline, covering sporting behaviour and the manner in which players carry out set-piece plays.

General Concepts

Co-operation by all four players can make the concept that the ball does more work than the ponies (see Figures 1 and 2 in Chapter 1) into a reality. This will be easier to achieve if players know what length of shot to expect, and between them they are always in reach of short, average and long passes.

Where possible, two players should try to provide options for a striker, by *playmaking* in two different areas at the same moment. This will be even more effective, if a fourth player is also involved at that time. For example, when A has the ball, B and C could move to separate places in open ground to receive, while D moves between them, ready to go laterally into space, in either direction. This makes it easy for another pass to be collected by D from either B or C and creates the possibility of D receiving directly from *A*. In this way, all four players can have a role at the same time, and the necessity to make the pony race for goal is replaced by the velocity of the ball. Hence there is more time for a slow swing, which results in accurate striking.

Defence can be maintained by either *B* or *C* – whoever does not receive from *A* – adjusting to be behind the barrier with *A* as No. 3 or 4, in conjunction with the positioning of the others. Alternatively, *D* could opt for the defensive role, while *B* and *C* combine in front of the barrier.

On some occasions, in order to win a match, a player has to place the team first, in front of self, by taking on a task that has no glory, or by changing positions in order to counter a known tactic of the opponents. Often this will involve *hidden playmaking*, as previously mentioned. This includes riding-off an opponent in the 75% in order to allow another team member to keep the ball for several hits (see Figure 61).

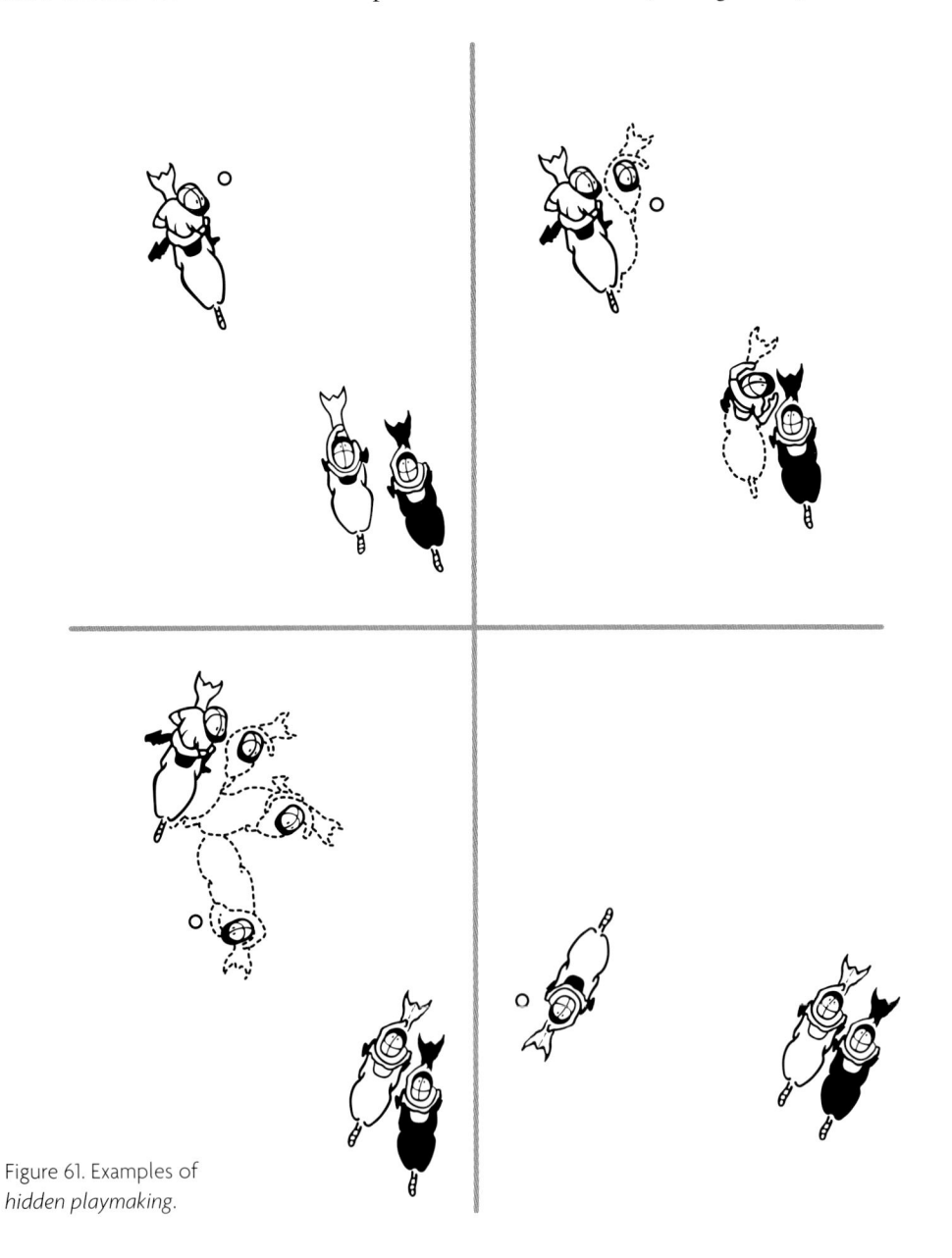

Figure 61. Examples of *hidden playmaking*.

Ride-off in the 75%.

Pre-match Preparation

There are distinctly different opinions as to how much pre-match preparation should be done. Some people argue that too many plans produce confusion, but clearly if no thought is given to how to combine, chaos can easily ensue.

Time will be saved by agreeing a regular pre-match agenda that examines:

1. Relative strengths of both teams.
2. Strong and weak points about each player.
3. Order of play for ponies. Inside information about the opponents' ponies, if obtainable, will assist here, but otherwise it is important not to allow all the players in a team to ride their weakest link, if there is one, in the same chukka.
4. Code words for set-piece tactics. It is even better if these are practised beforehand.
5. Marking arrangements for defence plans, with possible alternatives.

Practice Sessions

Team practice sessions are normally carried out in chukkas against organized strong opposition. There could also be practice sessions without opposition, which include all the set-piece situations and penalties. However, the problems of bringing all the players and ponies together on yet another day seem to be difficult to overcome, and it seldom happens. But, if it is possible to organize a place and time for constructive practice, the benefits outweigh the inconvenience and the instigator will have been a valuable *playmaker*, away from the polo field.

Coaching Contributions

All types of practice should produce better results if they are attended by a coach who can make the following contributions:

1. Assess and mix players of different technical abilities and powers of anticipation.

2. Prevent team friction, which can be caused by blame of one player by another being bandied about without recourse to an independent observer.

3. Compliment and advise on pony control in relation to the carrying out of tactics.

4. Provide a constant revision of the discipline of the striking technique.

5. Suggest improvement of *playmaking* roles and introduce new ideas for them.

Without coaching assistance, a high-handicap player is prone to expect others to have his ability and reactions. The whole team then suffers and his own play deteriorates considerably, because he cannot assess others while producing his best anticipation and tactical hitting. However, a non-playing coach can concentrate fully on the actions of all team members without such distractions. It must be a false economy to play without a coach and, with a little thought, a way can surely be found to include this facility within the team's budget. Coaches, like players, need experience and it should be noted that there are a number of potentially good coaches who have done the work to become qualified, but have less experience than they would like of team coaching, simply because it is seldom requested. In these circumstances, some very capable people may agree to work for a small fee, or it may even be possible to make some kind of mutually beneficial arrangement, such as coaching in return for stabling, transport, etc. As mentioned earlier, arrangements of this nature can constitute a very successful form of *playmaking* off the field.

Finally, it should be noted that many teams have sponsors and it could be beneficial for them as well as the teams, if they encouraged the employment of an independent adviser. Most other sports gain much respect from the coaching dimension and this is confirmed by the fact that it is highlighted in various ways, including interviews by the media.

Patron's Role

Where a patron is involved as a team member, his general attitude and the relationship between him and the other players can affect the cohesion of the team enormously. Without a patron, it is a difficult to have a team, because of the costs involved. Yet many teams play as if the patron is more like a spectator than a competitor.

A professional player will often cover two positions, thereby doing much of the job belonging to the patron's position. This prevents valuable involvement and the improvement that can be gained from a small degree of real participation – although simply experiencing the extra speed of fast polo may be of some benefit.

However, much of this situation is often self-inflicted by a patron who exhorts his team to win at any cost, with the result that the better players try to do too much, in the false belief that this is the way to gain a victory.

Surely it would be more constructive if the patron exercised greater control through employing a coach, who could organize rehearsals of situations in which the patron could play a part, however small. Furthermore, there could be a plan for the professionals to combine in such a way that the patron is protected and used at appropriate times to give one constructive pass. To do this, one player could clear away the closest opposition, while another positions himself to make it easy for the patron to send a simple pass that can be received.

Positions and Marking

Normally, teams are assembled with each player in the position that he prefers to play. Except in the best standard of polo, the lowest handicap is normally put in the No. 1 position. Some teams are sensible and adjust their line-up to that of the opposition, so that the weakest members of both teams are against each other. This demands that at least two players be briefed for the dual roles of Nos. 1 and 4.

One decision, which should be made before each game, is whether marking will be done through the system of counting heads (taking the nearest relevant opponent) or, alternatively, that each player tries to stay continually with the same person. Both systems can involve frequent interchanging, but this must include a continual awareness of which positions you have changed to. However, when the No. 3s are by far the two best players on the field, they often mark each other for much of the game, yet remain as the pivots behind their barriers at all significant times.

Team Discipline

The sporting behaviour of the players in relation to winning, losing and various umpiring decisions can have a decisive effect on the result. Any time a player loses self-discipline in one of these situations, the team is weakened and confidence is eroded.

In addition to its role in the context of sportsmanship, discipline is also important in tactical terms, especially in maintaining preparedness to counter unexpected actions by the opponents. Examples of the need for tactical discipline are given below.

Rapid Relocation

Many players are unaware of the importance of reacting quickly, when the ball goes out over the back line or sideline, or a foul has been blown. When the whistle blows or the ball goes out of play, the majority of players automatically stop where they are, to take a deep breath and relax temporarily. However, a much better discipline is to keep moving, until you arrive in the expected new location of the ensuing set piece.

Then, while breathing and relaxing, you can watch and take in what all the other players are doing, in preparation for marking an opponent or *playmaking* to receive the ball – or even combining the two actions. At the same time, any signals or code words for initiating a strategy can be sent and understood, so that the required tactic can be implemented.

Rather than being caught flat-footed, this will assist in achieving the vital dimension of mobility at a set piece. Moving before the ball is struck at a hit-in or a penalty from the spot is ten times better than remaining static to watch where the ball goes. In attack, this is essential for keeping possession and, in defence, it can be necessary to counter the speed of the opponents. However, this discipline can so easily be forgotten, and all players and teams require constant reminders.

Countering Surprise Moves

When the opposition are taking a hit-in or penalty, the aim should be to prevent them from springing a surprise move while, at the same time, covering the expected. The vigilance required can only be achieved by prompt positioning and careful observation of what all the other seven players are doing.

Historical Examples

Deauville

In 1993, when I was *'Capitan de Jeu'* at the annual August tournament in Deauville, France, professionals from *all* the teams told me that the patron was *not* in their plans. At the same event, a massively wealthy American patron told me that it was impossible for him to hit well, when he received the ball so seldom.

Palm Beach

At Palm Beach, where the costs of entering a team are probably the highest in the world, I continually noticed that patrons who hit an occasional ball would then hurtle after it with their mallet waving like a fishing rod, in an unbalanced manner, which gave them no chance of a second strike. This uncontrolled excitement, which ruined their technique, was clearly the result of no guidance coupled with ball starvation.

Argentina

In Argentina I once watched an 18-goal team play in a tournament, and noticed that they stood still at the hit-ins. At half-time, the team was only leading by 1 goal. I took the courage to tell the players that perhaps they should be more mobile before the ball was hit. They accepted this and corrected the fault and then won the match by 6 goals.

Cowdray

In a Gold Cup match I watched Gonzalo Pieres (10) mark Carlos Gracida (10) at all the set-piece situations. When Carlos took a hit and tried for a second shot he was frequently robbed of the ball. This was a classic example of No. 3s opposing each other.

Royal Berkshire

I was asked by a lady, whom I had coached many years ago, to drop in and watch her play in a 12-goal tournament at the Berkshire. At the end of the chukka, her team was 3 goals behind. I suggested that her 6-goal player should switch to marking the best opponent, who had the same handicap, and her team then won the match. The opposition had no idea that this had happened and, after the game, invited me to have some involvement with their 15-goal team!

Sotogrande 2003

That year, I enjoyed watching the final of the 20-goal Sotogrande Gold Cup. There was some brilliant play for the winners by Miguel Astrada, the newest 10-goal player in the world. He frequently protected his 8-goal No. 2 by engaging opponents so that his teammate was left free to score. His patron also played an effective part in the victory. It was a delight to see such unselfish play by a new polo star and he was duly given the most valuable player award.

SUMMARY

Polo is a glorious team game, which gives incredible scope for tactical co-ordination by using the speed of the ball through *playmaking*. But this can be destroyed by selfish players, who try to win through individual skill and the speed of their ponies. These problems are exacerbated by the difficulties encountered in arranging the time and place for practising together, and by the lack of coaching.

Team play requires good discipline, which could be greatly improved by more coaching involvement. If the standard of the patron were raised, then all four players could participate in mobile open play for attack, while maintaining a solid defence.

Clear planning for marking, together with a definite intent to *playmake* where possible, will give any team an advantage over opponents who are not so well prepared.

REVISION

Concept of play
- **U** — special **U**nderstanding of positions, set-piece play, covering, interchange, *playmaking*.
- **B** — **B**all works harder than ponies; control of length of shot; player in reach of weak hit.
- **R** — ideally, two *playmakers* give options from different places to **R**eceive passes.
- **N** — fourth player *playmakes* to receive in the **N**ext play, or to cover the defence.

Preparation

S — examine relative **S**trengths both teams; strong and weak points of own players.

O — plan ponies' **O**rder of play; obtain information on opponents' ponies; separate weakest links.

T — codewords and signals for specific **T**actics and change of plans.

M — defence system, **M**arking arrangements with alternative plan, 'no glory' role.

Practice and coaching

N — chukkas against good opponents assisted by practice with **N**o opponents if own players available.

M — coach **M**ixes abilities, prevents friction, helps pony control to execute tactics and striking.

P — set-piece rehearsals to revise, improve and extend ***P**laymaking* roles with new tactics.

R — high-goal players wrongly expect equal skills from others; coach brings **R**espect; needs experience.

Patron's role

F — no patron, no **F**inance; must not be spectator but give team spirit through own attitude.

I — professional to allow patron to **I**mprove by participation, plus benefit of fast polo.

W — excitement controlled, no 'fishing rod' before second shot and **W**in priority not inflicted.

P — rehearsal can give patron a small **P**art; could be **P**rotected receiving and giving passes.

Team discipline

C — good behaviour and self-discipline help **C**onfidence and team results.

N — when ball goes out, all move to **N**ext position where they relax and plan marking.

M — codes and signals before set piece; **M**obility for possession and countering opponents' speed.

S — prompt positioning to observe and face opponents' hits to cover both the expected and **S**urprises.

Positioning and marking

P — players normally in favourite **P**ositions, lowest handicap No. 1 except in high-goal.

W — some teams put **W**eakest against each other, this requires two players both briefed as Nos. 1 and 4.

D — marking **D**ecision needed; whether to count heads or stay mainly with same opponent.

B — often **B**est players mark each other, although mainly pivoting from behind the barrier.

31

Tactics 'K' — How to Beat a Better Team

Match-winning Components — Tactics against Superior Opposition — Historical Examples

Match-winning Components

Polo matches have been won over the years in many different ways. Team play that allows all four players to contribute, within their abilities, to planned tactics (including tight marking) is the most likely to succeed.

A system which positions all of your players against opponents whom they are able to control, and away from those who would be too strong for them, has to be effective. Also, if the outstanding opponent is neutralized, or greatly restricted, by one unselfish member of your team, the probability of defeating the opposition is increased.

The possession of fast and easy ponies, which give your players an advantage over all the opponents, will be an enormous help to any team in executing good tactics.

The total domination of the polo field by your best player may, on some occasions, produce a winning formula. But, of itself, this is negative polo, which prevents the other players from developing their games and, if that one player has an off day, or the opposition find a way to upset his confidence, the result will be disastrous.

Tactics Against Superior Opposition

On occasions, your team may have to play against opponents who are obviously superior in every dimension of polo, including pony power, and clearly none of the standard plans or systems would have any effect whatsoever. In this case, the only tactic that may, in some way, counterbalance the difference in abilities, is to slow down the game by keeping the ball on the outside of the field as much as possible.

The other team will be quicker than you in anticipation, at the gallop, and when adjusting to deviations and mistakes. However, this big advantage can be significantly reduced if you make the pace of play slower than they are expecting or are accustomed to, and prevent them from attacking down the middle of the field.

It will be even more effective if the opposing players become confused by not realizing what is happening, while your players understand the tactics and can react earlier than them to the different strategy. The opponents are less likely to recognize the change from normal tactics if a combination of ways to reduce the speed of play are employed and, hopefully, they may fail to adjust to these, which can include the following:

1. Use of widely angled backhands, the majority hit towards the sideline.

2. Persistent engaging of all opponents.

3. Changing the direction of play.

Wide-Angled Backhands

Reason for altering the angle

In any circumstances, when in possession and defending, it is normally disastrous to strike a straight backhand, because it is difficult for anyone in your team to receive it, as a pass, and it will be easy for the opposition to meet the ball. Hence the reason for hitting the angled tail or open backhand, in most situations.

But, against a superior opposition, the normally angled shot will not succeed. They will either anticipate, in order to meet the angled backhand, or arrive first on the line of that shot, to strike a return backhand. However, if the angle is *increased*, to be close to 90 degrees, it will be difficult for any opponent to interfere without fouling. If they do manage to regain possession, they will have lost the momentum that is needed to make a quick attack, and the game will be successfully slowed down.

Backhands to the side

This tactic is intended to keep the ball away from the centre field. Ideally, to perfect it, until the opponent's sixty-yard line is reached, nearly all backhands must be sent towards the nearest sideline. The aim is not to hit the ball out, but to prevent a fast, direct attack on your goal. Therefore, for most of the time, *playmaking* for this tactic should involve turning out – seldom inward, towards the centre. For your other team members, this should simplify anticipation. Yet, if the sideline area is crowded, with the midfield unoccupied, one of your team could *playmake* to receive the ball near the centre and then hit it in the direction of the corner flag on the *other* sideline. The effect of this can be equally good – if not better, in some situations.

Robbed on the turn

Too many players like to turn the ball with forehand half-shots, instead of backhanding. While this can also be a means of slowing the play, beware that turning the ball requires skill. One mistake will allow superior opponents to steal the ball and initiate a fast attack against you. Even if there is no other player to pass to, it is better to backhand wide than to be robbed while turning the ball. When there is a team member free on the outside of the field, then it is criminal not to send a backhand there.

Persistent Engaging

Marking exaggerated

As explained in LATET (Chapter 5 and elsewhere), in order to win the ball, opponents have to be engaged in the 25%, and it is important to control them effectively in the 75%, even though the ball is not being directly competed for. The object of doing this is to dominate the opposition, through physical contact, during most of the playing time, especially when close to them. When you deliberately want to slow down a game, this concentrated marking must be extended and exaggerated. If the opposing **Nos. 3** and **4**

Closing down the opposition. Antonio Herera (9), a Mexican who is a great team player on the field.

have their mobility and anticipation impeded in this way, the players behind your barrier will be better able to initiate these tactics, and the results should be highly beneficial.

Delaying the strike

Even when the ball is in front of you, with the ride-off won, you should push the opponent further to the side, instead of accelerating to dispatch a shot, thereby delaying the execution of the strike. Not only will this blunt the speed of the opposition, by giving them something to which to react, but it will also give your team more time to adjust to their next positions.

Extreme delay

Cool defenders go to the extreme to cause delay, by dribbling the ball towards their own goal before striking a widely angled backhand. This tactic should only be used when, for a moment, there is no one to pass to, or if a team member needs more time to adjust into the best position, before receiving the ball.

Control in the 75%

When opponents are engaged in the 75%, they can be pushed that extra bit further to the side to curb their ability to anticipate the next play. The better the opposing player, the more valuable such treatment will be, and the greater the potential for confusion. But such control of opponents requires good riding, especially when the game suddenly turns in a new direction. Then the tail trick (Chapter 15) will assist you enormously in staying together.

Changing the Direction of Play

Lateral backhand

You are in attack and, as planned, your team has taken the ball close to a sideline. Then you see that, as expected, the stronger opponents are all positioned between the goal and your team. If your next striker makes a conventional play, with a forehand, either to continue along the sideline or to hit towards goal, those quicker opponents will almost certainly regain possession of the ball and will probably start their own attack. A better alternative would be a well-directed backhand, which travels more laterally than vertically towards the midfield, especially if it can be anticipated by your other players, who should then take the ball to the other sideline, causing extra confusion for the opponents. Because of the surprise change of direction, possession could be maintained but, even if the ball is given away, the opponents should find their velocity restricted, their intended attack thwarted and the play slowed down.

This tactic requires a very accurate execution of the backhand, which thereby provides an easy approach to the ball for the receiver, who must *playmake* very early, in order to be first to join the new line of the ball. This will also reduce the possibility of an opponent being crossed during the next play.

Tail backhand

On either side of the field, if the backhand is struck round the tail, it will be easier for the ball to be received without a foul being committed. Therefore, to receive an open backhand, it will be necessary for the receiver to *playmake*, even before the ball is hit, in order to make the extra lateral adjustment to reach the line in time. Alternatively, the *playmaker* may have to ride-off an opponent en route to the ball.

Forehand angled to side

The direction of play can also be changed if and when the weaker team surprisingly gains possession in the middle of the field, because of a mishit or any unexpected action. Then, the best shot could be a forehand neck or cut shot, which brings the ball away from the centre and towards the sideline, with little chance of committing a foul. Alternatively, if there is no opponent close enough to claim a foul, a change of approach that takes you off the line of the ball can be used to hit a wide-angled backhand across the field. In either case, one or more *playmakers* moving towards the sidelines *before* the shot is made will obviously help. But, in any case, it must be constructive to avoid giving the ball away to opponents who are waiting for it in a dominating position between you and the goal.

Backhands later

By producing unexpected changes in direction, the game will be further slowed down. This will be even more effective when applied by backhands, in lieu of forehands, because the strike will be made seconds later than that anticipated by the opponents. In addition, by striking wide-angled backhands, the fastest route to the goal, which opponents may anticipate being taken, will have been circumvented. Provided that teammates are primed to expect it, this tactic can both slow the game and retain possession, and may even conclude with a goal being scored.

Historical Examples

From tennis

In a Wimbledon final in the 1970s, Arthur Ashe surprisingly beat the title-holder and hot favourite, Jimmy Connors. During the first set, Connors appeared to be totally on top and he duly won it easily. Then Ashe surreptitiously changed his tactics, to slow down the game. The effect was stunning and when Ashe won the match point, it was clear that Connors could not believe that he had lost. This was a wonderful example to all sportsmen that it is possible to beat better players and stronger teams.

Wayne Gresky

I have encountered a few ice hockey players in my polo clinics. They all enjoyed comparisons between polo and their own sport and, without fail, mentioned their legendary player, Wayne Gresky. In his book, Gresky explained that many of his big hockey victories had been gained by slowing the game, for the benefit of his team, so that all members of the team were able to contribute to the successful tactics. Indirectly, this strategy must have affected his opponents, who had expected Gresky to use maximum speed.

Palm Beach

On several occasions during my time at Palm Beach, I witnessed surprising high-goal results, caused by slowing down the game by the methods explained above. Each time, it was clear that the tactic was successful because the opponents were not aware of what was happening. I was always amazed that the victims did not have a coach, who probably would have spotted the reason for the upset and could then have suggested a remedy.

One day, in a semi-final, I was the coach of a 22-goal team that was up against opponents who had been unbeaten for two months. I had helped my team to win their previous six matches and now suggested that they should employ these slowing down tactics. To my disappointment, the advice was initially ignored, as they battled in the middle of the field, to finish the first chukka 0–3. While changing ponies, an 8-goal player confessed to me that they had made a mistake. From then on, they tried to take the ball wide to the boards and slow down the play, which they did to such effect that they started the sixth and last chukka level. Then, a 5-goal player in our team felt feverish, but did not tell anyone and the opponents won by 1 goal. Such is polo.

Personal experience

I have been both the victim and the frequent perpetrator of these tactics in low-goal polo. Twice they worked sensationally, to give us surprise victories. On many other occasions, we avoided anticipated heavy defeats and kept our self-respect intact.

Once, when playing for a Hamburg team in Berlin, I received severe criticism from a pre-war Olympic German player, for ruining the flow of a match. But Hamburg had lost by only 2 goals, against much stronger opponents. Our British Army conquerors went on to win the final by 11 goals against the Dusseldorf team, who were of similar standard to mine, but had tried to compete down the middle of the field. Afterwards, I could not resist looking for my critic to ask him if that was a better result than our team had achieved. Not surprisingly, I received no answer.

SUMMARY

The aim must always be to win. It will help if you remember that your opponents can only play as well as they are allowed to. By using the strategy of wide angles, mainly to the side, and continual aggressive marking with subtle changes of direction, the speed of play must be significantly reduced, preventing a superior team from producing their best result against you. The resulting confusion and frustration may even upset the odds and bring you a win. If not, you can at least achieve a satisfying and enjoyable result, by avoiding an expected thrashing and losing by just a few goals.

REVISION

Normal method of play

C — teams allow all four players to **C**ontribute to a planned system.

O — each player marks controllable **O**pponent and is kept away from anyone too strong.

D — attempt to nullify best opponent; negative polo if won by one player **D**ominating.

E — provision of fast, **E**asy ponies for all team players a big factor for winning match.

Superior opponents

S — may discover that opponents are **S**uperior in every way, requiring **S**pecial plan.

S — important to **S**low down play and keep the ball on the **S**ide of the field when possible.

M — cause confusion by preventing oppositon from attacking down the **M**iddle of the field.

T — **T**hree **T**actics: wide-angled backhands, persistent engaging and changing direction of play.

 Wide-angled backhands

 S — bad play at any time includes backhanding *Straight* and giving the ball to the opposition.

 L — normally angled backhands can be met by opponents and ball, when turned, often *Lost*.

 W — with backhands angled extra *Wide*, opponents lose momentum and cannot interfere.

 S — normally sent to *Sideline* unless that area crowded; then hit laterally across midfield.

 Persistent engaging

 C — continual physical *Contact* during 25% and 75% of play reduces opponents' anticipation.

 E — *Exaggerated* contact takes all opponents further away from ball and slows down play.

 A — persistent contact and dribbling in wrong direction before backhand shot gives extra *Adjusting* time.

 T — priority to engage strongest opponent, assisted by use of *Tail trick* when turning.

 Changing direction of play

 B — lateral *Backhand*, instead of forehand, across field to *playmaker* keeps possession.

 E — tail backhand most *Effective*, easier to receive and less likely to be a foul.

 S — if opponents mishit, retain *Surprise* possession by hitting ball towards *Sideline*.

 L — if no opponent is close, ignore *Line* of ball approach to simplify backhand angle.

32

Tactical Critique

Questions — Answers — Remedies

After every game of polo it will be constructive if the way in which you have applied tactics is critically assessed and discussed, to highlight both good and bad points. Ideally, a qualified coach will have watched but alternatively another player can comment on specific points selected by you. In either case you will be *playmaking*, in that you initiated how you should be observed.

A critique of tactics could be divided in to the following headings:

LATET – **L**ook, **A**djust, **T**eam, **E**ngage, **T**urn.

SPS – **S**et **P**iece **S**ituations.

PRST – related to which position you played.

COPP – how well you **C**overed **O**ther **P**layers' **P**ositions.

GRP – **G**iving and **R**eceiving **P**asses.

These headings can then be used as the basis for relevant questions.

Questions

LATET

L — What percentage of the time did you **L**ook at the ball, the opponents and your team?

A — How well did you **A**djust to others with your speed, distances, and direction?

T — Out of ten, how did you relate to the rest of your **T**eam throughout the game?

E — Did you **E**ngage an opponent more times than you were controlled by an opponent?

T — Did you normally turn before or after the play changed direction?

SPS

Throw-in — Did you block an opponent and then emerge *playmaking* or marking?

Your Hit-in — Were you mobile and reachable or did you *playmake* for the receiver?

Their Hit-in — Were you quick to position correctly and did you mark or *playmake*?

Penalties — Did you assist your team by positioning correctly?

PRST

No. 1

Were you a link to goal in attack and defence?

- **P** — In the 75%, did you relate correctly from your team to a goalpost in attack and to the last opponent in defence?
- **R** — Were you always responsible with the ball in the 25%? Did you aim at a target halfway to the goal in the middle of the field and keep the ball in play near the side and back lines?
- **S** — Did you maximize speed in the 25% and adjust it correctly in the 75%?
- **T** — Were you turning to defend early enough and then distinguishing between the necessity:
  (1) to mark and engage an opposing **No. 4** who is close to you?
  (2) to stay free and in reach of a backhand while watching an opposing **No. 4** who was positioned some way behind you?

No. 2

Were you the link between the barrier and your No. 1?

- **P** — Did you stay in front of and close to the barrier in the 75% when not needed to be in a different position for *playmaking* or marking an opponent?
- **R** — Did you hit constructively to keep the ball in front of the barrier and pass to No. 1?
- **S** — How quick were you to switch between the two tasks of marking your relevant opponent and *playmaking* to receive passes?
- **T** — How early did you turn to defend and did you cover behind the barrier whenever your No. 3 crossed it, thereby securing defence and backing-up attacks?

No. 3

Did you pivot the team from behind the barrier?

- **P** — Were you always behind the barrier in the 75% unless covered by two players?
- **R** — Did you distribute the ball with angled passes to your team and were you able to limit *playmaking* to winning situations and careful to go to the next play when unable to gain possession?
- **S** — Did you use speed to engage in defence (normally the second opponent)? Were you quick to *playmake* in attack?

T — How ready to were you to defend when the opponents attacked? How quick were you to reposition behind the barrier after losing possession?

No. 4

Was the back door always shut? – If not, was it your fault?

P — Were you, in the 75%, always the last player in your team, except when covered by another player? If not, why not?

R — Did you, in general, wait to be *given* the ball at the next play, except when you saw that there was a secure opportunity to *playmake*?

S — Did you lock the door by rapidly engaging the first opponent, whenever an attack was mounted against your team?

T — How quick were you to reposition as last player, when possession had been or clearly was about to be lost by your team? When in attack, with the ball behind you and knowing that the No. 4 position was not covered by another player, did you recover ground quickly?

COPP

1. How many times did you change positions because:
    (a) You were covering another player?
    (b) You were *playmaking*, while being covered by another player?
    (c) You were ball-chasing or ball-watching, or not adjusting?

2. When you changed position:
    (a) Were you conscious of having to mark a different opponent?
    (b) Were you aware of which side of the barrier you had moved to?
    (c) Did you apply your actions in relation to which side of the barrier you were?
    (d) To what extent did you take over the job of your new temporary position?
    (e) Did you always take the first opportunity to readjust to your correct position?
    (f) Did you ever stay in a different position too long without realizing the damage?

GRP

1. When hitting forehands, how many times did you consciously try to pass the ball to another person?

2. Before backhanding, did you look behind:
    (a) To see who was available to receive a pass?
    (b) To choose between a tail or open backhand?
    (c) To avoid giving the ball to an opponent?

3. When receiving a pass:
    (a) Did you wait to see where the ball would be hit?
    (b) Did you *playmake* by trying to anticipate where the ball would go?

(c) When necessary, did you change direction before the ball was hit?

(d) When close to an opponent, did you engage before receiving the pass?

Answers

It is unlikely that all that has been mentioned under LATET, SPS, PRST and COPP can be referred to on any one day. Yet a good coach should be able to extract from them a number of important points which are relevant to you.

Any of your actions which complied with the given tactical principles and produced a successful result, should be *highlighted* to bolster your confidence.

Mistakes ought to be examined, to see what can be learnt from them and how they can be avoided in future matches.

Remedies

If you have asked a coach or another player to watch for only some specific points, then I suggest that you carry out self-examination on all the remaining questions listed. When you are told about, or recognize, a weakness, you can seek improvement in one or all of the following ways.

1. Mentally rehearse many times the correct anticipation and action.

2. Rehearse actual situations, on ponies, together with one or more other players.

3. In practice chukkas, deliberately seek similar situations to test your ability to carry out the necessary action.

SUMMARY

Remember that the most important part of coaching is revision. Therefore, it is necessary for you to hear the comments of others frequently, in order to cover any detail or even a major tactical point which, without realizing, you have started to overlook. By conscientiously listening to the initial critiques, you should be able to minimize the negative comments and maximize the complimentary ones. Added to that, by continually referring to all the sub-headings listed above, you will have a permanent reminder for your tactical thought processes.

Every time you take advantage of an opportunity to receive constructive criticism you will be *playmaking* away from the polo field, especially if the result improves your performance for the team.

33

Riding Critique

Establishing Areas for Improvement — Questions — Assessing Answers — Remedies

Establishing Areas for Improvement

I hope that, by the time this chapter is reached, less experienced riders will have benefited from the ideas, lessons and exercises given in Chapters 6, 9, 12, 15 and 18. I am confident that those who own ponies will have used what they have read to improve their relationships with them and will thereby have developed some useful pony partnerships. This training will be even more effective if informed criticism is sought and the advice given applied, so that mistakes on the field are corrected and good points are built upon.

There are some players who, despite a good tactical sense and an ability to hit the ball, cannot apply their skills because of their lack of pony control. Others have been simply unable to move a pony fast enough on a polo field to develop satisfactory tactical and striking prowess. But all could increase their riding confidence and ability from further experience, together with good critique. Concerning the better riders, I trust that they are now benefiting from one or more of my riding tips, which may never have occurred to them before. They, also, should listen to constructive comments. Whatever one's standard, surely there is always room for improvement?

Overcoming riding weaknesses and developing strength of seat should be part of an ongoing process, but it cannot happen without some *playmaking* off the field. Thought and planning are required to initiate improvement and to provide continuity during a season. Much depends on the availability of time, facilities and money. Yet it must be possible to arrange for someone to watch while you play polo, because there is a choice, according to circumstances, from a variety of people. These include a qualified coach, another player, a groom, or even a relation or a friend who has been briefed by you to observe and report on specific faults of which you are unaware in the heat of a game. The trained eyes of a coach should be best of all and, from an economic standpoint, an

RIDING CRITIQUE

above Wise players are always keen to improve their riding and tactical skills. A group of players at the Palm Beach polo clinic.

Graduation day at Palm Beach.

281

expert equestrian opinion should, in the long term, save money. This is because polo ponies can either appreciate in value or depreciate violently, depending how well they are ridden. Alternatively, the second best solution to being watched by a coach could be to use a list of points which were previously given by a coach, or were taken from these pages, that are used constructively on your behalf by an appropriately informed observer.

Questions

Having decided who will assess your performance, the next decision is how the subject matter should be examined. One way to simplify this would be to construct a list of questions that relate to all the chapters on riding under the five headings of SLOSH, as follows.

Seat

1. Are you riding on the front of the saddle, or do you tend to slip to back in the saddle?
2. How much of each chukka do you ride in the half-seat?
3. Is the length of your stirrup leathers correct?

Legs

4. Do you apply your legs correctly to accelerate, slow down and stop?
5. Do you think about and apply leg aids before:
    (a) Striking the ball?
    (b) Turning and changing direction?
    (c) Engaging in a ride-off?
    (d) Hooking an opponent's mallet?
    (e) Adjusting to receive a pass?
6. Do you kick the pony unintentionally?
7. Do you apply spurs correctly?

Outside the pony

8. How much do you see your pony during a chukka?
9. Are you able to watch the other seven players?
10. Do the ponies follow you?
11. When halting, are you looking behind?

Steering

12. On average, do you turn quicker than your opponents?

13. Do you clearly look in the new direction before turning?

14. Throughout a turn, do you maintain focus in the new direction?

15. Do you turn on a line or in a circle?

16. Can you gain control of an opponent who turns away from you?

Hands

17. Are you gentle and kind to the pony's mouth?

18. Do you keep the reins level and at a good length?

19. How much do you use both hands on the reins?

20. Can you carry and apply the whip effectively?

Assessing Answers

Honest answers to these twenty questions should tell you how well you are riding, whilst playing. But can you, by yourself, reply correctly to each one? It could be interesting to compare the answers of a qualified coach or a knowledgeable observer with yours. Naturally, you can combine the two systems and only occasionally seek the opinion of others, but in one way or the other the answers to these questions should be evaluated frequently. Hopefully, in time, the unsatisfactory answers will lessen sufficiently to show that ongoing improvement of riding skills is being achieved. To speed up the process further you could, on all of your ponies, frequently revise the drills and exercises given in the earlier chapters on riding, while bearing in mind any points thrown up by the answers. This can, of course, be combined with the task of schooling ponies between polo matches. Also, when warming up before playing, it is constructive to carry out various parts of the drills, such as stopping, turning and circling.

Remedies

If, despite the above, some problems persist, I have some remedies to suggest. These are numbered to relate to the questions posed earlier in this chapter.

Seat

1. While schooling, in order to stay forward in the saddle, you should exaggerate with your feet the action of the snow-plough, while taking most of your bodyweight on

your knees. This action helps to keep your centre of gravity forward but, if it is not sufficient, you should at times use the martingale strap to pull yourself forward.

2. To develop a secure half-seat you could:
   (a) Talk to yourself while playing and practising, continually saying 'half-seat'.
   (b) Canter up and down hills in the half-seat. Halt at the bottom of a slope without sitting down.

3. To check stirrup length, measure the leather and stirrup against your arm. If the stirrup fits comfortably into your armpit, it should be correct. Otherwise, perform a few turns and stops to investigate how comfortable you feel on the front of the saddle. Then lengthen or shorten the stirrup leathers until you are completely satisfied.

Legs

4. If your legs are not effective, they can be strengthened by an extra amount of time in the saddle and/or riding for periods without stirrups. However, beware of damaging your riding muscles, by doing too much too quickly.

5. To remember to apply your grip consistently, try verbalizing 'legs' before any specific action, especially stopping, during practice and play. Continue until you are confident that muscle memory has taken over the task of briefing your subconscious.

6. Kicking unintentionally is caused by what I call 'riding like a duck'. To remedy this you must concentrate on the snow-plough with your feet, which should stay parallel to the flanks of the pony. If this proves difficult, exaggerate the action by pointing your toes inwards at the pony's mouth.

7. If in doubt about your ability with spurs, cease wearing them until you are 100% certain that you have answered Question 6 satisfactorily.

Outside the pony

8. If you need to make yourself more 'outside the pony' you should design a programme and then try to complete it without seeing the pony. This could include figures of eight, circles, turns and halts, during which you exaggerate looking where you are going and all around.

9. To increase your view of other players, you should repeat the exercises in Chapters 9 and 12 with one or more other riders, and regularly call out the names of those around you. Then, in practice chukkas, try to talk to yourself about who you can see and, before hitting passes to players, call out their names.

10. To improve the way a pony follows you, repeat the exercises in Chapters 9, 12 and 15 and the programme suggested in Answer 9 above, until you are satisfied that it is happening perfectly.

11. To train yourself to look behind when stopping, you could select a marker like a tree, a goalpost, a ball, etc. Then canter past that marker and look behind you directly at it before applying legs to halt without taking your eyes off the marker. Repeat this drill, gradually increasing your speed until you can do it correctly at the gallop.

Steering

12. If you seldom out-turn opponents, you could invite others to compete with you in the mini-races described in Chapter 21. Then, in chukkas and matches, treat opponents as if they are against you in a mini-race.

13. Looking before turning should become an automatic, unconscious action. However, you may become accomplished at this for some time, but later find that you are forgetting to do it. Constant revision can prevent the problem and this could be achieved by repeating the exercises in Chapter 9 and 12, and also by using a marker as suggested in Answer 11, but this time *looking at it whilst turning*.

14. If it is difficult to keep your eyes in the new direction, refer to Chapter 9, where the exercises compelled you to pass between two other ponies after turning. Invite others to do this drill with you.

15. Unless you can turn sharply, to return on the same axis, you can practise doing this while carrying out all the exercises suggested above.

16. To take control of an opponent turning away from you, the secret is to focus on the tail of the opponent's pony and wait until that tail is next to your pony's head before commencing the turn. This can be practised with others as described in Chapter 15.

Hands

17. Examination of the mouth of a pony which you play regularly will answer this question. If the mouth has cuts or bruises and there are no rough edges on the bit to account for it, then you have to concentrate on using lighter hands. A longer rein, continual adjustment of your fingers in the reins and deliberately adding the second hand more often than before, may deal with the problem. If not, experiment by placing the tips of the fingers of the left hand in the martingale strap. Thereby, you should be able to dissipate the initial shock of your hands through the strap, instead of the pony's mouth. You can also protect the pony's mouth by employing the strap to support your bodyweight, when striking the ball.

18. If you are told or think that the reins are slipping, or altering in your hands too often without your knowledge, you must correct this. While doing some or all of the riding exercises, stop frequently to check whether the reins are the same length on both sides. Continue until you and (preferably also) your coach are confident that the fault has been cured.

19. Increase your use of both hands by deliberately applying the two hands on many occasions during the riding exercises. Then try to repeat this application when playing.

20. If you need to improve your use of the whip, there are several ways of doing so:
    (a) Always ride with a whip in your left hand, so that you learn to carry it without being conscious of holding it.
    (b) While riding, frequently change the reins between the left and right hand.
    (c) Start flourishing the whip in the left hand, while the reins are in the right hand.
    (d) Improve the strength of your left hand by playing table tennis or other sports with it.

SUMMARY

The many examples, given above, of ways in which you can interfere with a polo pony when you should be assisting it, suggest that there is little room for complacency. Yet I hope that the twenty remedies I have produced for those who cannot give satisfactory answers to the foregoing twenty questions, will demonstrate that it is possible to counteract most of the likely problems. But, unless you *playmake* away from the polo field, by determining that you are regularly given a critique, your stronger riding points will seldom be highlighted in a constructive manner and the weaknesses will remain undetected. You may be able to reduce costs by occasionally sharing a coach with your team, and then recording the points made for reference by yourself and by other observers in the future. However, you will benefit most – both financially and practically – by hearing regularly from a qualified coach as to how you could polish your riding skills.

34

Striking Critique

Problems and Their Diagnosis — Questions Related to PASSF — Answers — A Closer Look at Remedies

Consistent accuracy and length for all the ten shots covered in the chapters on striking are clearly demonstrated by the high-goal polo players. They have developed excellent timing as a result of the continual correct application of all five parts of PASSF. Many other players dream of being able to reach the same standard, but do not think and plan how to achieve it. In other words, away from the polo field, *playmaking* is required to plan a system that will bring about an ongoing improvement and prevent bad habits from being developed.

Problems and Their Diagnosis

Problems with the striking technique are inevitable at every level and can appear in many different ways, which may not be detected for a long time unless there is some organized method of assessment. This can take place when you play and/or practise. There are certain players who only hit badly under pressure and they must be watched in matches or put into pressured situations while practising. It is important to determine whether the root of the problem lies in wrong tactical positioning, poor riding or a bad striking technique.

An experienced coach should be able to diagnose the reason for any problem. Alternatively, you can try to assess yourself through the eyes of a willing observer as described in the previous chapter. In either case, the five parts of PASSF should be examined in detail and the questions which follow could help with the assessment.

above left Early strike by England's Charles Beresford.

above right Bartolomé Castagnola finding the sweet spot.

Questions Related to PASSF

Preparation

1. How often do you hit late?

2. Do you think about preparing for each specific shot?

3. Are you conscious of finding the circle with the mallet:
    (a) Before taking a shot (in the 25%)?
    (b) When not competing for the ball (in the 75%)?

4. Do you carry the mallet in a way that makes it feel light or heavy?

Approach

5. Do you adjust your route to the ball early enough, or when too close to it?

6. How often are you too near to, or too wide from, the ball?

7. Do you normally select a target before reaching the ball?

8. Do you pick the required spot on the ball and do you select it early enough?

Swing

9. Is your average swing slow?
10. Does your backswing for the half-shot keep straight?
11. For the full shot does the mallet, as a pendulum in the circle, point at the target?
12. Do your shoulders and hips turn enough to support the swing?

Sweet spot

13. Are you striking *through* or at the ball?
14. Are you finding the bottom of the ball?
15. On contact, do you focus on the exact spot?
16. How often do you lift your head and eyes before contact on the spot is made?

Follow through

17. Are you aware of the location of the target while making each stroke?
18. After hitting the ball, does the mallet head continue towards the target?
19. Does your head stay down until the follow through is complete?
20. Do you allow the mallet head's velocity to dissipate by completing another circle?

Answers

If there are positive answers to the twenty questions above, it should help to bolster your confidence for striking the ball, because all correct parts of your technique will be underlined and revised in your mind, for good continuity and gradual improvement. However, reasons for any bad shots should be clarified and the way to correct them will be highlighted. Then, when you do stick and ball exercises, or play in a practice match, you can address any problems constructively.

A Closer Look at Remedies

If, despite working through the questions and answers, there is no improvement and some of the poor shots continue without a satisfactory explanation, then you will have to look more closely at all parts of your technique. The following suggestions of how to do this are numbered to correspond with the twenty questions above. As applicable, repeat the exercises given in Chapters 10, 13, 16, 19 and 22, giving emphasis to any points below that could be relevant to a particular problem.

Preparation

1. Hitting late can be caused by:
   (a) Sitting back in the saddle and not in the half-seat.
   (b) Over-concentration on getting to the ball without thought of which shot is required.
   (c) Forgetting to prepare, or preparing late.
   (d) Allowing the mallet head to be out of the circle and heavy before starting to swing.

2. As a reminder to prepare, you could talk to yourself about the required mallet position for each of the ten shots while practising. Then repeat this when playing until you are confident that the subconscious has taken over the correct action.

3. To find the circle consciously:
   (a) In the 25%, you must initially start doing it a long way from the ball and then progressively commence the action a little closer to it.
   (b) In the 75%, to increase the number of times you find the circle, think about balancing yourself with the action whilst on the move.

4. Unless the mallet feels light, concentrate on alternating between:
   (a) Holding it vertically up (weightless).
   (b) Finding the circle.

Approach

5. During stick and ball, deliberately exaggerate adjusting your approach early.

6. To correct being too close to, or far from, the ball may require:
   (a) Applying the legs more throughout the approach.
   (b) Use of the whip and/or spurs.
   (c) Joining the line earlier.

7. Selecting a target must become an automatic habit through practice on a wooden horse and/or during stick and ball. Do it while *preparing*. This will help you to swing slowly and keep the head down.

8. Picking the spot as you select the target, will greatly assist in finding it again as you make contact with the ball. Accuracy will be improved by practising this.

Swing

9. To slow down your swing, you should experiment with:
   (a) Starting the swing earlier.
   (b) Shortening the backswing.
   (c) Verbalizing the word 'slow' while making the swing.

10. To straighten the half-shot backswing you must develop muscle memory by watching your own action until it is straight and then memorizing the exact feeling.

11. If a coach or observer tells you that the mallet is not pointing at the target, you should correct this by watching the mallet while making dummy shots. Apply extra weight:
    (a) On the right thumb for offside forehand shots.
    (b) On the V between thumb and index finger for offside backhand and nearside forehand shots.

12. To increase the use of shoulders and hips you could experiment by:
    (a) Pushing the relevant shoulder against your chin.
    (b) Assist the hips by turning the lower leg.

Sweet spot

13. Briefing yourself to go *through* the ball and making dummy swings at an imaginary ball should prevent hitting *at* it.

14. Noticing where your hand passes your leg assists you to find the bottom of the ball.

15. Looking up too soon prevents a focus on the spot. Therefore, pushing your head down to make the eyes relate to the ball clock will help. Also, seeking the spot with your right hand or verbalizing the word 'spot' can both be effective.

16. If you are always lifting your head, despite trying hard not to, an extreme remedy is necessary. So try looking in the *opposite* direction from which you are hitting while making the follow through.

Follow through

17. During stick and ball exercises, exaggerate locating the target by verbalizing the action.

18. To correct the path of the mallet head after hitting the ball you may need to freeze the follow through to see the exact error. Then repeat several times until you are confident that muscle memory has taken over to solve the problem.

19. To avoid looking up during the follow through, exaggerate the turn of the relevant shoulder until you feel the action is complete.

20. Application of the thumb and index finger during the follow through will produce extra rotation. Continual self-briefing and many dummy swings with a follow through should create an automatic action of completing another circle.

SUMMARY

It is impossible for any polo player to maintain a consistently high standard of striking, without constructive criticism and continuing practice. *Playmaking* away from the polo field is necessary in order to implement a plan in which both figure sufficiently frequently to achieve good results. If bad habits are kept in check and good technique rewarded with praise, ongoing improvement in accuracy and length should be achieved.

35

Polo Rules Test

Tick the answers which you think are correct. Then check, by reading the rules, to see whether you have made any mistakes. If in any doubt as to what is correct, you must refer to a coach, an experienced umpire, or a knowledgeable player, because it is irresponsible to play polo without a comprehensive understanding of the rules.

1. When can you, without the umpire's permission, leave the field?
   (a) At the end of a chukka.
   (b) Whenever the ball goes out of play.
   (c) Whenever the whistle is blown.

2. You have entered a team for a tournament and then, less than forty-eight hours before the first match, you have to replace one of the players. Who has to be informed?
   (a) The opposition.
   (b) The match referee.
   (c) The tournament committee.

3. If one player is late but will clearly arrive at some stage, when can he replace the agreed substitute?
   (a) At the end of any chukka.
   (b) Halfway through the first chukka.
   (c) At the end of the first chukka.

4. Can any of the following ride on or near the polo ground without a hat?
   (a) A groom.
   (b) An umpire.
   (c) A spectator.

5. Can you play a pony:
   (a) Without a martingale?

(b) That is blind in one eye?
(c) In a snaffle bridle?
(d) In a hackamore bridle?

6. In which of the following situations should an umpire award a goal if the ball goes through the goal before the whistle is blown for any reason?
    (a) When a foul had been committed by an attacking player.
    (b) When a foul was committed by a defender.
    (c) When a player had fallen off.

7. If the umpires cannot decide whether the ball went through the goal or not, do they:
    (a) Award a goal?
    (b) Tell the defenders to hit-in?
    (c) Throw-in from where the ball was last hit?

8. When should the referee consult with the umpires on general points?
    (a) At half-time.
    (b) After each chukka.
    (c) Before the match.

9. How wide are the goals?
    (a) Twenty feet.
    (b) Ten metres.
    (c) Eight yards.

10. When does the chukka finish?
    (a) After seven minutes.
    (b) When the ball is out and the first bell rings.
    (c) When the whistle has been blown once before the bell rang.
    (d) When the first bell rings as a goal is scored.

11. When is the clock stopped?
    (a) After a goal is scored.
    (b) When the whistle is blown once.
    (c) When a pony falls.
    (d) When the ball goes out of play.
    (e) When a player has fallen off and is not in danger.

12. When should a penalty be taken?
    (a) If, at the end of the second chukka, the bell rang two seconds before the whistle.
    (b) If, at the end of the third chukka, the whistle was blown two seconds before the bell.
    (c) If teams are not level when the first bell to end the last chukka rings, after which one player crashes dangerously into an opponent.

13. Where does the umpire stand for the throw-in after the ball breaks ten yards away from the boards?
    (a) Ten yards from the boards.
    (b) Twenty yards from the boards.
    (c) Thirty yards from the boards.
    (d) Outside the boards.

14. When are ends changed?
    (a) After a goal.
    (b) To start a new chukka.
    (c) When a penalty 1 is awarded.
    (d) After half-time, if no goals have been scored.

15. The hit-in is taken:
    (a) From where the ball crossed the line.
    (b) From close to the goalpost that was missed.
    (c) From anywhere you like.

16. Is penalty 6, a safety (a corner), after a defender hits behind, awarded:
    (a) If the ball also bounces off his own pony?
    (b) If the ball also hits a team-mate's pony?
    (c) If the ball also bounces off an opponent's pony?
    (d) If the ball also bounces off a goalpost?

17. Which of the following must always be blown as a foul?
    (a) Meeting an opponent while hitting on the nearside.
    (b) Crossing the line of the ball.
    (c) Changing to hit the ball on the other side to avoid a hook.
    (d) Crossing the line before meeting the ball on the offside.

18. A foul can be blown because you endangered an opponent by which of the following?
    (a) Crossing the line before hitting the ball.
    (b) Crossing the line after hitting the ball.
    (c) Stopping ten yards to the left of the line.
    (d) Crossing the line while hitting a ball
    (e) By hitting an offside backhand after he had hit a well-angled neck shot.
    (f) By crossing him after hooking another opponent.

19. Which of the following is allowed?
    (a) Hooking an opponent who is being ridden-off by another player.
    (b) Riding towards an opponent at an angle and then pulling away at the last moment.
    (c) Riding into an opponent who is already in a ride-off with another player.

(d) Riding-off an opponent continually for a hundred yards when not playing the ball.
(e) Hooking an opponent who is not playing the ball.
(f) Hooking an opponent who is trying to hook you.
(g) Hooking an opponent while the ball is under your pony.

20. The priority for the line should be given to which of the following?
    (a) The player hitting on the offside.
    (b) The player meeting an opponent following the ball.
    (c) Any two players riding together on the line.
    (d) Any player in a direct line from goal to goal.

21. There are several ways in which a ride-off is deemed to be a foul. Which of the following should be blown?
    (a) Riding-off at too steep an angle.
    (b) Riding-off at a speed not compatible with your opponent's speed.
    (c) The opponent is parallel to you and about to hit a half-shot as you ride-off.
    (d) The opponent is parallel to you and about to hit a full shot as you ride-off.
    (e) Pushing an opponent across a member of your team who has the right of way.
    (f) Pushing an opponent across another opponent who has the right of way.

22. Which of the following actions with the mallet should not be blown as a foul?
    (a) Supporting the mallet on your shoulder.
    (b) Carrying the mallet down and between you and an opponent when riding-off.
    (c) Reaching across the legs of another pony to hit the ball.
    (d) Taking a full swing at a neck shot when an opponent is in front of you.
    (e) Taking a full swing at a neck shot while riding-off an opponent.
    (f) Hitting an opponent's pony with a backhand when it had accelerated to catch up.
    (g) When competing for a static ball, hitting the legs of an opponent's pony.

23. Of the following rules for penalties, which are correct?
    (a) For the sixty-yard penalty, attackers can position anywhere and defenders anywhere thirty yards or more from the ball.
    (b) For a forty-yard penalty, attackers can position anywhere and defenders must be behind or in the goal.
    (c) For the thirty-yard penalty, attackers must be behind the ball and striker, and defenders behind the goal line and outside the goal.

36

Polo Riding 'G' — Pony Procurement

Buying — Breeding

Once you decide that you wish to play polo seriously, the days of renting and borrowing ponies are over. The time will have arrived for assembling a string of your own. A possible exception to this is if you are employed by a polo patron, who provides ponies for you to play. But observation suggests that situation is unlikely to last.

Furthermore, as your polo career proceeds, you will find that, for a variety of reasons, ponies have to be replaced. Thus you will require some knowledge of the factors involved in buying ponies. Also, if you have the facilities for keeping mares and foals, you could decide to breed from one or more of the ponies you have purchased, but beware – this is not so simple as you might think.

Buying

Some people have a natural talent for horse dealing. They seem able to acquire good ponies, which are not too expensive, easily, and then sell them on for a higher price. Without this ability, it is important to have some guidelines, or you will be at the mercy of dishonest players and dealers, who can mislead you in many different ways, so that you may suddenly find you have spent a small fortune on several worthless ponies. Instead, it is useful to learn and apply some common-sense points, as a way of *playmaking* when not on the polo field.

Four main factors should guide your actions.

1. The price you are willing to pay.

2. Your polo ability and the handicap level at which you expect to play.

3. Availability of ponies.

4. Soundness and health of a particular pony.

Price

There is a false economy in believing that only young ponies will suit, on the grounds that they should increase in value. Beware that the younger a pony is, the higher the probability that the legs, back, heart and lungs have not yet been physically tested and proved. Older ponies have to be cheaper and, if they pass a thorough veterinary examination, you will know that they can stand up to the hazards and roughness of polo. Therefore, it could be better to buy a fifteen-year-old for a small amount, which you accept as money written off, instead of paying a much larger sum for a five-year-old, in the risky hope of a long-term profit. Naturally, you have little choice if your budget is low, unless you accept half-trained ponies or those with known faults – which is like buying non-guaranteed products. But if funds are available, I believe the best bet is an eight- or nine-year-old that has played and survived at least three seasons of polo, without damage or serious blemish.

Normally, at the end of a polo season, the price of ponies for sale will be lower than at the beginning of, or during, a season. People are more prepared to sell at this time because, while they needed the ponies for the final tournaments, matches and club polo of the season, they may wish to avoid the expense and hassle of caring for them during the months when there is no polo. If you do take advantage of this situation, you must have the appropriate facilities and be fully prepared to look after the ponies, throughout the off season. This will involve either keeping them in a stable or at grass, in a field, where extra feed may have to be added if harsh weather is encountered.

Ability

It is equally foolish to own a pony that is not good enough, as it is to procure one that is too good for you. A beginner should learn polo on ponies that are easy to control, because there is enough to assimilate without the problem of managing a difficult pony. There might be an exception for experienced, strong riders who are new to polo, but even they will benefit more by riding obedient ponies. Also, however well you ride, ponies belonging to players of much higher handicap than you are unlikely to be suitable, because they are trained to react faster than you can read the game. Yet an old-timer, who has gradually descended through the ranks from high-goal through medium- and down to low-goal polo, can be perfect for lower handicap players.

Establishing that you have a definite accord with a pony is important. I have known good players dislike ponies that other people found to be absolutely brilliant. Even though a pony performs well for another player and appears to be the exact standard you require, it is advisable to insist, before buying, that you play that pony in a chukka. Also, do not accept, without playing, a pony that goes perfectly for you when stick and balling. Some ponies are fantastic, until tested for courage in a chukka and, only then, show an unsatisfactory trait of cowardice. Conversely, you can occasionally find a pony which is unpleasant to ride and practise on, but is wonderful in a game and worth purchasing.

With enough knowledge, you might be able to spot the reason why a pony plays badly, with the happy result that you have to pay only a little money for a potentially good pony. The current owner could be overlooking a very basic reason for some serious discomfort, which prevents the pony from playing well. Examples might include sharp teeth, wrong or badly fitting tack and careless work by a farrier. If you can diagnose such a situation you could benefit, but be very careful that there is not another, more deep-rooted reason, making that pony worthless.

Availability

A suitable pony may be hard to find, at the time you want to buy one. Another part of *playmaking*, when not actually playing, involves always keeping yourself informed about other people's ponies; their attributes, which ones are on the market and who is selling. Knowledge of the genuine reason for sale is most important, to help you avoid accepting a pony with a problem or bad habit, such as shying off the ball, pulling too hard or going sideways when under pressure. Always be suspicious of someone who has only had a pony for one season or less, unless that person is definitely giving up playing or regularly imports ponies as a business. Thus the safest buys are ponies newly arrived from abroad, or those that have been owned for several seasons.

A pony with strong front and quarters.

Every year there will be some polo pony auctions. These give you an opportunity to look at many ponies in one location, and save you from travelling to different places to try several ponies. The disadvantage is that you do not have much time, or the ideal situation, for testing the suitability of a pony. In this situation, prior knowledge will be a great help.

When you have the opportunity to try a pony that is for sale, in a chukka, beware that you are not fooled by a brilliant display for the first few minutes, which then suddenly declines at the end of the chukka. You can be tempted to discount the end of the chukka because you so enjoyed the beginning. However, such a performance normally signifies that the pony's training was wrongly rushed at a crucial time, from which the pony never recovered mentally. Also, you can be badly misled if the chukka never opens out into a gallop and this type of pony cannot be exposed. If in doubt as to whether there was a fair test for stamina, or any other problems, be sensible and ask for a further trial chukka.

Soundness

Good and bad points of conformation are shown in Figures 62 and 63. A good pony that cannot stay sound is worthless for polo. When a pony is being sold, it is possible that injuries have been concealed by the use of drugs. Before completing a deal, I suggest you employ an experienced polo vet, rather than one who specializes in any other dimension of equestrian sports. In addition to knowing how drugs are used on a polo pony to deceive (and taking blood samples accordingly), such a vet may also be able to advise on what state of health and soundness is acceptable in relation to price. However, it is advisable to confirm with your vet that the pony has been checked when cold and not only when warmed up, because lameness can be hidden when the blood is circulating after violent exercise.

To be extra safe, X-rays of the legs and possibly the back should be taken. But if an experienced polo vet suggests that it is not necessary, you can save the extra cost without taking more than a little risk.

Lastly, you must be aware of various pony vices, which are difficult to detect until a pony is living under your care. A vet might be able to spot one or more but I suggest that you personally investigate and check whether they exist. The following vices can add major problems to those which automatically go with horse ownership:

Weaving in the stable.

Crib-biting.

Kicking.

Being difficult to shoe.

Being awkward to load into a lorry or trailer.

Being difficult to lead from another pony.

Dislike of being tied up in the pony lines, or elsewhere.

You can, of course, watch the pony in the stable and when tied up outside, besides seeing it being loaded and led. Also, you could test the pony's demeanour for shoeing by lifting

PLAYMAKER POLO

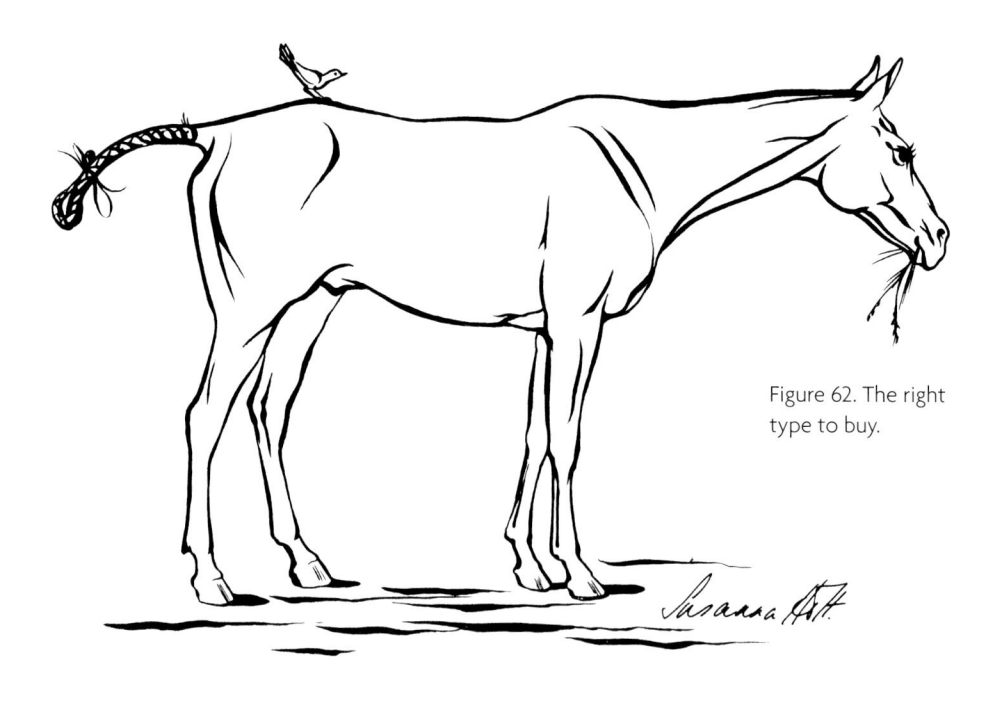

Figure 62. The right type to buy.

Figure 63. Reasons for caution when buying a pony:
A — Straight shoulder
B — Hollow back
C — Ewe neck
D — Shallow girth
E — Narrow second thigh
F — Narrow, hooked hind leg
G — Long and weak hind leg
H — Bony growth on pastern
I — Capped hock
J — Lack of bone
K — Over at the knee
L — Long pastern
M — Narrow in front.

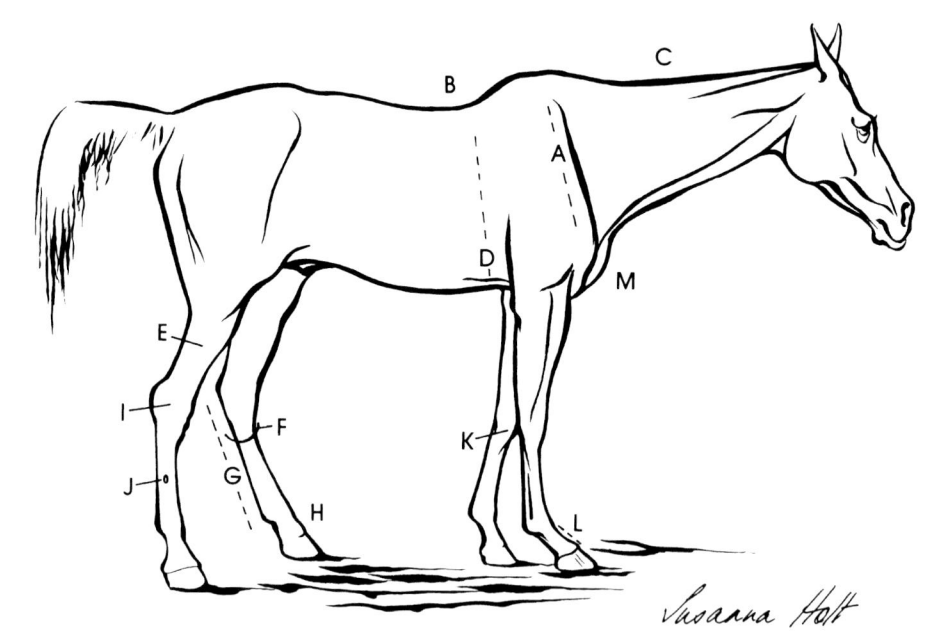

each leg in turn. But, to be completely safe, I suggest that you ask the owner whether the pony has any of the above vices. Then, before concluding the deal, you should request a contingency that, if you subsequently discover that any of them do exist, you can return the pony and be refunded in full. While a verbal contract is legally binding, it is still safer to have this agreement in writing.

SUMMARY

Every pony is different and you have to *playmake*, far from the polo field, by investigating in detail in order to find and buy one that will suit you. Do not be prejudiced against

300

older ponies and beware of false economy with young ones. Time can be saved by keeping yourself informed about all ponies within your budget, so that you are prepared when they come onto the market. Try to play the pony in at least one chukka that entirely satisfies you in every dimension, especially stamina. Ensure that the vetting is thorough and that there are no unacceptable vices being hidden from you.

Breeding

The operation of breeding can give enormous pleasure and may even make you feel as if you have another family. A good mare that breaks down at an early age, may (depending on the reason for breaking down) reimburse you with some valuable offspring. It is also a pleasant way of giving a faithful old mare a few extra years of life. But you must be sensible and not allow sentimentality to cloud your judgement, or you could end up with some worthless youngstock and an angry bank manager. There are many risks and expenses involved in the breeding process, which takes far longer to achieve results than you may expect.

At Whitfield Court I bred approximately sixty ponies over fifteen years, all from one stallion and a number of Argentinian mares which had played polo for us. I cannot be exact on numbers, because inevitably a few foals died. Thanks to the masterful breaking and training by one man, John O'Keeffe, only a few of the progeny failed to make the grade as polo ponies, although some three or four took an extra long time to accept the rigours of playing the sport. The breed had given us much enjoyment and served us extremely well. On three occasions our family team was completely mounted on them when winning tournaments. Some have also become replacements in the Polo School string and others have been bought by members of our Polo Club. A few were sold to play medium-goal polo in England and some for low-goal in Switzerland. Most rewarding of all was seeing my son Sebastian successfully break into the professional ranks of English polo, when playing six of them, including twins, in medium- and low-goal polo. In addition to these benefits, for at least ten years I did not have to write a cheque to buy a pony. Yet, inevitably, there were delays from factors outside our control, such as injuries, sickness and adverse weather, besides some losses and disappointments.

I trust that my own experience gives you a balanced view of the delights and problems that can be expected. To follow, I offer a few basic thoughts, which I hope will be helpful to anyone who wishes to breed polo ponies.

The Dam

If the dam has played polo satisfactorily, there is a strong possibility that the progeny will be good polo ponies. In the majority of cases, the genes that render a pony suitable for polo are passed on, which makes a young pony easier and quicker to train. The offspring of a dam that never played are more likely to reject the demands and abuses of polo athleticism. Furthermore, this may not be revealed until late in the training, when the big questions are asked. Other than the actual playing factor, the most important quality to look for is a quiet temperament, which will normally be inherited. A calm, good-natured pony will accept the schooling and training better than an excitable one. Another important consideration is conformation: good conformation gives a pony a higher chance of staying sound, and youngstock normally resemble their parents in this respect. Speed (that can be controlled) is incredibly valuable, but the owner of a mare which is excellent in every other way, while lacking top speed, could add this ingredient by using a suitably speedy stallion.

Playing the dam

After being covered, provided that there are no complications, a fully sound mare can be played for a whole season. Also, two or three months after giving birth and, before a foal is weaned, it is possible, if necessary, to play the dam. If doing so, it is a good idea to leave the foal in a stable, although it can be taken to the polo ground if it frets too much which, at this stage, is a distinct possibility. In either case, it is advisable that the foal is left alone once or twice before this is attempted.

The Stallion

A stallion that has previously covered polo mares with successful results, is obviously a safer proposition than one with no such record. If such a stallion is not available, an experiment has to be made. Our stallion was the son of one with a good record and out of a Thoroughbred mare, after an illicit union. Some tall Thoroughbred stallions have a reputation for reproducing offspring which are the same size as the dam. These should be very fast, strong and valuable but there will always be a risk that one or more will grow too big for polo. Once again, a quiet temperament is a priority, unless the mare to be covered is exceptionally passive, and good conformation is all-important for the reasons given in respect of the dam. You could regard it as another form of *playmaking* off the field, as you try to select a stallion with the required qualities for any of your breed.

Foaling

Spring is the best time for foaling, which must be planned to give the offspring the best chance of developing a strong body. This should bring about an early start with their handling and polo training. But a young pony must be sufficiently strong to take the strain and stress of being broken, trained and ridden. On the other hand, for the early maturers, the later the handling starts, the more wilful and difficult they can be. If in doubt, always postpone the start of breaking, but beware of the dangers from an obstinate, strong young pony.

Twins

If your mare has twins, both can often be saved and become good, strong polo ponies. We disproved the theory that one will die or be too weak to perform well, but only because we were lucky to receive some timely advice. A polo-playing guest, who happened to be an American vet, explained the solution to the normal twin problem. He prescribed medicines for the mother, to produce more milk, and extra vitamins for the twin foals, which helped to strengthen them at a vital time.

SUMMARY

Good planning, based on experience or sound advice, is essential. Much patience is required to deal with all the problems encountered at the various stages of breeding and training. The results can be very rewarding, but it is a long, expensive process, filled with the unexpected, that can easily bring losses and disappointments.

REVISION

Buying ponies

Price

- **Y** — **Y**oung ponies are more expensive and their long-term soundness has not been proved.
- **O** — **O**lder ponies are cheaper and fully proved if they pass a thorough vetting.
- **C** — **C**heaper ponies purchased at end of season – but need winter facilities – alternatives are not guaranteed, half-trained ponies.
- **S** — **S**afest value eight- or nine-year-old that has survived three long, hard seasons to pass vet.

Ability

- **E** — **E**qually foolish to buy a pony not good enough, as one that is too good.
- **B** — **B**eginners need obedient, easy ponies; polo hard enough without pony problems.
- **P** — **P**lay before buying; pony good in practice maybe coward; one bad at stick and ball may play brilliantly.
- **R** — **R**eason for pony playing badly, secretly diagnosed, could provide potential cheap buy.

Availability

- **I** — stay well **I**nformed about all ponies – what's for sale and reasons for sale.
- **S** — **S**afest buys have been owned for some time, or newly arrived from abroad.
- **A** — **A**uctions save travelling time, but difficult to try ponies fully, so information important.
- **R** — stamina in trial chukkas may not be **R**evealed; beware brilliant pony that later fades.

Soundness

- **D** — experienced polo vet can protect against injuries concealed by **D**rugs.
- **C** — check pony after **C**ooling down in case it was deliberately warmed up beforehand.
- **X** — **X**-rays advisable if there is any doubt, but heed vet's advice.

V — **V**ices should be checked out, or ask for contingency arrangement if later displayed clearly.

Breeding

Difficulties

W — beware not to keep **W**orthless youngsters from sentimentality.

R — over long period of time **R**isks can be excessive, expenses can add up.

N — after a few years **N**umbers of youngstock to be trained can grow out of control.

D — many **D**elays from injuries, sickness and weather hamper commercial success.

Mare

P — better if she has **P**layed; progeny easier to train and accept rough moments more readily.

T — quiet **T**emperament inherited gives big advantage in tricky polo situations.

C — good **C**onformation produces more sound and strong, versatile performers.

S — **S**peed valuable in mare, but not essential, as the stallion can give input to compensate.

Stallion

R — safer if he has proven **R**ecord with progeny already playing well.

S — better if not too tall unless known to give mares foals of their own **S**ize.

T — excitable **T**emperament unlikely to work unless mare very passive.

C — bad **C**onformation comes out in youngstock too often.

Additional points

S — **S**pring foaling best for planning breaking and training when older.

D — if young not well **D**eveloped, better to postpone breaking

M — **M**ares can play polo after being covered and before foal weaned if badly needed.

T — **T**wins can often be saved if given extra milk and special care from vet.

37

Preparation — Playmake Before the Season Starts

The Need for Preparation — Playing Plans — Pony Management — Tack — Mallets — Clothes and Equipment

The Need for Preparation

There are many different things to think about and plan before you can say confidently 'I am ready for the new season'. To look for your equipment the night before, or even on the day of your first game is to invite major problems.

Even so, you can be perfectly dressed, with enough polo mallets to cover all requirements, but if you have not made firm arrangements about where and with whom you will play, there will be major difficulties even in getting the season started. It is not possible to play regularly without belonging to a polo club and a team.

Any problem with the condition of your ponies could also limit your early participation. The consequences arising from lack of play could mean that ponies may struggle later in the season, especially if many commitments to play in tournaments are accepted. The fittening process must be designed to produce ponies that can stand the strain of playing throughout a season that lasts for several months.

Thoughtful preparation can be another form of *playmaking*, because good polo administration and personal organization reduces pressure away from the field, which should allow you to play to your best and enjoy it. Another consequence of thorough preparation is that it should provide you with flexible plans, which can be referred to at any time.

Playing Plans

This is an enormous subject, which would require a whole book to cover all the factors that might need to be dealt with. Therefore, I will touch on only a few basic points that should help you to understand what you have to think about.

Where to Play

Factors concerning your place of work in relation to your home, and the standard of polo you are seeking, will affect the decision of where to play. These can be straightforward, or be complicated by distances. If you are lucky enough to be able to keep your ponies at home, you should then be able to enjoy combining their and your pre-season preparation, but the means of transporting them to the polo ground will have to be arranged. If your ponies are in livery, the responsibility for getting them fit is taken from you, but you could have difficulties preparing yourself to be physically ready to play and you may find it is hard to maintain a satisfactory relationship with each pony.

Amount of Play

Your budget, time available and desire to compete will govern the amount you play. You may simply want to play club chukkas every week and enter just one or two tournaments. For this approach, arrangements could be left until close to each match. Or you may wish to plan a programme of many tournaments, for which you will have to sit down with at least one professional to make a detailed plan, which will require constant updating during the season. In this latter case, there is much scope for *playmaking* on the telephone, etc. to ensure that you can extract maximum value from the time and money that you invest. It is a mistake to expect club officials to put you in teams and plan all your tournaments – although their advice and assistance should be available to you and can be extremely helpful.

Pony Management

Pre-season

At grass

Ideally, a pony should start work looking just a little fat, so that weight can be lost as muscle is developed, and condition is maintained as fitness is built up. To achieve this, depending on the climate, extra feed should be available to ponies at grass. Hay, haylage, or even oaten straw can be sufficient, but if nuts or oats are added during the latter weeks, before coming in to start work, the ponies will become ready to play in a shorter time. The larger the area in which the ponies can roam, the less it is necessary to augment the basic grass and the more helpful it will be to the process of fittening them for the first day of play.

Worms

On the assumption that your ponies have just had a rest session out at grass before the new season, many important points have to be covered. Some of these will also apply to ponies that have been in stables, whether or not in work. The biggest enemy encountered in the battle to keep any horse in good condition is the worm. It is highly preferable to anticipate worm infestation rather than waiting for the first signs of deterioration which worms can cause. By giving regular doses of a recognized wormer, and following the manufacturer's instructions, problems such as the dreaded sight of a pony with colic or a twisted gut ought to be avoided. For the sake of continuity, records should be kept of worm doses given, and these should be checked frequently, with additional reference to the looks of the ponies.

Legs

Do not presume that ponies' legs will automatically recover from the stresses of the previous season during a rest period. Once any swelling has disappeared and cuts have fully healed, while resting, some form of blister ought to be considered. A mild application can usefully strengthen the tendons against future strain and injury. A strong treatment will be necessary if there has been any serious damage and in this case the length of rest should be longer and even last for one year. However, it is always safer to seek veterinary advice and to be aware that treatments are constantly being revised and even changed significantly.

Coats

Ponies should be inspected closely to check their coats. Any nasty infiltrators, such as lice, must be dealt with by treatment with an appropriate powder. Then a decision must be taken whether to clip out, trace clip or allow the summer coat to come through the winter one. A full clip, followed by rugging, is the best way to prevent excessive sweating as the exercise increases, and it helps to keep the coat clean. The trace clip is unattractive to look at, but it is a good compromise, which can reduce the need for rugs and allows a pony to be put out in the day, and possibly at night, in a suitable temperature. The summer coat will come through earlier and look a little better if no clipping takes place, but initially the grooming will involve very hard work.

Injections

Shortly before exercise is about to start, is as good a time as any to give the necessary injections. It is obligatory for the flu injection to be given every year and a certificate showing that the course has been kept up to date must be carried, ready to be shown at all venues. The tetanus injection (which often combined with the flu injection) should always be kept up to date in case of cuts and invasive injuries.

Teeth and shoes

Also, at this time, you would be wise to have all the ponies' mouths checked to assess the state of their teeth and, if in doubt, an accredited horse dentist should be employed. Naturally, shoeing is a necessity and booking the farrier as required is important in preventing any delay with the fittening process. Studs or calkins may not be needed on the first set of shoes (and, without them, you will be able to work the ponies on any surface), but for tournaments they should be added.

As the Season Begins

Food and exercise

There are many alternative ways in which you can mix food and exercise leading up to the first tough match. Too much of one and too little of the other can easily happen if careful thought is not applied, and the ensuing problems may include over-fresh ponies which are out of control. The other extreme is poor condition, which will result in weak performance on the field. Therefore, each individual pony should be watched to see if the general plan works for them, and changes must be made if necessary. The scope for altering the amount of work for the ponies will obviously vary according to your situation, but a little ingenuity, that produces positive results, is another form of *playmaking*. However, if you ever progress to high-goal polo the preparation for your ponies will have to be entirely different, with a vast increase in exercise, training and food. This is because extreme levels of stamina and fitness have to be built up. Gallops the length of the field happen far more often at this level, and the speed of play is very much faster throughout a match.

Chukkas

The fitness required of a pony in order to be ready for chukkas depends completely on the discipline of the rider during play. A careful, considerate player, who can resist the temptation to be fully competitive all the time, by cantering rather than galloping, can participate on a half-fit pony. In this way, much of the fittening process can take place on the polo field, but many slow chukkas must be played before the ponies are asked to meet the speed, strain and stress of a match. Alternatively, by exercising twice a day, with the ponies out of the stable for close on two hours every day, while receiving larger feeds, they could be ready to play fast chukkas immediately the season starts. Clearly, there are many different compromise methods between these two extremes but, unless due care is taken, all of them can cause problems such as leg injuries, girth galls and sore backs. By varying which ponies are ridden and which are led during exercise, it is possible to ensure that all become hardened to the saddle, the weight of the rider and the girth pressure.

Training

The characteristics of each pony should be used as a guide when deciding how much schooling and stick and ball each pony needs before being played. The young, inexperienced ponies require many sessions, while the older ones, with many seasons behind them, may need none. The training and exercises suggested in the chapters on riding can be used as appropriate in the sessions, for the mutual benefit of pony and rider.

Tack

Before the start of the season, the equipment for the ponies will probably have to be taken out of storage. Where applicable, oil must be cleaned off, everything should be examined and the leather made soft with saddle soap.

With unsuitable or broken tack, you will find it difficult to be a *playmaker*. I have seen a team, in the American Open, lose the semi-final because a girth broke.

Many parts of a saddle may need repair and most damage should be easy to detect. But a broken tree can go unnoticed for long enough to cause a serious back injury to a pony. Before the season begins, every saddle should be thoroughly inspected to ensure that none of the trees are faulty and that no rough edges exist. Similarly, the bits on all bridles require checking to confirm that the surfaces are smooth. Also, the condition of all straps and buckles on every piece of equipment must be satisfactory. Other forms of damage that can miss detection are broken curb-chain hooks and parts of a girth that are frayed or weakened.

To be fully prepared, a reserve stock of stirrup leathers, straps, reins and bandages should be assembled for emergencies, because even new pieces of tack can break without warning. To ensure that you have minimal problems with tack, a careful check of all items, before and periodically during the season, should prevent any emergency arising.

Mallets

Length and Weight

The off season is the ideal time to buy mallets and to arrange for all the repairs to be done to existing ones. You should always be considering making changes to the weight, length and stiffness of the mallets as your game develops. It is simpler and costs much less if you can use the same length on every size of pony, but it could be disastrous if this does not suit you and it affects your accuracy. There are no dogmatic rules for length other than a well-controlled long mallet strikes further and a shorter one is more accurate. Nonetheless, with many people something different can apply, and I have seen small men handling the long, 53-inch mallet effortlessly and big men preferring a heavy 50-inch one.

If you ever pick up what feels like the *perfect* mallet, you must try to take it to your stick maker to be copied. In this way all dimensions can be covered, without having to specify each individual one but, even so, it would still be advisable to take note of every detail of that mallet for the future.

Type of Head

The type of mallet head that is ideal depends on individual abilities. The cigar, shaped as described by the name, is best for accuracy; the RNPA, with both ends of the head angled, assists you to loft the ball and the Skene (named after the famous Australian player), provides a compromise between the two. The weight of head can be increased as confidence improves, stopping just short of when the balance clearly feels incorrect. Repairs and replacements should be planned to ensure that you have some scope for change to suit different conditions and your own state of fitness. Finally, it is advisable to put some form of marking on the mallets to prove ownership and as a deterrent to theft.

Clothes and Equipment

Breeches

For polo matches, white breeches or jeans must be worn. A careful examination might discover that one or more pairs have shrunk, or that repairs are needed. Trying them on may save time and clarify whether replacements have to be purchased.

Boots

Riding boots, when not in use, should have been kept clean and soft. A further application of saddle soap or polish will add an extra shine for the first game of the season. Any type or make can be worn but, ethically, black ones are not accepted because they can cause permanent stains on opponents' clothes. For your own protection, strong leather boots which reach up to your knees are advisable. Most players have boots with zips, but beware that these can break at unfortunate moments.

Gloves

Some people always wear gloves when playing but, if you do not, it is sensible to be prepared for the unexpected event that makes them crucial. For example, it can be difficult to hold the reins satisfactorily in the cold, the wet and the heat. Rain and hand-freezing conditions can appear when not predicted, and a pony may surprise you by sweating excessively onto the reins. In such adverse conditions, a blister could start on either hand at any time and, without protection, this can degenerate into an injury that interferes with play for a considerable time. Since the gloves themselves can become soaked or need repair, why not start the season with two or more pairs? Then, to cover all eventualities, one pair can be in your pocket and another in your bag.

Helmets

It is very important to have good protection from a helmet. It must feel comfortable and not impede the view of the game. New shapes and colours keep appearing, with different forms of face masks being worn by an increasing number of players. Yet the high-goal players still do not use any protection for the face, in order to have maximum vision, even though 10-goal player Horacio Heguy lost an eye from being struck by a ball. Ironically, his twin brother Gonzalo recently died in a car crash when not wearing a safety belt. There is a close comparison between the two gadgets, in that both can save you or kill you. The face mask protects you from mallets and balls but, should you fall from the pony in nosedive fashion, the injury might be serious, because a rigid, peaked mask might possibly force your head back. Whichever type of helmet you have, before the start of the season it should be checked carefully, to ensure that the chinstrap is in good condition and holds the headgear firmly in place. Also, while I believe that you can clean the helmet in a dishwasher, a simpler way to combat the head sweat is to spray it with aftershave.

Knee Pads

In situations where your knees might be crushed, knee pads can give you confidence. They also protect you from a blow by a pony, a ball or a mallet. But, if they are uncomfortable, with straps digging into the backs of the legs, they will do more harm than good. They can be of leather or cloth and secured by buckles or Velcro. For reasons unknown, some people dress up in them just to go riding. At Palm Beach, to my surprise and amusement, a few of my clients mounted a wooden horse wearing them. As with all equipment, some form of maintenance is required from time to time to ensure that the knee pads do not suddenly fall apart.

Spurs

All players should definitely own spurs, but they must be worn selectively. The buckles and straps can need repairs or renewal and the metal must be examined for sharp edges, which are illegal. Weak riders should not use spurs to compensate for their lack of strength, because they will goad the pony at the wrong moment, with disastrous results. They should wait until they have improved enough to be confident of having an excellent seat on a horse. The majority of polo ponies will benefit from the correct application of spurs, on an important day in a match, especially if they *have not* been used in practice and during chukkas. However, ponies that must be disciplined can benefit from their use in all situations, in order to prevent bad habits forming.

Whips

Managing four reins, a whip and a mallet is not simple, but it is important for a polo player to learn to carry a whip and to be able to apply it in all situations. The length allowed is 48 inches, which enables you to slap the pony's neck and tickle behind the girth while holding the whip and reins together in the left hand. To apply a strong slap on the pony's quarters, you have to take the reins, together with the mallet, in the right hand, while the left hand strikes firmly. These actions, employed judiciously, can make the pony accelerate minutely or greatly – whichever is required – and often this results in either scoring a goal or saving one against you. In fact, the whip assists you to tell a pony what you want to do and, in most situations, it will not cause pain but simply emphasize your directions. It is now a *foul* to use the whip when the ball is not in play.

SUMMARY

You need to *playmake* both on and off the polo field to achieve good results as a player. Careful preparation will never be wasted and must enhance the performance of your ponies and your contribution to a team. To go onto the polo field at the beginning of the season fully fit, on ponies that are physically ready to battle for your team, with all the necessary tack and equipment in good condition, requires detailed planning. To continue to play regularly, throughout a year, necessitates ongoing thought and *playmaking* in every dimension that has been mentioned in this chapter.

REVISION

New season

- **P** — **P**lan in many dimensions before being fully prepared and ready to play.
- **C** — **C**heck and repair equipment, tack, clothes and mallets.
- **W** — decide **W**here and **W**ith **W**hom to play and then prepare ponies to be in the best condition.
- **V** — thoughtful preparation for team, ponies and personal items is **V**ital *playmaking*.

Plans for playing

- **C** — location of home and work, plus level of polo wanted, affects which **C**lub to join.
- **T** — preparation of ponies and player may be combined at home base, but **T**ransport of ponies to polo is required.
- **R** — ponies can be prepared for play at livery, but this is hard for player fitness and good player/pony **R**elations.
- **V** — many plans for tournaments updated for maximum **V**alue, but fewer plans if mainly playing chukkas.

Pony management

Prior to season

- **R** — worming instructions obeyed and **R**ecorded, plus weak or strong leg blister as needed.
- **C** — **C**oats inspected, treated and clipping decision taken during initial fittening process.
- **F** — extra **F**ood at grass, less in large area, and hard **F**ood for latter days for faster fitness.
- **I** — flu and tetanus **I**njections, horse dentist and farrier booked and stud-fitting plan for later.

As season begins

- **C** — mix of food and exercise for pony strength and **C**ontrol, plus individual pony attention.
- **A** — fitness built by slow chukkas or by extra exercise related to player's **A**ttitude.
- **H** — ponies alternated between leading and riding to **H**arden all legs, girth areas and backs.

E — schooling and stick and ball related to ponies' Experience, plus riding Exercises for players.

Polo mallets
A — buy and repair in off season, and weight, length and stiffness Adjusted to player's development.
M — longer Mallets for distance, shorter for accuracy; let maker copy favourite mallet.
H — cigar Heads for accuracy, RNPAs for loft and Skene as compromise between the two.
C — weight increase with confidence; all Conditions catered for and mallets marked.

Tack
R — storage oil cleaned off, breakages Repaired and unsuitable parts discarded.
S — careful check of saddle trees, Surfaces on bits, girths, straps and buckles.
R — unexpected damage and breaks Replaced by collection of spare items.
C — problems minimized by frequent Checks of the Condition of all pieces.

Clothes and equipment
B — two pairs of white Breeches or jeans, serviceable boots and gloves always carried.
H — Helmets must protect and be comfortable, chinstraps secure and face masks are optional.
S — knee pads protect for confidence; Spurs used selectively and not by weak riders.
W — learn to carry Whip and use on wither and quarters for acceleration and pony discipline.

38

Playmaker Conclusion

Have I succeeded in converting you, the reader, to the ideology of *playmaking*? There is no such word, my computer tells me, every time I do a spell check. Yet, throughout this book, I have tried to explain that there are many dimensions of *playmaking*, which all polo players at every level can and should use. In all of them, a streak of initiative, which pushes you to act *constructively*, *early* and, hopefully, *before others*, is required.

On the polo field, the ultimate *playmaker* dimension is achieved by those who move to be free in space or, by controlling an opponent, become available to receive a pass *before* the ball is struck in their direction by another player. This is an act which helps keep possession in the most economical way, by making the ball do the work, instead of the ponies. It can be done by itself, in isolation, but if combined with the correct principles of tactics, riding and striking, it will produce the very best results.

Furthermore, if all dimensions of *playmaking* – including those involving administration, relationships, preparation and practice – are applied throughout a season, the effect will impress and surprise everyone you meet on and around the polo field.

This comment about application throughout the season brings me to my next point – that facet of human weakness, which is forgetfulness. Frequently, I have found myself watching players whom a year or more previously I had enjoyed coaching. They had, once, appeared to understand most of the important principles that I teach, and had demonstrated an ability to apply many of them. Yet, with the passage of time, I noticed that, although they were using some of the ideas that I had given them with success, they failed to apply many of the others. I have asked myself whether the problem was caused by lack of understanding – which suggests poor explanations by me – or simply through them forgetting from lack of practice and revision.

I always emphasize that, without constant reminders, the mind cannot hold too much information and recall how to apply it, when necessary. Yet, sadly, it is clear that the majority of polo players regard revision as a low priority. This must be an enormous mistake, because by mentally or practically repeating a technique or a tactical drill, the subconscious is not only given the opportunity to retain the details involved, but is also given a further chance to understand exactly what is required and why. Experience has now brought me to the conclusion that *80% of coaching should be REVISION*. Yet, although there are qualified coaches available, relatively few polo players employ one at any time, and only a small percentage of those that do, regularly revise what they have learnt from their instructor. (To assist those who are looking for a simple way to revise, I am publishing separately a small booklet that includes all the Revision sections at the ends of the chapters in this book – please see Appendix 1 for details.)

My realization of the significance of personal revision recently widened, when I again became the pupil, in an attempt to learn to play the piano. Initially, I felt humbled by the number of times the piano teacher had to remind me of the most fundamental and simple points. Then I began to excuse myself by thinking that, with so much to learn, until I have revised by practising frequently, it is clearly inevitable that I will often fail to apply some of the easy-to-understand basics. This, in turn, provided me with the explanation as to why low-handicap players and polo beginners take so long to assimilate all that I wish to teach them. It also highlighted the advantage which qualified coaches have over other players, in that they should be continually hearing the basics, guidelines and principles from their own mouths. Furthermore, when demonstrating and participating with clients, coaches should know if they are obeying the maxim 'Practise what you preach'. If not, cheeky students will quickly speak out – and the opinions of the more respectful ones can always be sought. It is even better if, from time to time, another coach is asked to pass judgement.

In Chapters 32, 33 and 34, I suggested ways in which you can be the subject of critiques for tactics, riding and striking. The results and the answers, derived from this constructive criticism, should tell you what urgently needs revising, and also the positive points will help to build your confidence. But, in due course, other important basics will be forgotten, if they are not revised in some form. The minimum required is to read about or discuss them, but it would be better to cover the details in a practical manner, by working with others. By doing the relevant exercises, which I have suggested in the chapters on tactics, riding and striking, you could ensure that very little is forgotten and that vital details are retained. If and when you do practise, in order to correct faults that were noticed, or simply to revise tactics and techniques, you should begin by reminding yourself of my three essential principles:

1. *Playmake for the ball to follow you* by applying LATET.

2. Make the *pony follow you* by riding as described by SLOSH.

3. Strike the ball *early* with a *slow swing* by using PASSF.

It is even better if you are watched by a coach when playing and practising, because you cannot see yourself, or assess yourself properly without hearing the opinion of someone who is qualified. It is debatable which of the following is worse:

1. Accumulating bad habits with no coach to correct you.

2. Learning bad habits from an ignorant. non-qualified coach.

In the same way as players must play, in order to learn and improve from experience, qualified coaches need to work to maintain and better their skills, and hence payment is not their primary motivation. Therefore, arrangements can be made to reduce the economic factor of coaching, and it is even better if all team members are involved and share the cost.

It has always been my vision that the day will come when an important member of one country's Polo Association will become a *playmaker of lasting stature*, by discovering a way to make all members of that Association accept regular coaching, in order that skills and techniques are frequently revised. The results would be stunning and would ensure a vastly improved standard of play, behaviour and *playmaking*. Then, large audiences could be attracted to give polo the reputation it deserves. In time, all other polo-playing countries would surely follow suit.

A practical way to bring about a substantial improvement in team and individual standards would be to introduce some constructive skills competitions. To do this would require a *playmaker* with considerable courage, prepared to raise sufficient funds to provide attractive prize money, and to arrange dates, venues and deal with other aspects of organization. However, if such an initiative were successful, it could have enormous *playmaking* dimensions, incorporating fund-raising for deserving charities, and also assisting the redistribution of wealth within the world of polo. To enter such competitions, *playmakers* would have to make a big effort to prepare properly, and even then risk making fools of themselves. However, those who did compete would gain enormously from the practice and revision beforehand – especially if assisted by a coach – and from the valuable exposure to pressure both during rehearsals and in the actual events. If any readers are interested in supporting the concept of such skills competitions – whether as competitors, sponsers, organizers or audience, please contact me or my son, Sebastian, as detailed in Appendix 2.

Appendix 1 — Playmaker Polo Revision Booklet

As mentioned in the concluding chapter of this book, I am publishing separately, in the form of a small booklet, all the Revisions sections that appear at the end of each chapter. This can be carried around in one's pocket, and it will be very easy to refer to it regularly, if not daily. Readers who would like the opportunity to keep tuned in to the many details of tactics, riding and striking given in *Playmaker Polo*, are invited to contact me, or my son Sebastian, and we will be pleased to send you a *Revision Booklet* on request.

Appendix 2 — Constructive Skills Challenge

At the end of the concluding chapter of this book, I outlined my concept of using constructive skills competitions as a practical way of bringing about a substantial improvement in team and individual standards. Properly administered, such an initiative could have enormous *playmaking* dimensions, incorporating fund-raising for deserving charities, and also assisting the redistribution of wealth within the world of polo.

This is a project close to my heart and I would welcome approaches from any *playmakers* who are interested in contributing, whether as competitors, sponsors or organizers, or in some other relevant capacity. If you would like to discuss any aspect of this project, please contact me, or my son Sebastian.

Since Hugh Dawnay is an international polo coach and Sebastian Dawnay is a professional polo player, both are constantly on the move and do not have a permanent contact address. However, they are widely known throughout the world of polo and it should be possible to contact them at major events. At the time of publication, their mobile phone numbers are:

Hugh – 3538 72470086   Sebastian – 4477 88798687

Hurlingham Polo Association Rules 2004

Reproduced by kind permission of the Hurlingham Polo Association.

THE RULES OF POLO

All matches, games and chukkas within the jurisdiction of the HPA are to be played under the HPA's Rules of Polo and the annexes thereto.

TEAMS, PLAYERS AND PLAYERS' EQUIPMENT, SUBSTITUTION

1. TEAMS
   a. **Composition.** A team may have no more than 4 players.
   b. **Entries.** The team captain or manager must complete an entry form to play in a tournament. The team must be qualified to play in the tournament and the entry form must contain the names of at least three players whose total handicap adds up at least to the minimum handicap of the tournament. Any player who is entered on the entry form or whose name is added subsequently must:
   (i) Be qualified by handicap and status to play in the tournament.
   (ii) Be a registered member of the HPA and a club having submitted a CV form where necessary at least 3 days before the match.
   (iii) Play for one team only in the tournament (but see Rule 3d).
   The entry form will contain a declaration which the team captain or manager must sign to the effect that the players nominated on the form or subsequently to be added or changed are qualified to play in the tournament or match and that the handicap and status of the player is correctly recorded (See also Annex D – Conditions for Official HPA Tournaments).
   c. **Team Changes.** Should a team captain or manager wish to change or add a player at any time before a match is about to start, he must submit an application to the Tournament Committee. Should the club official responsible be unable to check the eligibility of that player for whatever reason, then that player cannot play. The Club Official should inform the opposing team of any changes or addition as soon as possible. If the match is about to start or has started, then that player is a substitute (see Rule 3).
   d. **Handicap Limits.** Certain limits are placed on the handicap of teams and players within the team. If the handicap of a player or players has been raised during the season, a team may enter one goal above the tournament limit, with the goal or goals awarded on handicap being recorded on the scoreboard at the outset. Similarly, a player may play one goal above the individual limit e.g. a player raised to 5 mid season may play in a 6 goal tournament if entered but not as a substitute. Note: This rule does not apply to high goal in 2004 for which a Stewards' Directive has been issued.
   e. **Withdrawal or Disqualification.** Once the draw for a tournament has been published, a team may not withdraw without the authority of the Tournament Committee. This will only be

granted in exceptional circumstances at their discretion. Withdrawal by a team prior to or during a match without permission will invoke a charge of misconduct. A Tournament Committee has the right to disqualify a team at any time.

f. **Team Shirts.** Shirts will be in team colours with the number of the player no less than 9 inches high and in contrasting colour on the back. If, in the opinion of the Umpires or Tournament Committee, the colours of two competing teams are so alike as to lead to confusion, the team lower in the draw or second named in a league competition shall be instructed to play in another colour. Teams must have available a second set of shirts of contrasting colour.

g. **Umpire Ponies.** Teams are normally required to provide one pony for umpiring but two for high goal. Green or unfit ponies must not be offered.

h. **Handicap Calculation.** In all matches played under handicap conditions the handicap of each player in each team will be totalled. The lower total will then be subtracted from the higher and the resulting difference will be multiplied by the number of chukkas to be played in the match and divided by 6. This will give the number of goals to be given to the team with the lower total handicap. All fractions will count as half-a-goal. Any objection to the score posted on the score board at the start of the match must be made before the ball is thrown in.

j. **Team Captain.**
 (i) A captain will be appointed by each team. The umpires should identify the captain before the start of any match.
 (ii) The team captain or the team manager may not appeal against the appointment of any particular umpire, referee or other official nor against the time or venue of a game.
 (iii) The team captain has the right to ask the umpires to clarify a decision they may have made. However, once the umpires have, in their opinion, answered the team captain's query, he may not continue to question or dispute the decision in any way.
 (iv) A team captain may complete a report form detailing any irregularities by the Tournament Committee or the officials and submit it within 12 hours to the Tournament Committee who will forward it to the HPA.

k. **Not Trying.** Both teams in a match must try to win. If in the opinion of the Umpires or the Referee or the Tournament Committee, a team is believed to be not trying, the team should be warned by the Umpires. If the team fails to comply with this instruction, the Umpires shall submit a report using a report form and the team or individual players may be subject to a Disciplinary Enquiry by the Club Tournament Committee who may take any action considered appropriate, including the suspension of the team and its members from playing in the rest of the tournament. If it is considered appropriate by the Tournament Committee to refer the matter to the HPA, the team will be suspended pending adjudication by the HPA.

2. PLAYERS AND PLAYERS' EQUIPMENT

a. **Membership.** No person may play in matches, practice games and chukkas at or conducted by a club affiliated to the HPA in the UK or Ireland unless they are a registered member of a club and the HPA in accordance with Regulation 3 (see also Rule 1b).

b. **Left Handed Players.** No player shall play with his left hand.

c. **Dismounted Player.** A dismounted player may not hit the ball nor interfere with the play.

d. **Leaving the Field.** No player shall leave the field of play in the course of a match without the consent of the Umpires. Any player doing so may be subject to a charge of misconduct.

e. **Coaching.** Coaching of players is forbidden during play.

f. **Appealing.** A player may not appeal in any manner to the umpires for fouls, nor may he discuss or dispute a decision with the umpires during the game.

g. **Smoking.** No player or official shall smoke on the ground during a game or match.

h. **Drink and Drugs.** No player may play in any match, practice game or chukka under the influence of any illegal stimulant or drug including any substance referred to in Annex A to the Regulations (Human Doping).

j. **Equipment and Turnout.** Players are expected to be well turned out so that the reputation of the sport is enhanced. Umpires should inspect spurs and whips before a game.
 (i) **Headgear.** Everybody must wear protective headgear when riding on polo grounds or the surrounds and the headgear must be worn with a chin strap properly fastened and correctly positioned (see Note and Rule 27a).

(ii) **Breeches.** For matches, white breeches or jeans are to be worn.

(iii) **Spurs.** Spurs, including any rowel must be blunt, with the shank of no more than '1.25 inches' (3 cm) pointing downwards and to the rear. Any spur likely to wound a horse is forbidden and Umpires should inspect spurs before a match and have removed any sharp ones. They should fill in a report form to ensure that the same spurs do not appear at other clubs.

(iv) **Boots and Knee Pads.** For matches, brown boots are to be worn. Knee pads are usually worn. Buckles or studs may not be worn by a player on the upper part of his polo boots or knee pads in such a way as to damage another player's boots or breeches.

(v) **Whips.** Whips must not be more than 48 inches long including any tag. Broken whips are not allowed.

Note: The British Horse Society recommends "that hats which comply with PAS 015, EN 1384 or ASTMF 1163, ASTM F1163 and KOVFS 77.7, with either the Kitemark or SEI offer the best protection".

3. SUBSTITUTION

a. **General.** In order to start a match with each team having 4 players or to finish it, certain modifications to Rule 1 as detailed below are permitted. If a match is about to start or has started and a player is late or unable to play through accident, sickness or duty, he may be replaced by a substitute. The substitute must be qualified to play in the tournament and the team must remain qualified after the substitution has been made (see also Rule 28b).

b. **Captain's Choice.** The Tournament Committee, having been satisfied that there is a genuine need for a substitute, will ask the Captain of the team requiring the substitute for his choice. They must check the eligibility of the chosen substitute against Rule 1b.

c. **Chosen Substitute Not Eligible.** Should the chosen substitute not be eligible, the Tournament Committee must establish if there is another eligible substitute readily available. This is to include a player of the same handicap or one goal less than the player he will replace.

d. **No Eligible Player Available.** If no eligible player is readily available, the Tournament Committee may agree to any qualified player being used although he may have played or be due to play in another team. A player who is no longer in the tournament should be played in preference to one who is still in it. However, the Tournament Committee may authorise an OSP to substitute for an EU player if no qualified EU player is available.

e. **Handicap of Substitute.** If the substitute is of the same handicap as the player he has replaced or lower, then the score will not be altered. A team whose total handicap was below the upper limit of the tournament is not obliged to take a substitute of a higher handicap. However, if they choose to do so, up to the tournament limit, then the score will be altered immediately to reflect the increased total handicap of the team irrespective of when the substitution occurs. If a player who has been replaced by a substitute is subsequently able to play, the handicap of the higher player will stand.

f. **Player Raised in Handicap.** If a team is playing above the handicap limit of a tournament by virtue of including a player raised in handicap during the season, and that player has to be substituted during a match, the team must revert to within the handicap limit. However, if another player in that team is substituted, the original total handicap of the team may stand (see also Rule 28).

g. **Player who is Late.** Should a player who is late subsequently arrive, he may replace his substitute at the start of but not during any chukka in the match.

h. **Playing a 3 man Team.** If a player is late or unable to play as a match is about to start, then a team may play with 3 players but the team aggregate handicap must remain within the tournament limits. The team will start with the aggregate handicap of the three players but if the fourth player or his substitute subsequently joins in, then his handicap will be added to the score of the opposing side but will not be subtracted if he has a minus handicap.

j. **Substitution in a 3 man Team.** If a team has been reduced to 3 men as a result of a player being sent off by the umpires under Rule 28b(ii) or Penalty 10b, it must remain qualified in the event of any further substitution with the handicap of the sent off player included in the calculation.

k. **Effect on the Substitute.** A player who has substituted for another in an emergency should not be disqualified from continuing with his original team, or from joining another team if he is not already in one. He may also continue to play in the team in which he has played as a substitute if the original player is still not available and his own team is no longer in the tournament.

l. **Ponies.** It is the responsibility of the team to mount the substitute.

PONIES, TACK AND PONY WELFARE

4. PONIES, TACK AND PONY WELFARE

a. **General.** The overall responsibility for care and welfare of a pony rests at all times with the owner. The Stewards, Tournament Committee and match officials have a duty to enforce the Rules and may call in veterinary advice. Additional matters on the welfare of ponies, particularly on serious injury and the administration of drugs, are covered in Annex B of the Regulations.

b. **Veterinary Cover.** Clubs must have an arrangement for cover with a local veterinary practice. For all polo matches a veterinary surgeon should either be present or on immediate call and a club official should be in attendance from all games in case a welfare problem arises.

c. **Pony Passports.** All ponies are required by law to have a passport. These are available from the HPA.

d. **Vaccination.** All ponies playing in the UK must have a current annual certificate of vaccination against flu.

e. **Contagious or Infectious Diseases.** Any pony owner, stable manager or polo club which has a suspected case of a contagious disease such as ringworm or an infectious disease such as strangles or equine herpes must inform the HPA immediately with details of the action being taken. No infected pony or others in contact will be brought to a polo ground until clearance is given by a veterinary surgeon.

f. **Turnout and Prohibited Tack.** Ponies are expected to be well turned out and poor or badly fitted tack which is causing physical damage to the pony is not allowed (See Note for best playing or turned out pony). Each pony must be protected by bandages or boots on all four legs and it must have its tail put up. Ponies for umpiring should be equipped for polo except their tails need not be put up. The following are not allowed to be used during any game:

(i) A noseband, headpiece or headcollar which incorporates wire or any sharp material.

(ii) A hackamore or bitless bridle (may be used in practice chukkas at the discretion of the club).

(iii) Blinkers or any form of noseband or other equipment which obstructs the vision of the pony.

(iv) The mouthpiece of any bit, whether single or double, of not less than 0.25 inch (6.50 mm) in diameter at its narrowest point.

g. **Condition.** A pony may not be played if:

(i) Lame. Any pony that is seen to be lame should be referred to the duty veterinary surgeon before resuming another chukka. (If a pony does resume play, it is suggested that a public announcement should be made). If a pony is not sound, it is the Umpire's responsibility in the absence of a vet, to see that the pony is taken off the ground in the most humane way possible.

(ii) Showing signs of distress.

(iii) Blind in one eye.

(iv) Not under proper control or showing vice.

(v) It has had any form of tracheotomy or tracheostomy.

(vi) Showing blood, whether from the mouth, flanks or any other part. Ponies seen with blood in their mouths or excess spur or whip marks should be reported to the umpire or the referee, who should then request that the pony be inspected by the veterinary surgeon. If no veterinary surgeon is present, the pony should be inspected by an official or representative of the club; if in doubt about the severity of the wound, the pony should not be allowed to play until a veterinary surgeon's report has been received. A report form should be completed for (iii), (iv), and (v) above. Should any of the above symptoms become apparent during a game, then it will be stopped immediately and restarted as soon as the player has returned (see Rules 29 and 30).

h. **Shoes and Shoeing.** The Farriers' Registration Act, which has been law since 1975, states that any person who shoes a horse, including their own, must be a registered farrier. Ponies should therefore only be shod by a registered farrier. Frost nails, road studs, screws and fancy spikes or any protruding nails or sharp edges on a shoe are not allowed except as below:

(i) Rimmed shoes may be worn but the rim must be on the inside of the shoe only.

(ii) A calkin or stud must be of less than 0.5" (13 mm) cubed and be fitted on the last inch (25mm) of the outside heel of the hind shoe. A non-slip plug or road plug may be fitted. A plug is sunken into the shoe by a farrier and is not to be confused with any form of stud.

- (iii) If a shoe has a calkin or fixed stud it must be balanced by a raised and feathered inside heel tapered for a minimum of 1.5" (40 mm).
- (iv) A removable stud, which is the type strongly recommended, should be removed before the pony leaves the ground.
- (v) A pony may be shod with a maximum of two road nails or non-slip nails per shoe in order that it may be exercised safely on the roads. Such nails must not be on the widest part of the shoe.

j. **Injections.** A pony may not be injected in the surrounds of a polo ground except by a qualified vet or by an experienced individual with the permission of an official of the host club or the HPA. If a local anaesthetic is used to repair a wound, the pony is not allowed to play unless passed fit to do so by a veterinary surgeon.

k. **Water.** Clubs must ensure that fresh or running water is readily available at all pony and horse-box lines. Water should not be withheld for an extended period and should be offered to ponies after they have played.

l. **Number of Chukkas.** In the normal duration of a match, a pony must not be played for more than two full non consecutive chukkas, or the equivalent time; a pony which has played in more than half a chukka may not be played again for at least ten minutes. A pony must not be played in more than three full chukkas or the equivalent time in any one day.

m. **Use by Another Team.** In high and medium goal tournaments, a pony played by one team cannot be played by any other team in the same tournament. For intermediate goal tournaments, this rule applies except dispensation may be granted by the Tournament Committee.

n. **Drugs.** The administration to a pony of any drug or substance that is not a normal constituent of horse feed and is listed as banned in Annex B to the Regulations is prohibited.

o. **Horse Ambulance.** Either a trailer with motor vehicle attached or a low loading lorry each with ramp equipped with a winch and screens must be available near to the ground at all times during play.

Note. Best Playing or Turned Out Pony. Clubs are encouraged to award a prize for the best playing or best turned out pony. They must however ensure that the pony is in a fit state to collect its prize – i.e. that it is not distressed, looks well and does not have spur or whip marks, a cut mouth, sore back or any other signs of ill treatment. If a pony has received an accidental injury, such as a tread, then it should not be excluded from collecting its prize, provided that the injury has been properly treated. If a veterinary officer is present he should be asked to inspect the pony prior to the presentation

TOURNAMENT COMMITTEE, PRIVATE GROUNDS, UMPIRES AND REFEREES, GOAL JUDGES, TIMEKEEPER/SCORER AND MEDICAL COVER

5. TOURNAMENT COMMITTEE

a. **Requirement.** For any tournament the host club will appoint a Tournament Committee of three or more individuals, who preferably should have little or no vested interest in the outcome of the event. In the absence of a Tournament Committee, the Polo Manager of the Club or his representative with the Umpires and Referee shall act as the Tournament Committee.

b. **Duties.** The Tournament Committee will be charged with the overall responsibility for the running of the tournament. This will include;
- (i) checking the eligibility of each entry and any subsequent substitution.
- (ii) informing a team of a change in the entry of an opposing team.
- (iii) the structure of the tournament and the draw (See Annex E).
- (iv) the scheduling of matches.
- (v) the appointment of officials (but see Rule 7c and Annex D Paragraph 4).
- (vi) the provision of the grounds and the necessary equipment.
- (vii) dealing with any disciplinary matters or irregularity.

c. **Authority.** The authority of the Tournament Committee will exist at all times except that immediately before, immediately after and during play the authority of the Referee and the Umpires will be absolute on matters regarding the conduct of play. The Tournament Committee may receive a report from the umpires, referee or from the team captain which they will forward to the HPA. The decisions of the Tournament Committee will be final.

6. PRIVATE GROUNDS

a. **Inspection.** All private grounds must be inspected by an official of the HPA and passed before they may be used for matches played in official HPA tournaments.

b. **Matches.** A Tournament Committee that, in agreement with the owner and both teams, schedules a match to be played on a private ground, must contact the Polo Manager of the Club designated as the overseeing club for that ground. The Polo Manager should inform the Tournament Committee of the matches and teams that have been played at that ground in previous tournaments. If in agreement, then the designated club has the responsibility for all matters referring to the match. This includes the officials, the necessary medical and veterinary cover, any substitution and disciplinary action and finally to send in an authenticated score sheet.

7. UMPIRES AND REFEREES (see also Annex B)

a. **Authority.** There shall normally be two mounted umpires and a referee who have the duty to control the game according to the Rules of the HPA. Their authority as to the conduct of play shall be absolute immediately before, immediately after and during play. They will complete a report form with details of any irregularities or incidents of misconduct and submit it to the Tournament Committee immediately after the game. The report form should be signed by both umpires and the referee before submission.

b. **One Umpire.** The Tournament Committee may stipulate in the tournament conditions that there will only be one Umpire or, if this has not been done and in order to get a match started, invite the two Captains to agree to only one. When there is only one Umpire, there will normally be a Referee but he too on occasion may be dispensed with.

c. **Professional Umpires.** The Chief Umpire will appoint Professional Umpires to officiate at matches as laid down but he must inform the Tournament Committee of his choice. In the event of any disagreement, his decision is final.

d. **Consultation.** The Referee should have the means to contact the umpires at the end of each chukka to report any misconduct such as excessive whipping which the umpires may not have seen. The umpires should, in any event, report to the Referee at half time to discuss their conduct of the game.

e. **Umpires Disagree.** The decision of the Umpires shall be final, except where they disagree, in which case they should consult the Referee whose decision shall be final.

f. **Umpires' Discretion.** Should any incident or question not provided for in these rules or in the Supplementary Rules of the Polo Association concerned arise in a game, such incident or question shall be decided by the umpires. If the Umpires disagree, they must consult the Referee whose decision shall be final.

g. **Dress.** Umpires must wear a shirt or jacket with distinctive black and white vertical lines with clean white breeches or jeans and polished brown boots. They must wear a hard hat with a chin strap properly fastened and correctly positioned when mounted. The host club will normally provide an umpire shirt, whistle, pick up stick and ball bag (already on the umpire pony) for each umpire.

8. GOAL JUDGES (See also Annex B)

a. **Requirements.** A goal judge shall be appointed for each goal. On occasion, two may be used at each goal. Each shall give testimony to the umpire at the latter's request as to the goals scored or other points of the game near the goal, but the umpire shall make the final decisions.

b. **Goal Scored.** When a goal is scored (see Rule 20), the goal judge should wave his flag vigorously above his head to signify that a goal has been scored.

c. **Ball Crosses Back Line.** When the ball crosses the back line wide of the goal, the goal judge should signal by holding up a ball above his head, and then quickly place a ball on level ground one foot within the field of play where it crossed the line except that it must not be nearer than 4 yards from the goal posts or sideboards.

d. **Instructions.** Goal judges must be properly briefed, in particular:
   (i) To wear distinctive clothing such as white coats and protective riding or cricket hard hats, but not cycle helmets.
   (ii) To remain behind a white line, which must be drawn 20 yards behind each goal, until the ball is out and the ponies have slowed down.

(iii) To keep all impedimenta, e.g. chairs, ball boxes, spare goal posts, at least 30 yards behind goal posts. Other items such as bicycles should be placed well away from the ground so that they are not a danger to players or loose horses.

e. **Back to Back Goals.** Goal judges should not be used when there is play on two grounds with back to back goals.

9. TIMEKEEPER/SCORER (See also Annex B)

A Timekeeper/Scorer (referred to hereafter as "the Timekeeper") shall be employed in all matches with an Assistant Scorer who shall man the scoreboard. The Timekeeper shall be conversant with Rules 14–17 which govern his responsibility.

10. MEDICAL COVER

Clubs must ensure that at all matches listed in the Blue Book as "Fixtures Played Under HPA Official Tournament Conditions", there will be present 2 people with First Aid qualifications. Clubs should inform their local ambulance service in advance that the match is taking place and ensure that the correct telephone number is readily available. A First Aid qualification means having completed and passed a British Red Cross "Basic First Aid Course (Module 7)" or a St. John Ambulance "Emergency Aid for Appointed Persons Course" or an equivalent qualification, and completed such post-training refresher courses as are required to maintain a current certificate. Should the Umpire require medical assistance for an injured player, he should signal by waving his stick above his head.

GROUND, BALL AND ACCESS DURING PLAY

11. THE GROUND

a. **Ground.** The ground shall be a prepared surface to include the field of play and the safety zone (see also Rule 6 and Annex A).
b. **Field of Play.** A full size field of play shall be 300 yards (275 metres) in length (goal posts to goal posts) by 200 yards (180 metres) in width if unboarded; and by 160 yards (140 metres) if boarded. The minimum length shall be 250 yards (230 metres).
c. **Goal Posts.** The goal posts shall be 8 yards (7.3 metres) apart (inside measurement) and able to be widened to 16 yards (14.6 metres) to decide a tie (Rule 16) and centered at each end of the field. The goal posts shall be at least 10 feet (3 metres) high, and light enough to give way if collided with.
d. **Boards.** The boards shall not exceed 11 inches (28 centimetres) in height. They may be curved at the ends.
e. **Safety Zone.** The Safety Zone is recommended to extend at least 10 yards beyond the sidelines/boards and at least 30 yards beyond the back line. Clubs should ensure in any case that the safety zone behind the goals is of sufficient length and texture so that a player going through the goal at speed can stop with safety. Any incident of the game which occurs in the safety zone shall be treated as though it occurred on the field of play.

12. THE BALL

The size of the ball shall be 3 to 3.5 inches (76 to 89 millimetres) in diameter; the weight of the ball shall be within the limits of 4.25 to 4.75 ounces (120 to 135 grams).

13. ACCESS DURING PLAY

a. **Field of Play.** No person is allowed on the field of play during play for any purpose whatsoever, except the players and umpires. If play has been halted, no person may come onto the ground to assist except as authorized by the umpires.
b. **Safety Zone.** During play, the safety zone is restricted to the players, umpires and goal judges except that:
  (i) A stick holder may enter the safety zone but not the field of play to hand over a stick to a player.
  (ii) A pony may be ridden back to the pony lines providing it is safe to do so.

(iii) Ponies may be stationed and changed at the side (but not in the safety zone) providing there are no spectators in the area or at the ends of the ground in the corners of the safety zone. The area in which ponies are to be changed must be fair to both sides and be agreed between the umpires and the Polo Manager or Tournament Committee. The umpires must help to police it.

START, DURATION AND END OF PLAY

14. START OF PLAY

a. Five Minute Bell. The timekeeper will ring the bell five minutes before the advertised time for the start of the match to alert the teams and officials.

b. Line-up and Throw-in. At the start of the match the two teams shall line up in the middle of the ground, each team being on its own side of the half-way line. After calling for ends, the umpires should ask the team captains if they are happy with the score posted on the scoreboard (see Rule 1h for handicap calculation). The ball is then thrown in in accordance with Rule 21.

c. No Redress. After the ball has been thrown in there can be no redress even if the Umpires have failed to ask team captains if they are happy with the scores posted. (See also Annex B – Notes for Umpires – Preparation).

15. DURATION OF PLAY

a. Match. A match may be played over 4, 5 or 6 chukkas as stated in the Tournament Conditions.

b. Unfinished Match. Once a match has started it shall be played to a finish unless stopped by the umpires for some unavoidable cause, such as darkness or the weather, in which case it shall be resumed at the point at which it has stopped (score, chukka and position of the ball) at the earliest convenient time, to be decided upon by the Tournament Committee (see also Annex E, Rules for League Matches, paragraph 5).

c. Chukka. Chukkas are normally $7\frac{1}{2}$ minutes playing time with the exception of the last which will end on the bell after 7 minutes unless teams are tied and the Tournament Conditions require a result (see also Rule 17).

d. Intervals. In all matches there shall be a half-time interval of 5 minutes. For 5 chukka matches, this should be taken after the third chukka. All other intervals shall be of 3 minutes except 5 minutes shall be allowed if extra time is to be played or goals widened. A bell or hooter should be rung at the end of these intervals as a signal to the teams that the umpires are about to restart play.

e. Continuous Play. Play should be continuous except for the specified intervals and when an umpire blows the whistle for whatever reason. Play will not be stopped for changing ponies during play unless a pony is injured (see Rule 30).

f. Unnecessary Delay. No player or team may cause unnecessary delay before or during play.

g. Stopping Play. Play will be stopped by the umpires blowing one firm blast of the whistle. The clock is stopped and the ball is then dead until either the ball is hit or hit at if a penalty is awarded, or the ball is thrown in.

16. END OF TIME

a. The Bell. Where the bell or hooter ends play, play will stop immediately on the first sound, irrespective of where the ball may be and even if the Umpires fail to hear the bell or confuse the second with the first.

b. Normal Chukka. In a normal chukka, the first bell or hooter will be sounded after 7 minutes and play will continue until either a goal is scored or awarded, the ball goes out of play or hits the boards, the Umpire blows his whistle, or the second bell is rung after a further 30 seconds. Any penalty awarded after the first bell shall be taken at the beginning of the next chukka.

c. Last Chukka. In the last chukka play shall end at 7 minutes on the first bell except as below. If a penalty is awarded in the last chukka, it shall be taken in that chukka.

d. Last Chukka – Teams Tied. When the scores are tied and the Tournament Conditions require a result, play will continue until either a goal is scored or awarded, the ball goes out of play or hits the boards, or the second bell is rung after a further 30 seconds. If no goal is scored, extra time will be played.

e. **Last Chukka – Five Second Rule.** If a penalty has been awarded within the last 5 seconds of either the 7 minutes or the extra 30 seconds, the Timekeeper must allow a further 5 seconds of play from the time the ball is hit or hit at. e.g. if there were 3 seconds left, the timekeeper will allow 5 seconds from the time that the penalty is taken; thus 2 seconds will have been added to the game. The bell will be rung if a goal is scored or when 5 seconds have elapsed unless another penalty is awarded in which case the process is repeated. If the whistle is blown and no penalty is awarded, then play shall continue for the time remaining before the whistle was blown.

f. **Foul on The Bell.** If the bell rings for the end of the chukka or match just after a foul has been committed but before the Umpire has had time to blow his whistle, then the penalty must be taken in accordance with the above if the foul is confirmed.

17. EXTRA TIME TO BE PLAYED

a. **Interval.** There will be an interval of five minutes
b. **Sudden Death.** The team that scores or is awarded the first goal wins the match
c. **How Started.** The first chukka may be started with either:
   (i) Normal goals at the spot from where the previous chukka ended; ends are not changed; or
   (ii) Widened goals if the Tournament Conditions so state or team Captains agree in order to save ponies and time. The first chukka with widened goals will be started with a throw in from the centre, ends having been changed (but see Rule 18c). In any event, goals will be widened for the second chukka of extra time.

CHANGING ENDS, WRONG LINE-UP, SCORING GOALS AND WINNING

18. CHANGING ENDS

a. **After Goal Scored.** Except in the case of a goal awarded from a Penalty 1, ends shall be changed after every goal and the game re-started from the middle of the ground with a throw in. The players shall be allowed a reasonable time in which to reach the middle of the ground at a canter and take up their positions. However, no team should be disadvantaged by delaying tactics of the opposition. If this should happen, then the whistle should be blown and the clock restarted when the ball is thrown in.

b. **No Score at Half-Time.** Ends shall also be changed if a goal has not been scored by half-time, and play shall be re-started at a corresponding position in the other half of the ground

c. **Score Level: Widened Goals.** If the score is levelled at the very end of a match and the bell is rung before the ball has been thrown in, and the next chukka is due to begin with widened goals (Rule 17), then ends shall be changed once only.

19. WRONG LINE UP

a. **By Teams.** If the Umpires inadvertently allow the teams to line up the wrong way at any time play will continue. However, if at the end of the chukka no goal has been scored, ends shall be changed and the game restarted with a throw in or hit from a corresponding position in the other half of the ground.

b. **By Player.** If a player is on the wrong side of the line up, he may not make a play until he is behind a member of his own team.

20. SCORING GOALS AND WINNING

a. **To Score.** A goal is scored from play when the ball passes between the goal posts or the imaginary vertical lines produced by the inner surfaces of the goal posts and across and clear of the goal line. A ball on the line is still in play. A ball hit directly over the top of either goal post shall not count as a goal because it does not pass between their inner vertical lines. If a ball lodges in the goal post, a hit in will be awarded. If a ball splits, see Rule 31.

b. **Disputed Goals.**
   (i) If the two Umpires are unable to decide as to whether a goal was scored or not, having consulted the goal judge, they must give the benefit of the doubt to the defending team without consulting the Referee.

(ii) If it is considered that an error has been made in the recording of a goal, this may be brought to the attention of the Umpires during the match but once the match has ended, there shall be no redress as to the score.
c. **Whistle Blown as Goal Scored.** If a whistle is blown for a foul at approximately the same time as a goal is scored:
(i) The goal will be disallowed and a penalty awarded to the defending side if it is decided that the attacking side have committed a foul.
(ii) The goal will be allowed if it is decided that the attacking side have not committed a foul or the foul was blown against the defending side, whether or not the foul is confirmed.
d. **To Win.** The side that scores the most goals, including goals awarded on handicap and by penalties, wins the match.

RESTARTING PLAY

21. BALL NOT OUT: THROW IN
a. **When Thrown In.** The ball will be thrown in by the umpire in the following circumstance:
(i) At the start of the match (Rule 14) or on restarting after an interval (Rule 23) if a Penalty has not been awarded.
(ii) After a goal has been scored (Rule 18a) or Penalty 1 awarded (Rule 40a).
(iii) If the ball has gone out of play over the side lines or boards (Rule 22).
(iv) After an accident or injury or any forced stoppage (Rules 26 – 31).
(v) If the umpires award Penalty 7 for breach of Rules 34(c) or 39(c).
(vi) If the whistle has been blown for a foul and the umpires or the referee rule 'No Foul' (Rule 26b).
(vii) If the ball has been carried unintentionally (Rule 36c).
b. **Where Thrown In.** The umpire shall stand at the spot as laid down in the specific rule or where the incident took place, facing the nearer side of the field, but at least 20 yards from the boards or sideline.
c. **Position of Teams.** Both teams shall line up at least 5 yards from the umpire parallel to the back line with an appreciable distance separating each team.
d. **Play Restarted.** The umpire, having been satisfied that the teams are apart and ordered, will bowl the ball in underhand, low and hard between the opposing ranks of players; the players to remain stationary until the ball has left his hand.

22. BALL HIT OVER SIDE LINE
The ball must go over and clear of the sidelines or boards to be out. When the ball is hit over the side line or boards, the Umpire will throw in the ball in accordance with Rule 21 with his pony just inside the boards or line where it went out. A reasonable time must be allowed for players to line up.

23. RESTARTING AFTER INTERVAL
On play being resumed after an interval, the ball shall be thrown in or a hit taken as if there had been no interval. The Umpire must not wait for players who are late.
a. **Ball hit the boards or went out.** If the ball hit the boards without going over them it shall be treated as though it had been hit over them.
b. **Ball close to boards.** If the ball is close to the boards or sideline, the throw in must still be towards the boards but from 20 yards within the field of play.

24. ATTACKER HITS BEHIND – HIT IN
a. **Attacker Hits Behind.** The ball must go over and be clear of the back line to be out.
b. **Hit In.** When the ball is hit behind the back line by the attacking side, it shall be hit in, once the umpire has called 'Play', by a defending player from the spot where it crossed the line, but at least four yards from the goal posts or boards. The striker may not circle once 'Play' has been called. The umpire shall give the attacking side reasonable time to get into position before calling 'Play'. The ball is in play the moment that it has been hit or hit at if missed (see also Rule 32a(iii)). None of the attacking side shall be behind the striker nor within 30 yards of the back line until the ball is hit or hit at; the defenders being free to place themselves where they choose.

c. **Foul.** If the whistle is blown for a foul at approximately the same time as the ball is hit behind the back line by an attacker and the foul is over-ruled, the ball shall be hit in.
d. **Hitting Before 'Play' is Called.** If the player hitting in, hits or hits at the ball before 'Play' is called the umpire shall blow his whistle and allow the hit to be taken again. For persistent breach of this Rule, he may respond as in Rule e below.
e. **Delay by Defending Side.** In the event of unnecessary delay by the defending side hitting in, the umpire shall call on the defending side to hit in at once. If the umpire's request is not complied with, he shall award a Penalty 6.
f. **Delay by Attacking Side.** In the event of unnecessary delay by the attacking side, the hit in shall be moved up to the 30 yard line.

25. DEFENDER HITS BEHIND – PENALTY 6 (SAFETY 60)
a. **Defender Hits Behind.** If one of the defending side hits the ball over his back line either directly or off his own pony, or after glancing off the boards or goal posts, Penalty 6 shall be awarded. However, if the ball strikes any other player or pony, or the umpire, before going behind, it shall be a hit in.
b. **Foul.** If the whistle is blown for a foul at approximately the same time as the ball is hit behind the back line by a defender as above and the foul is over-ruled, a Penalty 6 shall be awarded.

PLAY STOPPED/NOT STOPPED

26. PLAY STOPPED FOR A FOUL
a. **Foul.** A foul is defined as any infringement of the Rules. Should a foul be committed, the umpires will blow the whistle to stop play except when he considers that the side fouled would be clearly disadvantaged if he did so. However, umpires should use this rule (**the Advantage Rule**) with discretion as often the side fouled would prefer the penalty, and serious or dangerous fouls should not go unpunished.
b. **No Foul.** If the Referee rules 'No Foul' or the umpires themselves agree after consultation that a foul was not committed, then the throw-in will be taken from the spot where the ball was when the whistle was blown. If the Referee is unable to see the play, then he should rule 'No Foul'.

27. PLAY STOPPED FOR PLAYER'S EQUIPMENT
a. **Loss of Headgear.** If a player loses his headgear the Umpire shall stop the game to enable him to recover it, but not until an opportunity occurs that neither side is favoured thereby.
b. **Illegal Equipment.** If any player infringes Rule 2j (Players' Equipment), the player shall be sent off the ground by the umpires and may not re-enter play until the offence has been rectified. Play shall be started or restarted as soon as the player has left the ground.

28. PLAY STOPPED FOR INJURY TO PLAYER
a. **Player Falls Off.** If a player falls off his pony, the umpires shall not stop the game, until the ball is in a neutral position, unless he is of the opinion that the player is injured or is liable to be injured. What constitutes a fall is left to the decision of the Umpire. The Umpire shall re-start the game with a throw in directly the player concerned is ready to resume play and shall not wait for any other player.
b. **Player Injured.**
   (i) If a player is injured, the umpires shall stop the game immediately and signal for medical assistance by waving the pick-up stick above their head. A period not exceeding 15 minutes shall be allowed for the recovery of the injured player. If it is likely that the player will not be able to continue, then an eligible substitute should be alerted during this period (see also Rule 3 and Annex B, Para 4g). If he is unfit to continue, the game shall be restarted as soon as possible with a substitute.
   (ii) If a player be disabled by a foul, and a qualified player cannot be found to substitute (see Rule 3c), the Umpires, in consultation with the Referee, may decide to remove a player from the team that has fouled. The player removed shall be the one whose handicap is nearest above the disabled player. If the disabled player is equal to or higher than that of any of his opponents, the captain of the team fouled will designate the one to retire. The game shall

continue and no change in handicap shall be made: if the team that has fouled refuses to continue, it shall forfeit the game.

c. **Concussion.** In the event of a player being or seeming to be concussed the Umpires, or if no Umpires are present the senior player on the ground, will stop the game and arrange for the player to see a doctor as soon as possible. If no doctor is present when the accident occurrs it will be the sole responsibility of the Umpires or the senior player present to decide if the player was actually concussed. The HPA must be notified within 24 hours by fax or email and the player will not be permitted to play again for a minimum of one week from the date of the concussion without a certificate of fitness from a doctor.

29. PLAY STOPPED FOR TACK

a. **Play to Continue.** Players are responsible for the serviceability of their tack. Hence time out will not be given for lost or broken tack such as a martingale, stirrup leather or iron, lost bandages or boots. A player may change onto another pony.

b. **Play Stopped.** The game will be stopped immediately however, in the interest of safety, for tack which presents a danger to any player or pony such as a broken girth or broken martingale if the end trails on the ground, broken rein if single, broken or loose bit, broken curb chain, or loose bandages or boots.
The umpire may allow the player to rectify the fault immediately on the ground if it can be done quickly. Otherwise the player must leave the ground and play will be restarted as soon as the player has done so. The player may change onto another pony.

30. PLAY STOPPED FOR INJURY TO PONY

a. The Umpires have a responsibility during play for the welfare of the ponies. Thus, if a pony is suffering from any of the conditions outlined in Rule 4g, in particular lameness, distress or showing blood, then the game will be stopped immediately:
   (i) If a pony falls (a pony is judged to have fallen if its shoulder touches the ground) the Umpire should ensure that it is trotted up and is fit to play before the player remounts.
   (ii) If a pony is not sound, it must be led off the ground to the pony lines as quietly as possible.
   (iii) If a pony is seriously injured, then every effort must be made to take it off the ground in a horse ambulance. Players shall be instructed to shield the pony from the spectators as far as possible (see also Annex B to the Regulations, Para 7, and Annex B, Para 4g).

b. If a pony throws a shoe and if requested by the player, the umpires will allow that player to change his pony the next time the whistle is blown. In both a and b the umpires shall re-start the game with a throw in directly the player concerned is ready to resume play and shall not wait for any other player who may not be present.

31. PLAY STOPPED FOR TRODDEN IN OR SPLIT BALL

a. **Trodden In.** If the ball is trodden into the ground, the Umpires shall stop play, remove the ball and re-start with a throw in (Rule 21).

b. **Split.** If the ball splits, the Umpire should stop play:
   (i) Immediately if in equal parts.
   (ii) When play is in a neutral position if the larger part can still be played.
   The umpires will award a goal if it is clear that the larger part of the ball has gone through the goal.

LINE OF THE BALL, RIGHT OF WAY AND PRECEDENCE

(See Appendix pages 350–353 for Figs i to xxv)

32. LINE OF THE BALL AND RIGHT OF WAY

The Right of Way (ROW) is not identical to and must not be confused with the Line of the Ball (LOB), and does not depend on who last hit the ball.

a. **Line of the Ball.**
   (i) When the ball is struck or thrown in, the path along which it travelled to a stop or is travelling, and its extended path, is known as the LOB.

(ii) The line does not change if the ball deviates only for a short distance and the player with the original ROW can still play the ball without changing direction.

(iii) If a player hits at and misses a dead (out of play) ball the line is taken as that which the player was riding.

b. **Right of Way.**

(i) At each moment of the game, there shall exist as between any two or more players in the proximity of the ball a priority referred to as the ROW. This shall be considered to extend ahead of the player who has established himself on it, and in the direction in which that player is riding. The ROW entitles a player to proceed down it freely (subject to a legitimate ride-off or stick hooking) and without danger to hit the ball on his off side. The width of the ROW is taken to be approximately 5 feet measured from the ball to the player's near side leg. No player shall enter the ROW except at such a distance that not the slightest risk of a collision or danger to either player is involved.

(ii) If the LOB changes and as a result the ROW changes, a player must clear the new ROW immediately without making a play on the ball. In this case, it is not a play if a pony kicks the ball.

(iii) The ROW entitles a player to take the ball on the offside of his pony. If he places himself to hit it on the nearside and thereby in any way endangers another player he has no ROW and can only make a play if he does not unlawfully impede or endanger a player with the ROW.

(iv) If two players ride from opposite directions, they must hit the ball on the offside.

33. PRECEDENCE OF PLAYERS

a. A player following the ball on its exact line and taking it on his off side has the ROW over all other players (Fig i), save as in 33g below.

b. A player meeting the ball on its exact line and taking it on his off side has the ROW over all players riding at an angle from any direction (Fig ii).

c. Any player riding towards the LOB at an angle to it and in the same direction that the ball is travelling has the ROW over any player riding from the opposite direction, irrespective of who is at the lesser angle. (Figs iii and iv)

d. When two or more players ride in the direction that the ball is travelling, the player that has precedence, and consequently the ROW, is the one whose approach to the ball is at the lesser angle to the LOB provided that he plays the ball on the offside (Figs v and vi). If the players are at equal angles, the player that has the LOB on his off side has the ROW (Fig vii).

e. When two or more players ride to meet the ball, the player that has precedence, and consequently the ROW, is the one whose approach to the ball is at the lesser angle to the LOB provided that he plays the ball on the offside (Fig viii). If the players are at equal angles, the player that has the LOB on his off side has the ROW.

f. Two opposing players already making a play on each other and following the ball on its exact line have the ROW over all other players (Fig ix).

g. Two players riding in opposite directions on the exact LOB each have a ROW. Both players must take it on their respective off sides (Fig x).

h. Two opposing players already making a play on each other and following the direction of the ball at an angle have priority over a player meeting unless he is on the exact LOB (see Rule 33b) (Fig xi).

j. A player may surrender his ROW if, having hit the ball, he deviates from its exact line Fig xii).

34. THE PLAYER WITH THE RIGHT OF WAY

Checking is a deliberate and sudden reduction in speed.

a. An opponent may only enter the ROW if he does so at a distance and speed that does not endanger either player nor cause the player with the ROW to check. If an opponent enters the ROW safely with the ball ahead of him, he has the ROW and the player cannot ride into him from behind and only has a play on his nearside (Fig xiii).

b. If the player hits the ball past the offside of an opponent who is on the exact LOB, the opponent has the right to play the ball on his offside. The player who hit the ball only has a play on the near side (Fig xiv).

c. If an opponent is in a position to attempt a defensive play, the player must continue to move the ball. If he is moving at walking speed or stops he may tap the ball once only and then must leave it, accelerate with it or hit it away (Fig xv). A Penalty 7 (throw in) should be awarded for the breach of this rule. The opponent is considered to be in a 'position to attempt a defensive play' if he is within one horse's length on either the off or the nearside of the player with the ball.

d. The player surrenders the ROW if he checks to avoid what would have been a legitimate ride off (Fig xvi).
e. The ROW entitles the player to play the ball on his offside. If he switches to play it on the nearside he loses the ROW and has fouled if he endangers any other player or causes a player to check (Fig xvii).

RIDING OFF, DANGEROUS RIDING, INTIMIDATION, HOOKING, MISUSE OF WHIP, SPURS AND STICK, ROUGH OR ABUSIVE PLAY

(See Appendix pages 352–353 for Figs xviii to xxv)

35. RIDING OFF, DANGEROUS RIDING AND INTIMIDATION

A player may not ride in a manner which creates danger to another pony, player, official or any other person or which places the welfare of his own pony at undue risk. A player must ride off shoulder to shoulder and may push with his arm above the elbow provided the elbow is kept close to the side. In particular, a player may not (Fig xx):

a. Ride off at such an angle or speed as to endanger a player or his pony.
b. Ride into an opponent behind the saddle.
c. Ride an opponent across or into the ROW of another player at an unsafe distance (Fig xix).
d. Ride off an opponent who is already being ridden off by another member of his team (sandwiching)(Fig xx). However, it is not a foul for a player to hook legitimately an opponent's stick while the opponent is being ridden-off by a team mate of the player hooking.
e. Continue to ride off another player over the goal line, thereby endangering a goal judge.
f. Ride his pony from behind into the forehand or backhand stroke of an opponent (Fig xxi).
g. Spare.
h. Use his pony to spoil a stroke by riding over the ball and into an opponent who has already started the downward swing of a full forehand or backhand stroke (Fig xxii).
j. Zigzag in front of another player in such a way as to cause the latter either to have to check his pace or risk a fall.
k. Pull across or over a pony's legs either in front or behind in such a manner as to risk tripping either pony.
l. Ride at an opponent in such a manner as to intimidate, causing him to pull out or miss his stroke, although no foul actually occurs.

36. HOOKING, MISUSE OF THE STICK AND CARRYING THE BALL

a. **Hooking.** For a player to make a legitimate hook, the following conditions must apply:
   (i) He must be on the same side of his opponent's pony as the ball (Fig xxiii), or in a direct linebehind (Fig xxiv and xxv), and his stick must be neither over or under the body nor across the legs of an opponent's pony.
   (ii) All of his opponent's stick must be below the level of his opponent's shoulder.
   (iii) His opponent must be in the act of striking the ball.
b. **Misuse.** A player may not hold his stick in such a way as to interfere with another player or is pony or use his stick in a manner that creates danger to another pony or player such as:
   (i) Reaching over and across or under and across any part of an opponent's pony to strike a the ball.
   (ii) Hitting into or amongst the legs of a pony.
   (iii) A player who is holding the ball through dribbling should be penalised if he is judged to have created the danger by then playing a full shot.
   (iv) Taking a full swing at the ball from the throw in or in a melee in such a way as to endanger other players or ponies.
   (v) Taking a full swing under a pony's neck in such a way as to endanger another player or pony riding alongside.

(vi) "Windmilling" or "helicoptering" his stick either as an appeal or in celebration of scoring a goal.

(vii) Dropping the head of the stick on the pony's rump.

c. **Carrying the Ball.** A player may not catch, kick or hit the ball with anything but his stick. He may block with any part of his body but not with an open hand. He may not carry the ball intentionally. If the ball becomes lodged against a player, his pony or its equipment, in such a way that it cannot be dropped immediately, the Umpire shall blow his whistle and restart the game with a throw in (Rule 21) at the point where it was first carried.

37. ROUGH OR ABUSIVE BEHAVIOUR

A player may not:

a. Use his whip other than in exceptional circumstances when the ball is not in play. For this offence the umpires should award as a minimum a Penalty 5 (b).

b. Use his whip or spurs unnecessarily or in excess at any time.

c. Intentionally strike his own pony with his stick at any time.

d. Intentionally strike another player or another player's pony with his stick, whip or fist.

e. Abuse his pony by hauling or jabbing it unnecessarily in the mouth.

f. Use foul or offensive language or a gesture of abuse in such a way as to bring the game of polo into disrepute.

g. Seize with the hand, strike or push with the head, hand, arm, or elbow another player (see also Rule 35).

h. Knowingly strike the ball when it is off the field of play or after the whistle has been blown. If a hit is made after the whistle for a foul, the umpires should increase the severity of the penalty if the hit is by a member of the fouling team, or cancel the penalty or decrease its severity if the hit is by a member of the team fouled.

PENALTIES

38. PERSONAL FOULS AND TECHNICAL PENALTIES

A personal foul involving unsportsmanlike conduct such as, but not limited to:
- Disrespect towards officials
- Arguing with the umpire or other official
- Foul or abusive language
- Appealing for fouls verbally or with the stick must at minimum be penalised by a technical progressively as follows:
- Penalty for first offence
- A more severe penalty if a penalty has already been awarded

This does not preclude an umpire awarding Penalty 10(a) or 10(b) at the first offence.

Note: If a Penalty 2 has been awarded and a defending player offends, then the penalty will be taken as normal, but if missed, will be taken again. If successful on the first attempt then play will be restarted with a Penalty 5b.

39. TAKING OF PENALTIES

a. **Ball In Play.** The ball is in play the moment it has been hit or hit at and missed (see also Rule 32a (iii)).

b. **Team Taking the Penalty.** The team taking the penalty or hit (the attacking team) must:

(i) **Position the Ball Quickly.** Making a tee is not allowed: one player only may position the ball, provided he takes no longer than five seconds. The ball may be repositioned once only and not after 'Play' has been called.

(ii) **Not Circle.** Once the Umpire has called 'Play', the striker must immediately start to take the hit. The ball must be hit at on the first approach without any circling at the beginning of or during the run up.

(iii) **Not Cause Unnecessary Delay.**

(iv) **Not Strike the Ball a Second Time with a Full Shot.** When taking a penalty on or within the 60 yard line, the striker and his team members, after the initial hit or hit at the ball, may not subsequently hit or hit at the ball with more than a half shot until the ball has been hit or hit at by an opponent or in such a way that the umpires consider dangerous. A half shot is defined as the head of the stick starting the downward swing below the shoulder of the striker.

c. **Infringement by Team Taking the Penalty.** If the team taking the penalty infringe the rules, the umpires will normally award a Penalty 7 except for infringement as in Rule 39b(iv) when Penalty 5a will be awarded from the spot where the offence occurred. If the rules pertaining to Penalty 2 or 3 are infringed other than in Rule 39b(iv), then the defending team shall be awarded a hit from the middle of their own goal.

d. **Infringement by Team Facing the Penalty.** If the team facing the penalty (the defending team) infringe the rules whilst the penalty is being hit, then another hit will be taken unless goal has been scored or awarded. In the case of a Penalty 2 or 3, if a member of the defending team comes out between the goal posts or crosses the back line before the ball is hit and stops the ball, and in the opinion of the umpires a goal would have been scored, then the goal will be awarded. If, however, the umpires consider that a goal would not have been scored, then the hit will be retaken. If the player who stopped the ball did not infringe the rules but another member of his team did, a goal or another hit will be awarded as above.

40. SPECIFIC PENALTIES

a. **Penalty 1 – Penalty Goal**
If, in the opinion of the Umpire, a player commits a dangerous or deliberate foul in the vicinity of goal in order to save a goal, the team fouled shall be allowed one goal. The game shall be restarted at a spot ten yards from the middle of the goal of the team that has fouled (defending team) with a throw in. Ends shall not be changed.

b. **Penalty 2 – 30 Yard Hit**
The umpires will give the captain of the team fouled (team that is taking the penalty) the choice between:
Either: a free hit from the spot where the foul occurred; none of the defending team to be within 30 yards of the ball,
Or: a free hit from a spot 30 yards from the goal line of the team that has fouled, opposite the middle of the goal.
In both cases, all the defending team to be behind their back line or off the field of play until the ball is hit or hit at, but not between the goal posts; nor when the ball is brought into play may any of the defending team enter the field of play between the goal posts. The team taking the penalty to be behind the ball at the moment it is hit or hit at (Note 1).

c. **Penalty 3 – 40 Yard Hit**
A free hit from a spot 40 yards from the goal line of the team that has fouled opposite the middle of the goal.
All the defending team to be behind their back line until the ball is hit or hit at, but not between the goal posts, nor when the ball is brought into play may any of the defending team enter the field of play from between the goal posts. The team taking the penalty to be behind the ball at the moment it is hit or hit at (Note 1)

d. **Penalty 4 – 60 Yard Hit**
A free hit at the ball from a spot 60 yards from the goal line of the team that has fouled opposite the middle of the goal. All the defending team to be behind the 30 yard line. The team taking the penalty shall be free to place themselves where they choose.

e. **Penalty 5(a) – Free Hit from the Spot**
A free hit at the ball from the spot where the foul took place, but not nearer the boards or side lines than four yards.
None of the defending team to be within 30 yards of the ball, nor behind the ball (Note 1).
The team taking the penalty shall be free to place themselves where they choose.
A Penalty 5a should not be awarded against a defending team within their own 60 yard line.
A Penalty 2, 3 or 4 is to be awarded as appropriate. This does not rule out the option of the spot hit for a Penalty 2.

f. **Penalty 5(b) – Free Hit from the Centre**
A free hit at the ball from the centre of the ground.
None of the defending team to be within 30 yards of the ball, nor behind the ball (Note 1).
The team taking the penalty shall be free to place themselves where they choose.

g. **Penalty 6 – 60 Yard Hit (Opposite where ball crossed the back line – Safety 60)**
   A free hit at the ball from a spot 60 yards distant from the back line, opposite where the ball crossed it, but not nearer the boards or side lines than four yards.
   All the defending team to be behind the 30 yard line.
   The team taking the penalty shall be free to place themselves where they choose.
h. **Penalty 7 – Throw In**
   A throw in in accordance with Rule 21 from the point where the foul occurred.
j. **Penalty 10(a) – Player Sent Off for the Rest of the Chukka**
   The Umpires may send off a player for the rest of the chukka in progress in addition to any other penalty (Note 2).
k. **Penalty 10(b) – Player Sent Off for the Rest of The Match**
   The umpires may send off a player for the rest of the match, in addition to any other penalty (Note 2).

Note 1: *Behind the ball is interpreted as being behind a line parallel to the back line and running through the point where the ball has been placed.*

Note 2: *Penalty 10(a) and (b) may be given for any breach of the Rules but the Umpires must agree that a player should be sent off. If not in agreement, the Referee must be asked to decide. The side to which the sent off player belonged shall continue with three players only and any player sent off must return to the pony lines. Umpires should make it clear to the player(s) penalised and to the captain of the teams which penalty has been given and, in both cases, a report form must be completed by the umpires.*

ANNEX A – SUGGESTED LAYOUT OF A POLO GROUND

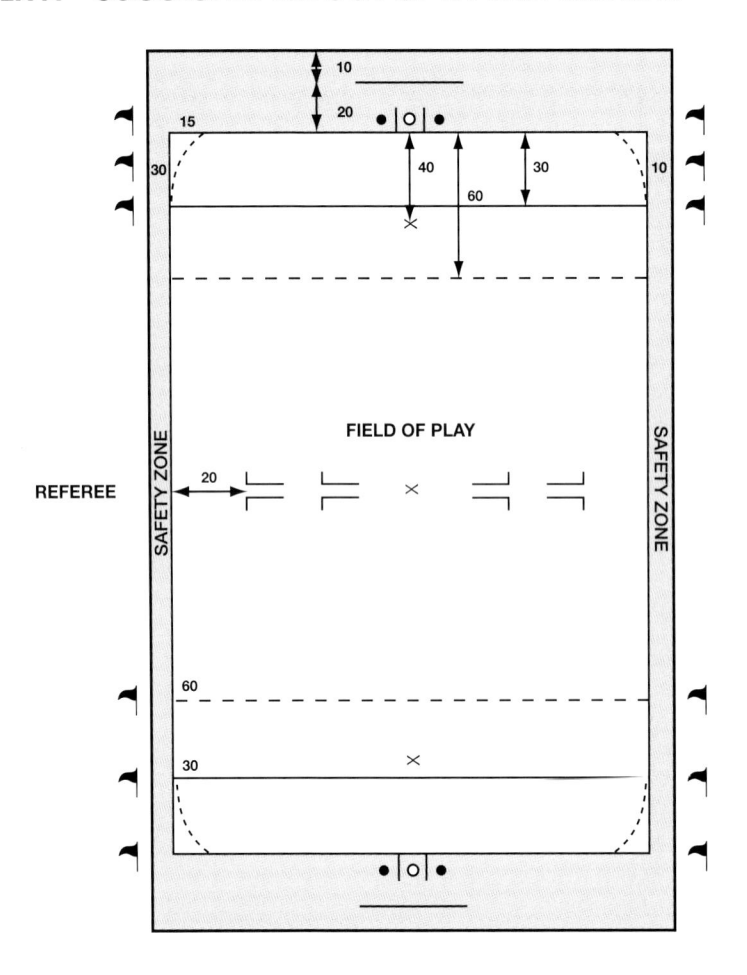

Sockets for widened goals 4 yards out from each goal post

Length: 300 yards maximum, 250 yards minimum.
Width: 200 yards maximum unboarded, 160 yards maximum boarded.
Safety Zone: At sides about 10 yards, at ends about 30 yards.
Markings: Broken lines or full marking may be used across the grounds. Marks on the boards or flags (clear of the safety zone) are useful as a guide to the umpires.

A line of tees clear of the centre spot should be marked on the centre line. A double tee as shown will help keep teams apart at the throw in.

Boards:
Boards keep the ball in play, allow the ground to be narrowed and spread the game more evenly across the field. They should not exceed 11 inches in height and be of treated timber at least one inch thick. A metal peg should be inserted down the middle to secure them to the ground. They should be tongued and grooved at the ends or joined by a metal plate. A board should be easily replaceable during a match if damaged. A triangular arris rail (4 x 2in) may be fitted at the base of the board to deflect the ball back into play. Boards may be curved from the 30 yard line to 15 yards into the back line.

ANNEX B – NOTES FOR OFFICIALS

1. **Introduction.** These notes are included in order to explain some of the tasks of referees, umpires and other officials. They are also designed to clarify and elaborate on some of the Rules of Polo and the penalties to be taken subsequent upon the infringement of these rules. The notes do not attempt to interpret all the incidents of play which are covered in the rules. They are not comprehensive and where there is apparent confliction the Rules of Polo take precedence.
2. **The Referee.** The Rules shall be administered by a referee and two mounted Umpires as laid down in Rule 7. The Referee has a very responsible position and he should have considerable polo experience at least to the level of the match that he is refereeing. He must be in an elevated and isolated position at the centre of the ground from which he can best observe the play. He must make his position known to the umpires before a match. He will be consulted if the two Umpires disagree as to the foul or as to what penalty to award. Thus he must concentrate throughout the game, as the decisions he will make will have a bearing on its outcome. He must avoid distractions such as talking to neighbours or using a mobile phone. If an Umpire appeals to the Referee, he will in the first instance raise a hand and if the Referee is satisfied that he saw and understood the play then he will confine his decision as to whether a foul occurred or not. If he considered that a foul did occur and it is obvious which side fouled, then he should raise one hand above his head and point with the other in the direction in which the hit is to be taken. If however he considers no foul occurred, or he could not see the incident because his sight was obscured, he should stand and make the wash out signal by moving his hands horizontally across his body.
    a. **Consultation.** If the Referee is in any doubt as to the nature of the foul or direction in which it should be given, he should make the come hither signal and move onto the ground. The Umpires should canter towards him for consultation. This should be kept as brief as possible and be carried on out of earshot of the players and spectators. Alternatively, the Umpires might wish to consult with the Referee in their own right in which case they should proceed as above. On occasion the Umpires will agree that a foul has occurred but disagree as to the penalty to be awarded. They will then point to the two alternative spots (e.g. centre or sixty) and the Referee will point to the spot at which he considers the penalty should be taken.
    b. **Radios.** Ideally, the Referee will be able to talk to at least one umpire by radio during the match. This will save time and allow the Referee and, through him, the commentator to know what is happening on the ground; eg, when a technical penalty is awarded or there is a stoppage owing to injury. In any event, he should have some form of contacting the umpires after each chukka and they should report to him at half time to discuss any particular aspects of play.
    c. **One Umpire.** The Tournament Conditions may stipulate that there will be only one umpire in which case the Referee has to act as a second umpire to whom the mounted umpire can appeal for assistance. In certain cases the Referee too may be dispensed with.

3. The Umpires

a. General. The authority of the Umpires should be absolute in all matters affecting the conduct of play immediately before, immediately after and during play. Polo is one of the hardest games toumpire due to the complexity of the Rules, the speed at which it is played and the need to make immediate decisions based on an assessment of speed, angle and distance. The good Umpire must therefore know the rules, concentrate on the play throughout and be consistent, clear and decisive in his judgements. In this way he will earn the respect of the players and make his task much easier. He should treat the players with fairness and under standing being ready to defuse any potentially explosive situation; he should be a dictator without being dictatorial. The Umpires should do all that they can to make a game flow and minimise delays but at the same time punish offences and maintain firm control. It is not in the gift of the team captains to agree time out except if agreed for friendly matches or if one or other team is on borrowed ponies.

b. Selection. There will normally be two umpires but the Tournament Committee may stipulate that there be only one umpire. They should select the umpires for a match with care. For preference, those who have an interest in the outcome of the match and those who have a relative playing should not be asked to umpire. The Committees should use discretion when selecting umpires avoiding as far as possible those who have a record of dissent from certain teams. There are never enough experienced Umpires to go round so a pairing with one less experienced is to be encouraged, not least to give the latter a chance to learn. A team captain may inform the Committee that his team is not happy with a certain umpire before the tournament but once the umpire has been appointed he may not appeal in any way against the appointment.

c. Preparation. An Umpire should arrive at the ground at least ten minutes before the match is due to start. He should be smart in appearance; dressed in white with boots and helmet. He must report to the club official in charge of umpires for his match and be issued with an umpire shirt, whistle and pick up stick. He should then check the pony which he has been allocated to ensure that it looks up to the job and that it is fully tacked for polo with ball bags (tails bandages are optional). It is extremely important that the umpires are well mounted on reliable and fit ponies. It is not sensible to allocate a green or unfit pony as the Umpire will not be able to carry out his duties effectively and the pony may be damaged. The Polo Manager will give the Umpires the go ahead when the teams are ready and all his officials, including medical and veterinary, are in place. He should also brief the Umpires if there is going to be a parade before the match. If so, it is advisable for the Umpires to have tossed up to decide ends before going onto the ground. The Umpires should take the following action at this time –

- Ride onto the ground together at least two minutes before the scheduled start time of their match, with the teams if there is to be a parade.
- Blow their whistles to check their efficiency and alert the teams.
- Check on the teams' colours to ensure that there is sufficient contrast. The Polo Manager should have already done this but the Umpires have the ultimate say.
- Check on the Referee and locate him.
- Check on the location of the medical support.
- Check that the Time-keeper and Scorer are alert.
- Check the scoreboard to ensure any handicap difference has been correctly credited.
- Decide on which side and back line each is to take. They may swap at half time if the sun is troublesome
- Establish who are the two team captains, call them together and toss for ends. The captain of the visiting team is normally asked to make the call. The captains should also be asked at this time if they are happy with the score as posted. Once the ball has been thrown in there is no redress.
- Be prepared to penalise any player who whips his pony before the ball has been thrown in.
- The Umpires should now be ready to throw in the ball. Should however one Umpire be late the team captains on being asked by the Polo Manager, may agree for the game to be started with one umpire.

d. Working Together. The Umpires are a team and must work together. The more experienced Umpire of the pair must do all that he can to bring his partner with him and encourage him to make his own decisions. If the more experienced Umpire takes upon himself the decision as to a foul without consulting his partner he will undermine his position and allow the teams to drive a wedge between them. Umpires will inevitably disagree but they must be aware that too frequent reference to the Referee will delay the game unnecessarily and serve as above to undermine their authority. The Umpires after discussion are perfectly entitled to throw the ball in without reference to the Referee.

e. **Umpire Positioning.** Having agreed before the start which side and back line each should take, the Umpires should try to complement each other in order to cover the whole ground, similar to partners in a doubles tennis match. The correct position should be one Umpire trailing the play on the line of the ball and the other level and parallel with the play. Not withstanding an Umpire's position on the ground, he must not hesitate to blow his whistle if he sees a foul as his partner may have been unsighted or be in the act of turning. It is above all imperative that the umpires keep up with the game to make the correct decisions swiftly and to maintain control. However the umpires should try to keep out of the game keeping on a flank or behind as far as possible. Should the ball hit an umpires' pony, play will continue.

f. **Stopping The Play.** The whistle must be blown decisively and loudly with one long blast which will stop the play and the clock. The Umpire should have the whistle in his mouth or his hand ready for instant use. If the decision to blow is delayed the moment will have past and the foul may go unpunished or, if blown late, the call will cause confusion and loss of confidence.

- The Umpires must remember that the Time-keeper acts on their whistle and unless blown loudly he may not hear it, particularly if there is a strong wind or background noise. In general terms the whistle should not be blown when the ball goes over the boards, back line when hit by an attacker or when a goal is scored. The Umpire, particularly if he is alone, may however blow the whistle to stop the clock after suitable elapsed time to allow himself to get into position for a throw-in.

- Umpire A having blown his whistle should check quickly that Umpire B agrees with the foul and the proposed penalty. This should be done by pointing or other pre arranged signal. Discussion between the Umpires should only take place if there is disagreement so that delay is cut to a minimum. If they still cannot decide then they must refer to the Referee by raising a hand and cantering over towards him. This procedure can be short-circuited by Umpire B if he believes Umpire A has made a wrong call, by raising his hand to obtain a decision from the Referee. As an overall consideration nothing is more damaging to the authority of the Umpires and to the flow and enjoyment of the match than delays caused by excessive consultation between the Umpires and the Referee. Decisive, immediate and firm action is to be preferred to shilly-shallying and consultation which often results in no more than a throw-in.

- Once they have agreed that one or other side has fouled then the Umpires must decide on the penalty to award. In doing so they must remember that the side defending the penalty, i.e. the side that has fouled, have the opportunity to regroup and get into the best position for defence. Thus the penalty should be made to count, being moved up the ground if the defending team have fouled and, at the very least, a hit from the spot if the attacking side fouled. Having agreed on the penalty to be awarded, Umpire A should announce 'Cross against Red, free hit from the spot' and without waiting canter to the spot where the foul occurred drop the ball and take up his position

- Should the referee signal 'No Foul' then the umpire should throw in the ball at the spot where it was when the whistle was blown (Rule 26b).

- The Umpires should use the Advantage Rule (Rule 26a) with discretion as the side fouled would often prefer a penalty rather than to have play continue. It should never be invoked for a very dangerous or deliberate foul.

- If a player is disabled by a foul, every effort should be made to find a qualified substitute. On occasion this may not be possible in which case the umpires, in consultation with the Referee, may decide to remove a player from the side that fouled. (See Rule 28b (ii))

g. **Appealing.** Rule 2f states that "a player may not appeal in any manner". This is probably the most frequently broken rule in the book and one in which Umpires must use a certain amount of discretion. If a player sees an opponent about to commit a foul which may endanger him or his pony, his instinctive action is to raise his stick, and sometimes his voice as a warning; that is to say I am more interested in self preservation than hitting the ball and inter alia as a signal to the Umpires that he thinks a foul is about to be committed. The Umpires must be aware that appealing with a stick or verbally is a foul and thus under normal circumstances must be penalised. Any form of frantic waving of the stick in the air (helicoptering) must always be a foul as it constitutes a danger to other players and their ponies. The Captain of each team has the right during the game to ask the Umpires for clarification of a decision but this does not include the right to challenge the Umpires on that or any other decision they may make. Sometimes the Umpires can pre-empt a potentially explosive situation by calmly explaining why the foul was given. They should not under any circumstances, either during or after a game, enter into discussion with the captains or any other player as to their conduct during the game.

h. Report Forms. The Umpires are required to fill in a Report Form (Rule 7a) for any irregularities or incidents of misconduct and submit the form to the Tournament Committee immediately after the game. The Tournament Committee will take such action as they consider necessary and forward the form to the Chief Umpire or HPA Welfare Officer as appropriate. The umpires are required to fill in a report form when implementing Penalty 10a and b or if a pony is seen to be blind in one eye or showing vice.

j. Pony Welfare. Umpires are responsible for the welfare of the ponies during play in particular they must check the length and serviceability of whips, length and sharpness of spurs and studs. A pony showing signs of distress or with blood in its mouth or on its flanks must be sent off.

k. Throw-in. (See Rule 21).
   (i) General. Umpire A, who is to throw-in the ball, must ensure that the teams are lined up on a T or equivalent with the nearest players at least five yards from him and with a distinct gap separating the two teams who must remain stationary. Umpire B will be about forty yards away at the back of the throw-in ready to move parallel and level with the play. The ball should be thrown-in hard and under hand so that it remains low to prevent players hitting wildly in the line-out. All rough and dangerous play should be penalised instantly. Umpire A will take up position as trailing Umpire.
   (ii) Centre. Used when starting or restarting after a goal has been scored or the goal posts have been widened. Umpires should allow a reasonable time i.e. a canter, for the teams to return to the centre after a goal has been scored. Should the Umpires inadvertently allow the teams to line up the wrong way there is no redress but if by the end of the chukka no further goal has been scored, then ends should be changed and play started at a corresponding position in the other half of the ground.
   (iii) Boards. Used when the ball is hit across the boards or sidelines. Umpire A stands with his pony inside the boards with the teams lined up at least 10 yards from the boards and separated until the ball is thrown in. Thereafter proceed as above.
   (iv) Towards the Boards. Used to restart the game at any spot if a Penalty has been awarded, a foul has been overruled, the ball is buried or damaged, after an accident or incident which has caused play to be stopped, unnecessary delay in taking a penalty or as the second element of Penalty 1. Proceed as from the centre.

l. Hit In. Umpire A, on whose side the ball has been hit out over the back line, should be behind the ball but clear of the goal so that he can see the exact line and get a clear view of a opposing player coming in for a meet. He will become the trailing Umpire. When he is satisfied that both sides are in position, and no unnecessary delay has occurred, he should call 'Play'. Umpire B should be keeping an eye on the 30 yard line to see that the opposing side do not cross the line before the ball is hit or hit at. Umpire B is in the parallel position and should move up the ground level with the play. Should there be unnecessary delay by the side hitting in, a Penalty 6 shall be awarded. If the opposing side cause unnecessary delay then the hit in is moved up to the 30 yard line.

m. Penalties. There are ten specific penalties listed which Umpires will use to penalise players for breach of the Rules. They should know both the number and name of the penalties but in any event they must know the name. The majority of penalties in common use involve a hit by the side fouled but the Umpires may award a throw-in if a penalty is incorrectly taken, after the ordering off of a pony or player or sending off a player. Umpires must ensure that any penalty awarded is appropriate to the foul committed, taking into account the direction of play, severity, position on the ground at which it occurred and prevalence. They must be consistent in their award, showing equal disfavour to both sides within the above parameters. Rule 39 covers the correct taking of penalties. In brief, teeing up is not allowed and only one player may position the ball, provided he takes no longer than 5 seconds. If the ball rolls into a hole, it may be repositioned once but not after 'Play' has been called. Nor is the striker allowed to circle once the Umpire has called 'Play'. Failure to comply is penalised with a throw-in from the spot (Penalty 7) where the penalty was to have been taken. The ball is in play the minute it has been hit or hit at.

When taking Penalties 2, 3, 4, 5(a) or 6 on or within the 60 yard line, the striker and his team members, after the initial hit or hit at the ball may not hit or hit at the ball with more than a half shot i.e. the head of the stick not starting above the shoulder of the striker. Failure to comply is to be penalised with a free hit from the spot (Penalty 5a).

(i) **Penalty 1 (Dangerous or Deliberate Foul to Save a Goal).** The Umpires, having awarded Penalty 1, shall instruct the goal judge to wave his flag to signify a goal. Umpire A will throw in the ball towards the side of the ground where the foul took place. Teams line up ten yards out from and opposite the centre of the goal.

(ii) **Penalty 2 (Thirty Yard Hit or Hit from the Spot).** Umpire A must ask the Captain of the team fouled if he would like a hit from the spot where the foul took place or a hit from the 30 yard line opposite the centre of the goal. Umpire A then places the ball. Umpire B should meanwhile take up position on the back line or equivalent distance to the ball ensuring that the defending players are correctly positioned (i.e. 30 yards from the ball behind the goal line or off the ground and not between the line of the goal posts extended) and that no player crosses the back line or equivalent before the ball is hit or hit at or enters play through the goal. Umpire A should call 'Play' when he is happy that the stage has been set.

(iii) **Penalty 3 (Forty Yard Hit).** Umpire A drops the ball on the cross at 40 yards from the goal and then proceed as for Penalty 2.

(iv) **Penalty 4 (Sixty Yard Hit).** Umpire A drops the ball on the 60 yard line opposite the middle of the goal and takes up position behind the striker. Defending players to be behind the 30 yard line. Umpire B will be behind the right hand goal post as he looks out from the back line with the goal judge on the left post. The Umpires must watch the flight of the ball carefully as many disputes arise as to whether the ball went between the posts projected vertically upwards or not. In the event of dispute, their decision, not the goal judge's, is final but they should give the benefit of the doubt to the side defending. They should be on their guard to penalise a full shot after the initial hit (Rule 39b(iv)).

(v) **Penalty 5a (Hit from the Spot).** Umpire A drops the ball where the foul took place. Umpire B positions himself down field to ensure that none of the defending side are closer than 30 yards to the ball or behind it. Penalty 5a should not be awarded against a defending team within their own 60 yard line. The Umpires should award a Penalty 2, 3 or 4 as appropriate taking into account the point where the foul took place, the severity of the foul and the likelihood of a goal being scored if the attacker had not been fouled. There is no rule to say that the ball may not be taken back for a Penalty.

(vi) **Penalty 5b (Hit from the Centre).** Umpire A places the ball on the centre line opposite the centre of the goal. Umpire B acts as in Penalty 5a.

(vii) **Penalty 6 (Ball hit behind by Defender).** This penalty is awarded if a defender hits the ball over his own back line (Rule 25) either directly or off his own pony or after glancing off the boards or goal post. If however it strikes any other player or an umpire before going behind it is a hit in. A free hit is given on the 60 yard line opposite to where the ball crossed the back line but at least 4 yards from the boards. None of the defending side to be forward of the 30 yard line. The attacking side can be where they choose.

(viii) **Penalty 7 (Throw-in).** The Umpire may award a Penalty 7 for the incorrect taking of a penalty from the spot where the penalty was due to be taken (Rule 39c) and for infringement of the one tap rule (Rule 34c). They may also award a Penalty 7 for unnecessary delay or for any other offence which would penalise too severely the team against whom it was awarded. However, for unnecessary delay by a side hitting in, a Penalty 6 should be awarded.

(ix) **Penalty 10 (a) (Player Sent Off for Rest of the Chukka).** The Umpires may send off a player for the remainder of a chukka, in addition to any other penalty, for a foul or conduct prejudicial to the game (Rule 38). The player sent off must return immediately to the pony lines and the game will continue with three players on the side penalised. Before they send off a player, the umpires must be in agreement. If not then the referee must decide. The umpires must make it clear to the player being sent off and his team captain whether they have awarded Penalty 10(a) or 10(b), particularly in the last chukka. The umpires must complete a report form at the end of the match and hand it to the Polo Manager of the host club.

(x) **Penalty 10 (b) (Player Sent Off for Rest of the Match).** The Umpires may send off a player for the remainder of the match for a similar but more serious offence than Penalty 10(a). The same restrictions will apply but in addition any substitution must comply with Rule 3j.

4. **Explanation of Some Rules**
a. **Prolongation of Last Chukka in Event of a Tie (Rule 16).** The last chukka shall normally end, although the ball may be still in play, at the first stroke of the 7 minute bell. However if the scores are tied and the match is to be played to a result, then the chukka shall continue until the ball goes out of play or the second bell (7 ½ minutes) is sounded. If still a tie then after an interval of 5 minutes, the match shall be continued until sudden death. Ends are not changed. If, however, goals are to be widened by agreement of the Captains, because the Tournament Rules require it or because the extra chukka has been scoreless, then ends are changed and the ball is thrown in from the centre. Play with widened goals must not start with a Penalty. Any such awarded will be played out in the previous chukka.

b. **Prolongation in Case of Penalty Awarded (Rule 16e).** If the Umpires award a penalty with in 5 seconds of the end of the match, whether in normal or extra time, they must ensure that the time-keeper is aware of their decision and he knows that 5 seconds of play must be allowed from the moment the penalty striker hits or hits at the ball. On occasion, another penalty can be awarded during the 5 seconds period, in which case the clock should be reset to allow a further 5 seconds of play and so on.

c. **Line of Ball and Right of Way (Rule 32) and Precedence of Players (Rule 33).** The Umpires must watch the play very closely so that they are certain of the line of the ball each time it has been hit and thus know which player has the Right of Way. The moment the line of the ball is changed they must know who is entitled to the new Right of Way and in what direction it lies. A player who was on the old Right of Way must be given sufficient room to pull up or turn otherwise a foul should be blown (Rule 32b (ii)). This Rule has become increasingly difficult to apply with the current form of play in which a player taps the ball to the side and follows round on the new line.

It is very important that Umpires understand the meaning of the Right of Way, which is set out in detail in Rule 32b. In general terms, it follows the line of the ball with the player parallel to it following down the exact line taking the ball on his off side having priority over all others. A player riding in the direction the ball is travelling at an angle to its line has the Right of Way over a player meeting the ball at an angle but two players riding to meet exactly on the line or lines projected have equal rights. The player who strikes the ball and then deviates from its line surrenders his right to the Right of Way. Two players riding in the direction in which the ball is travelling and simultaneously making a play against each other, have the Right of Way over a single player coming from any direction (Two against One Rule). The Umpires, as well as establishing in their mind the Right of Way at every moment of the game, must also assess the relative speed and distance when a player crosses or enters the Right of Way. If there is no danger whatsoever and no requirement for the player already on the line to check, then no foul will have been committed.

d. **The Player with the ROW (Rule 34).** Umpires must read and understand Rule 34c which allows a defended player, proceeding at walking pace or slower, only one tap of the ball. In particular a player who taps the ball under an opponent's pony, then turns onto the new line and claims the foul must be penalised. Umpires must make a judgement as to whether a player is being blocked by an opponent and thus cannot go forward or is deliberately restraining his pony in order to gain advantage. Equally the Umpires must use their judgment in the application of Rule 34d (old soldiering). They must decide if a player has given up his Right of Way by checking and that it is safe for an opponent to ride in front of him to take the ball. A player has not got a licence to blunder at an angle into an opponent on the ball causing him to hook up to avoid a nasty ride off.

e. **Riding Off, Dangerous Riding and Intimidation (Rule 35).** At all times the Umpires must have the welfare of the players and their ponies uppermost in their mind. Thus Rule 35 contains a list of examples of dangerous riding which could cause injury to player or pony. A player carrying out one of these actions must be immediately penalised. A player may ride off an opponent who is making a half shot providing he is parallel, level and travelling at approximately the same speed. Should the player ride into a full shot he is hazarding himself and his pony and should be penalised. Umpires have to be alert to police the rules of dangerous riding and if in doubt should penalise a player who is seen to endanger another player or pony. A ride off that causes a pony to lose it balance or stumble is likely to have been too severe and should be penalised.

- f. **Hooking and Misuse of Stick (Rule 36).** The Rule states that a player may only hook or strike at an opponent's stick when the opponent is in the act of striking the ball and his stick is below the level of the shoulder. Some examples of the dangerous use of the stick are:
  - Taking a full swing at the ball from the throw in or in any scrimmage in such a way as to endanger another player.
  - Striking hard into the legs of a group of ponies in the scrimmage.
  - Striking the ball in the air so as to endanger other players.
  - Taking a full swing under the neck in such a way as to endanger a player riding alongside.
  - Striking an opponents stick in such a way as to cause injury. Any player intentionally hitting his own pony with his stick, or abusing his pony by excessive use of the whip or spurs, must be the subject of a report, a copy of which should be sent to the Chairman of the Welfare Committee. Furthermore any player intentionally striking another player or his pony shall be severely penalised to the extent that the umpire may award Penalty 10(a) or (b).
- g. **Accident or Injury to Player or Pony (Rule 27, 28, 29 and 30).** The Umpires have a responsibility to do all that they can to prevent accident or injury to players or ponies. For example, if a player is behaving dangerously so as to be a hazard to himself or other players he must be warned, penalised and if necessary sent off. Common faults are dangerous use of the stick particularly in a melee, zigzagging in front of another pony, slowing down on the ball and hitting the ball hard into a crowd of players. Equally a pony which is out of control or has dangerous tack must be ordered off to prevent injury to others. Should an accident to a player or pony occur then the Umpires must immediately take charge. If a player is injured then the Umpires should stop the game and summon medical assistance by waving the pick up stick above the head. They should keep players and any others who come onto the ground away from the medical team except those who are actively helping. They should consult with the Team Captain of the injured player about possible substitutes and keep the commentator informed as to what is happening. Taking into account the paramount need to treat the injured player in the best conditions possible, the Umpires should endeavour to restart the match as soon as possible. They must get clearance from the Medical Officer before allowing a player, who could have suffered concussion, to play. If there is no Medical Officer present then this responsibility devolves onto the Umpires. If a pony falls or appears to be lame, the Umpires must stop the game and see that the pony is trotted up. If not sound it should be taken off the ground in the most humane way possible. Should a pony be badly injured or stay down the Umpires should ask the players to form a circle to shield the pony from spectators. If a Veterinary Officer is present, then he will take charge otherwise the Umpires should ensure that screens are erected, if necessary, and the pony is removed by trailer from the ground as humanely and speedily as possible. Try to keep the commentator informed to cover up as best he can.

5. **Umpire Grading Committee**
   Every Associate Member of the HPA as well has being allocated a handicap should also have an Umpire Grade. Each member is assessed by an Umpire Grading Committee annually and the grade published in the Blue Book. It is incumbent on all those who play polo not only to know the rules but also to take their turn as umpires. Once a player has reached -1 handicap he is eligible and should be encouraged to take his C grade umpire test. Umpire tests are held in April and May and also at other times on demand. On passing the test he will be graded CP until he has umpired a sufficient number of games to satisfy his club that he be recommended to the Umpire Grading Committee for upgrading to C.

6. **The Timekeeper/Scorer**
- a. **General.** Rule 9 states: 'A Timekeeper/Scorer (referred to hereafter as 'The Timekeeper') shall be employed in all matches with an Assistant Scorer who shall man the scoreboard'. In many cases, the Timekeeper and Scorer will be the same person.
- b. **Timekeeper.** The Timekeeper should be conversant with Rules 14, 15, 16 and 17 which govern his responsibilities.
  - (i) **Clocks.** The Timekeeper must be provided with a proper polo stop-clock, which can be stopped and started at will. This clock will govern the time, the clock on the scoreboard is

for guidance only. He will also require an ordinary stopwatch as a back up and to time the extra 5 seconds of play (see below).

(ii) **Five Minute Bell.** The timekeeper will ring the bell five minutes before the advertised time for the start of the match to alert the teams and officials. If the players are not responding, he may be requested to ring the bell again to help get the match underway. He should not start the clock until play actually starts.

(iii) **Stopping the Clock.** The time during which a penalty is being exacted or an accident being dealt with does not count in the 7 minutes playing time. The fact that the time is not to be counted (i.e. the clock is to be stopped) is indicated by the Umpire blowing one firm blast on his whistle. The time starts to count again when the Umpire says 'Play' and the ball is hit or hit at. Note that the clock is not stopped when a goal is scored or the ball goes over the back or sideline.

(iv) **Ringing the Bell.** It is the Timekeeper's duty to ring the bell when 7 minutes of playing time has elapsed, and again 30 seconds later if play has not already stopped. Great care must be taken that the stroke of the bell coincides exactly with the termination of the 7 and 7½ minutes. In the case of a close match, a ball may pass between the goal posts a second before or after the correct time of the conclusion of the final chukka. The Timekeeper's responsibility in this matter is therefore of great importance.

(v) **Intervals.** Between each chukka there is an interval of 3 minutes. In all matches there is a half-time interval of 5 minutes. In a 5 chukka match, the interval is taken after the 3rd chukka. Should play begin before the 3 minutes are up, it is unnecessary to ring the bell but the clock should be started at the moment that play begins. If the play has not begun at the end of each interval, then the Timekeeper shall ring the bell, but he must not start the clock until play actually begins. In the event of a tie requiring that an extra chukka be played, the interval shall be 5 minutes. In this case it is the Umpire's duty to see that the game is not started again until the 5 minutes interval has been taken.

(vi) **Additional 5 Seconds.** Rule 16(e) is extremely important to the Timekeeper, as he is the only official who can carry out this rule.

c. **Scoring**

(i) **Before Match.** The Polo Manager should provide a score sheet completed as far as possible. From this sheet the handicap received by a team will be put on the board by the Assistant Scorer. The Scorer will particularly note the colours in which the teams are playing and alter details on the score sheet if necessary.

(ii) **During Match.** The Scorer will record the goals scored (noting if possible the name of the player scoring the goal, the time at which the goal was scored and the direction of play). He will instruct the Assistant Scorer to put up the score on the board being particularly careful to check that the correct team has been credited. At all times it is the Scorer's figures that count.

(iii) **End of Match.** At the end of the match, the Timekeeper will add up the goals received on handicap and scored, fill in such details as weather, the time the match was completed and any unusual occurrences, sign the form as correct and hand it in to the Polo Manager. This score sheet will then act as the official record of the match.

(iv) **Objections.** No objection may be lodged after the game to the Tournament Committee, Umpires or the Goal Judges as to whether a goal was scored or not, or an error was made in recording the score or team handicap. Note, however, that it is the duty of the Umpires to draw team captains' attention to the score as posted before a match (i.e. any goals received on handicap) and changes may be made as agreed. However, thereafter no objection may be raised. If the Umpires fail to carry out this duty, there can be no objection from either team.

d. **Assistant Scorer.** The Assistant Scorer is responsible for preparing the scoreboard before the match, and updating goals scored and chukka numbers during the match. He should have communication with the Timekeeper if they are not sitting together.

7. **The Goal Judges**

a. **General. Rule 8 covers the role and duties of goal judges.** Under the rules the Club has the responsibility to ensure that goal judges are fully trained, are fit and active, of an age as laid down by the Health and Safety at Work Executive, and have parental permission if required. It is recommended that Clubs draw up their own set of standing orders to be issued on signature to all goal judges. The Club must also ensure that a line is drawn 20 yards away and parallel to the goal line behind which the goal judge must stay during play and that spare goal posts and ball boxes are left no nearer than 30 yards from the goal line. Other items such as bicycles should be placed well away from the ground so as not to be a danger to horses. Goal judges must not be used when play is in progress simultaneously on two grounds with back-to-back goals.

b. **Equipment.** The Club must issue goal judges with protective headgear (a cricket helmet is recommended) and distinctive clothing, normally white, and ensure that they are worn during play. Goal judges require a bag or box of balls, a white flag and access to spare goal posts.

c. **Before Match.** Goal judges should be in position 10 minutes before the scheduled start of a match and should check that they have:
- A flag.
- Sufficient balls in a box or bag.
- Immediate access to spare goal posts.
- The ability to change a goal post if it is broken and widen the goals if required.
- The goals post in the correct position and that they are vertical.
- No impedimenta, other than balls, on the ground or within 30 yards of the goal line.
- Distinctive clothing and are wearing a hard hat. Wet weather clothing should also be available.
- Knowledge of the team colours so they can distinguish which side is attacking and which is defending.

d. **During Match.** Once the match is started, the goal judge must observe the play carefully at all times as the situation can change very quickly. When play comes down the left hand side of the ground, the goal judge should begin to move to the right to keep the ball in his sight between the posts and if the play comes from the right, he should move to the left. At all times however, he must remain behind the 20 yard line until the ball is out of play and the ponies have slowed down. The goal judge must also keep his eye on the ponies as they approach to see which way they are turning or swinging. Evasive action should be taken if essential but it is often better to stand still as the player will turn away. It is an offence for two players to ride each other off over the goal line.

e. **Goal Scored.** In normal play, if the goal judge is certain that a goal has been scored (i.e. the goal went over and clear of the goal line), even though play continues, he will wave his flag vigorously over his head until receiving acknowledgement from the score-keeper. It is some times difficult for the goal judge to be certain that a goal was scored as his view may be obscured, he may be taking evasive action or he may be confused by the flight of the ball. In this event, he should make no signal at which point an umpires should come to him to consult and then make their decision. The goal judge should never get into discussion with a player as he is answerable only to the umpires who should protect him from pressure and abuse. Once a decision has been made by the umpires, they will instruct him either to wave his flag to signify a goal or to place the ball for a hit in. The goal judge must also be on the alert for an umpire's whistle which will render the ball dead and thus, if it subsequently goes through the goal or over the back line, no action should be taken by him. In the normal course the umpires will award a penalty and play will continue with a hit or throw in.

f. **Penalties.** When Penalties 4 or 6 are being taken, the goal judge should be behind the left hand post as he looks onto the ground and one of the umpires will take the right hand post. For Penalty 6 the goal judge and umpire should be on the straight line drawn between the ball and the goal post. He should then be able to tell if the ball went over the goal line and inside the goal post projected vertically. Judgement may be required if the ball hits a flag blowing in the wind, if the ball swerves in the air or goes over the post. Before making a signal, the goal judge should receive confirmation from the umpire who will normally raise his hand if he is satisfied it was a goal. If the umpires award a Penalty One or a goal as a result of a foul by a defender, they will instruct the Goal Judge to wave his flag as if a goal had been scored.

g. **Hit Over Back Line by Attacker.** If the ball was hit over the back line by an attacker, then the goal judge should signal by holding a ball above his head. When the ponies have slowed down he should run forward and place a ball just in front of the back line where it crossed but no nearer than 4 yards from a goal post or the boards. He should make a good lie for the ball otherwise time will be wasted as the striker tees it up. Remember that the clock is still running. Then pick up any loose balls and return swiftly behind the 20 yard line.

h. Hit Over Back Line by Defender. If the ball was hit over the back line by a defender, then the umpires will award Penalty 6 which is taken on the 60 yard line opposite where the ball went out of play. The umpires might ask the goal judge for help in deciding if a defender or attacker hit the ball over the back line (see Rule 25).

j. During Match. The goal judge may relax a little between chukkas and at half time although he must remain alert to players coming onto the ground to stick and ball. He can usefully tread-in in front of his own goal, collect up any stray balls and be prepared for the umpires to come up to him at this time to replenish their ball bags.

k. Two Goal Judges. Should there be two goal judges for each goal, they will work as a pair covering each goal. They must be particularly alert to avoid being ridden down as the options for the players are reduced.

ANNEX C – GUIDELINES FOR TOURNAMENTS

1. General. The Fixture List of tournaments is laid out in Section 4 page 254. The HPA Rules for Polo will apply to all matches which should be played under 'Conditions for HPA Official Tournaments' (see Annex D) unless marked with an asterisk. Those likely to count for the Victor Ludorum are in bold italics.

2. Entry. A Club wishing to run a tournament must prepare an entry form which should include the following:
- Name of tournament.
- Handicap level.
- Inclusive dates.
- Status (eg, official or if not, any special conditions that apply).
- Entry fee and note of any additional cost of officials, medical cover etc.
- Closing date of entry.
- Blank line so team can enter dates on which they would prefer not to play.
- For leagues or groups whether matches are to be played to a result or may finish in a draw.
- Any disclaimer and additional information.
- Declaration as to eligibility of those entered.
- Signature Block.

As a general rule Clubs should accept all entries although they have a right to refuse an entry and use their discretion as to how many teams will be accepted. Some tournaments may be run solely on an invitation basis.

To enter the team captain/manager must complete the entry form (see Rule 1b) and submit it, together with the entry fee, to the Club before the closing date. Clubs should whenever possible accept all entries although they have the right to refuse an entry or ballot out teams. They may arrange for qualifying rounds to be played at other clubs. See also Annex D.

3. Schedule. Once entries have been received, the Polo Manager must decide, if it is not in the tournament conditions, whether the tournament should be run as a knockout, league, group or combination of both. He will know how many entries have been received, how many playing days are available and days on which teams would prefer not too play and have an idea of the constraints on the players. Based on all this he can decide the format of the tournament and can produce a schedule of the matches which should include where appropriate nominated umpires and referees. It has become increasingly popular to start a tournament on a league or group basis, finishing with a knockout, as this guarantees each team a number of matches and also enables a time table to be drawn up.

4. Withdrawal or Disqualification of a Team. See Rule 1(e). If a team is disqualified or its withdrawal is accepted by the Tournament Committee and the team has already played in the tournament then, in a knockout, the team that they were due to play will be given a bye to the next round. In a league or group those matches which the team has played will be declared null and void and points and goals gained by their opponents subtracted from their total.

5. Knockout Tournament. A knockout tournament is one in which teams are drawn to play preliminary rounds, quarter finals, semi finals and finals. Unless there are eight or sixteen teams in the tournament there will be a requirement to have bye rounds. The method of placing these is shown in the table below. It is often popular to have a subsidiary to the main tournament to give the teams beaten in the first round a minimum of two matches. The subsidiary matches should be scheduled so that they fall as close as possible to the time and date of the equivalent matches arranged for the winning teams.

Method of Drawing Byes in Tournaments
All Byes are in the first round.

No of Teams	Byes at Top	Byes at Bottom
5	1	2
6	1	1
7	0	1
8	0	0
9	3	4
10	3	3
11	2	3
12	2	2
13	1	2
14	1	1
15	0	1
16	0	0

6. League and Group Tournaments. In a league tournament, teams are placed in a league and each plays the other in that league. Teams can also be placed in paired groups with an equal number of teams in each so that each team in one group plays each team in the other. The league and group system can be combined, for example if there are fourteen teams in a tournament there can be two leagues of four and two groups of three so that every team plays three matches during this phase. The order of merit can be established using the system laid out in Annex E (Rules for League Matches). Once an order of merit has been established then a knockout phase may be held starting with quarter finals, semi-finals or going straight to a final.

7. Round Robin or American Tournament. If three teams are to play on one day, then a Round Robin is a good answer. Normally each team plays two or three chukkas against the other. Two of the teams play consecutively e.g. the first four chukkas or the last four and the third team has a break in the middle. It is recommended that each match should end on the final bell whether the score is level or not and that two points are awarded for a win and one for a draw. To decide the order of merit refer to Annex E.

8. Expenses. The Council has approved the following arrangements for the guidance of Club Secretaries when making arrangements for visits from other Clubs:-
a. At all tournaments or matches, official or unofficial, the Host Club may provide stabling, straw, hay and board and lodging for grooms on a repayment basis if prior arrangements have been made between the Secretaries of the Host Club and the visiting teams.
b. It is suggested that the charges to be made are set out by the Host Club in their Schedule of Conditions for the tournament.
c. The Captain of a team winning any challenge cup is expected to have the name of theteam and of its members engraved upon the cup at his own expense.

ANNEX D – CONDITIONS FOR OFFICIAL HPA TOURNAMENTS

1. General. Official HPA Tournaments take priority over non-official Tournaments and as a general principle the higher goal tournament takes priority over the lower goal. Any queries may be referred to the Stewards of the HPA whose decision will be final.

2. Team Composition. All entries will be checked by the host club against the restrictions for official tournaments as set out below:

Level	Term	Max no of Chukkas	Min H'cap	Max OSP*	Max no of OSP*	Min H'cap
22+	High Goal	6	0	10	4	2
17–22	Hgh Goal	6	0	10	2	4
15–18	High Goal	5	0	10	1	4
12–15	Medium Goal	5	0	10	1	3
8–12	Intermediate Goal	4	-1	7	1	3
4–8	Low Goal	4	-1	6	1	2**
0–6	Low Goal	4	-2	4	1	
-2–5	Low Goal	4	-2	3	1	

*OSP = Overseas Sponsored Player (see Status Guidelines for Overseas Players)
**Victor Ludorum Tournaments only. For all other Official HPA tournaments an OSP of any handicap may play.

3. National Teams. No team may have four overseas players unless it is an invited national team which has been approved by the Stewards. However, the Stewards are likely to waive the condition for an established overseas patron who wishes to play with an immediate family member who is also from overseas. In the case of a substitution in such a family team, normal tournament conditions and rules will apply.

4. Officials. Below are the recommended minimum grades for officials for Official HPA Tournaments which clubs should, where possible, follow.

LEVEL	FIRST UMPIRE	SECOND UMPIRE	REFEREE	Grade or Minimum H'cp
22 +	P	P	A	6
18	P	P	A	5
15	A	A	A	3
12	B	B	B	2
8	B	C	C	1
6	C	C	C	1
4	C	C	C	1
2	C	C or CP	C	0

For example: A 3 goal player may referee medium goal even though he may be only a C grade umpire.

5. Entry Fees

a. As a guide, Clubs should graduate the entry fee to the suggested maximum according to the matches to be played in the tournament. The suggested maximum, which does not include fees for umpires or other officials, is:

High Goal 17–22	£5,000
High Goal 15–18	£2,500
Medium Goal	£1,500
Intermediate Goal	£1,000
Low Goal	£750

b. The host club may arrange for qualifying rounds of its tournament to be played at another club in which case the host club will refund 75% of the entry fee of those teams that do not qualify to the club holding the qualifying rounds. A team that plays only one qualifying match will be refunded 50% of the entry fee by either the host club or the club holding the qualifying rounds.

c. When a single match is played away from the host club, then 20% of the entry fee shall be paid by the host club to the club holding the match.

ANNEX E – RULES FOR LEAGUE AND GROUP MATCHES

(See also Annex C)

1. General. The methods to be used to determine the order of merit within a league or group are set out below.

a. **Points System.** In each league or group a points system will operate for matches as follows:
   (i) **Played for a Result:** Win = 1   Lose = 0
   (ii) **Draw Acceptable:** Win = 2   Draw = 1   Lose = 0

b. **Teams Tied.** If teams are tied as a result of the points system, the following methods are used to establish an order of merit.
   (i) **Who Beat Whom Rule:** the team that won the match between the teams.
   (ii) **Net Goals:** the sum of the goals 'for' minus the goals 'against'. Goals awarded on handicap should be included.
   (iii) **Gross Goals:** the sum of goals 'for'. Goals awarded on handicap should be included.

c. **Group System.** If the group system is used, then take the results of all the matches in the paired groups rather than within one group. Thus, with two groups of two teams playing across, the result of all four matches should be taken together.

2. Order of Merit within a League or Paired Groups.

a. **Points.** The order of merit is established firstly by the number of points scored by each team in its league or paired groups. But teams may be tied on points.

b. **Two Teams Tied on Points.**
   (i) If two teams are tied on points, the first placed team will be according to the 'who beat whom' rule.
   (ii) However, if the result of that match was a draw or the teams have not played each other, then the first placed team will be the one with the highest 'net goals' score, counting all the matches played by the two teams in their league or group.
   (iii) If still tied on 'net goals', then the first placed team will be the one with the highest 'gross goals' score, again counting all the matches played by the two teams in their league or group.

c. **Three Teams Tied with Same Points.**
   (i) If three teams are tied on points, establish the first placed team by recalculating the points scored, counting only the matches played between the tied teams. If this results in two teams still being tied on points, the 'who beat whom' rule will apply.
   (ii) If the three teams remain tied, the first team is established according to highest 'net goals', again counting only the matches between the tied teams. If this results in two teams still being tied on net goals, the 'who beat whom' rule will apply. If the result was a draw, or the two teams have not played each other, then proceed as in 2b above.

- **(iii)** If the three teams remain tied on 'net goals', the first team is established according to highest 'gross goals', again counting only the matches played between the teams tied. If this results in two teams being tied, the 'who beat whom' rule will apply. If the result was a draw, or the two teams have not played each other, then proceed as in 2b above.
- **d. Four or More Teams Tied.** In the unlikely event that four or more teams are tied on points, then proceed as in paragraph 2c above.
- **e. Teams Still Tied.** If two teams still remain tied having applied all the methods, then the Tournament Committee shall determine the order of merit by using a play off, other equitable test such as penalty shoot out, or the toss of a coin.

3. Order of Merit across Leagues and Groups. It may sometimes be necessary to establish an order of merit across leagues or groups if teams are to go forward to a knockout phase.
- **a. First in League or Group.** The first team in each league or paired group has an automatic place in the knockout phase
- **b. Discounted Team.** Equalise the number of teams to be counted in each league or group by taking out the lowest placed team in the larger league(s) so that the calculations following are based on teams having played an equal number of matches.
- **c. Order of Merit.** Excluding those matches played against a discounted team but taking into account the result of all other matches played, establish the order of merit according to points. Should two teams be tied, apply the 'who beat whom' rule. If however tied teams have not played each other (which is probable) then proceed as outlined in 2c above.

4. Placing of Teams. The order of merit as outlined in paragraph 3c above will normally be used to place teams within a tournament as follows:

Quarter Finals: 1st v 8th   Semi Finals: 1st v 4th
3rd v 6th   2nd v 3rd
4th v 5th
2nd v 7th

It may be necessary to vary this formula so those teams that have played each other in the league stage are not drawn to play each other in the early rounds.

5. Match Not Played or Completed. If a league match cannot be played or, if started, cannot be completed, and in either case cannot be re-scheduled, then a result should be calculated as follows:
- **a. If not played:**
  - Taking all the matches played in the league or group concerned, establish the 'net goals' for each team. The score is then calculated by dividing the net score of each team by the number of matches played by each team; all fractions to count as half.
  - If this produces a tie in a tournament in which matches are to be played to a result then a similar calculation will be made taking account of gross goals scored.
  - If two teams remain tied then Para 1d will apply.
- **b. If started but not completed:**
  - The score will be calculated by taking the score of each team at the time the match was abandoned. These scores are then each divided by the number of chukkas completed and multiplied by the total number of chukkas due to be played in the match to give the score; all fractions to count as half.
  - If the teams were equal when the match was abandoned, each team will be awarded half a point.

6. Tournament Played Both Open and Handicap. If the tournament is played both open and on handicap:
- **a. Scoreboard.** The scoreboard should show the 'Open' score with any goals awarded on handicap displayed separately below the appropriate team.
- **b. Last Chukka.** Matches must be played for a result in both the open and handicap sections. Although there may be a result in one section at the end of 7 minutes in the last chukka, play may have to continue in order to get a result in the other section. When the result of one section has

been established, that result will not be altered by the subsequent play that may have been required to get a match result in the other section It is important that umpires and time-keepers are briefed on this requirement.

c. **Order of Merit.** A team that wins both the open and handicap section in a league must go for the open final. When the order of merit is being calculated, all matches are counted. If two or more teams are tied on points, only matches between the tied teams are counted as in Para 2b above, except that a team that has won the open section of the league shall not be considered as a tied team.

7. Cancellation. If the result of a league is known before the last matches are played and the result cannot be influenced by those matches, they may be cancelled provided the Tournament Committee, the club where the matches were due to be played and both team captains all agree.

APPENDIX TO THE RULES

Rule 33a

A player following the ball on its exact line and taking it on his offside has the ROW over all other players save as in 33g. (See figure x).

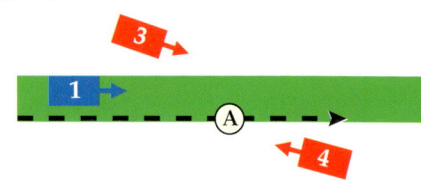

Fig i. Blue 1 is on the exact LOB and has the ROW over all other players including two players meeting, even if they are on the exact LOB.

Rule 33b

A player meeting the ball on its exact line and taking it on his offside has the ROW over all players riding at an angle from any direction.

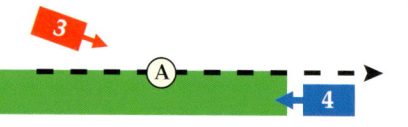

Fig ii. Ball is hit to A. Blue 4 is meeting on the exact LOB and has ROW.

Rule 33c

Any player riding towards the LOB at an angle to it and in the same direction that the ball is travelling has the ROW over any player riding from the opposite direction, irrespective of who is at the lesser angle.

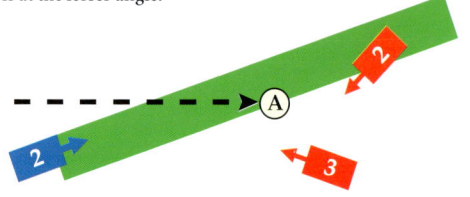

Fig iii. Blue 2 has the ROW as he is travelling in the same direction as the ball. If Red 3 was on the exact LOB, he would have the ROW on meeting (see Rule 33b) Red 3 may attempt to hook Blue 2's stick. If Blue 2 takes the ball on the near side, he will lose his ROW and foul because he endangers Red 3 and 2.

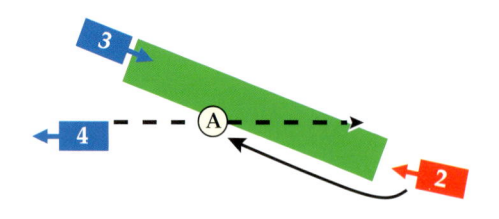

Fig iv. Blue 4 backs the ball to A. If Red 2 is not on the exact line of the ball, then Blue 3 has the ROW as he is travelling in the direction that the ball was hit. To make a play without fouling, Red 2 must move to A without endangering or impeding Blue 3 who has the ROW.

Rule 33d

When two or more players ride in the direction that the ball is travelling, the player that has precedence, and consequently the ROW, is the one whose approach to the ball is at the lesser angle to the LOB provided that he plays the ball on the offside (Figs v and vi). If the players are at equal angles, the player that has the LOB on his off side has the ROW (Fig vii).

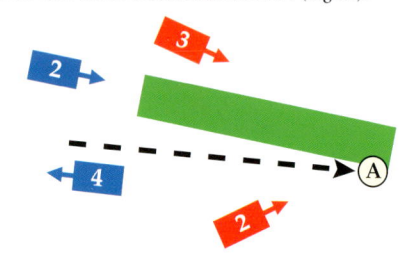

Fig v. Blue 4 hits long backhander to A. Blue 2 has ROW over both Red players.

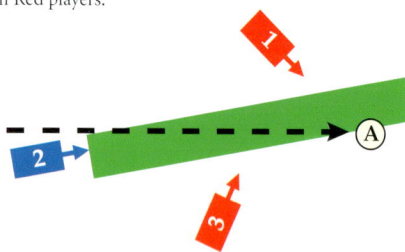

Fig vi. Blue 2 is riding at a lesser angle to the LOB than either Red 1 or 3 and therefore has the ROW to take the ball on his offside as shown. Red 3 could make a legitimate ride off or a nearside play. However, Red 1 has no play on Blue 2 as he is at too acute an angle to ride off and cannot hook from that side.

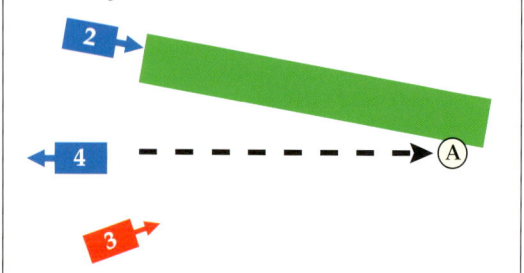

Fig vii. Blue 4 hits backhander to A. Blue 2 and Red 3 appear to be at equal angles. Blue 2 has the LOB on his offside and has the ROW.

Rule 33e

When two or more players ride to meet the ball, the player that has precedence, and consequently the ROW, is the one whose approach to the ball is at the lesser angle to the LOB, provided he plays the ball on the offside. If the players are at equal angles, the player that has the LOB on his offside has the ROW.

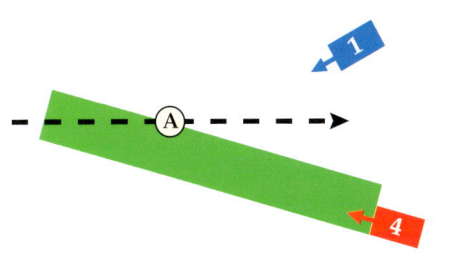

Fig viii. Red 4's approach is at the lesser angle to the LOB and he has the ROW. If Blue 1 was considered to be approaching at an equal angle, Red 4 still has the ROW because the LOB is on his offside.

Rule 33g

Two players riding in opposite directions on the exact LOB each have a ROW. Both players must take it on their respective offsides.

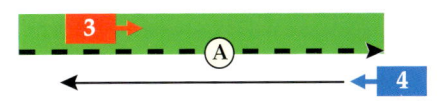

Fig x. Red 3 is on the exact line following the ball and has the ROW but Blue 4 would still have the right to meet him right hand to right hand as he also is on the exact line.

Rule 33j

A player may surrender his ROW if, having hit the ball, he deviates from its exact line.

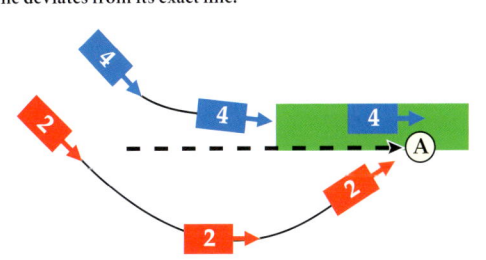

Fig xii. If Red 2 hits the ball under the neck to A but does not manage to stay on the exact LOB then the player on the lesser angle to LOB has the ROW. Blue 4 is at a lesser angle to the LOB and has the ROW. Red 2 can play the ball on the near side, or make a legitimate ride off or hook on Blue 4. (See Rules 35j and 36a).

Rule 33f

Two opposing players already making a play on each other and following the ball on its exact line have the ROW over all other players.

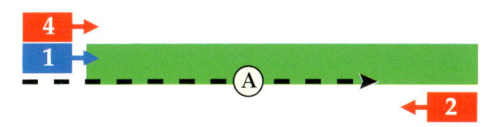

Fig ix. Red 4 and Blue 1 are on the exact LOB and have the ROW over all other players. Red 2 has no play. If Red 4 starts to make a play on Blue 1 when Red 2 is already established to meet Blue 1, then Red 4 will have fouled.

Rule 33h

Two opposing players already making a play on each other and following the direction of the ball at an angle have priority over a player meeting unless he is on the exact LOB. (see Rule 33b).

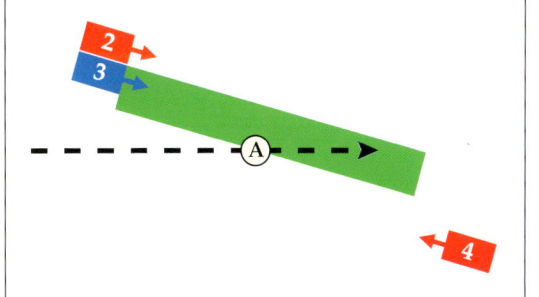

Fig xi. Blue 3 and Red 2 have the ROW and Red 4 has no play. If Red 4 was meeting on the exact LOB, Red 4 would have ROW.

Rule 34a

An opponent may only enter the ROW if he does so at a distance and speed that does not endanger either player nor cause the player with the ROW to check. If an opponent enters the ROW safely with the ball ahead of him, he has the ROW and the player cannot ride into him from behind and only has a play on his near side

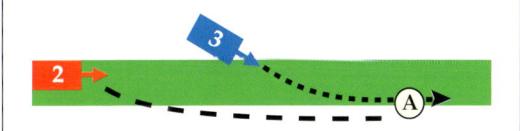

Fig xiii. Red 2 has possession and hits to A. Red 2's ROW is as shown. Blue 3 may enter the ROW provided he does not endanger or impede Red 2. Red 2 must not ride into Blue 3 (including riding him off from behind) and only has a play on his nearside.

Rule 34b

If the player hits the ball past the offside of an opponent who is on the exact LOB, the opponent has the right to play the ball on his offside. The player who hit the ball only has a play on the near side.

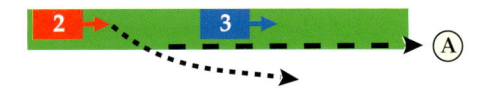

Fig xiv. Red 2 has possession and hits the ball to A. Red 2's ROW is as shown. Blue 3 may play the ball once it has passed his stirrup, providing he has not slowed down to wait for the ball. Red 2 must not ride into Blue 3 from behind but must take the ball on the near side.

Rule 34d

The player surrenders the ROW if he checks to avoid what would have been a legitimate ride off.

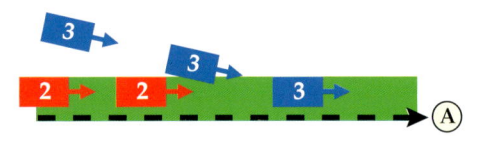

Fig xvi. Blue 3 goes to ride off Red 2 legitimately. If Red 2 checks to avoid a legitimate ride off, he surrenders the ROW and Blue 3 can come onto the ROW, provided it is safe to do so.

Rule 35a, b

A player may not ride in a manner which creates danger to another pony, player, official or any other person or which places the welfare of his own pony at undue risk. A player must ride off shoulder to shoulder and may push with his arm above the elbow provided the elbow is kept close to the side. In particular, a player may not:

a. Ride off at such an angle or speed as to be dangerous to a player or his pony.

b. Ride into an opponent behind the saddle.

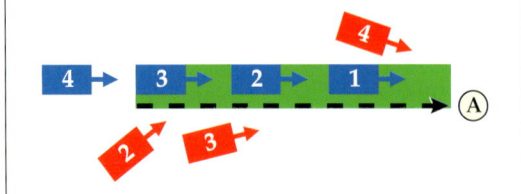

Fig xviii. Blue 4 hits ball to Blue 1 who is on the line of the ball and has the ROW. Red 4 can make a legitimate ride off on Blue 1.

Red 3 can play the ball on the nearside, (provided he does not impinge the ROW before or after playing his shot), or he can hook Blue 2 if he is playing a shot, or ride off Blue 2 legitimately; he can not ride in behind the saddle or from behind.

Red 2 is at too severe an angle to ride off Blue 3 or 4 legitimately.

Rule 34c

If an opponent is in a position to attempt a defensive play, the player must continue to move the ball. If he is moving at walking speed or stops he may tap the ball once only and then must leave it, accelerate with it or hit it away. A Penalty 7 (throw in) should be awarded for the breach of this rule. The opponent is considered to be in a 'position to attempt a defensive play' if he is within one horse's length on either the off or the nearside of the player with the ball.

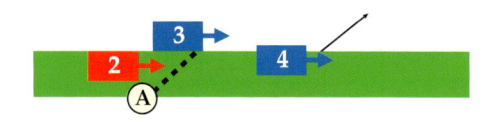

Fig xv. Red 2 has possession; Blue 3 is in a defensive position between Red 2 and the goal. Blue 4 must clear the ROW and Red 2 must continue to move the ball. He may tap the ball only once and must then leave it, accelerate with it or hit it away. If Red 2 hits to Blue 3, Blue 3 must clear the new ROW immediately without making a play on the ball. It is not a play if the pony kicks the ball.

Rule 34e

The ROW entitles the player to play the ball on his offside. If he switches to play it on the nearside, he loses the ROW and has fouled if he endangers any other player or causes a player to check.

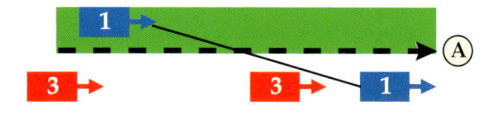

Fig xvii. Blue 1 has the ROW as shown. Blue 1 fouls if he switches to take the ball on his nearside and endangers Red 3 or causes Red 3 to have to check.

Rule 35c

A player may not ride an opponent across or into the ROW of another player at an unsafe distance.

Fig xix. Blue 3 has the ROW. If Red 3 rides Blue 2 into the ROW, thereby impinging or endangering Blue 3, Red 3 has fouled.

Rule 35d

A player may not ride off an opponent who is already being ridden off by another member of the team (sandwiching). However, it is not a foul for a player to hook legitimately an opponent's stick while the opponent is being ridden-off by a team mate of the player hooking.

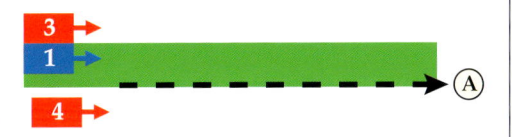

Fig xx. Blue 1, who has the ROW, is already being ridden off by Red 3. If Red 4 rides off Blue 1, it is a sandwich. However, Red 4 can hook Blue 1 when he is making a shot. If Red 3 pushes Blue 1 across the line to make contact with Red 4 it is also a foul against Red.

Rule 36a

For a player to make a legitimate hook, the following conditions must apply:
(i) He must be on the same side of his opponent's pony as the ball (Fig xxiii), or in a direct line behind (xxiv and xxv), and his stick must be neither over or under the body or across the legs of an opponent's pony.
(ii) All of his opponent's stick must be below the level of his opponent's shoulder.
(iii) His opponent must be in the act of striking the ball.

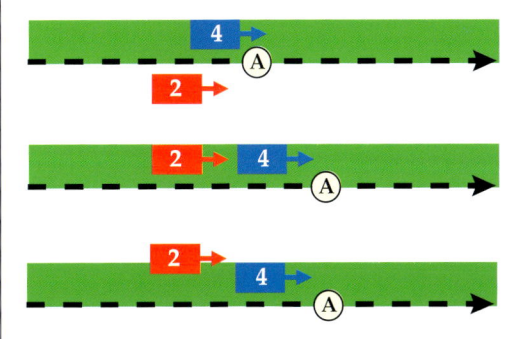

Rule 35f

A player may not ride his pony from behind into the forehand or backhand stroke of an opponent.

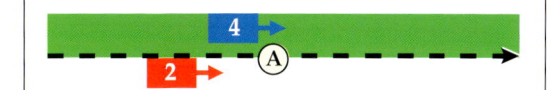

Fig xxi. Red 2 can not ride from behind into the forehand or backhand stroke of Blue 4.

Rule 35h

A player may not use his pony to spoil a stroke by riding over the ball and into an opponent who has already started the downward swing of a full forehand or backhand stroke.

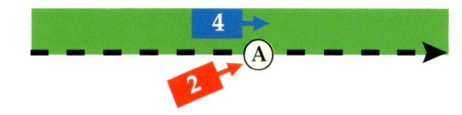

Fig xxii. Red 2 can not ride over the top of the ball if Blue 4 has already started the downward swing of a full forehand or backhand stroke.

Fig xxiii. Red 2 may only hook if Blue 4 is making a stroke and all of Blue 4's stick is below the level of his shoulder.

Fig xxiv. Red 2 may hook Blue 4 if Blue 4 is making a stroke and Red 2 is directly behind.

Fig xxv. Should Red 2 not be directly behind, then he will foul

Index

Note: Page numbers in **bold** refer to figures or illustrations

adjust 33–4
advantage, assessing 65–7
Aguerre, Martin **29**
Arab ponies 19
arcs 57–8
Argentina 9, 16–18, 23, 157, 266
Ashe, Arthur 273
Astrada, Tayo 21, 22
    see Novillo Astrada brothers
Azzaro, Michael 72, **154**, **215**

backhand
    avoiding straight 50
    nearside open 192–5, 197
    nearside tail 214–18
    offside open 137, 141–4, 146
    offside open half-shot 86–8
    offside tail 170–3, 175, 273
    wide-angled 270–1
Baig, Brigadier Hesky 20
ball chasing 4
ball clock 57
ball speed 4–5
    ball, sweet spot 61–62, 116, 236, 289, 291
    ball, striking, see striking
Barantes, Hector 72
The Barrier 96–7, 103
Barry, Joe 258
Bennett, James Gordon 12
Beresford, Charles 60, **288**
Berney, Tom **141**
Blue Book video 91
boots, riding 310
The Box 241–3, 247
breeches 310
breeding, ponies 301–3, 304
Brett, Henry **199**
British Army 12–13, 203

Cambiaso, Adolfo 17, 23, 72, **123**, **217**, **235**, **255**
car driving analogy 251
Castagnola, Bartolomé **224**, **288**
'catch a bus' 166, **167**, 170, 171

cavalry charge 163–4
Cernandas, Dickie 202–3, 230
Chukka 11
chukkas
    length 250
    number played by pony 206–7, 308
Churchill, Winston 7
circles 48–9
    arcs 57–8
    behind tail of pony 170–1
    finding 51–3
    nearside front (fourth) 190–6
    nearside rear (fifth) 212–18
    offside front (second) 137–46
    offside rear (third) 166–74
    straight full shots (first) 111–21
circling, exercises 75, **76**, 78, 81
clocks, pony and ball 57–8
clothes, riding 74, 310–11
co-ordination 8–9
coaching 6, 9
    Hugh Dawnay 20–4, 26, 129
    practice sessions 264, 267
    qualification system 26
    value of revision 279, 314–15
competition, constructive skills 316
Connors, Jimmy 273
constructive skills competitions 316, 317
Costa Careyes, Mexico 24
Cowdray Gold Cup **8**, 267
critique 315
    riding skills 280–6
    tactics 276–9
cut shots 174, 273
    nearside forehand 212–14, 218
    offside forehand 166–70
Cyprus 22–3

dam, polo pony 301–2
dangerous play 251
Dawnay, David 21, **25**
Dawnay family team 21, 24, **25**
Dawnay, Major Hugh
    authorship 26

coaching 20–4, 26, 129
    contacting 317
    marriage 21
    penalties 259
    playing apprenticeship 20
    starting polo 19
Dawnay, Sebastian 21, **25**, **42**, **69**, **83**, **105**, **115**, **140**, **154**, **171**, **173**, **250**
Deauville 266
delaying tactics 272
The Diamond 97–101, 103
direction of play, changing 272–3
disadvantage, assessing 65–7
disparity of skills 7, 37, 67, 203
distance, between players 35, 94
Dixon, Jason 157
Donovan, Silvestre **85**
Dora 157
Dorignac, Francisco 157
dress, riding 74, 310–11

engaging 36–7, 125, 271–2
    see also ride-offs
equipment 74, 249, 310–11

fast track system 8–9
Fernandez, Tomás **77**
The Field 11
Field Rules 37
figure of eight exercise 160–2
Firdausi 6
foaling 302, 302–3
follow through 62–3
    for hitting further 236–7
    improving 289
forehand
    angled to side 273
    nearside cut shot 212–14, 218
    nearside straight shot 117–20, 120–121
    offside cut shot 166–70
    offside half-shot 82–6
    offside straight shot 112–17, 120–121
Forsyth, Cody **178**
fouls 37, 66, 67, 250, 251, 259
    see also penalties

France 266
full shots 111–12
    exercises 120–1
    preparation 111
    straight nearside forehand 117–20, 120–121
    straight offside forehand 112–17, 120–121
    sweet spot 116
    see also different full shots

game
    slowing 273, 274
    timing and duration 249–50
Gaztambide, Santiago **29**
Germany 20–1, 274
gloves 310
goalpost, relationship to 105–6
goalpost drill 180–2, 183, 184
Gracida, Carlos **114**, **119**, **168**, 201–2, 267
Gracida, Memo 29, 178, 201–2
Great Britain 8–9, 23–4
Gresky, Wayne 273–4
grip, mallet 51, **52**, 82

half-seat 42, **83**, 284
half-shots 82
    exercises 88, **89**
    offside forehand 82–6
    open offside backhand 86–8
hammer grip 52
handicap factor 7
hands, use of 45–6, 285–6
Harriott, Alfredo 157
Harriott, Juan Carlos 182
Heguy brothers 17, 229
    Eduardo **84**
    Gonzalo 310–11
    Horacio 182, 310
helmet 310–11
Heythrop Pony Club team 246
hidden playmaking 3, 6, 262
Hill, Sinclair 229
Hipwood, Julian 182
history of polo
    Argentina 16–18
    British Army 12–13

354

INDEX

game spread by playmakers 12
India 11
Olympic Games 14, **15**
regimental tournaments 12
USA 15–16
hit-in 98–9, 239–47
    box system 241–3, 247
    The Diamond 97–101
    historical examples 246–7
    meeting the ball 243–6
    one on one marking 240–1, 247
    opponents' strategy 239
Hitchcock, Tommy 15, 16, 129, 156, 182
hitter 2
'hold a sword' 112–13, 192, 193
hooking sticks 70–2, 73
    rules 70
    technique 71–2
HRH Prince Charles 157, 230
Hurlingham Association Year Book 37
Hurlingham Polo Association (HPA) 26
    rules 91, 318
Hussars, 10th Royal 11, 12–14, 246

ice hockey 273–4
India 11
Ines, Maria 21, 24, **25**
interchanging positions 183, 223–8, 231–2
    examples 224–7
    exercises 227–8
    see also reverse rope move
international teams 9

Kennedy, George **251**
Kenya, Nairobi Polo Club 163
knee pads 311
knowledge, exchange of 26

LATET mnemonic 30, 39–40
    adjust 33–4
    changing positions 223–4, 231
    engage 36–7
    look 31–2
    tactical critique 276
    team 34–6
    turn 38–9
'Leave It' call 35
legs, use of 43, 55, 207
    assessing/improving 282, 284
line of the ball 37, 251
    crossing 67
    engaging 36–7
look 31–2
mallet
    grip 51, **52**, 82

hooking 70–72
    types/design 309–10
marking 265, 267, 271–2
    exercises 108
    one on one 240–1, 247
match-winning components 269
Merlos, Pite **29**, **46**
Mexico 24
Milburn, Devereux 156
mistakes, reaction to 33
mnemonics, *see* LATET; PASSF; PRST; SLOSH
Moore, Bobby 230
Morgan, Tommy 61
Mullins, Brian **251**

Nairobi Polo Club 163
nearside shots
    exercises 195–6
    forehand cut 212–14, 218
    neck 191–2, 196, 217
    open backhand 192–5, 197
    straight forehand 117–20, 120–121
    tail shot 214–18
    value of 190
    when to avoid 190–1
neck shots
    exercises 144–6, 174
    nearside 191–2
    offside 137–41, 146
No. 1 position
    facing the hit-in 240–1
    historical examples 129–30
    as link to goal 122–4
    position 124–6
    responsibility 126–7
    speed 127
    tactical critique 277
    throw-in 222
    turn to defence 127–8
No. 2 position 35, 176–81
    demands of 176
    historical examples 182–3
    passing to No. 1 177–8
    role 176–9
    tactical critique 277
No. 3 position 198–204
    covering by No. 2 179
    historical examples 201–3
    pivotal role 198
    position 199
    responsibility 200
    speed 200
    tactical critique 277–8
    turn to defence 200–1
No. 4 position
    historical examples 156–7
    job/roles 147–8, 158
    position in the 75 148–9
    responsibility 149–50

reverse rope tactic 153–6, 158–9
    speed 151–2
    tactical critique 278
    throw-in 222–3
    turn to defence 152–3, 228–9
Notley, Roland 203
novice players 6
Novillo Astrada brothers 17–18, **29**, **169**
    Ignacio **169**
    Javier **186**
    Miguel 267

obstruction, legal 7–8
offside backhand
    open 137, 141–4, 146
    tail 170–3, 175, 273
offside forehand
    half-shot 82–6
    straight full shot 112–17, 120–121
offside neck shot 137–41, 146
Olympic Games 14, **15**
one on one 240–1, 247
opponents
    as partners 132
    superior teams 269–74, 275
    turning inside 133
'outside the pony' 43–5, 164
    assessing and improving 282, 284–5
overtaking in attack 227
own-team awareness 34

pair exercises
    coaching assistance 135
    joining as foursome 133–4, **135**
    joining in pairs 108–9
    turning 132–3
    turning inside an opponent 133
Palm Beach 23–4, 129–30, 201–2, 258–9, 266, 274, **281**
'pane of glass' image 84
passes, receiving 65–7, 73, 278
PASSF mnemonic 30, 63–4
    adaptation for greater length 233–7
    approach 56–8
    follow through 62–3
    preparation 50–6
    questions related to 288–9
    sweet spot 61–2
    swing slowly 58–60, **61**
patron, role of 264–5, 266, 267
Pedley, Eric 129
penalties 252–8
    historical examples 258–9
    penalties 3 and 2 254–8, 260

penalty 1 258, 260
penalty 4 252–4, 260
penalty 5 252, 260
Persians 6
physical contact 7–8
Pieres, Gonzalo 3, 23, 72, **113**, **143**, 201–2, **235**, **245**, 267
plans, playing 305–6
playmaker
    defined 1
    sparing of pony 4–6
playmaking 10
    away from polo field 2
    coaching 6
    hidden 3, 6, 262
    practice and revision 314–16
polo, unique dimensions 6–9
polo field, away from 2
Polo Vision (Dawnay) 9, 20, 26, 43
ponies 74, 249
    ability 297–8
    avoiding hitting 137
    breeding 24, 301–3, 304
    buying 297–300, 303
    control 104
    fitness and number of chukkas played 206–7, 211, 308
    injuries 209
    management **208**, 306–8
    match considerations 206, 207, 211
    mouth 46, 207, 285
    performance analysis 209
    post-match care 208, 211
    practice days 206
    pre-match preparation 205–6, 211
    preserving stamina 4–6, 34, 207
    schooling 206, 209–10, 211, 308
    speed of 4–6
    steering 45
pony clock 57
Pony Club 8–9, 24, 26, 157, 246
position
    No. 1 124–6
    No. 2 177
    No. 3 199
    No. 4 148–9
positions
    interchanging 183, 223–8
    tactical critique 277–8
    team 265, 267
    see also different positions
practice sessions 206, 263–4, 267
preparation
    before new season 305
    pre-match 263
PRST mnemonic 122–4
    position 124–6

responsibility 126–7
speed 127
turn to defence 127–8

races, riding short 187–9
Ramsey, Sir Alf 230
'reach into the fridge' 138
'rear view mirror' simulation 43
receiver 2
receiving passes 65–7, 73, 278
recovering ground 228–9, 232
regimental teams 246
regimental tournaments 12
reins, holding and use 45–6, 285
relocation, rapid 265–6
Rendez-Vous II 19
responsibility
   No. 1 position 126–7
   No. 2 position 177
   No. 3 position 200
   No. 4 position 149–50
reverse rope move 153–9, 174, 218
revision, value of 279, 314–15
Revision Booklet 317
ride-offs 7–8, 37, 67, 73, 271–2
   elements of 68–70
   No. 1 position 125
riders, novice 41
riding 41–5, 185–7
   critique 280–3
   hands 45–6, 285–6
   'outside the pony' 43–5, 164, 282, 284–5
   remedies for problems 283–6
   seat 41–2
   SLOSH mnemonic 30
   standards 207
   use of legs 43, 55, 207, 282, 284
   use of whip 74, 185, 187, 286, 311
riding exercises 79–80
   circling individually 75, **76**, 78, 81
   conforming to playmaker in two parallel lines 78–9, **80–1**
   copying playmaker in horizontal line 78, **79**
   figure of eight 160–2
   joining in pairs 108–9
   joining vertical lines 109
   parallel vertical lines 106–7
   short races 187–9
   turning and halting individually 75, **76**, 81
   working in a vertical line 104–6

see also pair exercises; team exercises
right of way 7, 250–1
ripple turns 162–3
Rope exercise 92–5, 102
Royal Berkshire 267
rugby 96, 130, 230
rules of polo 318
   learning 91–2, 249
   test 292–5

saddle 309
safety 249, 310–11
'sandwiching' 251
seat
   description 41–2
   improvement 282, 283–4
set piece situations
   critique 277
   see also hit-in; throw-in
shape of team 92
shoulders, use of 50, 59–60, 118
'shutting the back door' 148–53
sire, of polo pony 302
skills
   constructive competitions 316, 317
   disparity of in polo 7, 37, 67, 203
SLOSH mnemonic 30, 46–7
   assessment questions 282–3
   hands applied softly 45–6
   legs 43
   'outside the pony' 43–5
   remedies for problems 283–6
   seat 41–2
   steering 45
soccer 230
Soft Diamond 101, **102**, 103
Sotogrande 2003 267
speed
   of ball 4–5
   No. 1 position 127, 178–9
   No. 2 position 178–9
   No. 3 position 200
   No. 4 position 151–2
   of ponies 4–6
speed of play, slowing 273, 274
Spencer, Herbert 11
sporting analogies 96, 130, 230, 273–4
spurs 74, 311
star exercise 144, **145**
steering the pony 45, 283, 285
striking 233
   approach 56–8
   avoiding hitting pony 137
   circles 48–9

clocks 57–8
construction of shot 51–4
follow through 62–3
hitting further 233–8
PASSF mnemonic 30, 48–50
preparation 50–6
problems and diagnosis 287–9
procedure 55–6
sweet spot 61–2
use of shoulders 50, 59–60
see also different shots
Superstars Circus 22–3
surprises
   adjustment to 34
   countering 266
Suto, Jose **42**
sweet spot 61–2
   critique and improvement 289, 291
   hitting further 236
   see also under different shots
swing 54, 61
   assessment 289
   for greater length 236
   slow 48, 58–60, 61

tack 309
tactics
   against superior opposition 269–74
   The Barrier 96–7, 103
   critique 276–9
   The Diamond 97–101, 103
   interchanging positions 183, 223–8
   LATET mnemonic 30–40
   look 31–2
   match-winning components 269
   penalties 252–8
   pre-prepared 97–8
   PRST mnemonic 122–8
   reverse rope move 153–6, 158–9, 174, 218
   rope exercise 92–5, 102
   soft diamond 101, **102**, 103
tail shot 166
   nearside backhand 214–18
   offside backhand 170–3, 175, 273
'tail trick' 133, 272
Tanoira, Gonzalo 182
team 6, 34–6
team discipline 265–6, 268
team exercises
   cavalry charge 163–4
   figure of eight 160–2
   joining in pairs 108–9

joining vertical lines 109
parallel vertical lines 106–7
relay races 188–9
ripple turns 162–3
working in a vertical line 104–6
team play 269
   general concepts 261–2
   historical examples 266–7
   patron's role 264–5, 266, 267
   positions and marking 265, 267
   practice sessions 263–4
   pre-match preparation 263
tennis 273
10th Hussars 11, 12–14, 246
thought processes 28–30, 35, 38–9
throw-in 219–23, 231
   historical examples 229–30
   line-up order 221–2
   problems 221
   rules 220
   strategy 222
'throwing salt' 117, 118, 191, 213
Tommy Hitchcock (Pedley) 129
trigger (pistol) grip **52**
Trotz, Ernesto **195**
Turkomans 6
turn to defence
   No. 1 position 127–8
   No. 2 position 179
   No. 3 position 200–1
   No. 4 position 152–3, 228–9
   turning 38–9
   exercises 75, **76**, 81
   inside an opponent 133, 272
   in pairs 132–3
   in the saddle 31, **32**
   thought processes 38–9

umpire 252, 258
unique dimensions of polo 6–9, 10, 37
United States 15–16, 156
United States Polo Association 91

wealth, redistribution 2
whip 74, 185, 187, 286, 311
Whitfield Court 21–2, 24, 28, 30, 301
Williams, J.P.R. 230
Wright, John 24